AMONG THE BELIEVERS

Other Books by V. S. Naipaul

FICTION
Miguel Street
The Mystic Masseur
The Suffrage of Elvira
A House for Mr Biswas
Mr Stone and the Knights Companion
A Flag on the Island
The Mimic Men
In a Free State
Guerrillas
A Bend in the River

NON-FICTION
The Middle Passage:
the Caribbean Revisited

An Area of Darkness:
an Experience of India

The Loss of El Dorado:
a History

The Overcrowded Barracoon
and other Articles

India: a Wounded Civilization

The Return of Eva Perón
with The Killings in Trinidad and Two Other Reports

Among the Believers

An Islamic Journey

V. S. NAIPAUL

ANDRE DEUTSCH

First published 1981 by
André Deutsch Limited
105 Great Russell Street London WC1

Printed in Great Britain by
Ebenezer Baylis and Son Limited
The Trinity Press, Worcester, and London

ISBN 0 233 97416 4

Contents

Now in earlier times the world's history had consisted, so to speak, of a series of unrelated episodes, the origins and results of each being as widely separated as their localities, but from this point onwards history becomes an organic whole: the affairs of Italy and Africa are connected with those of Asia and of Greece, and all events bear a relationship and contribute to a single end.

Polybius (died 118 BC), on the rise of Rome (translated by Ian Scott-Kilvert)

'But it was not alone in poetry that I excelled. I had a great turn for mechanics, and several of my inventions were much admired at court. I contrived a wheel for perpetual motion, which only wants one little addition to make it go round for ever. I made different sorts of coloured paper; I invented a new sort of ink-stand; and was on the high road to making cloth, when I was stopped by his majesty, who said to me, "Asker, stick to your poetry: whenever I want cloth, my merchants bring it from Europe." '

James Morier: *The Adventures of Hajji Baba of Ispahan* (1824)

I

◆◇◆◇◆

IRAN
The Twin Revolutions

◆◇◆◇◆

'This Kom is a place that, excepting on the subject of religion, and settling who are worthy of salvation and who to be damned, no one opens his lips. Every man you meet is either a descendant of the Prophet or a man of the law . . . Perhaps, friend Hajji, you do not know that this is the residence of the celebrated Mirza Abdul Cossim, the first *mushtehed* (divine) of Persia; a man who, if he were to give himself sufficient stir, would make the people believe any doctrine that he might choose to promulgate. Such is his influence, that many believe he could even subvert the authority of the Shah himself, and make his subjects look upon his firmans as worthless, as so much waste paper.'

James Morier: *The Adventures of Hajji Baba of Ispahan* (1824)

1

◆ ◆ ◆ ◆

Death Pact

SADEQ was to go with me from Tehran to the holy city of Qom, a hundred miles to the south. I hadn't met Sadeq; everything had been arranged on the telephone. I needed an Iranian interpreter, and Sadeq's name had been given me by someone from an embassy.

Sadeq was free because, like many Iranians since the revolution, he had found himself out of a job. He had a car. When we spoke on the telephone he said it would be better for us to drive to Qom in his car; Iranian buses were dreadful and could be driven at frightening speeds by people who didn't really care.

We fixed a price for his car, his driving, his interpreting; and what he asked for was reasonable. He said we should start as soon as possible the next morning, to avoid the heat of the August day. He would take his wife to her office – she still had a job – and come straight on to the hotel. I should be ready at 7.30.

He came some minutes before eight. He was in his late twenties, small and carefully dressed, handsome, with a well-barbered head of hair. I didn't like him. I saw him as a man of simple origins, simply educated, but with a great sneering pride, deferential but resentful, not liking himself for what he was doing. He was the kind of man who, without political doctrine, only with resentments, had made the Iranian revolution. It would have been interesting to talk to him for an hour or two; it was going to be hard to be with him for some days, as I had now engaged myself to be.

He was smiling, but he had bad news for me. He didn't think his car could make it to Qom.

I didn't believe him. I thought he had simply changed his mind.

I said, 'The car was your idea. I wanted to go by the bus. What happened between last night and now?'

'The car broke down.'

'Why didn't you telephone me before you left home? If you had telephoned, we could have caught the eight o'clock bus. Now we've missed that.'

'The car broke down after I took my wife to work. Do you really want to go to Qom today?'

'What's wrong with the car?'

'If you really want to go to Qom we can take a chance with it. Once it starts it's all right. The trouble is to get it started.'

We went to look at the car. It was suspiciously well parked at the side of the road not far from the hotel gate. Sadeq sat in the driver's seat. He called out to a passing man, one of the many idle workmen of Tehran, and the man and I began to push. A young man with a briefcase, possibly an office worker on his way to work, came and helped without being asked. The road was dug-up and dusty; the car was very dusty. It was hot; the exhausts of passing cars and trucks made it hotter. We pushed now with the flow of the traffic, now against it; and all the time Sadeq sat serenely at the steering wheel.

People from the pavement came and helped for a little, then went about their business. It occurred to me that I should also be going about mine. This – pushing Sadeq's car back and forth – wasn't the way to get to Qom; what had begun so unpromisingly wasn't going to end well. So, without telling anybody anything then or afterwards, I left Sadeq and his car and his volunteer pushers and walked back to the hotel.

I telephoned Behzad. Behzad had also been recommended to me as an interpreter. But there had been some trouble in finding him – he was a student footloose in the great city of Tehran; and when the previous evening he had telephoned me, I had already closed with Sadeq. I told Behzad now that my plans had fallen through. He made no difficulties – and I liked him for that. He said he was still free, and would be with me in an hour.

He didn't think we should take a car to Qom. The bus was cheaper, and I would see more of the Iranian people. He also said that I should eat something substantial before leaving. It was Ramadan, the month when Muslims fasted from sunrise to sunset; and in Qom, the city of mullahs and ayatollahs, it wasn't going to be possible to eat or drink. In some parts of the country – with the general Islamic excitement – people had been whipped for breaking the fast.

Behzad's approach, even on the telephone, was different from Sadeq's. Sadeq, a small man on the rise, and perhaps only a step or two above being a peasant, had tried to suggest that he was above the general Iranian level. But he wasn't, really; there was a lot of the Iranian hysteria and confusion locked up in his smiling eyes. Behzad, explaining his country, claiming it all, yet managed to sound more objective.

When, at the time he had said, we met in the lobby of the hotel, I at once felt at ease with him. He was younger, taller, darker than Sadeq. He

9

was more educated; there was nothing of the dandy about him, nothing of Sadeq's nervousness and raw pride.

We went by line taxis – city taxis operating along fixed routes – to the bus station in south Tehran. North Tehran – spreading up into the brown hills, hills that faded in the daytime haze – was the elegant part of the city; that was where the parks and gardens were, the plane-lined boulevards, the expensive apartment blocks, the hotels and the restaurants. South Tehran was still an eastern city, more populous and cramped, more bazaar-like, full of people who had moved in from the countryside; and the crowd in the dusty, littered yard of the bus station was like a country crowd.

Somebody in a grimy little office told Behzad that there was a bus for Qom in half an hour. The bus in question was parked in the hot sun and empty. No bags or bundles on the roof, no patient peasants waiting outside or stewing inside. That bus looked parked for the day. I didn't believe it was going to leave in half an hour; neither did Behzad. There was another bus service from Tehran, though, one that offered air-conditioned buses and reserved seats. Behzad looked for a telephone, found coins, telephoned, got no reply. The August heat had built up, the air was full of dust.

A line taxi took us to the other terminal, which was in central Tehran. Boards above a long counter gave the names of remote Iranian towns; there was even a daily service, through Turkey, to Europe. But the morning bus to Qom had gone; there wouldn't be another for many hours. It was now near noon. There was nothing for us to do but to go back to the hotel and think again.

We walked; the line taxis had no room. The traffic was heavy. Tehran, since the revolution, couldn't be said to be a city at work; but people had cars, and the idle city – so many projects abandoned, so many unmoving cranes on the tops of unfinished buildings – could give an impression of desperate busyness.

The desperation was suggested by the way the Iranians drove. They drove like people to whom the motor-car was new. They drove as they walked; and a stream of Tehran traffic, jumpy with individual stops and swerves, with no clear lanes, was like a jostling pavement crowd. This manner of driving didn't go with any special Tehran luck. The door or fender of every other car was bashed in, or bashed in and mended. An item in a local paper (blaming the Shah for not having given the city a more modern road system) had said that traffic accidents were the greatest single cause of deaths in Tehran; two thousand people were killed or injured every month.

We came to an intersection. And there I lost Behzad. I was waiting for the traffic to stop. But Behzad didn't wait with me. He simply began to cross, dealing with each approaching car in turn, now stopping, now hurrying, now altering the angle of his path, and, like a man crossing a forest gorge by a slender fallen tree trunk, never looking back. He looked back only when he had got to the other side. He waved me over, but I couldn't move. Traffic lights had failed higher up, and the cars didn't stop.

He understood my helplessness. He came back through the traffic to me and then – like a moorhen leading its chick across the swift current of a stream – he led me through dangers which at every moment seemed about to sweep me away. He led me by the hand; and, just as the moorhen places herself a little downstream from the chick, breaking the force of the current which would otherwise sweep the little thing away forever, so Behzad kept me in his lee, walking a little ahead of me and a little to one side, so that he would have been hit first.

And when we were across the road he said, 'You must always give your hand to me.'

It was, in effect, what I had already begun to do. Without Behzad, without the access to the language that he gave me, I had been like a half-blind man in Tehran. And it had been especially frustrating to be without the language in these streets, scrawled and counter-scrawled with aerosol slogans in many colours in the flowing Persian script, and plastered with revolutionary posters and cartoons with an emphasis on blood. Now, with Behzad, the walls spoke; many other things took on meaning; and the city changed.

Behzad had at first seemed neutral in his comments, and I had thought that this was part of his correctness, his wish not to go beyond his function as a translator. But Behzad was neutral because he was confused. He was a revolutionary and he welcomed the overthrow of the Shah; but the religious revolution that had come to Iran was not the revolution that Behzad wanted. Behzad was without religious faith.

How had that happened? How, in a country like Iran, and growing up in a provincial town, had he learned to do without religion? It was simple, Behzad said. He hadn't been instructed in the faith by his parents; he hadn't been sent to the mosque. Islam was a complicated religion. It wasn't philosophical or speculative. It was a revealed religion, with a Prophet and a complete set of rules. To believe, it was necessary to know a lot about the Arabian origins of the religion, and to take this knowledge to heart.

Islam in Iran was even more complicated. It was a divergence from the main belief; and this divergence had its roots in the political-racial dispute about the succession to the Prophet, who died in AD 632. Islam, almost from the start, had been an imperialism as well as a religion, with an early history remarkably like a speeded-up version of the history of Rome, developing from city state to peninsular overlord to empire, with corresponding stresses at every stage.

The Iranian divergence had become doctrinal, and there had been divergences within the divergence. Iranians recognized a special line of succession to the Prophet. But a group loyal to the fourth man in this Iranian line, the fourth Imam, had hived off; another group had their own ideas about the seventh. Only one Imam, the eighth (poisoned, like the fourth), was buried in Iran; and his tomb in the city of Mashhad, not far from the Russian border, was an object of pilgrimage.

'A lot of those people were killed or poisoned,' Behzad said, as though explaining his lack of belief.

Islam in Iran, Shia Islam, was an intricate business. To keep alive ancient animosities, to hold on to the idea of personal revenge even after a thousand years, to have a special list of heroes and martyrs and villains, it was necessary to be instructed. And Behzad hadn't been instructed; he had simply stayed away. He had, if anything, been instructed in disbelief by his father, who was a communist. It was of the poor rather than of the saints that Behzad's father had spoken. The memory that Behzad preserved with special piety was of the first day his father had spoken to him about poverty – his own poverty, and the poverty of others.

On the pavement outside the Turkish embassy two turbanned, sun-burnt medicine-men sat with their display of coloured powders, roots and minerals. I had seen other medicine-men in Tehran and had thought of them as Iranian equivalents of the homoeopathic medicine-men of India. But the names these Iranians were invoking as medical authorities – as Behzad told me, after listening to their sales talk to a peasant group – were Avicenna, Galen, and 'Hippocrat'.

Avicenna! To me only a name, someone from the European middle ages: it had never occurred to me that he was a Persian. In this dusty pavement medical stock was a reminder of the Arab glory of a thousand years before, when the Arab faith mingled with Persia, India and the remnant of the classical world it had overrun, and Muslim civilization was the central civilization of the West.

Behzad was less awed than I was. He didn't care for that Muslim past; and he didn't believe in pavement medicines. He didn't care for the Shah's architecture either: the antique Persian motifs of the Central Iranian Bank, and the Aryan, pre-Islamic past that it proclaimed. To Behzad that stress on the antiquity of Persia and the antiquity of the monarchy was only part of the Shah's vainglory.

He looked at the Bank, at the bronze and the marble, and said without passion, 'That means nothing to me.'

Was his iconoclasm complete? Was he Persian or Iranian in anything except his love of the Iranian people? Had his political faith washed him clean?

It hadn't. Tehran had had a revolution. But normal life went on in odd ways, and amid the slogans and posters with their emphasis on blood there were picture-sellers on the pavements. They offered blown-up colour photographs of Swiss lakes and German forests; they offered dream landscapes of rivers and trees. They also offered paintings of children and beautiful women. But the women were weeping, and the children were weeping. Big, gelatinous tears, lovingly rendered, ran half-way down the cheeks.

Behzad, whose father was a teacher of Persian literature, said 'Persian poetry is full of sadness.'

I said, 'But tears for the sake of tears, Behzad –'

Firmly, like a man who wasn't going to discuss the obvious, and wasn't going to listen to any artistic nonsense, he said, 'Those tears are *beautiful*.'

We left it at that. And from the topic of tears we turned once more, as we walked, to the revolution. There were two posters I had seen in many parts of the city. They were of the same size, done in the same style, and clearly made a pair. One showed a small peasant group working in a field, using a barrow or a plough – it wasn't clear which, from the drawing. The other showed, in silhouette, a crowd raising rifles and machine-guns as if in salute. They were like the posters of a people's revolution: an awakened, victorious people, a new dignity of labour. But what was the Persian legend at the top?

Behzad translated: '"Twelfth Imam, we are waiting for you."'

'What does that mean?'

'It means they are waiting for the Twelfth Imam.'

The Twelfth Imam was the last of the Iranian line of succession to the Prophet. That line had ended over eleven hundred years ago. But the Twelfth Imam hadn't died; he survived somewhere, waiting to return to earth. And his people were waiting for him; the Iranian revolution was an offering to him.

Behzad couldn't help me more; he couldn't help me understand that ecstasy. He could only lay out the facts. Behzad was without belief, but he was surrounded by belief and he could understand its emotional charge. For him it was enough to say – as he did say, without satirical intention – that the Twelfth Imam was the Twelfth Imam.

Later on my Islamic journey, as difficult facts of history and genealogy became more familiar, became more than facts, became readily comprehended articles of faith, I was to begin to understand a little of

13

Muslim passion. But when Behzad translated the legend of those revolutionary posters for me I was at a loss.

It wasn't of this hidden messiah that Iranians had written on the walls of London and other foreign cities before the revolution. They had written – in English – about democracy; about torture by the Shah's secret police; about the 'fascism' of the Shah. *Down with fascist Shah*: that was the slogan that recurred.

I hadn't followed Iranian affairs closely; but it seemed to me, going only by the graffiti of Iranians abroad, that religion had come late to Iranian protest. It was only when the revolution had started that I understood that it had a religious leader, who had been in exile for many years. The Ayatollah Khomeini, I felt, had been revealed slowly. As the revolution developed his sanctity and authority appeared to grow and at the end were seen to have been absolute all along.

Fully disclosed, the Ayatollah had turned out to be nothing less than the interpreter, for Iranians, of God's will. By his emergence he annulled, or made trivial, all previous protests about the 'fascism' of the Shah. And he accepted his role. It was as the interpreter of God's will that he addressed 'the Christians of the world' in an advertisement in the *New York Times* on 12 January 1979, three weeks before he returned to Iran from his exile in France.

Half the message consisted of blessings and greetings from God. 'The blessings and greetings of Almighty God to the Blessed Jesus . . . his glorious mother . . . Greetings to the clergy . . . the freedom-loving Christians.' Half was a request for Christian prayers on holy days, and a warning to 'the leaders of some of the Christian countries who are supporting the tyrant shah with their Satanic power.'

And it was as the interpreter of God's will, the final judge of what was Islamic and what was not Islamic, that Khomeini ruled Iran. Some days after I arrived in Tehran, this was what he said on the radio: 'I must tell you that during the previous dictatorial regime strikes and sit-ins pleased God. But now, when the government is a Muslim and a national one, the enemy is busy plotting against us. And therefore staging strikes and sit-ins is religiously forbidden because they are against the principles of Islam.'

This was familiar to me, and intellectually manageable, even after a few days in Tehran: the special authority of the man who ruled both as political head and as voice of God. But the idea of the revolution as something more, as an offering to the Twelfth Imam, the man who had vanished in AD 873 and remained 'in occultation', was harder to seize. And the mimicry of the revolutionary motifs of the late twentieth century – the posters that appeared to celebrate peasants and urban guerrillas, the Che Guevara outfits of the Revolutionary Guards – made it more unsettling.

Behzad translated; the walls spoke; Tehran felt strange. And North Tehran – an expensive piece of Europe expensively set down in the sand and rock of the hills, the creation of the Shah and the large middle class that had been brought into being by the uncreated wealth of oil – felt like a fantasy. There were skyscrapers, international hotels, shops displaying expensive goods with international brand names; but this great city had been grafted on to South Tehran. South Tehran was the community out of which the North had too quickly evolved. And South Tehran, obedient to the will of God and the Twelfth Imam, had laid it low.

Muslims were part of the small Indian community of Trinidad, which was the community into which I was born; and it could be said that I had known Muslims all my life. But I knew little of their religion. My own background was Hindu, and I grew up with the knowledge that Muslims, though ancestrally of India and therefore like ourselves in many ways, were different. I was never instructed in the religious details, and perhaps no one in my family really knew. The difference between Hindus and Muslims was more a matter of group feeling, and mysterious: the animosities our Hindu and Muslim grandfathers had brought from India had softened into a kind of folk-wisdom about the unreliability and treachery of the other side.

I was without religious faith myself. I barely understood the rituals and ceremonies I grew up with. In Trinidad, with its many races, my Hinduism was really an attachment to my family and its ways, an attachment to my own difference; and I imagined that among Muslims and others there were similar attachments and privacies.

What I knew about Islam was what was known to everyone on the outside. They had a Prophet and a Book; they believed in one God and disliked images; they had an idea of heaven and hell – always a difficult idea for me. They had their own martyrs. Once a year mimic mausolea were wheeled through the streets; men 'danced' with heavy crescent moons, swinging the moons now one way, now the other; drums beat, and sometimes there were ritual stick-fights.

The stick-fights were a mimicry of an old battle, but the procession was one of mourning, commemorating defeat in that battle. Where had that battle taken place? What was the cause? As a child, I never asked; and it was only later that I got to know that the occasion – in which Hindus as well as Muslims took part – was essentially a Shia occasion, that the battle had to do with the succession to the Prophet, that it had been fought in Iraq, and that the man being especially mourned was the Prophet's grandson.

Islam, going by what I saw of it from the outside, was less metaphysical and more direct than Hinduism. In this religion of fear and reward, oddly compounded with war and worldly grief, there was much that reminded me of Christianity – more visible and 'official' in Trinidad; and it was possible for me to feel that I knew about it. The doctrine, or what I thought was its doctrine, didn't attract me. It didn't seem worth inquiring into; and over the years, in spite of travel, I had added little to the knowledge gathered in my Trinidad childhood. The glories of this religion were in the remote past; it had generated nothing like a Renaissance. Muslim countries, where not colonized, were despotisms; and nearly all, before oil, were poor.

The idea of travelling to certain Muslim countries had come to me the previous winter, during the Iranian revolution. I was in Connecticut, and on some evenings I watched the television news. As interesting to me as the events in Iran were the Iranians in the United States who were interviewed on some of the programmes.

There was a man in a tweed jacket who spoke the pure language of Marxism, but was more complicated than his language suggested. He was a bit of a dandy, and proud of his ability to handle the jargon he had picked up; he was like a man displaying an idiomatic command of a foreign language. He was proud of his Iranian revolution – it gave him glamour. But at the same time he understood that the religious side of the revolution would appear less than glamorous to his audience; and he was trying – with the help of his tweed jacket, his idiomatic language, his manner – to present himself as sophisticated as any man who watched, and sophisticated in the same way.

Another evening, on another programme, an Iranian woman came on with her head covered to tell us that Islam protected women and gave them dignity. Fourteen hundred years ago in Arabia, she said, girl children were buried alive; it was Islam that put a stop to that. Well, we didn't all live in Arabia (not even the woman with the covered head); and many things had happened since the seventh century. Did women – especially someone as fierce as the woman addressing us – still need the special protection that Islam gave them? Did they need the veil? Did they need to be banned from public life and from appearing on television?

These were the questions that occurred to me. But the interviewer, who asked people prepared questions every day, didn't dally. He passed on to his next question, which was about the kind of Islamic state that the woman wanted to see in Iran. Was it something like Saudi Arabia she had in mind? Fierce enough already, she flared up at that; and with her *chador*-encircled face she looked like an angry nun, full of reprimand. It was a mistake many people made, she said; but Saudi Arabia was *not* an Islamic state. And it seemed as if she was saying that Saudi Arabia was an acknowledged barbarism, and that the Islamic state of Iran was going to be quite different.

It was of the beauty of Islamic law that I heard a third Iranian speak. But what was he doing, studying law in an American university? What had attracted these Iranians to the United States and the civilization it represented? Couldn't they say? The attraction existed; it was more than a need for education and skills. But the attraction wasn't admitted; and in that attraction, too humiliating for an old and proud people to admit, there lay disturbance – expressed in dandyism, mimicry, boasting, and rejection.

An American or non-Islamic education had given the woman with the *chador* her competence and authority. Now she appeared to be questioning the value of the kind of person she had become; she was denying some of her own gifts. All these Iranians on American television were conscious of their American audience, and they gave the impression of saying less than they meant. Perhaps they had no means of saying all that they felt; perhaps there were certain things they preferred not to say. (It was only in Iran that I understood the point the woman with the *chador* had made about Saudi Arabia. It was a sectarian point and might have been thought too involved for a television audience: the Arabians and the Persians belong to different sects, have different lines of succession to the Prophet, and there is historical bad blood between them.)

From an accomplished Iranian novel, which I read about this time, I learned more. People can hide behind direct statements; fiction, by its seeming indirections, can make hidden impulses clear. The novel, *Foreigner*, described by its American publisher as the first novel in English by an Iranian, was by a young woman, Nahid Rachlin. It was published in 1978, while the Shah still ruled. It avoids political comment. Its protest is more oblique; the political constriction drives the passion deeper; and the novel, with all its air of innocence, is a novel of violation, helplessness and defeat.

The narrator is Feri, an Iranian woman of thirty-two living in Boston. She has studied in the United States, is married to an American university teacher, and works as a biologist in a research institute. Feri, on an impulse, goes back to Tehran for a two-week holiday. The city she goes back to is full of cars and 'western' buildings ('western' rather than 'new' or 'modern' is the narrator's curious word); but it is not a city of glamour. The streets can be thuggish; and family life in the hidden courtyards of old houses is cramped and squalid, with memories for Feri of incestuous advances, women's talk of menstruation and rape, and memories of women listening to a monthly sermon by a Muslim priest and wailing as they once again heard of the tragedies of the Shia heroes of Iran.

For Feri the life of her own family house is incomplete. Her mother is living with another man in another town; her father has married again. Feri decides to cut short her holiday and go back to Boston. To do that she needs an Iranian exit visa, and to get that she needs the permission of her husband. It begins to seem that she has trapped herself and that she will never return to the clarity and light of suburban Boston.

She goes looking for her mother, and in a broken-down country town she finds a sad, broken-down mother. The mother needs help; but Feri, the biologist from Boston, needs love more. Finding her mother, she becomes like a child again; she falls ill. She is taken to the local hospital. She is nervous about its standards, but the doctor in charge reassures her. The equipment is modern, he says, and he himself was trained in the United States. He could have stayed there but – for reasons he cannot give, except that Iranians who go to the United States become unsettled – he preferred to come back; and then for a month, he says, he soothed himself by visiting mosques and shrines.

Feri is half-seduced by the doctor's understanding, and in the hospital she reflects on her time in the United States. She has always been a stranger, solitary in spite of husband and friends, always at a loss sexually and socially; she cannot say why she has done anything, why she has lived the American life. She has worked hard, but now even that work – of experiment and research – seems pointless, work for the sake of work, work for the sake of fitting in. Her time in the United States, in spite of study, work and husband, has been a time of emptiness. And then the doctor tells Feri that the pain in her stomach comes from an old ulcer. 'You brought it with you,' the doctor says. 'Now you have no right to be afraid of the hospital, me, or your country. What you have is a western disease.'

Feri's American husband, previously summoned, arrives to take her back. He is seen as a stranger, but fairly (and this fairness is part of the novel's virtue): a man of work and the intellect, private rather than solitary, self-sufficient, a man made by another civilization, his marriage to an Iranian his single unconventional act. It is impossible for Feri to go back with someone so remote to the American emptiness. She will lose her research job. But she doesn't mind.

She will, in fact, lay down that anxious, all-external life of work and the intellect. She will do as the doctor did; she will visit mosques and shrines, and to do that she will put on the *chador*. She feels she has never really been happy. Tranquillity comes to her with her renunciation (and oddly – a good stroke of the novelist's – ideas for research which she will now never carry out).

And – though the novelist doesn't make the point – it is as if Feri and the doctor, turning away from the life of intellect and endeavour, have come together in an Iranian death pact. In the emotions of their Shia religion, so particular to them, they will rediscover their self-esteem and wholeness, and be inviolate. They will no longer simply have to follow after others, not knowing where the rails are taking them. They will no longer have to be last, or even second. And life will go on. Other people in spiritually barren lands will continue to produce the equipment the doctor is proud of possessing and the medical journals he is proud of reading.

That expectation – of others continuing to create, of the alien, necessary civilization going on – is implicit in the act of renunciation, and is its great flaw.

2

❖❖❖❖❖

The Rule of Ali

IN AUGUST 1979, six months after the overthrow of the Shah, the news from Iran was still of executions. The official Iranian news agency kept count, and regularly gave a new grand total. The most recent executions had been of prostitutes and brothel-managers; the Islamic revolution had taken that wicked turn. The Ayatollah Khomeini was reported to have outlawed music. And Islamic rules about women were being enforced again. Mixed bathing had been banned; Revolutionary Guards watched the beaches at the Caspian Sea resorts and separated the sexes.

In London the man at the travel agency told me that Iran was a country people were leaving. Nobody was going in; I would have the plane to myself. It wasn't so. The Iran Air flight that day had been cancelled, and there was a crowd for the British Airways plane to Tehran.

Most of the passengers – the international mish-mash of the airport concourse sifting and sifting itself, through gates and channels, into more or less ethnic flight pens – were Iranians; and they didn't look like people running away from an Islamic revolution or going back to one. There wasn't a veil or a head-cover among the women, one or two of whom were quite stylish. They had all done a lot of shopping, and carried the variously designed plastic bags of London stores – Lilly-white, Marks and Spencer, Austin Reed.

In the plane I sat between two Iranians. The middle-aged woman in the window seat had a coppery skin and golden hair. Her hair looked dyed, her skin seemed stained; and the effect was eastern and antique, Egyptian: antique cosmetics aiding an antique idea of beauty. She spoke no English, and didn't behave like someone used to air travel. She was unhappy about the ventilation and spoke to the man on my left. She was big, he was small. I thought I was sitting between husband and wife, and offered to change seats with the man on my left.

He demurred, and said in English that his family were in the seats

20

across the aisle: his young son and daughter, and his handsome wife, who couldn't speak English, but smiled forgivingly at my error.

He was a physician. He and his family had just been to the United States to see their eighteen-year-old son.

I recognized that we were beginning to fall into an eastern, Indian kind of conversation, and I responded as I thought I should. I said, 'But that must have been expensive.'

'It was expensive. For the fare alone, 800 pounds per person. Except for the girl. She's under twelve. Over twelve you pay full fare. Have you been to the United States?'

'I've just spent a year there.'

'Are you a physician?'

I didn't feel, going to Iran, I should say I was a writer. I said, 'I am a teacher.' Then I felt I had pitched it too low, so I added, 'A professor.'

'That's good.' And, as though he drew courage from my calling and my time in America, he said, 'The revolution is terrible. They've destroyed the country. The army, everything. They've killed all the officers. Tehran was a nice city. Restaurants, cafés. Now there's nothing. That's why I sent my son away.'

The boy had been sent to the United States after the revolution, and he had already done well. He had got into a pre-medical school in Indiana. But the United States was more than a place to get an education. It was also – for the Iranian physician, as for the newly rich of so many insecure countries, politicians and businessmen, Arab, South American, West Indian, African – a sanctuary.

The physician said, 'I've bought a house there.'

'What did you pay?'

'Sixty-four thousand. Forty-four down, twenty on a loan.'

'Can foreigners buy property in America?'

'I will tell you. I bought it in my brother's name.' So the sanctuary had been prepared, and the migration begun, before the revolution. 'But now I've transferred it to my son's name. It's being rented now. Four hundred a month. Paying off the loan. How much do professors get?'

How much did they get? What figure could I give that would seem reasonable to a man who had just spent six thousand dollars on air fares for a family holiday? I said, 'Forty thousand dollars. How much do you make?'

'I have this government job in the mornings, in a hospital. I get fifteen hundred for that.'

'I thought they paid doctors more in Iran.'

'But then I have my own clinic in the afternoon, you see. I make about thirty thousand a year from that.'

'So you make about forty-eight.'

To the forty I had quoted for myself.

He said defensively, 'But I work hard. I am a man of forty-four. And now,' he added, wiping away his advantage, equalizing our chances, 'I don't know what will happen. These Muslims are a strange people. They have an *old* mentality. Very *old* mentality. They are bad to minorities.'

What was he then? Christian, Armenian, Zoroastrian, Jew? Eastern as our conversation had been, I couldn't bring myself to ask; and in the end, judging me to be safe, he told me. He was a Bahai. I knew the name, nothing more.

He had not lowered his voice when he had talked about the revolution and the wicked ways of Muslims. I assumed that he was sure of his fellow passengers; that I was among a group of Bahais. And in the stained-looking face and dyed gold hair of the woman beside me I saw a further, disquieting remoteness.

He said, 'We're international. We have a temple in America. Nice little temple.'

But, though open with me about money and job, the physician was less than frank about his religion. The Bahais – as I learned later from Behzad – had their own secret frenzy, and it derived from the Shia frenzy of Iran. The Shias were waiting for the Twelfth Imam; the Bahais believed that in the nineteenth century a deputy or surrogate, or the Twelfth Imam himself, had come and gone, and only they, the Bahais, had recognized him. Behzad told me that in the beginning they had been revolutionary, but then they had been corrupted by the British, competing with the Russians for control of Iran.

It seemed fanciful – I knew that Behzad valued only what was revolutionary. But it wasn't wholly fanciful. The Shia protest, occurring in the earliest days of the Islamic empire, was a political-racial protest among the subject peoples of that Arab empire; and the faith that had evolved with that protest had remained political, or liable to political manipulation. Recognizing their own line of succession to the Prophet, wailing every year for their martyrs, the men whose rightful claims had been denied, the Shias have remained suspicious of the authority of the state. The Bahai movement in the nineteenth century was subversive. An early call was for 'heads to be cut off, books and leaves burnt, places demolished and laid waste, and a general slaughter made'; in 1852 there was an attempt to kill the king.

Politically, though not in doctrine, the movement was like Khomeini's against the Shah. Politically, it didn't take; and the Bahais were left, or stranded, like many other Muslim sects, with the almost unapproachable intricacies of their faith: revelation within revelation, divergence within divergence.

The physician was right about the persecution, though. The Bahais' claim about the Twelfth Imam is to the Shias of Iran the most punishable kind of blasphemy; and after the Islamic revolution – proof of the rightness of the true faith – there were to be joyful popular outbursts against them, and sporadic 'revolutionary' executions. The sanctuary in the United States was necessary.

We made a technical stop at Kuwait, to refuel; no one left the plane. It was dark, but dawn was not far off. The light began to come; the night vanished. And we saw that the airport – such a pattern of electric lights from above – had been built on sand. The air that came through the ventilators was warm. It was 40 degrees centigrade outside, 104 fahrenheit, and the true day had not begun.

Tehran was going to be cooler, the steward said. It was an hour's flight to the north-east: more desert, oblongs of pale vegetation here and there, and here and there gathers of rippled earth that sometimes rose to mountains.

After all that I had heard about the Shah's big ideas for his country, the airport building at Tehran was a disappointment. The arrival hall was like a big shed. Blank rectangular patches edged with reddish dust – ghost pictures in ghostly frames – showed where, no doubt, there had been photographs of the Shah and his family or his monuments. Revolutionary leaflets and caricatures were taped down on walls and pillars; and – also taped down: sticky paper and handwritten notices giving a curious informality to great events – there were coloured photographs of the Ayatollah Khomeini, as hard-eyed and sensual and unreliable and roguish-looking as any enemy might have portrayed him.

The airport branch of the Melli Bank – rough tables, three clerks, a lot of paper, a littered floor – was like an Indian bazaar stall. A handwritten notice on the counter said: *Dear Guests. God is the Greatest. Welcome to the Islamic Republic of Iran.* Bits of sticky brown paper dotted the customs notice boards which advised passengers of their allowances. The brown paper did away with the liquor allowance; it was part of the Islamic welcome.

The luggage track which should have been rolling out our luggage didn't move for a long time. And the Iranian passengers (the physician and his family among them), with their London shopping bags, seemed to become different people. At London airport they had been Iranians, people from the fairyland of oil and money, spenders; now, in the shabby arrival hall, patient in their own setting and among their own kind, they looked like country folk who had gone to town.

The customs man had a little black brush moustache. He asked, 'Whisky?' His pronunciation of the word, and his smile, seemed to turn the query into a joke. When I said no he took my word and smilingly waved me out into the summer brightness, to face the post-revolutionary rapaciousness of the airport taxi-men, who after six months were more than ever animated by memories of the old days, when the world's salesmen came to Tehran, there were never enough hotel rooms, and no driver pined for a fare.

The colours of the city were as dusty and pale as they had appeared from the air. Dust blew about the road, coated the trees, dimmed the colours of cars. Bricks and plaster were the colour of dust; unfinished buildings looked abandoned and crumbling; and walls, like abstracts of the time, were scribbled over in the Persian script and stencilled with portraits of Khomeini.

On the outskirts of the city, in what looked like waste ground, I saw a low khaki-coloured tent, a queue of men and veiled women, and some semi-uniformed men. I thought of refugees from the countryside, dole queues. But then – seeing another tent and another queue in front of an unfinished apartment block – I remembered it was the day of an election, the second test of the people's will since the revolution. The first had been a referendum; the people had voted then for an Islamic republic. This election was for an 'assembly of experts', who would work out an Islamic constitution. Khomeini had advised that priests should be elected.

Experts were necessary, because an Islamic constitution couldn't simply be adopted. No such thing existed or had ever existed. An Islamic constitution was something that had to be put together; and it had to be something of which the Prophet would have approved. The trouble there was that the Prophet, creating his seventh-century Arabian state, guided always by divine revelation, had very much ruled as his own man. That was where the priests came in. They might not have ideas about a constitution – a constitution was, after all, a concept from outside the Muslim world; but, with their knowledge of the Koran and the doings of the Prophet, the priests would know what was un-Islamic.

My hotel was in central Tehran. It was one of the older hotels of the city. It was behind a high wall; it had a gateman's lodge, an asphalted circular drive, patches of lawn with shrubs and trees. It was in better order than I had imagined; there were even a few cars. But the building the driver took me to had a chain across the glass door. Someone shouted from the other side of the compound. The building we had gone to was closed. It was the older building of the hotel; during the boom they had built a new block, and now it was only that block that was open.

A number of young men – the hotel taxi-drivers, to whom the cars outside belonged – were sitting idly together in one corner of the lobby, near the desk. Away from that corner the lobby was empty. In the middle of the floor there was a very large patterned carpet; the chairs arranged about it appeared to await a crowd. There were glass walls on two sides. On one side was the courtyard, with the dusty shrubs and pines and the parked hotel taxis; on the other side, going up to the hotel wall, was a small paved pool area, untenanted, glaring in the light, with metal chairs stacked below an open shed.

The room to which I was taken up was of a good size, with sturdy wooden furniture, and with wood panelling three or four feet up the side walls. The glass wall at the end faced North Tehran; a glass door opened on to a balcony. But the air-conditioning duct was leaking through its exhaust grille, and the blue carpet tiling in the vestibule was sodden and stained.

The hotel man – it was hard, in the idleness of the hotel, to attach the professional status of 'boy' to him, though he wore the uniform – smiled and pointed to the floor above and said, 'Bathroom,' as though explanation was all that was required. The man he sent up spoke about condensation; he made the drips seem normal, even necessary. And then – explanations abruptly abandoned – I was given another room.

It was furnished like the first and had the same view. On the television set here, though, there was a white card, folded down the middle and standing upright. It gave the week's programmes on the 'international', English-language service of Iranian television. The service had long been suspended. The card was six months old. The revolution had come suddenly to this hotel.

It was Ramadan, the Muslim fasting month; it was Friday, the sabbath; and it was an election day. Tehran was unusually quiet, but I didn't know that; and when in the afternoon I went walking I felt I was in a city where a calamity had occurred. The shops in the main streets were closed and protected by steel gates. Signs on every floor shrieked the names of imported things: Seiko, Citizen, Rolex, Mary Quant of Chelsea, Aiwa; and on that closed afternoon they were like names from Tehran's past.

The pavements were broken. Many shop signs were broken or had lost some of their raised letters. Dust and grime were so general, and on illuminated signs looked so much like the effect of smoke, that buildings that had been burnt out in old fires did not immediately catch the eye.

Building work seemed to have been suspended; rubble heaps and gravel heaps looked old, settled.

On the walls were posters of the revolution, and in the pavement kiosks there were magazines of the revolution. The cover of one had a composite photograph of the Shah as a bathing beauty: the head of the Shah attached to the body of a woman in a bikini – but the bikini had been brushed over with a broad stroke of black, not to offend modesty. In another caricature the Shah, jacketed, his tie slackened, sat on a lavatory seat with his trousers down, and with a tommy-gun in his hand. A suitcase beside him was labelled *To Israel* and *Bahama*; an open canvas bag showed a bottle of whisky and a copy of *Time* magazine.

Young men in tight, open-necked shirts dawdled on the broken pavements. They were handsome men of a clear racial type, small, broad-shouldered, narrow-waisted. They were working men of peasant antecedents, and there was some little air of vanity and danger about them that afternoon: they must have been keyed up by the communal Friday prayers. In their clothes, and especially their shirts, there was that touch of flashiness which – going by what I had seen in India – I associated with people who had just emerged from traditional ways and now possessed the idea that, in clothes as in other things, they could choose for themselves.

The afternoon cars and motor-cycles went by, driven in the Iranian way. I saw two collisions. One shop had changed its name. It was now 'Our Fried Chicken', no longer the chicken of Kentucky, and the figure of the southern colonel had been fudged into something quite meaningless (except to those who remembered the colonel). Revolutionary Guards, young men with guns, soon ceased to be surprising; they were part of the revolutionary sabbath scene. There were crowds outside the cinemas; and, Ramadan though it was, people were buying pistachio nuts and sweets from the *confiseries* – so called – that were open.

Far to the north, at the end of a long avenue of plane trees, an avenue laid out by the Shah's father, was the Royal Tehran Hilton. It was 'royal' no longer. The word had been taken off the main roadside sign and hacked away from the entrance; but inside the hotel the word survived like a rooted weed, popping up fresh and clean on napkins, bills, menus, crockery.

The lounge was nearly empty; the silence there, among waiters and scattered patrons, was like the silence of embarrassment. Iranian samovars were part of the décor. (There had been some foreign trade in these samovars as decorative ethnic objects; two years or so before I had seen a number of them in the London stores, converted into lamp-stands.) Alcohol could no longer be served; but for the smart (and non-Christian) who needed to sip a non-alcoholic drink in style, there was Orange Blossom or Virgin Mary or Swinger.

Chez Maurice was the Hilton's French restaurant. It was done up in an appropriate way, with brownish paper, a dark-coloured dado, and sconce-lights. On the glass panels of one wall white letters, set in little arcs, said: *Vins et Liqueurs, Le Patron Mange Içi, Gratinée à Toute Heure*. In the large room, which might have seated a hundred, there was only a party of five, and they were as subdued as the people in the lounge. The soup I had, like the sturgeon which followed it, was heavy with a brown paste. But the waiters still undid napkins and moved and served with panache; it added to the embarrassment.

Every table was laid. Every table had a fresh rose, and pre-revolutionary give-aways: the coloured postcard (the restaurant had been founded four years before, in 1975); the little ten-page note pad that diners in places like this were thought to need: *Chez Maurice, Tehran's Most Distinctive Restaurant, Le Restaurant le Plus Select de Tehran*. Six months after the revolution these toys – pads, postcards – still existed; when they were used up there would be no more.

The pool at the side of the hotel was closed, for chemical cleaning, according to the notice. But the great concrete shell next door, the planned extension to the Royal Tehran Hilton, had been abandoned, with all the building materials on the site and the cranes. There were no 'passengers' now, the waiter said; and the contractors had left the country. From the Hilton you could look across to the other hills of North Tehran and see other unfinished, hollow buildings that looked just as abandoned. The revolution had caught the 'international' city of North Tehran in mid-creation.

And I thought, when I went back to my hotel, that there was an unintended symbolism in the revolutionary poster on the glass front door. The poster was printed on both sides. The side that faced the courtyard was straightforward, a guerrilla pin-up of Yasser Arafat of the Palestine Liberation Organization in dark glasses and checkered red headdress.

On the reverse was an allegorical painting of blood and revenge. In the foreground there was a flat landscape: a flat, featureless land bisected by a straight black road, marked down the middle by a broken white line. On this road a veiled woman, seen from the back, lay half-collapsed, using her last strength to lift up her child as if to heaven. The woman had a bloodied back; there was blood on the black road. Out of that blood, higher up the road, giant red tulips had grown, breaking up the heavy crust of the black road with the white markings; and above the tulips, in the sky, was the face of Khomeini, the saviour, frowning.

Khomeini saved and avenged. But the tulips he had called up from the blood of martyrs had damaged the modern road (so carefully rendered by the artist) for good; that road in the wilderness now led nowhere.

Also, in this allegory of the revolution, personality had been allowed only to the avenger. The wounded woman, small in the foreground, with whose pain the upheaval began, was veiled and faceless; she was her pain alone. It was the allegorist's or caricaturist's licence; and it wouldn't have been remarkable if there hadn't been so many faceless people in the posters and drawings I had seen that day.

In one election poster a faceless crowd – the veiled women reduced to simple triangular outlines – held up photographs of candidates of a particular party. In a newspaper the face of Ali, the Shia hero, the cousin and son-in-law of the Prophet, was shown as a surrealist outline, transparent against a landscape. In one poster Khomeini himself had been faceless, his features (within the outline of turban, cheeks and beard) replaced by a clenched fist.

Facelessness had begun to seem like an Islamic motif. And it was, indeed, the subject of protest in *Iran Week* (lettering like *Newsweek*), a post-revolutionary English-language paper I had bought in a kiosk. The paper was for the revolution, but it was protesting against what had begun to come with the revolution, all the Islamic bans on alcohol, western television programmes, fashions, music, mixed bathing, women's sports, dancing. The cover illustration showed a twisted sitting-room where walls had been replaced by iron bars. The family posing for their picture in this room – father, mother, two children – were dressed in western clothes; but where their faces should have been there were white blanks.

Individualism was to be surrendered to the saviour and avenger. But when the revolution was over, individualism – in the great city the Shah had built – was to be cherished again. That seemed to be the message of the *Iran Week* cover.

In the morning, traffic was heavy on the flyover to the left of the hotel. The mountains to the north were soft in the light, but fading fast in the haze.

I telephoned the editor-in-chief of *Iran Week* and he asked me to come over right away. I had to be careful, though, he said: there were two buildings in the street with the same number, 61. And when I had found the right 61, I had to remember that if I took the lift, the office was on the sixth floor; if I walked up it was on the fourth.

The hotel taxi-driver had trouble finding any 61; and the one we did find, after doing a number of Iranian turnarounds in Iranian traffic, was the wrong one. So we hunted, the morning melting away; and then we saw the second 61. Sixth floor for the lift, the editor had said; fourth if I walked up. But the board in the lobby said the paper was on the fifth; and there was no sign of a lift. The driver and I walked up and up.

The office was unexpectedly spacious, with a cool girl at a desk in the front room. And after all the time I had taken to get there, and after his own brisk invitation, Mr Abdi, the young editor-in-chief, was frankly disappointed in me. I represented no English or American paper, as he had thought. He said he could give me ten minutes; I shouldn't send the driver away.

But then, in his own office, he softened his executive manner and, becoming more Iranian, graciously ordered tea, which came in small glasses. He said that to understand Iran I should go to the holy city of Qom and talk to the people in the streets. I said I couldn't talk Persian; he said they couldn't talk English. So there we were.

Softening again, he said – but in a way which permitted me to see that nothing was going to happen – that he would try to get one of his researchers to make an appointment with me.

Just then the head researcher came in. He promised to see what he could do for me. Underground work had kept them all very busy for three years, the head researcher said; and they were still very busy. He was tall for a Persian, and grave, and he had a pretty leather briefcase. But he wasn't as stylish as his editor-in-chief, who was unusually handsome, and in whose executive manner there was a certain amount of mischievousness.

I asked about the *Iran Week* cover. Were Iranian families, even middle-class families, as 'nuclear' as the cover suggested? I had expected Iranian families to be more traditional, more extended. Sharply, as though to head me off the topic of Muslim polygamy, Mr Abdi said that Iranian middle-class families were as the cover had shown them.

There was a big map of the Caribbean and the Gulf of Mexico on the wall. I thought it might have been there for the sake of Cuba and Nicaragua, old and new centres of revolution. But no. Mr Abdi had gone to Cayenne, French Guiana, to write about Devil's Island for a Persian magazine that was doing a series on prisons.

He said, 'It's bad to travel alone. You should have a girl.'

He had had a girl on his Cayenne trip: West Indian women were lovely. West Indian? A black woman for Mr Abdi? He said, 'I am wrong. She wasn't West Indian. She was *mexique*.' He raised his head a little, as if remembering; and his black eyes went hollow.

This was the dandy side of the revolution. Even after a day in

Tehran – and in spite of the advice to go and talk to the people in Qom – I felt it was far from the revolution of Khomeini and the streets. And six months later, when I returned to Tehran at the end of my Islamic journey, *Iran Week* was hard to find.

The next day was going to be a public holiday again – Constitution Day, to mark Iran's first written constitution, achieved only in 1906 – and the commercial streets were busy.

On Nadir Shah Avenue – Nadir Shah was the Persian king who raided Delhi in 1739 and stole and broke up Shah Jahan's Peacock Throne, the jewels of which are still part of the Iranian state treasure – pavement hawkers and the sun and the dust made India feel close. And in Firdowsi Street, where the money-changers' booths faced the long blank wall of the British embassy compound, the atmosphere was a little like that of a red-light area, with everybody on the prowl, accosting or waiting to be accosted.

The money-changers offered better rates than the banks. They had their name-boards and some of them offered a window display of coins and facsimile notes; but, after that, their little booths were furnished strictly for business: desk, chairs, telephone, iron safes, a portrait of Khomeini. And their manners matched their rooms. They looked up, they said no, they looked away. They didn't want my signed traveller's cheques. Only Mr Nasser was interested; but then he wanted all the cheques I had; and then he wanted to sell me the old silk carpet hanging on the wall for 500 pounds.

Some of the changers worked from what were literally gaps in the wall. Some had no offices; they, more carefully dressed, prowled up and down Firdowsi with their briefcases.

At the top of the street, near a newspaper kiosk, I saw a small middle-aged man who looked more Indian than Iranian. At first I thought he was taking the air; then I thought he was a changer. I accosted him and he behaved as though I was a changer.

He was an Indian, a Shia Muslim from Bombay, and he had been living in Iran for twenty years. He wasn't a changer; he was a buyer; he had come to Firdowsi to buy dollars. He had been offered dollars at 115 rials. It was a good rate; but he was a man of business and he thought that if he stood his ground, if he continued to show himself, he might eventually tempt one of the ambulant changers to come down a rial or two.

A young man – Indian, Pakistani or Iranian – came and stood anxiously near us. He was a friend or dependent relative of the man from

Bombay. He had been brought out to help with buying the dollars and had been making inquiries on his own.

And, as though he felt some explanation was necessary, the man from Bombay said, 'In the old days these shops used to be stuffed with foreign currency. Stuffed. Nobody cared for any foreign currency here. Every body wanted rials.' But he wasn't grieving for the Shah's rule. 'You must forgive my language. The Shah was a bastard.'

It was a hard word; it encouraged the young man to shed his anxiousness and talk. The topic of foreign currency was laid aside; it was of the injustices of the Shah that the two men spoke, each man supporting the other, leading the other on, until – in that dusty street with the plane trees, the shoe-shine men, the pavement coin-sellers – they were both at the same pitch of passion.

When the Shah ruled, everything in Iran had been for him. He had drained the country of billions; he had allowed the country to be plundered by foreign companies; he had filled the country with foreign advisers and technicians. These foreigners got huge salaries and lived in the big houses; the Americans even had their own television service. The people of Iran felt they had lost their country. And the Shah never really cared for religion, the precious Shia faith.

'What a nice thing it is now,' the man from Bombay said, 'to see the rule of Ali! Getting women back into the veil, getting them off television. No alcohol.'

It was astonishing, after the passion. Was that all that there was to the rule of Ali? Did the Shia millennium offer nothing higher? The man from Bombay and his companion could say nothing more, had nothing more to say; and perhaps they couldn't say that the true rewards of the revolution – as much a matter of undoing dishonour to Ali and the true faith, as of overthrowing the wicked – lay in heaven.

And the man from Bombay had another surprise for me. He wasn't staying with the rule of Ali. He was leaving Iran, after his twenty good years under the bad Shah, and going back to Bombay. That was why he had come to buy dollars in Firdowsi. His excess air baggage – and I gathered there was a lot – had to be paid for in dollars.

He said, and it was like another man speaking, 'I don't know what's going to happen here now.'

At *Iran Week* I had been given ten minutes. At the *Tehran Times* I was almost offered a job. The *Times* was the new English-language daily; its motto was 'May Truth Prevail'. The office was new, well-equipped and busy, and there were some American or European helpers.

Mr Parvez, the editor, was an Iranian of Indian origin, a gentle man in his mid-forties. Galleys were being brought to his table all the time, and I felt I wasn't holding him with my explanation of my visit. Our conversation began to go strange.

He said, 'Are you a Muslim?'

'No. But I don't think it's necessary.'

'Islam is a touchy subject here.' On the wall behind Mr Parvez was a large, severe photograph of Khomeini.

'I know.'

'What is the money basis of this?' Mr Parvez said, bending over a galley.

'Of what, Mr Parvez?'

'Of what you want to write for us.'

We disengaged – in fact, as I learned later, money was the touchy subject in that office: there wasn't much of it – and I was passed on to the next desk, to Mr Jaffrey, an older man, who had a story or a feature or an editorial in his typewriter, but broke off to talk to me.

Mr Jaffrey, too, was an Indian Shia. He came from Lucknow. He said he was told 'rather bluntly' in 1948 that as a Muslim he had no future in the Indian Air Force. So he had migrated to Pakistan. In Pakistan, as a Shia, he had run into difficulties of another sort, and ten years later he had moved to Iran. Now he was full of anxiety about Iran.

He spoke briskly; everything he said he had already thought out. 'All Muslim people tend to put their faith in one man. In the 1960s the Shah was loved. Now they love Khomeini. I never thought the time would come when Khomeini would usurp the position of the Shah.' Khomeini should have stood down after the revolution in favour of the administrators, but he hadn't; and as a result the country was now in the hands of 'fanatics'.

Someone brought Mr Jaffrey a dish of fried eggs and a plate of *pappadom*, crisp fried Indian bread.

I said, 'What about Ramadan?'

He said in his brisk way, 'I'm not fasting.'

He had been for Khomeini right through the revolution, because during the rule of the Shah the alternatives had become simple: religion or atheism. Every kind of corruption had come to Iran during the Shah's rule: money corruption, prostitution, sodomy. The Shah was too cut off; he woke up too late to what was going on.

'And I thought, even in those days,' Mr Jaffrey said, 'that Islam was the answer.'

I couldn't follow. Religion, the practice of religion, the answer to a political need?

32

I said, 'The answer to what, Mr Jaffrey?'

'The situation of the country. Islam stands for four things. Brotherhood, honesty, the will to work, proper recompense for labour.'

Still I didn't follow. Why not call for those four things? Why go beyond those four things? Why involve those four things with something as big as Islam?

'You see,' Mr Jaffrey said, and he became softer, 'all my life I've wanted to see the true *jamé towhidi*. I translate that as "the society of believers".'

It was the rule of Ali again: the dream of the society ruled purely by faith. But Mr Jaffrey's faith was profounder than the faith of the man from Bombay; for him the rule of Ali was more than getting women back into the veil. Mr Jaffrey's society of believers derived from an idea of the earliest days of Islam, when the Prophet handed down the divine laws, led his people in war and prayer, when every action, however worldly, served the true faith.

That was the kind of society that had to come to Iran. And Mr Jaffrey – with his Indian-British education, and as if with another side of his personality – thought that such a society could be secured by institutions: by getting the mullahs back into the mosques, getting Khomeini to stand down, and putting politicians and administrators into the administration. So, though Mr Jaffrey didn't say it, to secure his dream of oneness, church and state were to be divided. Faith, education, and political instinct had locked Mr Jaffrey into that contradiction.

It was simpler for the man from Bombay. He was happy to see in the rule of Ali, and run. Mr Jaffrey was anguished that a dream, which had come so close, had been dashed by Khomeini.

And I had also to recognize that that dream of the society of believers excluded me. In that newspaper office – typewriters, galleys, the English language, telephones, 'May Truth Prevail' – nothing of the intellectual life that I valued was of account; the convergences of sentiment or reason that occurred from time to time were coincidental.

In the open space downstairs someone called out to me in an executive American voice, 'Can I help you?'

It was one of the Iranian 'directors' of the paper, and he was as unlikely a figure as could be imagined in the service of the *jamé towhidi*. He was young, handsome, well-barbered, with a black moustache. With the tips of his fingers he was holding down a chocolate-brown jacket that rested square on his shoulders, setting off the fawn trousers, the biscuit-coloured shirt, and the wide-knotted wide tie.

He must have thought I was another Indian Shia with the gift of the English language and with a need for a few rials; and in his executive-like way he began to walk me up and down, firing off questions, frowning at the floor, his skin a little moist from all the clothes he was wearing, and saying, 'Certainly, certainly,' to everything I said. When he understood that I didn't want to write for the paper, he stopped walking with me. And when I said goodbye he said, 'Certainly, certainly.'

Remember that director. Remember the busy newspaper office; Mr Jaffrey at his typewriter; and the galleys falling on the desk of the gentle editor who would have offered a stranger a job. Six months later, when I went back to Tehran, that office was desolate.

One of the English-language magazines I bought was published from the holy city of Qom. It was *The Message of Peace*, and, as its title warned, it was full of rage.

It raged about the Shah; about the 'devils' of the West and the evils of its technology; it even raged about poor old Mr Desai, the Indian prime minister, who banned alcohol (good, from the Muslim point of view) but drank urine (from the Muslim point of view, deplorable). But it wasn't for its rages that I bought the magazine, or for the speeches of Khomeini, or for the biographies of the Shia Imams. I bought the *Message of Peace* for an article on Islamic urban planning.

Could there be such a thing? Apparently; and more, it was badly needed. Islam was a complete way of life; it didn't separate the worldly from the spiritual. Hence it was necessary, in addition to avoiding materialist industrial excess, to plan for 'a theocentric society'. In this society women also had to be sheltered. Problems! But the very existence of these problems proved the need for sensible Islamic planning. And a solution was possible.

Build, at the corners of an imagined square, four residential areas. Give each a mosque, a clinic and a nursery: that is where the women will busy themselves. The men will go to work. They will go to work in the centre of the square. At the very heart of this working area there will be a mosque large enough to hold all the male population. With the mosque there will be an alms-giving centre, since the giving of alms is as important in Islam as prayer, or fasting, or the pilgrimage to Mecca.

In a circle around the mosque there will be a bazaar; around the bazaar will be a circle of offices; and at the perimeter of this office circle there will be hospitals, maternity homes and schools, so that men on their way to work can take their children to school, and on other occasions can rush to hospitals or maternity homes.

For recreation, women can meet and chat. Men can ride horses or take up flying. 'The idea is not to encourage such games which distract the religious consciousness of the community.'

There are certain other Islamic requirements. Water from recycled sewage is not to be used, except for irrigation. 'The concept of cleanliness, and water as the medium of bodily cleanliness, is strong in Islam. The purifying agent for water is water itself and the chemical and biological processes are not acceptable from the religious point of view.'

The houses in the residential areas are to be so aligned that the prayer call from the mosque can reach them without the use of an amplifier. There is a final detail. 'The toilet fixtures like water closets shall be so arranged as to make the user not to face the City of Mecca either from his front or back side.'

The mountains to the north of Tehran showed in the morning light, faded in the daytime haze, and at sunset became a faint amethyst outline. The lights came on; here and there neon signs did their little jigs. The traffic roared. But through all the hectic-seeming day the cranes on the unfinished buildings had never moved.

Technology was evil. E. F. Schumacher of *Small is Beautiful* had said so: *The Message of Peace* quoted him a lot, lashing the West with its own words. But technology surrounded us in Tehran, and some of it had been so Islamized or put to such good Islamic use that its foreign origin seemed of no account.

The hotel taxi-driver could be helped through the evening traffic jams by the Koranic readings on his car radio; and when we got back to the hotel there would be mullahs on television. Certain modern goods and tools – cars, radios, television – were necessary; their possession was part of a proper Islamic pride. But these things were considered neutral; they were not associated with any particular faith or civilization; they were thought of as the stock of some great universal bazaar.

Money alone bought these things. And money, in Iran, had become the true gift of God, the reward for virtue. Whether Tehran worked or not, seventy million dollars went every day to the country's external accounts, to be drawn off as required: foreign currencies, secured by foreign laws and institutions, to keep the Islamic revolution going.

But some people were scratchy. They could be scratchy in empty restaurants where they didn't have the food their old-time menus offered. They needed customers, but they couldn't help hating those who came. They were scratchy at my hotel, for an additional reason. After the revolution the owners had left the country. The hotel had been

35

taken over by a revolutionary *komiteh*, and it was important for every-one downstairs to display pride. (It was different upstairs. The chamber-maid told me by signs one morning that I wasn't to use the hotel laundry; she would wash my clothes. She did. When I came back in the afternoon I saw my damp clothes displayed in the corridor, hung out to dry on the door-knobs of unoccupied rooms.)

Nicholas, a young British journalist, came to see me one evening and – starting from cold – began absolutely to quarrel with the man at the desk about the hotel taxi charges. The quarrel developed fast in the empty lobby.

Nicholas, tall and thin and with a little beard, was jumpy from overwork: the long hours he kept as a foreign correspondent, the 'disin-formation' he said he had constantly to sift through, the sheer number of words he had to send back every day. He had also begun to be irritated by the events he was reporting.

The man at the desk was big and paunchy, with a sallow skin and curly black hair. He wore a suit and radiated pride. His pride, and Nicholas's rage made him lose his head. He went back to the manners and language of old times.

He said, 'If you don't like the hotel, you can leave.'

Nicholas, with the formality of high temper, said, 'It is my good fortune *not* to be staying at the hotel.'

I took the car at the stated price, to calm them both down.

Nicholas leaned on the desk, but looked away. The man at the desk began to write out the taxi requisition slip. In spite of his appearance, he was a man from the countryside. He had spent a fair amount of money to send his mother on the pilgrimage to Mecca; he was anxious about money and the future, and worried about the education of his children. During the boom an American university education had seemed possible for the boy, but now he had to think of other ways.

Nicholas was closed to pity. He remembered the boom, too, when hotels had no rooms, and he and many others had slept on camp-beds in the ballroom of a grand hotel and paid five dollars a night.

He said, 'For seven months no one in this country has done a stroke of work. Where else can you do that and live?'

The revolution continued. The election results showed – although there were charges of rigging – that the people had done as Khomeini had told them, and voted in mullahs and ayatollahs to the constitution-framing Assembly of Experts. A man was executed for having a two-month affair with a married woman. The Revolutionary Committee for Guild Affairs warned women hairdressers (mainly Armenian) to stop 'wasting their youth' and cutting the hair of men. And some frightened carpet-washers began to advertize an 'Islamic carpet-wash' – the carpet to be rinsed three times in water.

Five billion dollars' worth of American F-14 jets were written off, their missile system too 'difficult and uneconomical'. And other big pre-revolutionary projects were cancelled, in addition to the two West German nuclear power plants on which a billion dollars were owed. The six-lane highway to the southern port of Bandar Abbas was taken away from an American consortium and given to an Iranian contractor: 'In the first stage of the work two lanes will be constructed.' There were reports of sabotage: the Israelis had been sabotaging the 'normal operations' of the Arya National Shipping Line. The Kurds in the north-west were in rebellion; the Arabs in the south-west were restive.

The speeches never stopped. The Minister of Labour and Social Welfare made one and got his picture in the papers: the mosque, he said, was not only a place of worship but also 'a base for launching anti-colonialistic movements in a display of unity, thought and action'. Unity: it was the theme of a big Friday sabbath feature in the *Tehran Times*, 'Why has Islam the potential for revolution?'

Unity, union, the backs bowed in prayers that were like drills, the faith of one the faith of all, the faith of all flowing into the faith of one and becoming divine, personality and helplessness abolished: union, surrender, facelessness, heaven.

'How did you like the Hilton?' one of the hotel desk clerks asked me. He was less buttoned up than the others: he dealt in a small way in silver coins and was on the point of selling me two.

'It was empty.'

'All the hotels are empty. It will change in two months. There is no government now. In two months we will have a government. At least that's what we say.'

He was a devout man, like the others in the hotel. No sermon on television was too long for him.

They spoke, in Iran, of the oneness of faith and deed. That oneness had overcome the Shah and his armed forces. That oneness was all that was still needed. But they were fooling themselves. What, after the centuries of despotism, they really believed was that the state was something apart, something that looked after itself and was ever restored. And even while with their faith they were still pulling it all down – hotel, city, state – they were waiting for it to start up again, to be as it was before.

I decided then to go to the holy city of Qom; and that was when I met

Behzad. He led me through the traffic and said, 'You must always give your hand to me.' I liked the words; they answered my need. Without the language, and in the midst of these Iranian contradictions, I needed now to be led by an Iranian hand.

Then Behzad translated the legend in the revolutionary poster – 'Twelfth Imam, we are waiting for you' – and I was taken to another level of wonder.

3

❖❖❖❖❖

The Holy City

BEHZAD AND I went to Qom by car. It was past noon when we got back to the hotel; and the hotel taxi-drivers, idle though they were, didn't want to make the long desert trip. Only one man offered – he was the man who had made me listen to the Koranic readings on his car radio one evening – and he asked for seventy dollars. Behzad said it was too much; he knew someone who would do it for less.

We waited a long time for Behzad's driver, and then we found that between our negotiations on the telephone and his arrival at the hotel his charges had gone up. He was a small, knotty man, and he said he wasn't a Muslim. He didn't mean that. He meant only that he wasn't a Shia or a Persian. He was a 'tribesman', a Lur, from Luristan in the west.

Qom had a famous shrine, the tomb of the sister of the eighth Shia Imam; for a thousand years it had been a place of pilgrimage. It also had a number of theological schools. Khomeini had taught and lectured at Qom; and on his return to Iran after the fall of the Shah he had made Qom his headquarters. He was surrounded there by ayatollahs, people of distinction in their own right, and it was one of these attendant figures, Ayatollah Khalkhalli, whom I was hoping to see.

Khomeini received and preached and blessed; Khalkhalli hanged. He was Khomeini's hanging judge. It was Khalkhalli who had conducted many of those swift Islamic trials that had ended in executions, with official before-and-after photographs: men shown before they were killed, and then shown dead, naked on the sliding mortuary slabs.

Khalkhalli had recently been giving interviews, emphasizing his activities as judge, and a story in Tehran was that he had fallen out of favour and was trying through these interviews to keep his reputation alive. He told the *Tehran Times* that he had 'probably' sentenced four hundred people to death in Tehran. 'On some nights, he said, bodies of thirty or more people would be sent out in trucks from the prison. He claimed he had also signed the death warrants of a large number of people in

Khuzistan Province.' Khuzistan was the Arab province in the south-west, where the oil was.

He told another paper that there had been a plot – worked out in the South Korean embassy – to rescue Hoveyda, the Shah's prime minister, and other important people from the Tehran jail. As soon as he, Khal-khalli, had heard of this plot he had decided – to deal a blow to the CIA and Zionism – to bring forward the cases. 'I reviewed all their cases in one night and had them face the firing squad.' He told the *Tehran Times* how Hoveyda had died. The first bullet hit Hoveyda in the neck; it didn't kill him. Hoveyda was then ordered by his executioner – a priest – to hold his head up; the second bullet hit him in the head and killed him.

'Would this man see me?' I had asked an agency correspondent, when we were talking about Khalkhalli.

'He would *love* to see you.'

And Behzad thought it could be arranged. Behzad said he would telephone Khalkhalli's secretary when we got to Qom.

The telephone, the secretary: the modern apparatus seemed strange. But Khalkhalli saw himself as a man of the age. 'He said' – this was from the *Tehran Times* – 'the religious leaders were trying to enforce the rule of the Holy Prophet Mohammed in Iran. During the days of the Prophet swords were used to fight, now they have been replaced by Phantom aircraft.' Phantoms: not American, not the products of a foreign science, but as international as swords, part of the stock of the great world bazaar, and rendered Islamic by purchase.

There was a confusion of this sort in Behzad's mind as well, though Behzad was not religious, was communist, and had been kept away from religion by his communist father. Behzad's father had been imprisoned during the Shah's time, and Behzad had inherited his father's dream of a 'true' revolution. Such a revolution hadn't come to Iran; but Behzad, employing all the dialectic he had learnt, was forcing himself to see, in the religious fervour of Khomeini's revolution, the outline of what could be said to be true. And as we drove south through Tehran – at first like a bazaar, and then increasingly like a settlement in a polluted desert – it was the city of proletarian revolt that he was anxious to show me.

Low brick buildings were the colour of dust; walls looked unfinished; bright interiors seemed as impermanent as their paint. Tehran, in the flat land to the south, had been added and added to by people coming in from the countryside; and clusters of traditional square clay-brick houses with flat roofs were like villages.

We passed a great factory shed. Some kind of beige fur had adhered to the walls below every window. Behzad told me it was a cloth factory and had been a centre of the revolution. The army had gone in, and many workers had been killed.

After the oil refinery, puffing out flame from its chimney, we were in the true desert. There were no trees now, and the views were immense: mounds, hills, little ranges. The road climbed, dipped into wide valleys. Hills and mounds were smooth, and sometimes, from a distance and from certain angles, there was the faintest tinge of green on the brown, from tufts of grass and weeds which were then seen to be really quite widely scattered.

From the top of a hill we saw, to the left, the salt lake marked on the map. It looked small and white, as though it was about to cake into salt; and the white had a fringe of pale green. Behzad said that sometimes it all looked blue. Many bodies had been dumped there by the Shah's secret police, from helicopters. And the lake was bigger than it looked. It was a desolation when we began to pass it; the green water that fringed the white was very far away. The land after that became more broken. Hills were less rounded, their outlines sharper against the sky.

It was desert, but the road was busy; and occasionally there were roadside shacks where soft drinks or melons could be had. Behzad thought we should drink or eat something before we got to Qom; in Qom, where they were strict about the Ramadan fasting, there would be nothing to eat or drink before sunset.

We stopped at a bus and truck halt, with a big rough café in Mediterranean colours and a watermelon stall on a platform beside the road. The watermelon man, seated at his stall below a thin cotton awning that gave almost no shade, was sleeping on his arms.

We woke him up and bought a melon, and he lent a knife and forks. Behzad halved the melon and cut up the flesh, and we all three – the driver joining us without being asked – squatted round the melon, eating as it were from the same dish. Behzad, I could see, liked the moment of serving and sharing. It could be said that it was a Muslim moment; it was the kind of sharing Muslims practised – and the driver had joined us as a matter of course. But the driver was a worker; Behzad was sharing food with someone of the people, and he was imposing his own ritual on this moment in the desert.

Two saplings had been planted on the platform. One was barked and dead; the other was half dead. Between them lay an old, sunburnt, ill-looking woman in black, an inexplicable bit of human debris an hour away from Tehran. Scraps of newspaper from the stall blew about in the sand, and caught against the trunks of the trees. Across the road a lorry idled, its exhaust smoking; and traffic went by all the time.

We squatted in the sand and ate. The driver spat out the watermelon seeds on to the road. I did as the driver did; and Behzad – but more reverentially – did likewise. Abruptly, stabbing his fork into the melon, saying nothing, the square-headed little Lur jumped off the platform. He was finished; he had had enough of the melon. He walked across the dingy desert yard to the café to look for a lavatory, and Behzad's moment was over.

I had imagined that Qom, a holy city, would have been built on hills: it would have been full of cliff walls and shadows and narrow lanes cut into the rock, with cells or caves where pious men meditated. It was set flat in the desert, and the approach to it was like the approach to any other desert town: shacks, gas stations. The road grew neater; shacks gave way to houses. A garden bloomed on a traffic roundabout – Persian gardens had this abrupt, enclosed, oasis-like quality. A dome gleamed in the distance between minarets. It was the dome of the famous shrine.

Behzad said, 'That dome is made of gold.'

It had been gilded in the last century. But the city we began to enter had been enriched by oil; and it seemed like a reconstructed bazaar city, characterless except for the gold dome and its minarets.

Behzad said, 'How shall I introduce you? Correspondent? Khalkhalli likes correspondents.'

'That isn't how I want to talk to him, though. I really just want to chat with him. I want to understand how he became what he is.'

'I'll say you are a writer. Where shall I say you come from?'

That was a problem. England would be truest, but would be misleading. Trinidad would be mystifying, and equally misleading. South America was a possibility, but the associations were wrong.

'Can you say I am from the Americas? Would that make sense in Persian?'

Behzad said, 'I will say that you come from America, but you are not an American.'

We made for the dome and stopped in a parking area outside the shrine. It was mid-afternoon, and hotter in the town than in the desert; the gilded dome looked hot. The Lur driver, in spite of our sacramental watermelon feast, was mumbling about food. Ramadan or not, he wanted to take the car and go out of Qom to look for something to eat; and he wanted to know what our plans were.

Across the road, near the watermelon stall at the gateway to the shrine, there was a glass-walled telephone booth of German design. Behzad went to telephone Khalkhalli's secretary.

The high wall of the shrine area was aerosolled and painted with slogans in Persian. There were two in English – WE WANT REPUBLIC, KHOMEINI IS OUR LEADER – and they must have been meant for the foreign television cameras. The second slogan was a direct translation of *Khomeini e Imam*, but as a translation it was incomplete, suggesting only (with the help of the first slogan) a transfer of loyalty from the Shah to Khomeini, not stating the divine authority of the leader or the access to heaven that he gave. In Iran, where for eleven hundred years they were waiting for the return of the Twelfth Imam, *Imam* was a loaded word; and especially here at Qom, where the sister of the Eighth Imam was buried. Access to heaven, rejection of non-divine rule, was the purpose of the 'republic' proclaimed here.

Behzad, opening the door of the telephone booth, the telephone in his hand, waved me over.

When I went to him he said, 'The secretary says that Khalkhalli is praying. He will see you at nine this evening, after he has broken his fast.'

It was 3.30. We had told the driver we would be only three or four hours in Qom.

Behzad said, 'What do you want me to tell the secretary?'

'Tell him we'll come.'

Then we went to break the bad news to the impatient Lur – or the good news: he was charging by the hour. He said something that Behzad didn't translate. And he drove off to look for food, leaving Behzad and me to think of ways of spending five and a half hours in the torpid, baking city, where nothing could be eaten or drunk for the next five hours.

The shops opposite the shrine sold souvenirs – plates with Khomeini's face, cheap earthenware vases – and sweets: flat round cakes, brown, soft, very sweet-looking, breaking up at the edges. Food could be sold to travellers during Ramadan, Behzad said; but it wasn't worth the trouble. Not many people were about. A crippled old woman, a pilgrim no doubt, was wheeling herself slowly past the shops. We surprised a plump boy in a booth taking a nibble at a brown cake, part of his stock; but he judged us harmless and smiled (though a couple of people had been whipped some days before for eating).

The souvenir shops also sold little clay tablets stamped with Arabic lettering. The clay was from the Arabian cities of Mecca and Medina (good business for somebody over there); so that the faithful, bowing down in prayer and resting their foreheads on these tablets, touched sacred soil. High on the shrine wall, in glazed blue and white tiles, there was, as I supposed, a Koranic quotation. Behzad couldn't translate it; it was in Arabic, which he couldn't read.

Arabia! Its presence in Iran shouldn't have surprised me, but it did. Because with one corner of my mind I approached Iran through classical history and felt awe for its antiquity – the conqueror of Egypt, the rival of Greece, undefeated by Rome; and with another corner of my mind I approached it through India, where, at least in the north-west, the idea of Persia is still an idea of the highest civilization – as much as France used to be for the rest of Europe – in its language, its poetry, its carpets, its food. In Kashmir, *Farsi khanna*, Persian food, is the supreme cuisine; and of the *chenar*, the transplanted plane tree or sycamore of Persia (so prominent in both Persian and Indian Mogul painting) it is even said that its shade is medicinal. In Qom these ideas had to be discarded. Here they looked to spartan Arabia as to the fount.

Behzad suggested that we should visit the shrine. If anyone asked, I was to say I was a Muslim. I said I wouldn't be able to carry it off. I wouldn't know how to behave. Was it with the right foot that one entered a mosque, and with the left, the lavatory? Or was it the other way round? Was it the Sunnis who, during their ablutions, let the water run down their arms to their fingers? Did the Shias, contrariwise, run the water down from their hands to their elbows? And what were the gestures of obeisance or reverence? There were too many traps. Even if I followed Behzad and did what he did, it wouldn't look convincing.

Behzad said, 'You wouldn't be able to follow me. I don't know what to do either. I don't go to mosques.'

But we could go into the courtyard, and to do that we didn't have to take off our shoes. The courtyard was wide and very bright. At one side was a clock tower, with an austere modern clock that had no numerals. On the other side was the entrance to the shrine. It was high and recessed and it glittered as with silver, like a silver cave, like a silver-vaulted dome cut down the middle. But what looked like silver was only glass, thousands of pieces catching light at different angles. And here at last were the pilgrims, sunburnt peasants, whole families, who had come from far. They camped in the open cells along the courtyard wall (each cell the burial place of a famous or royal person), and they were of various racial types: an older Persia, a confusion of tribal and trans-continental movements.

One Mongoloid group was Turcoman, Behzad said. I hardly knew the word. In the 1824 English novel, *Hajji Baba* (which I had bought at the hotel in a pirated offset of the Oxford World's Classics edition), there were Turcoman bandits. I had once, in a London sale-room, seen a seventeenth-century Indian drawing of a yoked Turcoman prisoner, his hands shackled to a block of wood at the back of his neck. So the Turcomans were men of Central Asia who were once feared. How they fitted into Persian history I didn't know; and their past of war and banditry seemed far from these depressed campers at the shrine. Small, sunburnt, ragged, they were like debris at the edge of a civilization which had itself for a long time been on the edge of the world.

Near the mosque was the two-story yellow brick building where Khomeini had taught and lectured. It was neutral, nondescript; and nothing was going on there now. Behzad and I walked in the bazaar. For most of the stall-keepers it was siesta time. In one bread stall, stacked high with flat perforated rounds of sweet bread, the man was stretched out on a shelf or counter on the side wall and seemed to be using part of his stock as a pillow. Behzad bought a paper. It was very hot; there was little to see; Qom's life remained hidden. We began to look for shade, for a place to sit and wait.

We came upon a small hotel. It was cramped inside, but newly furnished. The two men seated behind the desk pretended not to see us, and we sat in the little front lounge; nobody else was there. After some minutes one of the men from the desk came and told us to leave. The hotel was closed for Ramadan; that was why, he added disarmingly, he and his friend hadn't stood up when we came in.

We went out again into the light and dust, past the souvenir shops again, with the brown cakes and the tablets of Arabian clay; and were permitted to sit in the empty café opposite the KHOMEINI IS OUR LEADER slogan. It was a big place, roughly designed and furnished, but the pillars were clad with marble.

There was nothing to drink – a bottled 'cola' drink seemed only full of chemical danger – and the place was warm with the raw smell of cooking mutton. But the shade was refreshing; and the relaxed exhaustion that presently came to me, while Behzad read his Persian paper, helped the minutes by.

At the table in the far corner, near the serving counter, there was a family group, as I thought: father, two boys, and a little girl in a long black dress and veil. So small, I thought, and already veiled. But she was active; she talked all the time, and was encouraged by the others, who seemed to find everything she said funny. From time to time the man smiled at me, as though inviting me to admire. Shrieking at one stage, the girl ran up the steps to the upper gallery, shrieked some more up there, encouraging fresh laughter downstairs. She came down again, showed the others what she had brought down. She turned – and for the first time we could see her face – and she came to Behzad and me.

She wasn't a girl. She was very small, about four feet, very old, and possibly mad. She showed us what she had brought down from upstairs: a plate of white rice with a little lozenge of brown-black mutton. Was she pleased with what she had been given, or was she complaining? Behzad didn't say. He listened while she spoke, but he said nothing to her. Then she went out.

I said to Behzad, 'I thought they were a family. I thought they owned the place.'

Behzad said, 'Oh, no. They're not the family. They're workers.'

We went out ourselves, to telephone Khalkhalli's secretary again, to see whether the appointment couldn't be brought forward. It was about half past five, and a little cooler. There were more people in the street. Our driver had come back; he hadn't found anything to eat.

Behzad telephoned. Then, coming out of the telephone booth, he got into conversation with two bearded young men who were in mullah's costume. I hadn't seen them approach; I had been looking at Behzad.

I had so far seen mullahs only on television, in black and white, and mainly heads and turbans. The formality of the costume in real life was a surprise to me. It made the two men stand out in the street: black turbans, white collarless tunics, long, lapel-less, two-button gowns in pale green or pale blue, and the thin black cotton cloaks that were like the gowns of scholars and fellows at Oxford and Cambridge and St Andrews in Scotland. Here, without a doubt, was the origin of the cleric's garb of those universities, in medieval times centres of religious learning, as Qom still was.

The costume, perhaps always theatrical, a mark of quality, also gave physical dignity and stature, as I saw when Behzad brought the young men over. They were really quite small men, and younger than their beards suggested.

Behzad said, 'You wanted to meet students.'

We had talked about it in the car, but hadn't known how to go about it.

Behzad added, 'Khalkhalli's secretary says we can come at eight.'

I felt sure we could have gone at any time, and had been kept waiting only for the sake of Khalkhalli's dignity.

The two young men were from Pakistan. They wanted to know who I was, and when Behzad told them that I came from America but was not American, they seemed satisfied; and when Behzad further told them that I was anxious to learn about Islam, they were immediately friendly. They said they had some books in English in their hostel which I would find useful. We should go there first, and then we would go to the college to meet students from many countries.

Behzad arranged us in the car. He sat me next to the Lur driver, who was a little awed by the turbans and gowns and beards; Behzad himself sat with the Pakistanis. They directed the driver to an unexpectedly pleasant residential street. But they couldn't find the books they wanted to give me, and so we went on, not to the college, but to an administrative building opposite the college.

And there, in the entrance, we were checked by authority: a middle-aged man, dressed like the students, but with a black woollen cap instead of a turban. He was not as easily satisfied as the students had been by Behzad's explanation. He was, in fact, full of suspicion.

'He is from America?'

Behzad and the students, all now committed to their story, said, 'But he's not American.'

The man in the woollen cap said, 'He doesn't have to talk to students. He can talk to me. I speak English.'

He too was from Pakistan. He was thin, with the pinched face of Mr Jinnah, the founder of that state. His cheeks were sunken, his lips parched and whitish from his fast.

He said, 'Here we publish books and magazines. They will give you all the information you require.'

He spoke in Persian or Urdu to one of the students, and the student went off and came back with a magazine. It was *The Message of Peace*, Volume One Number One.

So this was where they churned it out, the rage about the devils of the western democracies, the hagiographies of the Shia Imams. This was where they read Schumacher and Toynbee and used their words – about technology and ecology – to lash the West.

I said to the man with the woollen cap, 'But I know your magazine.'

He was thrown off balance. He looked disbelieving.

'I've been reading Volume One Number Two. The one with the article about Islamic urban planning.'

He didn't seem to understand.

'I bought it in Tehran.'

Grimly, he beckoned us in. And we went up to his office after taking off our shoes. The terrazzo steps were wide, the corridors were wide; the rooms were spacious, with carpet tiling.

The man in the woollen cap, the director, as I now took him to be, sat behind his new steel desk. One of the students sat on his left. Behzad and myself and the other student sat in a line on chairs against the far wall, facing the desk. And, as formally as we were seated, we began.

The student on the director's left said that Islam was the only thing that made humans human. He spoke with tenderness and conviction; and to understand what he meant it was necessary to try to understand how, for him, a world without the Prophet and revelation would be a world of chaos.

The director picked at his nose, and seemed to approve. On his desk there were rubber stamps, a new globe, a stapler, a telephone of new design. On the shelves there were box files, the Oxford English Dictionary, and a Persian-English dictionary.

There were 14,000 theological students in Qom, they told me. (And yet, arriving at the worst time of the day, we had found the streets empty.) The shortest period of study was six years.

'Six years!'

The director smiled at my exclamation. 'Six is nothing. Fifteen, twenty, thirty years some people can study for.'

What did they study in all that time? This wasn't a place of research and new learning. They were men of faith. What was there in the subject that called for so much study? Well, there was Arabic itself; there was grammar in all its branches; there was logic and rhetoric; there was jurisprudence, Islamic jurisprudence being one course of study, and the principles of jurisprudence being another; there was Islamic philosophy; there were the Islamic sciences – biographies, genealogies, 'correlations', traditions about the Prophet and his close companions.

I had expected something more casual, more personal: the teacher a holy man, the student a disciple. I hadn't expected this organization of learning or this hint of antique classical methods. I began to understand that the years of study were necessary. Faith still absolutely bounded the world here. And, as in medieval Europe, there was no end to theological scholarship.

One of the great teachers at Qom, a man who still lectured and led prayers five times a day, had produced (or produced materials for) a twenty-five-volume commentary on a well-known work about the Shia idea of the Imam. Seven of those volumes had been published. A whole corps of scholars – no doubt collating their lecture notes: the medieval method of book-transmission – were at work on the remaining eighteen. Khomeini himself, famous for his lectures on jurisprudence and Islamic philosophy, had produced eighteen volumes on various topics.

That ordered life of prayer and lecture, commentary and reinterpretation, had almost perished towards the end of the Shah's time. Khomeini had been banished; the security forces had occupied Qom; and even the Pakistani students had been harassed by the secret police.

The student sitting on the director's left said, his voice falling, 'If there had been no revolution here, Islam would have been wiped out.'

The students both came from priestly families in country towns in the Punjab, and had always known that they were meant to be mullahs. They were doing only eight years in Qom. They were taking the two-year Arabic course, with logic and rhetoric (rhetoric being no more

48

than the classical way of laying out an argument); but they weren't doing literature. History was no part of their study, but they were free to read it privately. It was for Islamic philosophy that they had come to Qom. In no other university was the subject gone into so thoroughly; and their attendance at Qom, Khomeini's place, and Marashi's, and Shariatmadari's (all great teaching ayatollahs), would make them respected among Shias when they got back to Pakistan.

The student on Behzad's left said, in Behzad's translation, 'I compare this place to Berkeley or Yale.'

I said to Behzad, 'That's a strange thing for him to say.'

Behzad said, 'He didn't say Berkeley and Yale. I said it, to make it clearer to you.'

The three Pakistanis, the director and the students, talked among themselves, and the student at the director's desk lifted the telephone and began to dial.

Behzad said, 'They want you to meet their teacher. Ayatollah Shirazi. He's telephoning him now to get an appointment.'

With the child's part of my mind I was again amazed, in this world of medieval schoolmen I had walked into, at this telephoning of ayatollahs, great men, for appointments. And I was nervous of meeting Shirazi – as I would have been at the sudden prospect (assuming such a thing possible) of a disputation with Peter Abelard or John of Salisbury or even some lesser medieval learned man. I knew nothing of Shirazi's discipline; I wouldn't know what to say to him.

The student who was telephoning put the modern receiver down. His shyness and reverence were replaced by elation. He said, 'Ayatollah Shirazi will see you at seven o'clock. As soon as I told him about you he agreed to meet you.'

The director's face lit up for the first time, as though Shirazi's readiness to receive me had at last made it all right for me to be in his own office, talking to guileless students. He had been picking his nose constantly, in a way that made me feel that the Ramadan fasting that had dried and whitened his lips was also affecting his nostrils and irritating him. Now he relaxed; he wanted to show me over the building. We all stood up; the formal interview was over.

I tried to find out, as we left the room, about the fees and expenses of students. But I couldn't get a straight reply; and it was Behzad who told me directly, with an indication that I was to press no further, that it was the religious foundation at Qom that paid for the students, however long they stayed.

In a room across the wide corridor a calligrapher was at work, writing out a Koran. He was in his forties, in trousers and shirt, and he was sitting at a sloping desk. His hand was steady, unfree, without swash or elegance; but he was pleased to let us watch him plod on, dipping his broad-nibbed pen in the black ink. His face bore the marks of old stress; but he was at peace now, doing his new-found scribe's work in his safe modern cell.

The director showed photographs of a meeting of Muslim university heads that had taken place in Qom two years before. And again, though it oughtn't to have been surprising, it was: this evidence of the existence of the sub-world, or the parallel world, of medieval learning in its Islamic guise, still intact in the late twentieth century. The rector of Al Azhar University in Cairo, the director said, had been so impressed by what he had seen in Qom that he had declared that Qom students would be accepted without any downgrading by Al Azhar.

We walked down the steps. Against one wall there were stacks of the centre's publications – not only *The Message of Peace*, but also two new paperback books in Persian. One was an account of the Prophet's daughter, Fatima, who had married the Prophet's cousin, Ali, the Shia hero; this book was called *The Woman of Islam*. The other book or booklet, with a sepia-coloured cover, was written, the director said, by an Iranian who had spent an apparently shattering year in England. This book was called *The West Is Sick*.

Shirazi's house was in a blank-walled dirt lane in another part of the town. The lane sloped down from both sides to a shallow central trough, but this trough was only full of dust.

We knocked at a closed door set in the wall; and children in the lane mocked the Pakistanis, threatening them with the anger of Shirazi when they got inside. It seemed a traditional form of play, a licensed mockery that in no way mocked belief: the 'clerk', the religious student in his student's costume, a recognized butt, as he perhaps had been in the European middle ages. It was a difficult moment for the Pakistanis, though, trying to shoo away the children, keep their dignity, preserve their courtesy to Behzad and myself, and prepare for the grave reception ahead.

The door opened. We entered a vestibule, took off shoes, went up carpeted steps to a gallery which ran right around a sunken paved courtyard to the left, with fig trees, all covered by a high white awning which cooled light and colour, so that, abruptly, after the dust and warmth of the lane, the midsummer desert climate seemed benign, perfect for men.

I would have liked to pause, to consider the shaded courtyard with the fig trees. But wonder almost at once turned to shock: there was a barefooted man just a few feet ahead in the carpeted gallery with an Israeli-made sub-machine-gun: Shirazi's bodyguard. He stayed in the gallery. We turned into the carpeted, empty room on the right and sat down in silence beside an electric fan, to wait. The Pakistani students smiled, at once expectant and encouraging.

'He is coming,' Behzad said. 'Stand.'

We all stood up. Ceremony assists an entrance, and Shirazi's entrance was impressive, regal. He was a big man, with a full, fleshy face; his beard, as neatly trimmed as his moustache, made it hard to guess his age. His two-button gown was pale fawn; his black cloak was of the thinnest cotton.

The students appeared to fall forward before him – a flurry of black cloaks and turbans. He, allowing his hand to be kissed, appeared to give them his benediction. And then we all sat down. He said nothing; he seemed only to smile. The students said nothing.

I said, 'It is very good of you to see me. Your students here have spoken of you as a man of great learning.'

Behzad translated what I had said, and Shirazi began to speak slowly, melodiously, with an intonation that was new to me. He spoke for a long time, but Behzad's translation was brief.

'It was good of them to say what they said. It is good of you to say what you said.'

Shirazi spoke some more.

Behzad translated: 'Education cannot begin too soon. I would like children to be brought as babies to school. There is a tape-recorder in the human brain. Hitler had that idea.' And Behzad added on his own, 'He wants to know what your religion is.'

'What can I say?'

'You must tell me.'

I said, 'I am still a seeker.'

Shirazi, his face calm, his large eyes smiling, assessing, spoke at length. His enunciation was clear, deliberate, full of rhythm. His full-lipped mouth opened wide, his clean teeth showed.

Behzad said, 'He wants to know what you were before you became a seeker. You must have been born into some kind of belief.'

It was of the Pakistani students that I was nervous. They had been told – with some truth, but more for the sake of simplicity – that I came from America but was not an American. For them to hear now that my ancestry was Hindu would, I thought, be unsettling to them; the Hindu-Muslim antagonisms of the Indo-Pakistani sub-continent went deep. They would feel fooled; and they had been so welcoming, so open. They had arranged this meeting with their great teacher, and even now never took their gaze – beatific rather than obedient or even awed – off Shirazi.

I said to Behzad, 'Can you tell him I never had any belief? Tell him I was born far away, in the Americas, and wasn't brought up to any faith.'

'You can't tell him that. Say you are a Christian.'

'Tell him that.'

And as soon as Behzad began to talk, I regretted what I had asked him to say. Shirazi hadn't been taken in by my equivocations; he knew that something was wrong. And I decided that I would never again on my Islamic journey, out of nervousness or a wish to simplify, complicate matters for myself like this, and consequently falsify people's response to me. Strain apart, it would have been more interesting now – it would have served my purpose better – to get Shirazi's response to me as a man without religion, and as a man of an idolatrous-mystical-animistic background.

Shirazi spoke in his special rhythmic way, the mullah's way, as Behzad told me later, his accent and intonation more Arabic than Persian. He made 'Islam' into 'Ess-lam'; and 'Allah' became a word of three syllables, with a round, open-mouthed pronunciation: 'Oll-lor-*huh*'.

He asked: 'What kind of Christian are you?'

I thought. 'Protestant.'

'Then you are closer to the truth.'

'Why?'

'Catholics are inflexible.'

He didn't mean that. He was only giving a Shia twist to Christian divisions. The Shias, with their own line of succession to the Prophet disregarded by other Muslims, see themselves as an embattled minority.

And conversation after that was as hard as I had feared. I asked whether history – the history of Islamic civilization – was something he had studied. He misunderstood; he thought I was asking a question about Muslim theology, and he said of course he knew Islamic history: when the Prophet first gave the message the people of his village didn't want it, and so he had to go to the next village. And always – whether I attempted to get him to talk about the scientific needs of Muslim countries, or about his ideas for Iran after the revolution – we slid down his theology to the confusion of his certainties. With true Islam science would flourish: the Prophet said that people should go out and learn. With true Islam there was freedom (he meant the freedom to be Islamic and Shia, to be divinely ruled); and everything came with freedom (this idea of freedom quite separate from the first).

There was a long pause.

I said, 'You look serene.'

He said, 'I thank you for that.' He didn't return the compliment.

I wanted to be released.

I said to Behzad, 'Tell him I feel I am taking up too much of his time.'

Shirazi said, with his smile, 'I am free until I break my fast.'

It was only 7.30. I said, just to keep the conversation going, 'Ask him when he is going to break his fast.'

Behzad said, 'I can't ask him that. You're forgetting. I am a Muslim. I am supposed to know these things.'

Someone else came in, a holy man in a white turban, a Turcoman, pale from his Ramadan seclusion, not as sunburnt or as meagre as the Turcoman pilgrim families camped in the courtyard of the shrine. With him was a very pale little girl. Shirazi was warm and welcoming. We stood up, to take our leave. The students fell again before Shirazi and kissed his hand. Shirazi smiled, and he continued to smile as – our own audience over – the little girl rushed to kiss his hand.

The awning over the courtyard and the fig trees had been taken down. The light was now golden; shadows were no longer hard. Our shoes waited for us at the bottom of the steps; and in the small room off the vestibule the barefooted bodyguard with the sub-machine-gun was bending down to play with another child.

Outside, in the dirt lane, where dust was like part of the golden evening, the Pakistani students turned bright faces on me, and one of them said, 'How did you like him?'

For them the meeting had gone well. They asked Behzad and me to dine with them, to break the fast together and eat the simple food of students. But that invitation (as the qualification about the simple food of students showed) was only a courtesy, their way of breaking off, of seeing us into the car and picking up again the routine of their Ramadan evening that we had interrupted.

The lane and the street at the end of it were full of busy, black-cloaked figures: it was like an old print of an Oxford street scene. But here the clerical costumes were not borrowed; here they belonged and still had meaning; here the Islamic middle ages still lived, and the high organization of its learning that had dazzled men from the dark ages of Europe.

And there was more than old Oxford in the streets. This desert town – with its blank walls that concealed sunken courtyards, its straight pavements lined with trees, its enclosed, thick-planted garden squares – was the pattern of small towns I had seen far away in Spanish America, from Yucatan in south-east Mexico to the pampa of Argentina. Spain had been the vehicle: conquered by the Arabs between AD 710 and 720, just eighty years after Persia, and incorporated into the great medieval Muslim world, the great universal civilization of the time. Spain, before it had spread to the Americas, had rejected that Muslim world, and gained vigour and its own fanaticism from that rejection. But here in Iran, five hundred years on, that world still existed, with vague ideas of its former greatness, but ignorant (as the article about Islamic urban planning in *The Message of Peace* showed) of the contributions it had once made, and of the remote continent whose fate it had indirectly influenced.

The Pakistani students had given our Lur driver directions. As we drove to Ayatollah Khalkhalli's, Khomeini's hanging judge, Behzad said, 'You know why I couldn't tell Shirazi you hadn't been brought up in any religion? He was trying to find out whether you were a communist. If I had told him that you had no religion, he would have thought you were a communist. And that would have been bad for you.'

Khalkhalli's house was the last in a dead end, a newish road with young trees on the pavement. It was near sunset; the desert sky was full of colour. There were men with guns about, and we stopped a house or two away. Behzad went and talked to somebody and then called me. The house was new, of concrete, not big, and it was set back from the pavement, with a little paved area in front.

In the verandah or gallery we were given a body search by a short, thickly-built young man in a tight blue jersey, who ran or slapped rough hands down our legs; and then we went into a small carpeted room. There were about six or eight people there, among them an African couple, sitting erect and still on the floor. The man wore a dark grey suit and was hard to place; but from the costume of the woman I judged them to be Somalis, people from the north-eastern horn of Africa.

I wasn't expecting this crowd – in fact, a little court. I was hoping for a more intimate conversation with a man who, as I thought, had fallen from power and might be feeling neglected.

A hanging judge, a figure of revolutionary terror, dealing out Islamic justice to young and old, men and women: but the bearded little fellow, about five feet tall, who, preceded by a reverential petitioner, presently came out of an inner room – and was the man himself – was plump and jolly, with eyes merry behind his glasses.

He moved with stiff, inelastic little steps. He was fair-skinned, with a white skull-cap, no turban or clerical cloak or gown; and he looked a bit of a mess with a crumpled long-tailed tunic or shirt, brown-striped, covering a couple of cotton garments at the top and hanging out over slack white trousers.

This disorder of clothes – in one who, given Shirazi's physical presence, might have assumed Shirazi's high clerical style – was perhaps something Khalkhalli cultivated or was known for: the Iranians in the room began to smile as soon as he appeared. The African man fixed glittering eyes of awe on him, and Khalkhalli was tender with him, giving him an individual greeting. After tenderness with the African, Khalkhalli was rough with Behzad and me. The change in his manner was abrupt, wilful, a piece of acting: it was the clown wishing to show his other side. It didn't disturb me; it told me that my presence in the room, another stranger who had come from far, was flattering to him.

He said, 'I am busy. I have no time for interviews. Why didn't you telephone?'

Behzad said, 'We telephoned twice.'

Khalkhalli didn't reply. He took another petitioner to the inner room with him.

Behzad said, 'He's making up his mind.'

But I knew that he had already made up his mind, that the idea of the interview was too much for him to resist. When he came out – and before he led in someone else to his room – he said, with the same unconvincing roughness, 'Write out your questions.'

It was another piece of picked-up style, but it was hard for me. I had been hoping to get him to talk about his life; I would have liked to enter his mind, to see the world as he saw it. I had been hoping for conversation. I couldn't say what questions I wanted to put to him until he had begun to talk. But I had to do as he asked: the Iranians and the Africans were waiting to see me carry out his instructions. How could I get this hanging judge to show a little more than his official side? How could I get this half-clown, with his medieval learning, to illuminate his passion?

I could think of nothing extraordinary; I decided to be direct. On a sheet of hotel paper, which I had brought with me, I wrote: *Where were you born? What made you decide to take up religious studies? What did your father do? Where did you study? Where did you first preach? How did you become an ayatollah? What was your happiest day?*

It didn't work. He was pleased, when he finally came out, to see Behzad with the list of questions, and he sat cross-legged directly in front of us. Our knees almost touched. He answered simply at first. He was born in Azerbaijan. His father was a very religious man. His father was a farmer.

I asked, 'Did you help your father?'

'I was a shepherd when I was a boy.' And then he began to clown. Raising his voice, making a gesture, he said, 'Right now I know how to cut off a sheep's head.' And the Iranians in the room – including some of his bodyguards – rocked with laughter. 'I did every kind of job. Even selling. I know everything.'

But how did the shepherd boy become a mullah?

'I studied for thirty-five years.'

That was all. He could be prodded into no narrative, no story of struggle or rise. He had simply lived; experience wasn't something he had reflected on. And, vain as he was ('I am very clever, very intelligent'), the questions about his past didn't interest him. He wanted more to talk about his present power, or his closeness to power; and that was what, ignoring the remainder of the written questions, he began to do.

He said, 'I was taught by Ayatollah Khomeini, you know. And I was the teacher of the son of Ayatollah Khomeini.' He thumped me on the shoulder and added archly, to the amusement of the Iranians, 'So I cannot say I am *very* close to Ayatollah Khomeini.'

His mouth opened wide, stayed open, and soon he appeared to be choking with laughter, showing me his gums, his tongue, his gullet. When he recovered he said, with a short, swift wave of his right hand, 'The mullahs are going to rule now. We are going to have ten thousand years of the Islamic Republic. The Marxists will go on with their Lenin. We will go on in the way of Khomeini.'

He went silent. Crossing his legs neatly below him, fixing me with his eyes, becoming grave, appearing to look up at me through his glasses, he said, in the silence he had created, 'I killed Hoveyda, you know.'

The straightness of his face was part of the joke for the Iranians. They – squatting on the carpet – threw themselves about with laughter.

It was what was closest to him, his work as revolutionary judge. He had given many interviews about his sentencing of the Shah's prime minister; and he wanted to tell the story again.

I said, 'You killed him yourself?'

Behzad said, 'No, he only gave the order. Hoveyda was killed by the son of a famous ayatollah.'

'But I have the gun,' Khalkhalli said, as though it was the next best thing.

Again the Iranians rolled about the carpet with laughter. And even the African, never taking his glittering eyes off Khalkhalli, began to smile.

Behzad said, 'A Revolutionary Guard gave him the gun.'

I said, 'Do you have it on you?'

Khalkhalli said, 'I have it in the next room.'

So at the very end he had forced me, in that room full of laughter, to be his straight man.

It was fast-breaking time now, no time to dally, time for all visitors to leave, except the Africans. For some minutes young men had been placing food on the verandah floor. Khalkhalli, dismissing us, appeared to forget us. Even before we had put our shoes on and got to the gate, he and the African couple were sitting down to dinner. It was a big dinner; the clown ate seriously.

And at last our Lur driver could eat, and Behzad could repeat the sacramental moment of food-sharing with him. We drove back to the centre of the town, near the shrine, and they ate in the café where we had waited earlier in the afternoon, in a smell of cooking mutton.

They ate rice, mutton and flat Persian bread. It was all that the café offered. I left them together, bought some nuts and dried fruit from a stall and walked along the river, among families camping and eating on the river embankment in the dark. Across the road from the embankment electric lights shone on melons and other fruit in stalls: a refreshing night-scene, after the glare and colourlessness of the day.

When I was walking back to the café, and was on the other side of the river, I passed an illuminated shoe shop. It had a big coloured photograph of Khomeini. I stopped to consider his unreliable face again: the creased forehead, the eye-brows, the hard eyes, the sensual lips. In the light of the shop I looked at the handful of nuts and *kishmish* raisins I was about to put in my mouth. It contained a drawing pin. Without that pause in front of Khomeini's picture, I would have done damage to my mouth in ways I preferred not to think of; and my own unbeliever's day in Khomeini's holy city of Qom would have ended with a nasty surprise.

The highway to Tehran was busy. There was a moon, but the lights of cars and buses killed the view. It was only in snatches that the desert and the moonlight and the outlines of hills could be seen. Behzad was tired; he dozed off. When he awakened he asked the driver to put on the car radio for the news.

The news was bad for Behzad. *Ayandegan,* the newspaper of the left, the paper Behzad read and had told me about, had been closed down by the Islamic Prosecutor in Tehran. The paper was charged with publishing 'diversionary ideologies and beliefs among the revolutionary Muslims of Iran'; with attempting 'to create dissent among the various Muslim groups of Iran' – a reference to the racial and non-Shia minorities; with falsifying its circulation figures; with sending out incomplete copies of the paper to some parts of the country, in order to save newsprint 'for publishing material aimed at dividing the nation'. The assets of the paper had been handed over to the Foundation for the Deprived; and Revolutionary Guards had occupied its offices.

Behzad – in spite of Shirazi and Khalkhalli – still claimed the revolution as his own, seeing in one popular movement the possibility and even the beginnings of another. The revolution, though, had now turned against him. But revolutionaries have to be patient; and Behzad had learnt patience from his revolutionary father. The loss of the paper was serious – it would have been shattering to me, if the cause had been mine – but Behzad bore his disappointment well.

He didn't go back to sleep. From time to time, as we drove through the moonlit desert, he went abstracted. We passed the white salt lake on the right, where he had said bodies had been dumped by the Shah's secret police; the cemetery, on the left, where martyrs of the revolution had been buried, which we would have visited if we had returned in daylight; and then Tehran Refinery on the right, puffs of flame leaping from its tall chimney – Iran making money while it slept.

About midnight we got back to the hotel. And it was at the hotel gate that the Lur slapped on the extra charges that he must have been meditating for hours. He charged both for distance and time; he charged for late hours; he was in the end more expensive than the hotel taxi we had turned down. But it had been a harder day than he had bargained for; he had been denied the lunch he badly wanted; I had studied, with growing tenderness, the back of his square little head for so long; his passion for his rice and mutton, when eating time had at last come for him, had been so winning; the lean and knobby face that he turned to me to ask for more was so appealing, in the dim saloon light of the car; he was so completely Behzad's ideal of the good and gentle worker; that I paid without demur.

4

The Night Train from Mashhad

BEHZAD came from a provincial town, one of the famous old towns of Persia. His father was a teacher of Persian literature. About his mother Behzad had nothing to say – he spoke of her only as his mother – and I imagined that her background was simpler. He had studied for some time at an American school and he spoke English well, with a neutral accent. Now, at twenty-four, he was a science student at an institute in Tehran. He had an easy, educated manner, and a Persian delicacy. He was tall, slender, athletic. He went skiing and mountain-walking, and he was a serious swimmer.

The provincial background, possibly purely traditional on one side, the American school, the science institute in the capital, the athletic pursuits: it might have been said that for Behzad, living nearly all his life under the Shah, the world had opened up in ways unknown to his grandparents.

But that was my vision. I was twice Behzad's age. I had been born in a static colonial time; and in Trinidad, where I spent my first eighteen years, I had known the poverty and spiritual limitations of an agricultural colony where, as was once computed, there were only eighty kinds of job. I therefore, in places like Iran, had an eye for change. It was different for Behzad. Born in Iran in 1955, he took the existence of national wealth for granted; he took the expansion of his society for granted; he had an eye only for what was still unjust in that society.

I saw him as emerged, even privileged. He saw himself as poor, and as proof he said he didn't own a jacket; in winter he only wore a pullover. The idea of poverty had been given Behzad by his father, who, as a communist, had been imprisoned for some time during the Shah's rule. And that idea of poverty was far from mine in Trinidad twenty-five years before.

When he was a child – it would have been in the mid-sixties – Behzad had one day asked his father, 'Why don't we have a car? Why don't we have a refrigerator?' That was when his father had told him about poverty and injustice, and had begun to induct him into the idea of revolution. In Behzad's house revolution had replaced religion as an animating idea. To Behzad it was even touched, like religion, with the notion of filial piety. And Behzad, in his own faith, was as rigid as any mullah in Qom in his. He judged men and countries by their revolutionary qualities. Apart from Persian literature, for which he had a special feeling, he read only revolutionary writers or writers he considered revolutionary, and I wasn't sure that he could put dates to them: Sholokhov, Steinbeck, Jack London. He had never been tempted to stray.

He told me, as were walking about central Tehran two days after our trip to Qom, that there was no true freedom in the West. The workers were oppressed, exchanging their labour for the barest necessities. True freedom had existed only once in the world, in Russia, between 1917 and 1953.

I said, 'But there was a lot of suffering. A lot of people were jailed and killed.'

He pounced on that. 'What *sort* of people?'

He had no religious faith. But he had grown up in Shia Iran, and his idea of justice for the pure and the suffering was inseparable from the idea of punishment for the wicked. His dream of the reign of Stalin was a version of the dream of the rule of Ali – the Prophet's true successor.

I said, 'Have some of your friends changed sides now and decided that they are Muslims?'

'A few. But they don't know what they are.'

He showed me the city of the revolution. On this tree-lined shopping avenue, in that burnt-out building (its blackened window openings not noticeable at first in the fume-stained street), the Shah's soldiers had taken up their positions. They had fired on demonstrators. And here, in this doorway, a man had died. After six months the blood was barely visible: just dark specks on the dirty concrete. In two places someone had written, with a black felt pen, in Persian characters of a size that might have been used for a private note: *This is the blood of a martyr.* 'Martyr' was a precise religious word; but Behzad could also read it politically.

On Revolution Avenue, formerly Shah Reza, opposite the big iron-railed block of Tehran University, were the publishers (mingled with men's shops) and the pavement booksellers and cassette-sellers and print-sellers. The cassettes were of speeches by Khomeini and other ayatollahs; they were also – in spite of Khomeini's ban on music – of popular Persian and Indian songs. Some booksellers had books in Persian about the revolution, its ideologues and its martyrs. Some had solider piles of communist literature, Persian paperbacks, with hardback sets of Lenin or Marx in English, from Russia. One revolution appeared to flow into the other.

And there were photograph albums of the revolution. The emphasis in these albums was on death, blood and revenge. There were photographs of people killed during the Shah's time; photographs of the uprising: blood in the streets, bodies in the morgues, with slogans daubed in blood on the white tiles; galleries of people executed after the revolution, and shown dead, page after page, corpse upon corpse. One corpse was that of Hoveyda, the Shah's prime minister, hurried out to death late one night by Khalkhalli's orders and shot twice, first in the neck, then in the head: and the black bullet hole in Hoveyda's old man's neck was clear in the photograph.

These were the souvenir books of the revolution, put out by competing publishers. It was the other side of Iranian sentimentality, also available here, in the stock of the print-sellers: dream landscapes of water and trees, paintings of children and beautiful women with thick, inexplicable tears running half-way down their cheeks. Behzad loved those tears.

All the buildings in the university block – founded by the Shah's father – were disfigured with slogans. The university was the great meeting place of Tehran, and even on a day like this, a day without any scheduled event, it was full of discussion groups. Behzad said, 'It goes on all the time.' What did they talk about? He said, 'The same things. Islam, communism, the revolution.' It looked a pacific campus scene; it was hard to associate these young men in jeans and pretty shirts with the bloodiness celebrated in the books and albums across the road.

But violence was in the air, and just after we came out through the main gate we saw this incident. A student in a white shirt, small and with glasses, inexpertly and with some comic effort taped a leaflet on to the iron rails of the gate. The leaflet was a protest about the closing down of *Ayandegan*, the paper of the left. A workman near a food stall at the edge of the pavement walked slowly over, drew a red hammer and sickle on the leaflet, crossed the whole sheet with an X, slapped the student twice, in the middle of the pavement crowd; and then, without hurry, taped up the defaced leaflet more securely.

The student had ducked to save his glasses and his eyes. No one moved to help him. Even Behzad did nothing. He only said, as though appealing to me for justice, 'Did you see that? Did you *see* that?'

The two revolutions appeared to flow together, the revolution of Khomeini, and what Behzad would have seen as the true revolution of the people. But they were distinct. The previous weekend Behzad and some of his group had gone to a village to do constructive work. They had run into trouble with the Revolutionary Guards: every village had its *komiteh*, young men with guns who were now the law in many parts of Iran. The Guards, Muslims, didn't want communists in the village.

Who were these Muslim militants? Behzad said, 'They're *lumpen*. Do you know the word?' The village Guards were *lumpen*, like the workman who had slapped the student. The doctrinal word helped Behzad; it enabled him to keep his faith in the people.

It was a different scene at the university the next morning. It was the Friday sabbath again, and this was the third successive Friday on which there were to be mass prayers in the university grounds.

Behzad and I walked from the hotel, and when we got to Revolution Avenue it seemed that half Tehran was walking with us. No buses or trucks had brought these people in; they had walked. The crowd was thick outside the university; cars moved carefully; separate little groups among the walkers shouted slogans that were barely audible in the deep hubbub.

We passed the pavement booksellers and print-sellers and at the end of the block we turned off to the right, following the university rails. The wide side street, sloping up to north Tehran, was lined on both sides with plane trees and narrow water channels, flowing fast. A bearded young man outside the university rails, a book-pedlar, was holding up a booklet in each hand and shouting, 'These books are against communism and imperialism.'

Behzad said pityingly, 'To them the words are the same.'

We passed the man and were continuing along the rails, when Behzad pulled me back. He said, 'Here we must follow Islamic law. This side of the road is for women.'

We crossed the road, walked up some way beside the fast water channel, and for an hour or more, on the pavement reserved for men (as we thought), in the contracting, thinning shade of a plane tree, we watched the crowd coming up from Revolution Avenue, the women black-veiled and black-gowned on one side, the men on the other. Fervent, frenzied men squatted by the water channel, did their ritual wash, and then pelted on; it was as if there was a competition in frenzy or the display of frenzy. Whenever Behzad and I stopped talking we heard the sound of feet, the chatter of the walking crowd, the occasional cry of a baby. A faint dust rose above the university grounds.

From time to time groups came up shouting slogans about unity; once there was a group in paratroop camouflage clothes with G-3 rifles. Revolutionary Guards appeared, keeping the flow moving, keeping men separate from women. Once I saw a Kurd or a man in Kurdish costume: the loosest kind of belted dungaree, with very baggy trousers tapering off at the ankles. Once, amazingly, on our pavement there passed by a plump young woman in tight jeans and high heels bound on some quite different business. She walked as fast as she could on her heels, looking at no one.

The crowd thickened, men and women now in distinct streams, the men moving, the women slowing down, bunching, checked by the crush at the women's entrance some way up. A speech began to come over the loudspeakers, in a breaking, passionate voice; it added to the frenzy. The pavement on the women's side filled up. Women began to settle down on newspaper and cheap rugs on the street itself, at first in the glare-shot shade of the plane trees, then anywhere. They invaded our pavement, or the pavement which we had thought was ours. Indifferent to us, they dug into their baskets, spread their bits of rug and cloth and pieces of paper at our feet; and after being part of the anonymous, impressive, black-gowned flow, they turned out to be peasant women with worn faces, fierce about their patch of pavement or street.

A Revolutionary Guard came and spoke roughly to Behzad and me. Behzad said, 'He says we must let the women pray.'

The Che Guevara outfit of the Guard, the dark glasses, the gun, the gear of revolution, serving this cause: the incongruity was at that moment irritating. But Behzad said gently, 'Let us walk with the people.'

At the gate for women it was black with women's veils and gowns, women inside unable to move, women outside waiting to get in. Dust rose from the black mass. The intersection at the northern end of the university block was kept clear by men in battle dress, with guns. The northern side of the university was reserved for men; already they had spread over half the road. Every gate was guarded. And it was through one of the northern gates (many more gates for men than women) that Behzad led me in, after telling a Revolutionary Guard, in reply to the Guard's casual question, that yes, I was a Muslim.

Behzad wanted to see the crowd. I was nervous of being caught by the prayers. Behzad understood. He said it would look bad for us to leave when the prayers started; and, of course, if we stayed we wouldn't know what to do, and it would look worse. But the prayers weren't going to start for a while. It was still only time for the speeches, and they could go on and on, as this first warm-up speech (by a lesser ayatollah, and not worth translating) had been going on, booming out over the loud-speakers.

The true crowd was in the centre, around the university mosque. But even a few yards in from the gates men had settled down for prayer in the half-shade of every little tree and shrub. Some had handkerchiefs or folded pieces of cloth on their heads; some wore newspaper hats and cardboard caps, like people in a sports stadium.

Two workmen came in, running, still acting out their frenzy. They jostled us deliberately as they ran, and one man shouted, 'If the Shah's father knew that the university was going to be like this one day, he would never have started it.'

The ayatollah at the microphone asked for chants from the seated multitude. And again and again the responses came, drowning the amplification from the loudspeakers. The chants were about unity. Unity, union, facelessness, in an immense human coagulation: what was joy to the crowd quickly became oppressive to me – if only because I had never before been in an enclosed space with nearly a million people – and it was a relief, when we went outside, through one of the eastern exits, and began to walk back to the hotel, to find that there were still other people about, doing other things.

We had something to eat in the hotel dining-room. A radio was on loud in the kitchen: the speeches at the university were still going on.

The only other people in the big dining-room were a party of stranded Italians who had been in the hotel for a few days. Their company must have been paying their hotel bills, and they possibly had no money of their own. They were elegant, in their thirties, and they all wore trousers of the feminine Italian cut: tight, high-waisted, hip-rounding. They seldom went out; they ate every meal in the hotel; and their liveliness and their consciousness of their style diminished from day to day, from meal to meal. The hotel, once known for its food, had lost its chef since the revolution.

And what, after the walking and the frenzy and the waiting in the sun, were the university crowds – and our uniformed waiters – hearing?

'Iranians should keep the flame of Islam burning.'

They had heard it before, but the familiarity was like ritual. And the speaker was the much loved Ayatollah Taleqani, the leader of the prayers. It was Taleqani who had decreed these mass prayers at Tehran University as a demonstration of revolutionary unity, unity as in the days of the Prophet and the desert tribes. Taleqani was an old man, and he was to die a few weeks later. He was thought, even by the left, to be the most moderate and intelligent of the ayatollahs; but at his death it was to come out that at this time he was the head of the Revolutionary Council.

The Prophet himself, Ayatollah Taleqani was saying, might have had the Iranian revolution in mind when he predicted that the Persians, the descendants of Salman-e-Farsi, were to be 'the pioneers of Islam at a time when the world had deviated from the faith'.

In AD 637, just five years after the death of the Prophet, the Arabs began to overrun Persia, and all Persia's great past, the past before Islam, was declared a time of blackness. Pride in Persia remained: the Persians had grown to believe that they were the purest Muslims. It was at the root of their Shia passion, their animosity to what was not Shia.

The ayatollahs, great prelates, had dispersed for Ramadan, each man, like a medieval baron during this month of retreat, staying close to the source of his power. Khomeini ruled from Qom; and in Qom Khalkhalli was close to Khomeini. Taleqani led the prayers in Tehran. And in Mashhad, five hundred miles to the north-east, near the Russian and Afghanistan borders, Shariatmadari cultivated his Turkish following and was reportedly sulking. It was said that he didn't like how the elections for the Assembly of Experts had gone.

Mashhad was a good base for an ayatollah. In Mashhad was a shrine more sacred than the tomb of the sister of the Eighth Imam in Qom; in Mashhad was the tomb of the Eighth Imam himself. He died in AD 817, one year after he had been nominated to succeed to the overlordship of the whole Muslim world; and the Shias say he was poisoned by a son of the Arabian Nights ruler, Harun al Rashid. Dynastic conflict, palace intrigue, the ups and downs of Persian fortunes within the Islamic empire: they are the stuff of Shia theology.

Behzad and I should have been on our way to Mashhad that day. But there had been problems. First it seemed that Behzad's mother was coming up to Tehran; then it seemed that Behzad's girl friend was coming for the weekend. The girl friend was important. She was twenty-five, with a degree in economics, but with no job in post-revolutionary Iran; and, as I understood, she had gone to spend some time in the provinces. Then, oddly, it turned out that she was in Mashhad.

So we could go to Mashhad, after all; and Behzad and his girl could travel back to Tehran together. But Mashhad received a lot of visitors during Ramadan, and the queues at the railway station at seven that morning had been for two days ahead. So we had decided to fly, and had been lucky, after waiting for Iran Air to open, to get the last tickets for the following day.

They were first-class tickets, but Behzad (who said he carried most of his wardrobe in his little briefcase) spread himself in the wide seat without embarrassment. There were stewardesses, unveiled: on Iran Air, at least up in the sky, a pre-revolutionary style still prevailed.

The land over which we flew was mainly brown. The flat green fields to the east of Tehran quickly went by; and soon we were flying over bare mountains, now with centipede-like ranges, now cratered, now hard and broken, now with great smooth slopes veined from the watercourses created by melted snow. The patterns and the textures changed continuously; the colours varied from ochre to dark red to dark grey. It was astonishing to see occasional green patches, to see the meandering of a road in a valley, or to see a road scratched straight across a brown waste. Everywhere that men could live was known; the land was old. An hour out of Tehran the fields occurred more often, dusty green on brown, or dusty green on pale red; and then, the mountains over, there was the wide plain where Mashhad lay: remote, isolated, and in this old part of the world perhaps always a meeting place and a centre of pilgrimage, long before Islam and the Eighth Imam.

The Hyatt Omar Khayyam Hotel was in business, in spite of its name. Upper-class pilgrim traffic maintained it in all its American-international opulence: a big marble hall, elaborate lighting, a swimming pool (different hours for the sexes), a sunny coffee shop separated by glass from the green, un-matured garden, a darker, carpeted, formal restaurant with a black-suited maître. Strange, this style in the holy city of Mashhad; and then stranger, in this hotel setting, to find among the give-aways in the room a cake of Meccan or Medinan clay tastefully folded over in a brown face-towel: the sacred soil of Arabia, courtesy of Hyatt.

But what was incongruous to me was less so to Behzad. In the restaurant he said, 'Look at that family. The old woman is holy or religious. Nobody else. The old woman has come here for the Imam. The daughters and the sons-in-law have come for the hotel, to swim and to relax and to eat. They can eat during this Ramadan period because travellers can eat, and in Mashhad they are travellers.'

So the Hyatt Omar Khayyam lived on in old splendour – in the bookshop there were still books in English that praised the Shah. But other hotels in the Hyatt chain were not so lucky; and, amid the bits and pieces of hotel literature in my room, the jaunty copy for the Hyatt Regency Caspian was like a sad American voice from a past that had hardly lasted. *Remember when the Caspian Coast had no meeting place?* BUT NOW THERE'S HYATT.

Behzad couldn't get through to his girl. So we went out after lunch. Much money had been spent by the Shah on the beautification of Mashhad. The great public works around the shrine area at the other end of the town were incomplete. The domes and minarets and courtyards stood at the heart of an immense, dusty, sun-struck circle.

Within the rails, but before the courtyards, we saw a drunken man being hustled off by Guards or policemen to a police building. A small crowd watched. Behzad said the man would probably be whipped, but not in public. Just after the revolution there had been public whippings, as part of the revived Islamic way, but the effect on the public hadn't been good.

'Not good?'

Behzad said, 'People didn't like the man doing the whipping. It became hard for him afterwards.'

The courtyards of the mosque and tomb were full of mountain people, camping in the open cells above the burial vaults at the side, sprawling in the shade, small, sunburnt, poor, perhaps poorer than the pilgrims we had seen in Qom.

Central Asia felt closer here, with the mountain faces. And into the shrine courtyard there came a vision: a tall, half-veiled woman in a short, flounced skirt of bright yellow, walking with her back arched, her shoulders thrown back, each high-heeled step measured, precise, steady, her gorgeous yellow skirt and all her under-skirts flouncing straight up from the thigh, swinging slowly then to one side, and then swinging back to the other: a dancer's steps, a performance. The Caucasian world of Lermontov and Tolstoy, still here!

Behzad didn't know where she came from; he only knew that she was poor, and from a village. We watched her cross the courtyard – an older, unveiled woman was with her, and a man – and saw her enter the booth beside the entrance to the shrine, to leave her high-heeled shoes with the attendant. We waited for her to come out, but in vain: there was a side door from the booth to the shrine. So many people from the mountains here, so many hard journeys; yet a journey for which, at least at the end, a village girl would put on her best flounced skirt.

Behzad said, 'You know what they pray for? They pray for money, a job, a son.'

In the museum, on the old brass gate of the shrine of the Imam, we saw relics of old, and still living, prayers. When a visitor to the shrine offered a prayer or asked a special boon, he tied a strip of cloth to the gate; and all the lower rungs or struts – brass cylinders linked to brass globes – were thick with these strips of cloth. When the cloth became untied, the prayer was granted; and even in the museum people rubbed their hands over the cloths, to cause one or two to fall off, to help a fellow Muslim get his wish. The floor behind the gate was littered with fallen pieces of cloth that had gathered dust. The lower parts of the gate had been handled so often that some of the brass sections had fallen off.

Some people with especially difficult prayers or wishes had put cheap padlocks (most of them made in China) high up, attaching them to holes in the brass globes. How would the padlocks be undone without the key? Had they thrown away the key? Wouldn't that be tempting providence? Behzad wasn't sure. He thought it more likely that the key would be given to a friend, who might one day come to Mashhad and, out of all the padlocks, pick the right one.

Behzad didn't have the address of his girl friend. He only had a telephone number, and that number never answered, not at lunch time, not now, in the evening.

The telephoning that he did on my behalf was just as fruitless. I had been given the name of an Islamic scholar at the university of Mashhad, but he was nervous of foreigners. He said he had been transferred to Tehran and was busy packing and couldn't receive. When I invited him to have coffee he said he was developing a migraine and was at that moment lying flat on his back. He might be better in two or three days; I should telephone in the morning.

So Behzad and I didn't separate in the evening, as we had planned. We went after dinner, and after more telephoning, to Ayatollah Shariatma-dari's Ramadan headquarters. The ayatollah's secretary said that the ayatollah received between ten and eleven at night, after breaking his fast. Then he lectured; then he went to sleep, to be up again for prayers before the pre-fast meal, at 4.30 sharp. Ramadan imposed on the pious this rhythm of food and fast and sleep and food.

The smiling, friendly maître said, when he heard where we were going, 'Be careful. Mashhad is a place where something bad can happen to foreigners at any moment.' The warning was good and well-intentioned. But then courtesy made the maître add, 'Not you, though. Indians are all right. Egyptians, Pakistanis – all right. Americans, Germans – that's bad. The Shah brought them here and made them lords of the country. He was bad.' He smiled again – moustache tilting up, eyes twinkling. 'Or stupid.'

The house where Shariatmadari was to receive was in a little, many-angled lane off the main road. After the evening traffic and the lights, it was dim and quiet. Dirt and dust muffled the footsteps of the faithful; but there was no crowd, no hurry.

The gate was guarded, but casually, by two young men who sat on chairs outside and didn't show their guns. They let us in after Behzad

68

explained. And it was like entering a little fairyland: an enclosed garden with electric lights in white globes illuminating peach trees in fruit, flowers, roses, patches of lawn. The level ground at the near end was carpeted and was being used for prayer by a few men; a strip of red carpet ran down one side of the garden next to the high, ivy-covered wall. At the far end, beyond a shallow, blue-tiled pool, there was a tent with more lights, and on carpets there people were sitting.

We took off our shoes and went right up, beyond the pool, and sat opposite the black cushions against which Shariatmadari, when he came, would recline. The house at the side of the tent was new, of concrete and glass; modernistic wrought-iron rails went up the tiled steps. It might have been Shariatmadari's own house, or the house of a religious foundation, paid for by the tithes of the faithful: Behzad wasn't sure. An old man and a young man went around offering tea and sugar and water; there were bowls with sugar lumps on the carpet.

Behzad said, 'Shariat wants to make himself more popular. He is using his opportunity. Khomeini is busy with the government. So Shariat is here, making himself more popular.'

We all stood up when Shariatmadari arrived. And it was hard to attribute political wiliness to the benign old man who came up the red carpet and appeared to be smiling but perhaps wasn't: it might have been no more than the combined effect of the glasses, his beard and the set of his mouth. His beard was white, his complexion pink and white, his cast of face oddly Scottish. His clerical costume was spotless. Among the mullahs in the crowd, so many of them paunchy and grubby and perhaps also (as in folk-legend) over wived, he was like a prince. His black gown was of very thin material, embroidered or patterned, with elegant tie-on ribbons at the top; the pale fawn under-gown showed through.

He looked what he was, a figure of high medieval learning. Philosophy and astronomy had been among the subjects he had studied in Qom in the 1920s under a famous divine: astronomy part of the Muslim intellectual expansion of centuries before, but long since frozen, with philosophy, into a theological discipline.

As soon as he sat down against his black cushions people ran to kiss his hand. Two men became crowd-controllers, marshalling the queue that went out of the tent and turned down the red carpet beside the ivy-covered wall. Boys and men took his right hand to their lips, their forehead, their eyes. One man kissed Shariatmadari's hand twice, the second time for the camera of a friend; there were many cameras.

Shariatmadari seemed to smile all the while, hardly seeing the people who dropped before him and did as they pleased with his hand. He was already preoccupied with the petitions that two or three people, braving the crowd-controllers and the mullahs, had given him. Mullahs with their fancy turbans, black and white, and beards, black and white, pressed around him. The leaning bodies, the pale colours of the gowns, the angled heads, the turbans, the beards, all against the blank end wall, in strong light: the effect was pictorial, almost posed.

Faith like this – faith in the faith, faith in the guidance of the good man – had made the revolution. Shariatmadari, in the conflict with Khomeini, was now on the losing side, the victim of the faith of others. But he had been one of the leaders of the revolution; and even Behzad was awed to be in his presence.

The queue of hand-kissers stopped moving when Shariatmadari began to write on one of the petitions. It was hard, while the ayatollah wrote, to lift and kiss his writing hand – though one or two people tried.

We were sitting right up at the front, and we had no clear cause. We had no petition, no camera; we weren't kissing the hand. We began to attract attention; once or twice Shariatmadari himself gave us a brief, questioning look. Behzad thought it was time to move. We recovered our shoes and picked our way to the back of the garden. Mullahs were still coming in. One was blind. He was doing the tiniest shuffle down the red carpet while making wide, circular gestures with both hands. No one paid him any attention; people just ducked his hands and let him be. On the other side of the garden, in something like darkness, women had gathered in their special area.

We waited until Shariatmadari began to speak. And after the splendour of the setting, the garden and the water and the lights and the peach trees with their illuminated furry green fruit, after the splendour of the man himself, Shariatmadari had little to say. The Shah was bad and he had done bad things. He had forbidden polygamy and had thereby damaged women. Islam protected women; it protected them especially in cases of divorce. It had been said many times before; it could have been said by any mullah.

But the occasion remained an occasion – a Ramadan evening with a lecture by an ayatollah; and when we went out, past the men with guns, into the alley, we found it full of people just arriving.

The main street was busy with cars and scooters; a shop selling all the Iranian varieties of nuts and dried fruit was dazzling with fluorescent lights and glass; exhaust fumes hung in the air like foul cooking smoke.

Again, when we got back to the hotel, Behzad telephoned and got no answer from his girl.

Next morning he could not hide his distress. He had stopped believing that the line was out of order.

He said, 'I hope she hasn't done something and been arrested. In a

place like Mashhad it can be dangerous, with these Revolutionary
Guards.'

'Why should they arrest her?'

'She's a communist.'

My own scholar, the man who had been transferred to Tehran and was
packing and had migraine and was flat on his back, still had his migraine.

He said, 'You know *The Encyclopaedia of Islam?* A Dutch publication.
It will give you all the information you want about Islam and Mashhad.'

Migraine or no, I didn't think I had come to Mashhad to be told to go
away and read an old book.

The scholar said, 'My head is bad. You've been to the shrine? The
museum? The library? Go to Firdowsi's tomb. Yes, go to that tomb.'

And that was where we went. It was some miles out of Mashhad, in
the wide, dry plain that turns green when irrigated: a desolate burial
place for Persia's great poet who, four hundred years after the Arab
conquest of Persia, wrote without Arabic words and, as Behzad told me,
was against the imposition of Arabic culture on Persia.

The tomb was not old, as I had expected. It was new, built by the Shah:
a square marble tower with pre-Islamic columns at the corners, part of
the Shah's attempt to recall the pre-Islamic Iranian past. On the wall
beside the steps going down to the vault there were sculptures in a
version of the old style of famous scenes from Firdowsi's epic. But all the
inscriptions had been defaced; every reference to the Shah or the royal
family or the monarchy had been obliterated. Where the letters were
raised they had been covered over with rough slaps of cement or
plaster. And there were photographs of Khomeini everywhere on the
marble.

It was as though the scholar in Mashhad had sent me to Firdowsi's
tomb less for the sake of Firdowsi than for this evidence of the people's
rage. And rage was what I saw – more clearly in this rich, reconstructed
town than in Tehran – when we returned to Mashhad: the burnt-out
buildings (among them the Broadway cinema, with its English lettering
and Las Vegas façade), the ruined, burnt pedestals in the gardens without their royal statues, all the Persepolitan, pre-Islamic motifs of the
Shah's architecture mocked. The holy city was also a city of rage.

Behzad was happier at lunch.

He said, 'I've spoken to my girl's sister. She's all right. The telephone's out of order. I talked to the operator and he gave me the number
of the sister. I'm going to see them this evening. I was worried.'

'Is the sister communist too?'

'My girl is the only communist in the family. All the others are
religious.'

You were religious or communist: there was no middle, or other, way in Iran.

We decided after lunch to go and buy tickets for the Tehran train that left on the following day. But the taxi-driver told Behzad that the railway station booking office opened at six and closed at twelve.

Behzad said, 'I will go and queue at six tomorrow morning.'

I said, 'Do you think it's true, what the driver says?'

'Why should he lie?'

'I didn't mean that. I only wanted to know whether what he said was correct.'

We didn't go to the railway station. We went to the shrine, to the library. It was closed.

Behzad said, 'What should we do?'

'Shall we go to the railway station?'

We went there. The booking office was open and they were selling tickets for the Tehran train. Behzad made no comment. There were four sleepers in a compartment. I thought we should buy all four. Behzad appeared to agree. But then he said, 'You don't like the poor classes, do you?'

Poor classes! Was it the poor who travelled first? But I gave in to his blackmail, and we bought three tickets, Behzad paying for the third, for his girl.

The train, of German or Swiss manufacture, was waiting at the platform. The outer panel of one of the double-glassed windows was smashed, as if with a pebble or stone. Behzad said, 'The revolution.'

We found our compartment, but there was no question of waiting there. The air-conditioning would begin to function only when the train was on the move; and the heat in the more or less sealed compartment was barely tolerable. A family scene in another compartment – complete with water in a big green plastic bucket – awakened some of my anxiety about our own vacant berth. But I kept that anxiety to myself and we went out to the platform, cool below its high, cantilevered concrete roof, to wait for Behzad's girl.

Almost at once Behzad left me, saying he would come back in good time. He didn't. I was alone in the compartment when, just before the train left, Behzad's girl turned up. She was small, with glasses, her skin rough (perhaps from the summer heat), not pretty or plain. She wore blue slacks and a shirt. And there was more than a sister to see her off. She seemed to have come to the station with a family or a large part of one. *Her* family! Religious people! I began to understand something of

Behzad's difficulties over the weekend, and the deceptions he had been practising on me as on others.

He came to the compartment after the train had left the station. He never really introduced me to his girl, never gave me her name; he only apologized for her, saying that she spoke no English. She acknowledged me but never looked directly at me. Old constraints worked on her, as they worked on Behzad.

And yet, with an unveiled woman in slacks in the compartment, free and easy and perhaps a little too restless with her legs, it was easy to forget that women wore the veil or head-cover in Iran, and that this day was the stillest in the Shia calendar, the day of the death of Ali: there had been no music that morning on the Hyatt Omar Khayyam bedside radio.

At the edge of Mashhad we passed a village of flat-roofed clay houses. Village boys at the bottom of the high embankment began fiercely, but with no malice, to stone the train. They were fierce only because the train passed so quickly, and they wanted to get in as many throws as possible. Behzad had said that the broken window in a coach had been caused by the revolution. And perhaps it had; perhaps the sport came from that brave time. But I was glad he was taken up with his girl, and didn't see.

With his girl he was as easy as a child; talk never stopped between them. Almost at once they began to play cards – she had brought a pack. She knew only one game, Behzad said, remembering me for a minute; and it was a very simple game. They played that game until it wearied them.

A landscape of mountains, hills, and irrigated plain. The hills were isolated, and the train curved between them. The fields were golden, after the harvest; and in the late afternoon the distant hills became warm brown. The land was dug up here and there by watercourses, which had sometimes cut right down, creating little bluffs; but now, in the height of summer, the watercourses had dwindled to rippled rivulets a couple of feet wide and a few inches deep. Flocks of lambs fed on the stubble. Sometimes men could be seen winnowing. But the modern road was never far away, and the brilliantly coloured trucks; and power pylons marched across the plain.

The villages were the colour of mud; and the houses had domed clay roofs (timber for beams not being easy to come by here), with slanting pipes at the bottom to drain the water off. From the train, the domes seemed to cluster together; the projecting pipes, with black shadows more sharply slanted on the clay walls, suggested miniature cannon; and at the angles of the village walls there were round towers, like watchtowers. The hills became smoother, and the folds and wrinkles in them

73

were like wrinkles in human skin. The desert came slowly. The ground was pitted with earth-rimmed wells, like giant molehills; and, often in the barrenness, mud walls enclosed wonderfully green groves of poplars.

The sun set, on Behzad's side of the coach. The land was dusty: Behzad said the desert was near. He didn't agree with me that the land was well cultivated and that much had been done about village roads and electricity. He was with his girl; with her he had a developed eye for injustice, a feeling for injustice being one of the things that bound them together. He told me – and translated what he had said for the girl – that seventy-five percent of the villages in Iran were without roads and electricity.

But the country was enormous, difficult, its villages widely scattered. And though Behzad said that we were now in unirrigated desert – and though he turned on the top light, imposing mirror reflections on the fading view – I could see the level plain still cultivated in strips and patches, until it became dark.

Behzad's girl offered food – waiting, perhaps out of habit, for sunset on this Ramadan day. Her Adidas bag was heavy with plastic sacks of pastries and doughnuts – which Behzad said he had never eaten before – and dried figs and other kinds of dried fruit. This was what she was taking from Mashhad to give to friends in Tehran. I had some dried fruit – a smaller kind of fig, wrinkled, cracked, the colour of clay on the outside, soft and sugary inside, a fruit that felt grown in the land we had been passing, and had suggestions of sun and desert and enclosed gardens. Behzad had a doughnut; his girl had a bun.

She leaned against the window, stretched her left leg out on the seat, and began to read a crisp new Persian booklet with a red star and a red hammer and sickle on the yellow cover. Behzad said the booklet had just been issued by the party – an independent party, not attached to Moscow – to explain why they hadn't taken part in the elections for the Assembly of Experts.

Behzad's girl read with determination, but what she was reading didn't seem to hold her. She stopped turning the pages. She put the open booklet face down on the seat, and she and Behzad talked. She took her leg off the seat, and they began to play cards again, the same simple game.

We stopped at a station. And – after Behzad's rebuke at Mashhad about my attitude to the 'poor classes' which had prevented me buying the fourth bunk – both he and his girl were now gigglingly anxious to keep out strangers. He drew the curtains on the corridor side.

The train started. There was a knock at the door, and almost at the same time the door was slid open. It was the sleeping-car attendant. He slung in blue sacks with bedding: a blanket, a pillow, sheets, a pillow-case.

There was another knock. Behzad drew one side of the curtain, I drew the other. It was a small young man in soldier's uniform, with a revolver. He slid the door open, spoke to Behzad, and closed the door. He wore black boots.

I said, 'Army man?'

Behzad said, 'He is from the *komiteh*. He said we were not to play cards. Do you know what he called me? "Brother". I am his brother in Islam. I am not to play cards. It is a new rule.'

After his shock, he was angry. So was his girl. She said nothing; her face went closed. To Behzad now fell his man's role; and it was to me, witness of his humiliation, that he turned, working his anger out in English.

'I don't mind about the cards. It's the power I mind about. He is only doing it to show me his power. To show me their power. I don't see how Mohammed would have known about cards. They weren't invented in his time.'

I said, 'But he spoke out against gambling.'

'He did. But we were not gambling.'

'The man from the *komiteh* wouldn't have known that.'

'He knew. Of course he knew.'

My own sense of shock was developing. The appearance of the man in khaki had altered the journey, given irrationality to a land which, while the light lasted, I had been studying with an interest that now seemed inappropriate and absurd: trucks, roads, pylons and villages were not what they had seemed.

Behzad said, 'You see what I've been telling you. The power has to belong to the people. The workers and the farmers. The upper classes are all just wanting to show their power.'

I thought that the power now did belong to the people, that what had just happened was a demonstration of that power.

I said, 'Was the man from the *komiteh* an upper-class man?'

'He is upper-class. The army always serves the upper classes. That is why I call him an upper-class man.'

We didn't argue. Neither of us wanted it; and his dialectic would have been as difficult for me as Ayatollah Shirazi's had been in Qom.

He hadn't wanted to play cards; his girl knew only the one simple game. Now they were like children forbidden to play. The cards lay on the seat between them, still not gathered up. The girl had simply dropped hers, with a gesture that was like a sigh. Her face, already closed, was hardening. I thought that it might have been easier for

75

both of them if they had been alone together, and much easier for Behzad if I hadn't been there as an extra witness. I was nervous of his pride.

I said, 'The *komiteh* man is not important. Forget him. You don't have to fight every battle. Fight only the important ones.'

It was a calming thing to say. He said, 'It isn't the cards I mind about. I'm not going to make a fuss about that. But if it comes to books — if they ask my girl why she is reading that book — ' He didn't finish the sentence.

The unread booklet still lay face down on the seat. It had struck me, even when she had put it down, that she was displaying the yellow cover with the red star and the hammer and the sickle, that she intended it to be noticed by people passing in the corridor.

Still saying nothing, and with a gesture of feminine weariness, she gathered up the cards.

Behzad said, 'You know what they object to, don't you? They see that my girl' – still, out of old constraints, avoiding the name – 'doesn't wear the *chador*. That is why they want us to feel their power.'

She stood up, nodded towards the corridor, and she and Behzad went out and moved away, to be alone, as I thought, and also to challenge people who mightn't approve of a veil-less girl in slacks and shirt, on this day sacred to Ali.

They were away for some time.

When they came back Behzad said, 'The man who brought the bedding – I believe he reported us. He saw us playing cards and reported us.'

He loved the people. But who, in Iran, were now the people?

Less than an hour later the girl said she wanted to go to sleep. Behzad asked me to suggest the arrangements. I suggested, thinking of her privacy, that she should sleep on one of the bunks above; that I should sleep below her; that Behzad should sleep on the lower bunk opposite mine; and that the bunk above his should be pulled down, so that there would be no reflection in the mirror.

She understood what I had said, and almost immediately began to climb up the ladder.

Behzad said, 'But – '

And, following his eyes, for the first time I saw, as she stood on the lowest rung of the ladder, that her left foot was bad, that her left leg, which I had thought too restless, was shorter than her right, that her left hip was slightly shrunken.

She insisted on climbing up. And Behzad didn't sleep on the lower bunk across from mine. He slept on the upper, with his girl near to him.

He wore no pyjamas; he had none or carried none in his little briefcase. He was amazingly daring, in Iran.

It had been desert and mountain late at night. In the morning there were earth-rimmed wells, irrigation channels, the mud walls of groves and gardens, people at work in the neat, rich fields; villages; the outskirts of Tehran. An attendant brought tea, served in glasses and meant to be drunk in the Persian way, through a lump of sugar held in the mouth.

Behzad hadn't slept well; he remained tormented. When we were almost in the city – air-conditioning units set into the backs of the unlikeliest houses – we saw the *komiteh* man in the corridor: boyish, very small, unfussed, with no apparent memory, when he looked into the compartment, of his intrusion the night before.

Behzad's girl said goodbye without seeming to see me. Through all the hours we had been together she had never looked directly at me. I let them walk ahead on the platform at Tehran station: she small and limping, he tall and athletic, protective, slightly inclined towards her. Friends were waiting for her; they took her away from Behzad. Young people of the revolution, people carrying danger with them; but the city they had come back to was for them that day a city of calamity.

There had been riots over the weekend, between Muslims and people of the left, and the left had suffered badly.

A week before, when Behzad and I were driving back from Qom, we had heard on the car radio about the closing down of *Ayandegan*, the newspaper of the left. Leftist protests had built up during the week; and Muslim groups had begun to counter-attack.

After the prayers at Tehran University on Friday – which Behzad, out of his own revolutionary emotion at the sight of the multitude, had seen as a political occasion, not a religious occasion – hundreds of Muslims had marched on the offices of *Ayandegan*. Thirty of the paper's press workers had refused to leave the building; now they were ejected by Revolutionary Guards. Five of the ejected *Ayandegan* men were injured and had to be taken to the military hospital; twenty were arrested. On Sunday, at a leftist demonstration at Tehran University, there had been serious fighting with sticks and knives; many more people had been injured. On Monday – while we were getting ready to take the train from Mashhad – Muslim groups had stormed the headquarters of Behzad's communist organization, thrown everybody out, thrown documents out, seized all the arms – grenades, mortars, teargas canisters, Belgian and Russian rifles.

This was the news Behzad and his girl returned to. They heard about it – as I learned later – from the friends who had come to meet the girl. But Behzad, after his humiliation of the previous evening, told me nothing. He saw me back to the hotel and – his own obligations to me then over – left me to find the news out myself, from the *Tehran Times*.

Newspaper items: set language, set phrases, that left everything to the imagination. But just a little while later, when I was on my way to the Intercontinental Hotel for their buffet lunch, the news items took on an actuality that was scarcely believable.

A skyscraper, with a garden and sculpture; a side road barred with a car with a flashing roof light; men in camouflage battle dress with guns; sand-bags at the corners of the skyscraper plot, with mounted machine-guns. And across the busy road, the dispossessed communists, young men looking like city workers, in trousers and open shirts. A Persian battle arrangement; both sides waiting and intently watching; the life of the town flowing around, as peasants in the old days attended to their peasant tasks while the armies fought, to decide who was to rule.

That afternoon on Firdowsi Street, the street of the money-changers, I heard a siren, and an open truck with Muslims with guns raced by, followed by a police-style car. Later, on the Avenue of the Islamic Republic, formerly Shah, the siren sounded again, and again I saw the Muslims with guns. No emergency had called them out. They were only driving fast round the town, the siren their battle-horn; and they were doing it, as Behzad might have said, to show their power.

Two days later, on my last evening in Tehran, I saw Behzad for a few minutes. He was dark with sunburn. He had been standing with the dispossessed communists across the road from the sand-bags and the machine-gun. He was sad but calm. He had found his battle. I asked after his mother, who had come to Tehran and was staying with him. But – old constraints still – he said little about her; and he said nothing about his girl.

Such emotion, such bravery; and, unavoidably in Iran, his cause was as simple as his enemy's, and in the end really no more than a version of his enemy's. Both sides depended on revealed truth and a special reading of historical events; both required absolute faith. And both were fed by the same passion: justice, union, vengeance.

I was going on to Pakistan. My first plan had been to go by bus, to drop down south and east in stages, through old towns with beautiful names: Isfahan, Kerman, Yazd (important to Zoroastrians, Persians of the pre-Islamic faith, long since expelled, their descendants surviving in India as

Parsis, Persians), Zahedan. But Qom and Mashhad had given me enough of desert travel in midsummer; I didn't want now to run into *komitehs* in out-of-the-way places; and I could get no certain information about transport across the Pakistan border. I decided to go by air, straight to Karachi.

There were not many flights. The one I chose left at 7.30 in the morning, and Pakistan International Airlines said it was necessary to check in three hours before. I was on time, and I thought I had done the right thing. I was quickly through, with my little Lark bag. Half an hour later, when dawn was breaking, the queue was long and moving very slowly.

Just as, at London Airport, the flight pen for Iran had been full of Iranians who had done their shopping in Europe and the United States, so now Tehran Airport was full of Pakistani migrant workers who had done their shopping in Iran. They were taking back a lot: boxes, trunks, big cardboard suitcases tied with rope, brown cartons stamped with famous names, Aiwa, Akai, Toshiba, National, names of the new universal bazaar, where goods were not associated with a particular kind of learning, effort, or civilization, but were just goods, part of the world's natural bounty.

The plane which was to leave at 7.30 didn't arrive until ten. We began to taxi off at 11.25 but then were halted for a further hour, while American-made Phantoms of the Iranian Air Force took off. I thought they were training. They were in fact taking off on Khomeini's orders to attack the rebel Kurds in the west. Later in Karachi I learned that two Phantoms had crashed, and the news was curiously sickening: such trim and deadly aircraft, so vulnerable the inadequately trained men within, half victims, yet men that morning obedient to the will of God and the Twelfth Imam and full of murder.

To Kurdistan, following the Phantoms, went Ayatollah Khalkhalli, Khomeini's Islamic judge, as close to power as he had boasted only ten days before in Qom. In no time, moving swiftly from place to place in the August heat, he had sentenced forty-five people to death. He had studied for thirty-five years and was never at a loss for an Islamic judgment. When in one Kurdish town the family of a prisoner complained that three of the prisoner's teeth had been removed and his eyes gouged out, Khalkhalli ordered a similar punishment for the torturer. Three of the man's teeth were torn out on the spot. The aggrieved family then relented, pardoned the offender, and let him keep his eyes.

It was Islamic justice, swift, personal, satisfying; it met the simple needs of the faithful. But we hadn't, in the old days, been told of this Iranian need. This particular promise of the revolution had been blurred or fudged; and we had read, mostly, *Down with fascist Shah*. Only Iranians, and some foreign scholars, knew that when Khomeini was a child – while the Qajar kings still ruled in Iran – Khomeini's father had been killed by a government official; that the killer had been publicly hanged; that Khomeini had been taken by his mother to the hanging and told afterwards, 'Now be at peace. The wolf has attained the fruit of its evil deeds.'

In his advertisement in the *New York Times* in January 1979, when he was still in exile in France, Khomeini had appealed to 'the Christians of the world' as to people of an equal civilization. It was a different Khomeini who said in August, on Jerusalem Day (the day the Phantoms were sent against the Kurds): 'The governments of the world should know that Islam cannot be defeated. Islam will be victorious in all the countries of the world, and Islam and the teachings of the Koran will prevail all over the world.'

That couldn't have been said to the readers of the *New York Times*. Nor could this, spoken on the last Friday of Ramadan (and a good example of the medieval 'logic and rhetoric' taught at Qom: certain key words repeated, used in varying combinations, and finally twisted): 'When democrats talk about freedom they are inspired by the super-powers. They want to lead our youth to places of corruption . . . If that is what they want, then yes, we are reactionaries. You who want prostitution and freedom in every matter are intellectuals. You consider corrupt morality as freedom, prostitution as freedom . . . Those who want freedom want the freedom to have bars, brothels, casinos, opium. But we want our youth to carve out a new period in history. We do not want intellectuals.'

It was his call to the faithful, the people Behzad had described as *lumpen*. He required only faith. But he also knew the value of Iran's oil to countries that lived by machines, and he could send the Phantoms and the tanks against the Kurds. Interpreter of God's will, leader of the faithful, he expressed all the confusion of his people and made it appear like glory, like the familiar faith: the confusion of a people of high medieval culture awakening to oil and money, a sense of power and violation, and a knowledge of a great new encircling civilization. That civilization couldn't be mastered. It was to be rejected; at the same time it was to be depended on.

II

PAKISTAN
The Salt Hills of a Dream

GONZALO	Had I plantation of this isle, my lord –
ANTONIO	He'd sow't with nettle seed.
SEBASTIAN	Or docks, or mallows.
GONZALO	– And were the king on't, what would I do?
SEBASTIAN	Scape being drunk for want of wine.
GONZALO	I' th' commonwealth I would by contraries
	Execute all things. For no kind of traffic
	Would I admit; no name of magistrate;
	Letters should not be known; riches,
	poverty,
	And use of service, none; contract,
	succession,
	Bourn, bound of land, tilth, vineyard, none;
	No use of metal, corn, or wine, or oil;
	No occupation; all men idle, all;
	And women too, but innocent and pure;
	No sovereignty.
SEBASTIAN	Yet he would be king on't.
ANTONIO	The latter end of his commonwealth forgets
	the beginning.

The Tempest

1

Displacements

THE RULE of Ali had come to Iran: the Iranian state was disintegrating. The outsider could make the connection. But the man of faith could juggle with these great events and keep one separate from the other; and even while he prepared to run he could continue to rejoice at the victory for Islam. Pakistan could be contemplated in the same way. It could be seen as a fragmented country, economically stagnant, despotically ruled, with its gifted people close to hysteria. But Pakistan was also the country that had been founded more than thirty years before as a homeland for the Muslims of India, and for that reason was to be cherished as a pioneer of the Islamic revival.

An article in the *Tehran Times* linked the two countries. 'The history of Pakistan and the Islamic Revolution in Iran is a reminder of the power of religion and the hollowness of secular cults. How the world works is the concern of science, and how society is to be governed is the affair of politicians, but what the whole thing means is the main concern of Iran and Pakistan. Politics is combined with religion in Islam. Iran and Pakistan can join hands to prove to the world that Islam is not just a faith of the past, practising ancient rituals.'

It was the logic of the faith. The writer acknowledged, and dismissed, what was lacking in both countries — science, the ability to run a twentieth-century state; and then by a kind of intellectual wipe, a verbal blur ('what the whole thing means'), he offered the honouring of the faith as an achievement that overrode everything else. To do that — and without irony to present chaos as its opposite ('a reminder of the power of religion and the hollowness of secular cults') — the writer had to leave out a lot.

He had referred to 'the history of Pakistan'. But he hadn't gone into that history, and he had ignored its nature: the uprootings and mass migrations after the state had been founded in 1947; the absence of representative government; the land of the faith turning into a land of plunder; the growth of regionalisms; rule by the army in 1958; the bloody secession of far-off Bangladesh in 1971. There was no hint in the article that the army ruled once again in Pakistan, that there was martial law once again; no hint that Mr Bhutto, the country's only elected prime minister, deposed by the army in 1977, arrested on a murder charge, tried and sentenced to death, had been hanged after nineteen months in jail; no hint that this hanging, just four months old, had shocked, demoralized and further divided the country.

All this history, all this secular failure and pain, had been conjured away by the logic of the faith.

The desert of Iran ran into the desert of Pakistan. From 30,000 feet up the wastes of Iranian and Pakistani Baluchistan showed brown and black, but pale, more glare than colour.

There was some natural gas in Baluchistan, but the desert of Pakistan was without oil. Iran was a land of oil and money; here desert was desert. Iran, with a population of 35 million, earned 70 million dollars a day from its oil; Pakistan, with twice the population, earned 140 millions a month from its exports of rice, leather and cotton. Iran had just won, in an American federal court, a repayment of 30 million dollars from the American Bell International company; Pakistan, in a year, could spend only 20 million dollars on the roads of Sind province, which was vast. Iran could write off billions in military equipment – oil turned to money to water; here it was news that Pakistan was approaching Iran for a loan of 150 million dollars.

Here – the world dwindling and dwindling – it was news that 140,000 dollars had been granted to thirty Pakistani sports organizations. A bigger country than Iran, but a dwarf economy, and it was reflected in the newspaper advertisements, which were for insurance, tropical clothes, TV sets, a cotton pesticide (made in collaboration with the British firm of May and Baker), cement, a voltage stabilizer, brass and copper triangles and rods, a cosmetic soap, a brand of razor blade.

Sophisticated administrative forms, surviving in a dwarf economy, could at times suggest a people at play. In *Dawn*, the leading English-language newspaper of Karachi, there was a double-column, four-inch tender advertisement from the Defence Science and Technology Organization (HQ), Ministry of Defence, for the supply of one refrigerator and four cupboards ('wooden with glass panel doors fitted with hinges').

Eight inches were given in that paper to the announcement of a government 'skill development plan for youths'. What was that plan? The government was giving 2,000 rupees, 200 dollars, to a thousand village schools to buy work-tables and hand tools. Eight inches for that?

How? Like this: '. . . The training programme will be adjusted to the immediate needs of the local community and matched with the interest of the learners in order to derive maximum benefit out of this programme. The Government officials explained that this programme will be based on modular concepts consisting of well-defined community-oriented skills . . .'

When money was short, language took up the slack. *Farm mechanisation being stepped up*: that was the reassuring headline in *Dawn*. This was the story: 'Agriculture mechanisation programme is being stepped up in Sind province by deploying more machinery in the fields for their development, it was learnt here yesterday . . .'

But then it was less funny to read the advertisements for workers, at 200 dollars a month, in Saudi Arabia. 'Candidates will be employed on single status basis regardless of their actual marital status. Bachelor air-conditioned accommodation on a double occupancy basis equipped with necessary items of furniture and communal cooking and toilet facilities will be provided against deduction of appropriate rental charges.' It was on foreign earnings like this, as much as on its exports of rice, leather and cotton, that Pakistan lived.

And yet there was also news of a Pakistan-manufactured 'Islamic' nuclear bomb; and there was a long article on the editorial page about opposition to this bomb by 'International Zionism'. Pakistan was poor; but it was a land of the faith, with the obsessions of the faith. *Indira gets money from Israel for KGB information*: this was a story from *Dawn*'s London correspondent: the KGB had passed on some information to Mrs Gandhi when she was prime minister of India, and she had passed on the information to Moshe Dayan, foreign minister of Israel, and he had given her six million dollars. The source for this story was said to be an unpublished book by a Ugandan diplomat (Uganda, under Amin, being part of the Muslim world).

Away from this Jewish-Indian-Russian underhandedness, pious Pakistanis were preparing for the pilgrimage to Mecca. The Pan-Islamic Steamship Company had arranged twelve sailings to the Arabian pilgrim port of Jeddah (280 dollars for the 'deck class' return fare, including twenty-six dollars for food; 420 dollars first class, including fifty-seven dollars for food); and General Zia, the President and chief martial law administrator, had decreed that each pilgrim ship should be seen off by a different provincial governor or federal minister. General Zia himself was going quietly by air in a day or so to Arabia, to perform his own devotions without fuss (and he was to return with a modest Saudi loan of 100 million dollars).

Off-stage there were rumblings which were like a continuation of events in Iran. Various people in Pakistan were calling for stricter Islamic laws, and at the university of Karachi there had been a gunfight with Sten guns between students of the left and right – words which have to be defined in every country, and here meant, on the right, people who were against Mr Bhutto and were using Islam to discredit him, and, on the left, people who grieved for Mr Bhutto and longed to pull down his enemies.

In Iran you felt, in spite of all that was said about the wickedness of the Shah, that the money had gone down far. Money, and the foreign goods and tools that it bought, gave an illusion of Islamic power. Seventy million unearned dollars a day kept the idle country on the boil, and fed the idea of the revolution. In Pakistan poverty had the same effect. The tensions of poverty and political distress merged with the tensions of the faith. Thirty-two years after its founding as a religious state, an Indian Muslim homeland, Pakistan remained on the boil, and Islam was still an issue: failure led back again and again to the assertion of the faith.

The idea of a separate Indian Muslim state, once it had been formulated, couldn't have been resisted. The idea was put forward in 1930 by a revered poet, Sir Mohammed Iqbal (1876–1938), in a speech to the All-Indian Muslim League, the main Muslim political organization in undivided India.

Iqbal's argument was like this. Islam is not only an ethical ideal; it is also 'a certain kind of polity'. Religion for a Muslim is not a matter of private conscience or private practice, as Christianity can be for the man in Europe. There never was, Iqbal says, a specifically Christian polity; and in Europe after Luther the 'universal ethics of Jesus' was 'displaced by national systems of ethics and polity'. There cannot be a Luther in Islam because there is no Islamic church-order for a Muslim to revolt against. And there is also to be considered 'the nature of the Holy Prophet's religious experience, as disclosed in the Koran . . . It is individual experience creative of a social order.'

To accept Islam is to accept certain 'legal concepts'. These concepts – revelatory, but not to be belittled for that reason – have 'civic significance'. 'The religious ideal of Islam, therefore, is organically related to the social order which it has created. The rejection of the one will eventually involve the rejection of the other. Therefore, the construction of a polity on national lines, if it means a displacement of the Islamic principle of solidarity, is simply unthinkable to a Muslim.'

Iqbal, in fact, is saying in a philosophical way that in an undivided India Islam will be in danger, will go the way of Christianity in Europe and cease to be itself. Muslims, to be true to Islam, need a Muslim polity, a Muslim state. The Muslims of India especially need such a state, Iqbal suggests; because 'India is perhaps the only country in the world where Islam, as a people-building force, has worked at its best'. And Iqbal's solution was simple: the Muslim-majority areas of north-west India should be detached and consolidated into a single Muslim state.

Seventeen years later (and nine years after Iqbal's death) it happened – and to the Muslim-majority north-west was added the Muslim-majority eastern half of Bengal, a thousand miles away. But that Muslim state came with a communal holocaust on both sides of the new borders. Millions were killed and many millions more uprooted. And it was only afterwards that it became clear that the plan for the creation of Pakistan, apparently logical, meeting Muslim needs, had a simple, terrible flaw.

Muslim passions were strongest among those Muslims who felt most threatened, and they were in that part of the sub-continent which was to remain Indian. Not all of those Muslims, not a half, not a quarter, could migrate to Pakistan. The most experienced Muslim political organizations were rooted in Indian India rather than in Pakistan. Indian Muslim politicians, campaigners for Pakistan, who went to Pakistan became men who overnight had lost their constituencies. They became men of dwindling appeal and reputation, men without a cause, and they were not willing to risk elections in what had turned out to be a strange country. Political life didn't develop in the new state; institutions and administration remained as they were in British days.

A special word began to be used in Pakistan for the migrants from India: *mohajirs*, foreigners. In the province of Sind, especially, where Karachi became a *mohajir* city, local resentment built up into separatist feeling.

In the new state only the armed forces flourished. They were seen at first as the defenders, and possible extenders, of the Islamic state. Then it became apparent that they were the state's only organized group. They became masters, a country within a country. The armed forces were mainly of the north-west, with the cultural prejudices of the north-west; in time they forced the eastern wing of Pakistan into secession as Bangladesh. It was Pakistan's luck then to get a national leader in Mr Bhutto, a man of Sind and the country's first native leader, as it were. He was a populist; he ruled despotically for nearly six years. Then he was deposed by the army and hanged, and the fragmented country was further riven.

Calamity was added to calamity. The Bengali Muslims had Bangladesh; the people of West Pakistan had Pakistan. The Bihari

Muslims had nothing. They had migrated from Bihar in eastern India to Pakistani Bengal. But by language and culture they were closer to the Muslims of the West. When Bangladesh became independent they were wanted neither by Bangladesh nor by Pakistan, and they became a lost community, cast into limbo by their dream of the Muslim polity.

The state withered. But faith didn't. Failure only led back to the faith. The state had been founded as a homeland for Muslims. If the state failed, it wasn't because the dream was flawed, or the faith flawed; it could only be because men had failed the faith. A purer and purer faith began to be called for. And in that quest of the Islamic absolute – the society of believers, where every action was instinct with worship – men lost sight of the political origins of their state. They forgot the secular ambitions of Mr Jinnah, the state's political founder, who (less philosophical than Iqbal) wanted only a state where Muslims wouldn't be swamped by non-Muslims. Even Iqbal was laid aside. Extraordinary claims began to be made for Pakistan: it was founded as the land of the pure; it was to be the first truly Islamic state since the days of the Prophet and his close companions.

At the end of my time in Pakistan I met a middle-aged man, a civil servant and a poet. He had sought me out to give me his books. But the condition of his country was closer to him than poetry now. It was of Pakistan that he spoke, with an unfocussed rage that took him almost to tears.

'When I was a child in India,' he said, 'and I heard we had got Pakistan, I cannot tell you what I felt. To me it was like God, this country of Pakistan.'

But wasn't that where the failure started? Wouldn't it have been better if the creation of Pakistan had been seen as a political achievement, something to build on, rather than as a victory of the faith, something complete in itself? Wasn't that the flaw in the Iqbal speech? 'One lesson I have learnt from the history of Muslims,' Iqbal said at the end of that speech. 'At critical moments in their history it is Islam that has saved Muslims and not *vice versa*.' Wouldn't it have been better for Muslims to trust less to the saving faith and to sit down hard-headedly to work out institutions? Wasn't that an essential part of the history of civilization, after all: the conversion of ethical ideals into institutions?

The poet didn't agree. The Muslim polity should have arisen naturally out of the faith. The feeling that Pakistan was God should have taken the country to the heights.

What had gone wrong then?

Men were bad, he said. They didn't live up to the faith.

In Pakistan that was nearly always where you ended.

Late one afternoon, in a dusty village in the interior of Sind, more than a hundred miles to the east of Karachi, I met the maulana or teacher of a theological school. It was a famous school, but for reasons I couldn't follow it had fallen into disrepair during Mr Bhutto's time.

The crumbling buildings, of sun-dried brick, were like village buildings, peasant buildings – nothing here of the grandeur of Qom: no steel desks or modernistic telephones or carpeted floors. The guest house was a little one-roomed hut with a walled courtyard, everything of sun-dried brick and uneven, everything returning to dust. The room had a ceiling fan, three string beds with rolled-up bedding, an arched niche in the wall with three shelves; and that was all. The brick floor was bare. Roughly-cut windows and doors, front and back, were open to dust. We were near the Indus River, and sub-surface water, seeping through from the river, fed fields and caused trees to grow, but everything seemed to grow out of dust.

The maulana's room was more enclosed than the guest house, but not less bare. He had been lying down on his string bed; he sat up to talk to me. He was turbanned and bearded, an old man, but still vigorous, and not gentle. In the late-afternoon gloom, soon made gloomier by a very weak electric bulb, in the dust and bareness of his peasant setting, he was alive with a religious passion that was like malevolence: the passion for the true faith running, as it can easily run, into the idea of Islam in danger, the need for the holy war, the idea of the enemy.

He asked me about myself and my travels. I told him I had been to Iran.

He said, 'Khomeini is a good man. He is Islamic.'

'Why do you say that?' I had expected him, so orthodox and fierce, to disapprove of Khomeini's Shia Islam as a deviation.

He said, 'He has banned women from appearing on television.'

It was all that he knew of Iran since the revolution.

He said, 'We don't have an Islamic government here.'

How could he say that? The government had ordered civil servants to break off every day and say their prayers. It had legislated for Koranic punishments like whipping and stoning to death. It was talking of levying a Koranic tax, to be paid out to the poor as alms. The President had just made the pilgrimage to Mecca. What more did the maulana want?

He said, 'They haven't abolished interest in the banks.' The Prophet had outlawed usury; a banking system that depended on interest was not Islamic.

What kind of banking system did he want? How did he want the financial affairs of the country to be managed?

He didn't know. He hadn't thought about it. But he didn't care. He said, 'If Pakistan makes money in an Islamic way, everything will follow.' He was pleased with that thought – logic was one of the subjects taught at his school – and he repeated it slowly.

He was half a politician, a man of local influence; and in his criticism of the government there was no doubt some local or personal grudge. But he was not being disingenuous; he lived by his rules. His world had shrunk to a hut in a crumbling village. He was prepared for even that to crumble away further, once the faith was served.

Some miles away, in the fading light, peasants were baiting a bear with dogs in a ploughed field. The yelping dogs were cradled by their handlers. The chained bear sniffed the upturned earth, and salivated. The dogs were released, four of them. They leapt and bit hard and threw the bear; the crowd shouted. But everything that got in the way of the bear's paws was damaged. The bear righted itself, and the crowd shouted again; and thereafter at every roll the bear did the crowd shouted. Then the bear, using its flexible spine, sitting on the ground and slumping forward, began to crush the two dogs it had dislodged and trapped, sitting on one, squeezing another to death with its forward slump; and the dog being killed looked out with a sudden blank mildness from the brown-black fur of the bear. The back of the dog being sat on was broken. The dog-handlers then went in to rescue the two dogs that survived, still holding on where they had bitten.

The fight lasted three minutes. It was a village entertainment and, like the faith, part of the complete, old life of the desert.

The British came late to Sind, in 1843, and after a small battle at a place not far from the bear-baiting field, ruled for just about a hundred years. The native towns of Sind were inland, on the Indus River. Karachi in 1843 was a fishing village on the coast. In 1947, when the British left, it was a modern port and the main city of the western half of the new Muslim state of Pakistan. It had a population then of 300,000. One third were Hindus or non-Muslims and had to leave; but there were millions of Indian Muslims waiting to come. Now, more than thirty years later, after the great Indian Muslim migration, and the continuing migration from within Pakistan, the population of Karachi was five or six million – no one knew the true figure.

I had seen Karachi before, in 1962, but briefly, and my memories of it were phantasmagoric. I was going to India, my ancestral land, for the first time — and going there in easy stages. I was travelling on a freighter from Alexandria to Bombay, and Karachi was a port of call.

There were Africans on the docks of Karachi, and they were a surprise: descendants of slaves set free after the British annexation in 1843, turned out into the streets, where they had more or less stayed. There were camel-carts, the first I had seen, with high, sloping shafts. There was a hotel with two dwarfs in white uniforms and green turbans at the entrance.

Africans, camel-carts, dwarfs in green turbans: they were not memories that could be trusted. They were more like ideas suggested by nerves, my nerves at being in the sub-continent for the first time, my confused unhappiness at the reminders (in buildings, in names) of British rule, nerves and unhappiness given a physical edge by the humid salt heat, from which, after only a couple of hours, I preferred to hide in the ship.

Now the floating memories focussed, and turned out to be true. There were Africans in Karachi, dock workers. Away from the motor traffic of main roads there were camel-carts. The camels trotted with their long heads held high. Their flapping mouths and big, round, cleft feet, picked up clean, gave each camel a triumphant air, as of a smiling athlete perpetually breasting a tape.

And more than camels. There were the donkeys, which I had forgotten, though they must have been the smallest donkeys I had ever seen, brisk, amiable, and so small that in a playful imagination they became smaller, with the size and character of red setters — almost. Their hind quarters, scored black with the harness strap, had a dog-like slenderness; their legs were delicate. When they were idle they stood still, in couples, on grassless ground; and, after their amiability on the trot, they looked sad, and sadder because of that forlorn companionship.

And the Metropole Hotel did have two dwarf doormen. They were no longer apparent, but nothing bad had happened to them. They had (I was told) only been taken inside. Club Road, where the Metropole was, was more hectic than in 1962; and the dwarfs were not as young as they had been. Time had told on the Metropole too. It had ceased to be the first hotel of Karachi. It had been overtaken by the Intercontinental. And other hotels of the new age were coming up — the Sheraton, the Hyatt Regency (pressing on Islamically, even after Iran), the Holiday Inn.

It was the city of the five million that I wanted to see. But the boy or young man the taxi service gave me had other ideas. He wanted to take me to the Chaukandi tombs, seventeen miles outside Karachi; it was necessary to say no.

He was short and moon-faced, the driver, spoilt and thuggish. He wore an outfit in slate-blue, loose cotton trousers and a full, long-tailed shirt. He gave me a feeling of danger: the dropout, the rustic with urban vanities. But he had undeniable style.

I said, 'I think you are a student?'

He liked that. He said, 'My story is sad. Because it is sad I will not tell you about it. I will show you the sights of Karachi.' And he sighed.

He stopped not far away, in one of the grand residential streets of the older, British-built town. The long wall of the house opposite which we had stopped was lined at the top with barbed wire.

The driver hugged the steering wheel, like a man suddenly weary, and said, 'Mr Bhutto's house.'

I would have preferred not to see it, the house of the man hanged four months before, the house where his wife and daughter still were. But it was hard in Pakistan, as I had already found, to stay away from the passion of Mr Bhutto, the degradations of his long months in prison, the manner of his death. That event was already more than political. It was like the legend of a saint or martyr, and it was a Muslim legend, with its mixture of piety and anger and its intimations of revenge.

In the jail in Lahore – I had been told – they had put him in a cell where the cruel summer sun fell for much of the day. He asked for his drinking water to be boiled; they brought him a vacuum flask of boiling water; it was evening before the water was cool enough for him to drink. He lived simply, eating one round of unleavened bread a day; but he spent 2,000 rupees, 200 dollars, every day on his fellow prisoners. He washed his own clothes, the man who had been a dandy. At every stage of his legal degradation the quality of his food declined.

In the jail at Rawalpindi – where he was to be hanged – his warders were constantly changed because they became too sympathetic. But then a warder was found who taunted the condemned man. 'Why do you want to read *Time* and *Newsweek*, when in a few days you will be dead?' At the time of his death he weighed eighty pounds. When they came to put the hanged man's clothes on him he said, 'I will wear my own clothes. If any of you want to put that on me, let him try.' In one story he walked to the scaffold. When his hands were tied he asked for them to be untied. He said, 'It hurts.' In another story he was carried to the gallows on a stretcher. In a third story he was killed in his cell: a prisoner, roused early one morning and told to go and wash a hanged man, went to a cell and saw Mr Bhutto dead, but so cold and stiff that the clothes had to be torn off. All this, just four months before.

The driver, ceasing to hug the steering wheel, said, 'I will show you the sights.'

We went to the sea front: breakers, breeze, the shining flat beach of a muddy bay and, at the far end of the bay, the concrete frames of new apartment buildings: money in the midst of economic stringency, a property boom in Karachi. The driver said, 'Apartments is the fashion now. No more bungalows.'

On the sand there were stalls selling toys and souvenirs. I thought of food. I said, 'Are you fasting?'

'No. I am angry with God. You are Muslim?'

'No.'

'Muslim people are bad. They lie too much. Too much lies from Muslim people. It is a sad story. I will not tell you about it.'

We drove further along the front. He showed me a big, marble-clad building at the end of the road. 'Guess what that is. You guess and tell me.'

I said, 'It is a hotel.'

'Casino. Mr Bhutto's time.'

It was unfinished. A smaller concrete frame beside it was also unfinished.

'Staff quarters. Mr Bhutto's time. No casino now. No gambling. No horse-racing. This government is bad. It is against *everything*.'

We drove on to a residential area: big plots, gardens, big concrete houses. 'Rich people live here. Foreigners, Arabs. Some Pakistanis too. That house is the house of the king of Abu Dhabi.' It was a big house in a big plot, and it had a high wall all around. 'Five hundred servants. That whole house is just for one month in the year. The king of Abu Dhabi comes for one month here just to shoot. In Pakistan there are too many of these birds. Now I will show you my house.'

'You live here?'

'I will show you. I tell you, it is a sad story.'

Some streets away – the plots here were smaller – we stopped in front of a house. Only the upper story could be seen above the wall. The driver sounded his horn. No one answered. He asked to be excused, got out of the car, and shouted. He pushed open the gate and I saw a fussy concrete house that was smaller than it pretended. No one came out of the house. But above the wall of the house opposite a servant's head appeared, amid the greenery of the garden. The servant and the driver spoke familiarly in Urdu.

The driver, getting back into the car, said, 'Nobody is there. It is all taken away now. All.'

'Who took it away?'

'This government. Who else? My father was with the last government.'

Was it true? One of the charges against Mr Bhutto was that during his time in office he had destroyed the social balance in Pakistan, had brought up riff-raff and given them authority. Was the driver's father one of the people Mr Bhutto had brought up? The house was in a rich area but wasn't grand, was certainly less grand than it might have seemed to the man who had built it. The driver seemed to know the house well; he knew the servant of the house opposite. What had happened to the father? The driver said it was he alone who now had to look after his mother, his two sisters, and a brother. He had given up his studies to drive the taxi. He didn't own the taxi. He got 350 rupees a month from the manager of the taxi company; and that was all.

Yet, having told his story, having shown me proof of his former wealth, he didn't seem too unhappy. He took me to a modern mosque with a big concrete dome ('No pillars,' he said proudly) and with a minaret like a church spire. He showed me the tomb of Mr Jinnah, the founder of Pakistan, and he told me the sad story (another sad story) of this leader who died just three months after the state had been established. If Mr Jinnah had lived, the driver said, it would have been different in Pakistan.

A sad story, but the tomb was impressive; the driver liked it. He liked the big new buildings of Karachi; he liked the modern style. He told me that Pakistani architects were the best in the world. The Arabs always wanted them to build mosques.

'We are Muslims in Pakistan. Muslim people like God. I like God.'

'But you told me you were angry with God.'

'Angry, yes. But God is God. God is not like people. Now I will show you before Pakistan.'

We drove in thick traffic into old, commercial Karachi. Scooters squalled and racketed. The hot air was grey and brown with smoke.

I said, 'What did your father do?'

He pretended not to understand.

'Was he a civil servant?'

'I told you, he was with the government.'

He made it sound like a job. But he was unwilling to say more, and I wasn't sure whether he was telling me that his father was a politician or someone who had somehow prospered under Mr Bhutto.

He stopped at a perfume shop to buy perfume and henna for his sisters for the festival at the end of Ramadan. Henna to redden the girls' palms, a gift for the festival – the family side of the elder son, spoilt by sisters and mother. He told me it was the only shop in Karachi where such things could be bought. He was a long time in the shop; he seemed to know the people.

Africans in workaday Sindhi clothes gave a touch of the Arabian Nights to the street, which was architecturally extravagant, oriental. They were simple concrete structures, the bazaar buildings of Karachi 'before Pakistan', but they were fantastically decorated: iron balconies, Saracenic arches, Corinthian or Doric columns, Gothic or mock-Gothic windows. All the available styles of the late British period were jumbled together in pure delight, as at some once-a-year feast where no delicacy could be left out. The inspiration for the Gothic – at first puzzling – was easy to spot later. It was the British-built Victorian Gothic memorial called the Mereweather Tower, in the middle of commercial Karachi. What was the point of that tower?

The driver said, 'It is a *tower*. Like the one in Paris.'

And then he took me to see the Mecca-bound pilgrims, in the reception centre the government ran for them near the docks. It was like an army camp, with the neatness; and walking up and down the well-swept lanes, like well-groomed stage figures in an artificial setting, were elderly men from all the provinces of Pakistan in their provincial dress: Punjabis, Baluchis (with a difference in the turban), Sindhis (with their flat caps), Pathans from the Afghan frontier. The faces were calm, contented. They were men for whom – whatever was happening outside, whoever ruled – heaven was at last within reach.

The driver said, 'It's only because we look like Pakistanis we can come here. If you were an American I wouldn't bring you here.'

Like the pilgrims, my driver had moved from passion to calm. And his religious emotions had risen on a contrary curve, after the mosques, Mr Jinnah's impressive white tomb, and the pilgrim centre. From being angry with God, and an indifferent Muslim, he had become at the end as passionate and secure a Muslim as any.

There remained his sad story. I had my doubts about it. But truth can be crude, and later I believed that in its outline the story was true. I believed that his father had risen fast in Mr Bhutto's time, had risen to being the near neighbour of an Arabian king, but had lost everything with Mr Bhutto's fall and had in some manner been put away: a peasant drama, the small change of Mr Bhutto's tragedy, part of the thuggish public life of the Muslim polity, where in practice the only morality (and also the eternal balm) was the possession of the faith.

'Now I will show you before Pakistan': it was one way of getting around the awkwardness of history. Before 1947 there was no Pakistan here;

there was only the Indian province of Sind and the British-built city of Karachi. That past survived in buildings, and in names: Club Road, Bleak House Road, Clifton, McNeil Road, Jutland Lines, Jacob Lines, Abyssinia Lines, Clayton Quarters, Napier Barracks, Soldier Bazaar. There were even purely Indian survivals· Tamil Colony, Ramswamy, Dadabhoy Nouroji Road. There was no longer a Motilal Nehru Road, but there was still a Gandhi Garden.

And one afternoon, walking from the Intercontinental down the two-mile road that led, through land reclaimed from mangrove swamp, to the Chinna Creek and the Napier Mole Bridge, I was surprised, at the edge of the creek, beside the bridge and amid the works for the new dock, to see a memorial plaque with Hindu names on a wall.

The wall was the front of a bathing ghat, bathing steps, built in 1943 — four years before Pakistan — by the Hindu Charitable Bathing Ghats Association. There were two carved wooden doors, still with their old signs: 'This Entrance Reserved for Hindu Women', 'This Entrance Reserved for Hindu Men'. One door was carved with elephants rampant, the other with serene swans.

The bathing steps still existed. They could be seen (the women's steps walled around with concrete, though) from the Napier Mole Bridge: the lower steps black with the refuse of the oily harbour creek. There were stone seats higher up; the wall on this side, facing the water and the mangrove across the creek, was painted bright green; there were pigeons on the Mogul-style domes. On the Napier Mole Bridge itself there was a stone recording the construction of the bridge in 1864, with the names of the British engineers.

A boy of about twelve came to me on the bridge. He had been watching me. He nodded towards the tainted bathing steps and said, 'Muslims can't go there. Hindus can go there, Parsis, English people. But not Muslims.' To him the prohibition was what was important about the ghat. He was a Hindu, a remnant of the Sindhi Hindu population, but he was innocent of history (and I was to see him a week or so afterwards at a Muslim wedding reception in a hotel).

The ghat clearly stood in the way of the new dock works. Later I was to meet the man who had intervened to prevent the ghat being pulled down. He said that the ghat had long ceased to be a ghat. There were two caretakers, and they used the place as their home. Someone had offered to put up a neon sign on the domed roof, to give the ghat some income for its maintenance; but the man who had saved the ghat thought it better for the place to stay as it was, washed by the polluted tides of the harbour, decaying at its own pace.

The Hindus had all but disappeared. But that was old history. And

95

there had been a greater dispossession since. Karachi, with its immigrant millions, was a city of Pakistan; it had ceased to be of Sind alone. Sind had received the bulk of the Muslims from India; and the Muslim polity as it had developed in Pakistan could not out-balance Sindhi feelings that they were being besieged and colonized, with their language and land under threat. Now, as against Sindhi talk of separatism, there was talk of detaching Karachi as a federal district from the province of Sind.

The dream of the Muslim homeland had had strange consequences. And strangest of all was this: the state which had appeared to some as God itself, a complete earthly reward for the faithful, lived not so much by its agricultural exports or by the proceeds of its minor, secondary industries, as by the export of its people. The newspaper advertisements called it 'manpower-export'.

The idea of the Muslim state as God had never converted into anything less exalted, had never converted into political or economic organization. Pakistan – a thousand miles long from the sea to the Himalayas, and with a population of more than 70 million – was a remittance economy. The property boom of Karachi was sustained in part by the remittances of overseas workers, and they were everywhere, legally and illegally. They were not only in Muslim countries, Arabia, the Gulf states, Libya; they were also in Canada and the United States and in many of the countries of Europe.

The business was organized. Like accountants studying tax laws, the manpower-export experts of Pakistan studied the world's immigration laws and competitively gambled with their emigrant battalions: visitor's visas overstayable here (most European countries), dependants shippable there (England), student's visas convertible there (Canada and the United States), political asylum to be asked for there (Austria and West Berlin), still no visas needed here, just below the Arctic Circle (Finland). They went by the planeload. Karachi airport was equipped for this emigrant traffic. Some got through; some were turned back. *Germans shoot 4 Pakistanis: Illegal entry*. This was an item in *Dawn*, sent from Turkey, on the emigrant route, and it was the delayed story of the humane disabling (men shot in the leg) and capture of one batch.

Abroad, the emigrants threw themselves on the mercies of civil liberties organizations. They sought the protection of the laws of the countries where the planes had brought them. They or their representatives spoke correct words about the difference between poor countries and rich, South and North. They spoke of the crime of racial discrimination and the brotherhood of man. They appealed to the ideals of the alien civilizations whose virtue they denied at home.

And in the eyes of the faithful there was no contradiction. Home was home; home wasn't like outside; ecumenical words spoken outside didn't alter that. The Muslim polity was like God itself, a thing apart, and had ceaselessly to be purified and defended. As the *Tehran Times* article said, speaking of the Islamic wave, 'With reformation and adaptation to present needs in full conformity with the holy Koran and Sunnah [the old, right way], Iran and Pakistan with a clarity of purpose and sincere cooperation can establish the truth that Islam is a complete way of life.'

2

◆◆◆◆◆

Karachi Phantasmagoria

PAKISTAN had a high reputation in the Muslim world. It was the twentieth-century Islamic pioneer, and for some time there had been reports of its 'experiments' with Islam. Pakistan, it was said, was experimenting with Islamic law, with a Koranic alms-levy that would eventually sustain an Islamic welfare state, and with a banking system that would do away with interest.

I wanted to have a look at these experiments. But after a few days in Karachi it became clear that I needed help, that by myself I would see nothing. The *Tehran Times* had said that an Islamic bank existed in Pakistan, 'established under the patronage of the great Pakistani Moslem scholar Maulana Maudoodi'. But in Karachi what I saw everywhere were the green signs of the Habib Bank. The main Habib building in central Karachi was a concrete tower of New York magnificence; and Habib had just opened a branch in Europe. The newspaper advertisements announcing this opening said it had come about 'by the grace of Allah'. But Habib was not an 'experimental' bank.

I needed help, and I went to see Mr Deen, the government information officer. His office was in a concrete shed in what looked like old British military barracks.

Off a wide central corridor, a bar-room-style swing door led to Mr Deen's room. The cotton carpet was worn, its red and white pattern faded with dust and sun. The distempered walls were ochre-coloured, flaking, erupting with lime; the windows, of the roughest carpentry, were protected with a diamond-patterned metal grille; and someone was running a scooter just outside, creating a tearing noise in a cloud of blue smoke. Two small windows cut into the top of the wall were meant to let out hot air; and a ceiling fan spun over the old, government-issue sofa set which, as I found when I sat down, was a little rickety: government on a shoestring.

And Mr Deen was bemused by my request. He had been courteous to me; he had sent the office van — he called it 'a thing on four wheels' — to

98

fetch me from the hotel. But he was a busy man. He was concerned that morning with the pilgrims going to Mecca – the government had decreed that to be a matter of importance – and he was going through the official photographs of the scene at the docks the previous day. It was clear that Mr Deen was finding some of the photographs unsatisfactory. And now: Islamic courts, Islamic banks, Islamic experiments? He seemed mentally to grope.

So I had read the wrong papers?

'People talk about these things,' Mr Deen said, with the weariness of a harassed official. 'But the people who talk expect other people to do the work.'

There was an Islamic Ideology Council that met ten days a month; but that was in Islamabad, the capital, far to the north. Mr Deen didn't know what he could do for me in Karachi. He was in his mid-fifties; he wore grey trousers and a white shirt, and the striped tie hanging on the wall behind him might, in another country, have been a club tie of some sort.

Mr Sherwani, a colleague, came in. He was heavy, looser in flesh than Mr Deen; his skin was smooth, and he was wearing a short-sleeved sports shirt. Mr Deen explained what I was after, and Mr Sherwani looked hard at me. He said to Mr Deen in Urdu, 'But he looks just like Qutub. When I came in the room I thought, "But it is Qutub."' Mr Deen looked at me with a new interest and said with sad affection that yes, I looked like Qutub. Qutub, they told me, was a Pakistani painter.

Mr Sherwani said, 'How old are you?'

I said, 'Forty-seven.'

'I am forty-eight. And I am healthier than you. No, you can't deny it. Your eyes are tired. They are the eyes of an old man. That indicates a vitamin deficiency.'

Mr Deen said, 'He wants to see Islam in action.'

I thought Mr Deen put it well.

Mr Sherwani said, 'He should read the Koran. Marmaduke Pickthall – that's the best translation for you.'

'It's more an interpretation,' Mr Deen said.

Mr Sherwani said, 'You must know the philosophy.'

I clung to Mr Deen's good words. I said, 'I want to see Islam in action.'

Mr Sherwani said that many people said they were Muslims, but there were very few true Muslims. Islam was a complete way of life and for that reason was too hard for most people. I mentioned Iran; Mr Sherwani said with immense, fatherly tolerance that the Shias of Iran were a deviation.

A man came into the office with some photographs. Mr Deen, withdrawing from the conversation, looked at the photographs and began to be vehement with the man who had brought them.

Mr Sherwani – ignoring the row at the desk, and the running scooter outside – asked whether I had any religious faith. I said I hadn't, and to my surprise he was delighted. He said it meant I wasn't prejudiced; it was important, in studying Islam, not to be prejudiced.

The man who had brought the photographs left the office, and Mr Deen followed him out.

Mr Sherwani said to me, 'A man like you – I am going to make a prophecy about you. When you have finished your investigations you will become a Muslim.'

Mr Deen came back and Mr Sherwani said to him, 'I've just been telling him: he is going to become a Muslim.'

Mr Deen, his handsome face still full of the cares of his office, smiled at me. And then he and Mr Sherwani began to discuss what could be done for me. I heard 'Ideology Council' a few times. I felt I was imposing on both of them, taking up their time with a non-official matter. But Mr Deen said, 'It makes a change from what journalists here usually want us to do for them.' And so the two of them talked on. How could they demonstrate Islam to a visitor?

Pilgrims, they decided. In the morning another pilgrim ship was going to Jeddah. Officers from the department would be going to cover the event, and I could go with them. Mr Sherwani thought it a very good idea: unless I saw and talked to the pilgrims going to Mecca I wouldn't understand the depth of their faith. And mosques, they decided. I should visit the mosques of Karachi that evening. No evening could be better, Mr Sherwani said; because this was the night in Ramadan when in AD 610 the Prophet received his first revelation; prayers offered on this night were worth a thousand times more than on other nights. In Shia Iran Ramadan was a month of mourning, full of the calamities of the Shia heroes who had failed to be recognized as the Prophet's successors. For the Sunni Muslims of Pakistan, Ramadan was a happier month, the month of the revelation and the foundation of the religion.

So that was the programme, then: the mosques in the evening with Mr Sherwani, and the docks and the Mecca-bound pilgrims in the morning.

Mr Sherwani said to me, 'I will tell you a story. Listen. An English lord had two sons. They started just like you. They thought they would travel and find out about Islam. So they travelled. They went to Ajmer in India, to the famous Muslim shrine there, and they began to study with a Muslim teacher. The teacher had two daughters. The two sons of the English lord became Muslims and married the two daughters of the teacher. When you become a Muslim you will remember this story.'

English lords, double marriages, Arabian kings with five hundred servants for one month: in Karachi – already with camels, dwarves and Africans – the Arabian Nights came easily.

Mr Deen gave me a lift in the office van back to the hotel. Mr Deen came from India; he had migrated from Delhi just after the partition. He had had many opportunities, official and unofficial, of seeing Delhi again. But for a reason he couldn't explain he had preferred not to. He had left India; the past was over; the wound was not to be reopened.

In the evening Mr Sherwani came for me with a junior colleague from Information, and we went in the office van to some of the mosques of Karachi. The junior colleague was silent; Mr Sherwani did the talking, and I felt that for him it was a good way of easing himself into the long night of prayer: going from mosque to mosque, and in between talking of the faith to someone who had volunteered to listen.

The mosques were crowded, and lit up. Fluorescent tubes were used decoratively, sticks of blue-white glitter; and strings of coloured bulbs were hung over walls like illuminated carpets. Breathless recitations in Arabic from the Koran – some of the mullahs showing off how well they knew the book, how fast they could recite, how little they needed to draw breath – were followed by expositions in Urdu. And at every mosque, like a bee sipping from every flower, Mr Sherwani prayed and, whenever the opportunity offered, joined in the responses of the congregation.

In the mosques in the better-off areas there was a feeling that men were separate, engaged in private devotions. In the poorer areas there was a feeling of community. At one mosque in a poor area sweets were distributed while the mullah chanted, and children so besieged the distributor of sweets that he seemed to lose the use of his legs and to be propelled about the courtyard, holding aloft his cardboard box, by the busy little legs of many children, like a dead cockroach being carried off, as though on hidden wheels, by ants. The scrimmage didn't affect the sanctity of the occasion; the occasion was also a communal one, and the children and the sweets were part of it.

Islam was each man's salvation; it was also the faith itself, the Prophet's story; it was also the community, stitched together by innumerable communal acts and occasions. Unity, faith and discipline: that was the theme of Islam, Mr Sherwani told me, and it was only later that I learned that he had borrowed the words from Mr Jinnah, the founder of Pakistan. Something else underlay the feeling of community: anxiety about the hereafter. It was important, it was fundamental, it locked all the components of faith together: the anxiety whether, on doomsday, one was going to torment or bliss. Mr Sherwani said that by his own pious exercises he had been given the merest glimpse of the hereafter; the truly pious could see further.

Mr Sherwani was steadily losing his joviality, his wish to explain. The prayers were holding him more and more; and soon, like a man who grudged the time, he took me back to the hotel and hurried away. On this night of revelation, when prayers were so precious, Mr Sherwani intended to pray right through until the morning fast began. To be a devout Muslim was always to have distinctive things to do; it was to be guided constantly by rules; it was to live in a fever of the faith and always to be aware of the distinctiveness of the faith.

But the world was going on. Another revelation was being prepared that night, and in the morning it burst on us, in a big front-page story in the government paper, the *Morning News*: PLOT TO MAKE PAKISTAN A FOREIGN STOOGE – *Benazir's bid to arrange US-backed coup – Photostat copy of letter to Murtaza released.*

What was reproduced, in six full columns of the paper, were letters from Mr Bhutto's daughter, Benazir, to her brother in London. They were written from that house which the taxi-driver had shown me; one letter had been written nine days before the hanging of Mr Bhutto, another four days before the hanging. They were family letters, and it was a violation to expose them; they were suggestions – in the circumstances, extraordinarily lucid – from a sister to a brother about what might be done in the way of petitions and pressure to save their father. The burden of the *Morning News* story was that, in return for American help in saving her father, Benazir Bhutto was offering to give up the Pakistan nuclear programme. The handwritten letters were presented as evidence; but they were poorly reproduced and no transcription was given. And in fact the newspaper story was a fabrication.

It was the other side of the life of faith. The faith was full of rules. In politics there were none. There were no political rules because the faith was meant to create only believers; the faith could not acknowledge secular associations or divisions. For everyone in open political life Islam was cause, tool, and absolution. It could lead to this worldly virulence.

Mr Sherwani must have had enough of me; or perhaps more official duties had claimed him. I found, when I went to Mr Deen's office in the morning, that another officer was to go with me to the docks to see the pilgrims leave for Mecca.

The officer was a young woman in a green sari. She was slender, almost thin, and her English was precise. She had, unusually, taken a degree in journalism at Karachi university. Afterwards she had passed the examination for the Pakistan civil service; and after that there had been an eight-month civil service course. She hadn't chosen Information; she had been allotted to the department, and she found it frustrating. In Information she just had to do whatever she was given to do; it wasn't good enough for someone who had done a degree in journalism and wished to do proper writing.

She said all this quite openly in Mr Deen's office, and she wasn't speaking to impress me or Mr Deen. She was as unhappy and tense as her thinness suggested; and I wondered why – as important as the federal civil service was in Pakistan – she kept on with the job. I asked what her husband did. She said all her family were service people, army people, and her husband too used to be in the service. Used? Yes; her husband was dead. 'He expired in a helicopter crash.'

Her husband's family gave some financial help now, but she did the job because she needed the money, especially for the education of her children. She was educating them in English as well as in Urdu, because in foreign countries – and she meant Saudi Arabia and the Muslim countries – you couldn't get a job unless you spoke English.

So, already, she was training her children to leave Pakistan, to become emigrants?

She said, 'I have to. We are a minority. We are non-Muslims.'

She was wearing a sari. Did that mean she was a Hindu or a Parsi?

Before I could ask, she said, 'We believe in the Prophet. But three years ago we were declared non-Muslims by the government. We are Ahmadis.'

'But why did they declare you non-Muslims? What were the pressures on them?'

'You must ask Benazir Bhutto. Benazir will tell you why her father declared us non-Muslims. He was very friendly with us, and then he went and did that.'

The sect began, she said, with a man called Ahmad, who was born in North India in the last century. In 1906 (she was wrong about the date; it was 1890; but I learned that some weeks later) he came to the realization, by many signs given him, that he was the Mahdi or the Promised Messiah. He was a pious man; he fought the conviction, but in the end couldn't resist it. There were Muslims who believed that the Messiah was going to come only at doomsday; but another interpretation of the prophecy was that the Messiah would appear when Islam had degenerated, and in 1906 Islam had degenerated.

I said, 'So you are like the Bahais of Iran? They believe that the Hidden Imam or someone like him appeared in the last century.'

But she had never heard of the Bahais.

She was an Ahmadi convert. And the Ahmadis themselves, she told me, were divided. Some – like herself – believed in the successor to the Messiah; others didn't.

But how had she, a Muslim, come to accept this idea of the Messiah? The idea was hateful to Muslims. Muslims believed that Mohammed was the final Prophet; this idea of the Indian Messiah came close to denying that finality, and therefore came close to denying something fundamental about the Prophet. As a Muslim, she would at one time have felt horror at the idea. How had she managed to make the jump?

Well, she said, her parentage was mixed. She was Shia on one side, orthodox Sunni on the other. So she was ready, it might be said, for heterodox belief. And – she had married an Ahmadi. It was necessary therefore for her to become one. Heresy, then, was something that had been given to her, something she had seen approaching and had deliberately embraced. Her husband had talked to her, instructed her; and she was now so convinced a believer that she spoke of the Messiah, Ahmad, with a little tremor: the good man, the pious man who had had Messiahhood forced on him, and couldn't deny the many signs of God.

The heresy – to which only Muslims could fully respond – now ruled her life; it might even take her out of the Muslim homeland. A government office with flaking distemper and shaky furniture: a girl in a green sari with a degree in journalism from Karachi university, a woman civil servant in a Muslim country: that was arresting enough. But just below appearances in Karachi, below what was easily graspable, was the faith and the fever of the faith, which took many forms, and nearly always gave a phantasmagoric quality to an encounter.

Phantasmagoria continued. I went out to the corridor to wait for the girl in the green sari. And I was so full of what I had just heard, and so confidently expecting to go with her at some stage to the pilgrim docks, that I paid insufficient attention to where I was being led by men who spoke no English, failed to see that I had been separated from her, missed the point of a short van-ride, failed to see that I was being taken to another department and another office, and found myself at the end in a big enclosed room, a much grander office than Mr Deen's, where an elderly man faced two or three other men across a crowded desk, and I was made to sit in a corner, in the draught of an air-conditioning unit, on a chair of a sofa set which was upholstered in PVC rather than Mr Deen's simple cotton.

This was Ahmed's office (another Ahmed, not the long dead visionary I had been hearing about). There was a shelf at the side of his desk with five telephones, and even Ahmed had trouble telling which one was ringing. By some bureaucratic intermeshing which I was in no position to follow, the Ahmed of this office had taken me over. Mr Deen and Mr Sherwani, harassed men, had quietly surrendered me – and with them had gone the Ahmadi girl in the green sari.

And it was with two men from Ahmed's office that I went to the docks. But their English was not good; they preferred to talk among themselves in Urdu; at the docks they were so taken up with their departmental duties, and so awed by the high official nature of the pilgrim send-off (the governor of Baluchistan was to attend), that I saw the whole scene without language, as it were, and as from a distance: the white ship that turned out to be British-built, old, and grubby where not painted white; bunks and bundles in the packed hold, elderly men and women at once like refugees and pilgrims, penitential and expectant; rubbish already being swept up into little piles; on the narrow upper deck, some old men – indifferent to the fussed officials, and piling piety upon piety – doing their ritual wash before prayer, devotion in Islam always also a correct and reassuring physical deed.

General Rahimuddin, the governor of Baluchistan, arrived. On the wharf the bagpipe band, in tartans, paraded and skirled: the inherited British military style, appropriate to a general with a peaked cap, dark glasses, stars and baton, imposed on this pilgrimage to Mecca, a pilgrimage older than Islam, rooted in old Arabian tribal worship, and incorporated by the Prophet into the practices of Islam: layer upon layer of history here.

A port official made a speech, and loudspeakers took his words to all parts of the ship and also to the wharf below where, outside the canopied, festive-looking enclosure with the pipers and soldiers, a small crowd of workmen had gathered. The general made a slightly longer speech. The official farewell to the pilgrims, as ordered by the President, was then over (the government hand-out made nine inches in *Dawn* two days later); and I was taken back to Ahmed's dark, air-conditioned office.

I never saw Mr Deen or Mr Sherwani again. I never saw the girl or widow in the green sari again. I was nagged by her story. But her Ahmadi sect was outlawed, held in horror by many; and it was only at the end of my time in Pakistan that I was able to learn more about them.

Ahmed took me over. His interest in me in the morning might have been an official interest – there was martial law in Pakistan, and a nervousness about foreigners and Pakistan's nuclear programme – but that changed almost as soon as I had been taken to his office. Sitting at his desk, facing his subordinates, he had looked at me carefully; and I had passed his scrutiny.

It would have been reported to him that there was a visitor asking about Islamic institutions. A strange story; but when he found it to be true he became more than interested. There was a reason. Ahmed, who was in his late fifties, was a penitent. By his own account he had lived loosely as a young man, and was still teased by the flesh. He had come late to religion and was now consumed by it. He was awed by his own faith. He wished not only to talk about it, like Mr Sherwani; I believe he also wanted to have a witness to it, someone from the other side, the side he had left behind.

He was well-built, erect and energetic, and still attractive, dark, hook-nosed, with a full, curved lower lip. He was a man of Sind, and he said (perhaps over-romantically) that he belonged to the original, pre-Aryan race of Sind, the builders of the great cities of Mohenjodaro and Harappa, the creators of the Indus Valley civilization that the migrating Aryans had overrun in 1500 BC. Most people in Pakistan, he said, behaved as though the world had begun in 1947, when Pakistan was created. With his Sind ancestry, he had another view of history.

And a feeling for history was at the back of his feeling for Islam. It was the world's youngest great religion and, being the youngest, was the most evolved. He didn't condemn the religions of the past; he saw them as stages in man's spiritual development. Consider the revealed religions. Moses, he said, was all law; that was too harsh. Jesus was all compassion. Ahmed said, 'In a world where there are people like Africans and Negroes, that doesn't make sense. If you turn the other cheek to a primitive fellow, it annoys him.' The beauty of Islam lay in its mixture of law and compassion. To see Islam at its best, to understand the charity of which it was capable, I should go to some of the old shrines in the interior of Sind – he would arrange it. There was one place, connected with a Muslim saint and mystic, that he especially wanted me to visit. There I would see a brotherhood, among them professional men, who had renounced the world to live in the desert and to serve and feed the poor.

That was how that afternoon, in one gulp, as it were, in one excited outpouring, Ahmed outlined his faith, his attitudes, and his plans for me. He drove me back to the Intercontinental and we talked in the parking lot until just before sunset. At the end, with a tenderness for which I wasn't prepared, he pressed his forefinger to the middle of my forehead. He said, 'That is where it gets you. If you were a businessman you would get blood pressure. You're an intellectual. You are concerned with the truth. So it gets you there, in the eyes. You must rest your eyes. You must look at green things.'

My eyes again! And what happened the next morning was that a lens fell out of my glasses and broke on the tiled floor of my room. So the first service Ahmed had to do for me was to take me to an oculist.

Our friendship was sudden, but I felt it as real; and while it lasted I leaned on it. My search for Islamic institutions and experiments – the search that had brought me to Ahmed – was still going on; and Ahmed was the rational man to whom I returned after venturing into other men's Islams.

Mr Mirza had been represented to me as one of the most distinguished men of Pakistan, one of the country's profoundest minds, and someone who would tell me all I wanted to know about the Islamization of institutions. But the man who told me that about Mr Mirza, and arranged the meeting, was one of Mr Mirza's lesser relations. And it was as a kind of family suppliant that I was received by the great man in his air-conditioned office, and addressed (when my turn came) as though I were a prayer meeting.

There were many books in the room, faded English political books of the 1930s and 1940s, indicating a time spent as a student in England. Two young men, attentive, leaning forward, bright-eyed, were seated in front of Mr Mirza's desk, and Mr Mirza said gently that he was exchanging a few words with 'young colleagues'. I thought the young men were just that, but it was only part of the great man's public humility. The young men, like myself, had been brought to receive wisdom.

And there was no exchange of words: a low, even, unceasing, uninterrupted babble poured out of Mr Mirza. We were living in a Satanic time; people were not interested in the truth; university professors were not interested in the truth. We had a lot of information now, but too much information was as bad as too little information. No one could foretell the future; the 'imponderables' were too many; the Tolstoyan view of history was correct. Was Mr Mirza the only one interested in truth? Where was all this leading? It was leading back to the Satanic nature of the age, to the need for Islamic belief.

The young men stood up, dazed with pleasure, and Mr Mirza, with extra gentleness, offered them a goodbye like a benediction. And then I began to get my dose. No Tolstoy for me, though; I got an obscure Arab. 'An Arab scholar of the tenth century – he was perhaps the greatest of the Arab philosopher-scholars of the Abbasid period – he died in 1011, so his writing falls at the turn of the century and belongs more to the tenth century rather than the eleventh – he says that prophets are not like other men.'

But I hadn't come to hear that from Mr Mirza. I had come to find out about the application of Islam to institutions, to government, to law.

'Let me finish,' Mr Mirza said; he couldn't bear to be interrupted. And he went on. Prophets were the ones through whom God expressed his will; Islam was dedicated to the idea that the time would come when prophets would cease to be necessary.

Where had that got us, or Pakistan? It had got us to this point: that the law and institutions of Pakistan, as they were, were not divine. In spite of his reputation and his books, Mr Mirza had not thought beyond that point. His education was part of his vanity; but he was like the simplest mullah. And in fact, as an Islamizer as pure as any, Mr Mirza had political ambitions. With the disappearance of Mr Bhutto and the suppression of Mr Bhutto's party, with an Islamizing military government, Mr Mirza was hoping to be lifted to the heights.

I said I was going. Mr Mirza was disappointed; he had more to say to me. He offered me his car. I accepted. Waiting for the car, he attempted to organize his own interview. He said, 'I suppose you are thinking that I should be in a monastery and shouldn't be in business.'

'I am not thinking that.'

'But in Islam, you see, there is no separation. It's a complete way of life.'

He took out some prayer beads and began clacking them, muttering. I looked past his left ear and then past his right ear. Clack-clack, went the beads, and he said, 'I am God-intoxicated.' I looked over his left shoulder and then over his right shoulder. Clack-clack, went the beads; and I let him mutter on until the car came.

Mr Salahuddin, the newspaper editor, had the reputation of being an Islamic 'hard-liner', like Mr Mirza. But he was without Mr Mirza's mystical or intellectual bent, and I preferred his directness.

In Pakistan, with its fifteen percent literacy, newspaper circulations were low. The English-language *Dawn* (a journalist from the rival *Morning News* told me) had a circulation of 30,000; the *Morning News* itself, having dropped to 4,000 in Mr Bhutto's time, had bounced up again and was now ticking away quite nicely at 10,000. So Mr Salahuddin, editing an Urdu-language paper with a circulation of 35,000, was a power in the land. The editorial assistant who met me told me that Mr Salahuddin had spent three years in jail in Mr Bhutto's time. Mr Salahuddin, the assistant said, was a man of principle.

The office was at the top of a newish concrete building of four or five storeys in central Karachi. A broken, bumpy dirt road off a bazaar street; black-skinned children playing football; a human derelict of some sort left out in the sun in a home-made box-cart. A rubbled, uneven yard, a lift door opening directly on to the yard. Odd that lift, being just there, slightly surreal.

But it worked. And at the top of the building, in the verandah, as in a parody of a waiting room (and a continuation of the modern urban parody of the street), there were three cane-bottomed chairs, all without bottoms. The rooms were divided by half-partitions into little cubicles, one leading into the other. Doors on either side of the editor's cell opened into offices, in one of which the calligraphers were at work, penning out edited copy on to transparent slips that were later to be off-set. Flies buzzed on the panes of the small windows; there was a pencil drawing of Mr Jinnah on the wall.

Mr Salahuddin was a small man in his early forties. He had a grey-streaked spade beard, a precise mouth, and bright black eyes. I tried to think of him in jail: I thought that jail would not diminish his fire. He was born in India and had come to Pakistan when he was twelve.

Muslims were free to worship in India, he said; it wasn't just for the freedom of worship that Pakistan was established. Pakistan was meant to be an Islamic state, run on Islamic principles. What did that mean? Had there been such a state? He said, 'The state that existed for thirty-two years at the time of the Prophet and the first four caliphs.'

So there it was again – the dream not only of the early Islamic state, the creation of the Prophet, but also of the time when Muslims were rightly guided, divinely ruled: a fusion of history and theology, the indestructible alloy of the faith. That pure time could come again; Muslims could live in such purity again. They had only to follow the rules. The rules were there; they could be found in the holy book and the traditions. The many rules of Islam were not handed down for the sake of God, Mr Salahuddin said; they were for the good of people. Freedom came with obedience; the rules made men free.

And – in his office in Karachi, with men coming in all the time on newspaper business, some of them with bundles of rupees, and with the calligraphers at their long desks in the next room preparing their copy for the press – that was Mr Salahuddin's cause: the Islamic state, and its special freedom. He had gone to jail in Mr Bhutto's time; I felt he was ready to go to jail again.

He gave me some booklets to take away. Some were old-fashioned: reissues, I felt, of Muslim missionary publications first put out in the days of European colonialism, when Islam, impoverished and politically null, needed all the European support it could get.

The Koran and Modern Science, by a Frenchman, showed that the Prophet had anticipated many modern European ideas. *Islam – the First and Final Religion* (an abridged and combined edition of *Charms of Islam* and *Islam Our Choice*) proved that all the other religions, in their holy books, had prophesied the coming of Mohammed. There was also a tribute and a statement of Islamic intent from Napoleon: 'I hope the time is not far off when I shall be able to unite all the wise and educated men of all the countries and establish a uniform regime based on the principles of the Koran which alone are true and which alone can lead men to happiness.'

After Napoleon, there were comments from Victorian Englishmen, 'statesmen and diplomats', all titled, whose names still apparently rang in the Muslim world, but were not as well known at home as they ought to have been: people like Al-Haj Lord Headley Al-Farooq (1855–?), 'Peer, Author and Statesman', an army man, an engineer as well, and also editor of the *Salisbury Journal*; Sir Abdullah Archibald Hamilton (1876–?), 'Statesman and Baronet', an army man again ('Lieutenant in the Royal Corp'); Sir Jalaluddin Lauder Brunton (no dates given), 'Statesman and Baronet', no career given ('an English Baronet and a public man of wide repute'). To them was added the English scholar, Professor Haroun Mustapha Leon, M.A., Ph.D., L.L.D., F.S.P., an 'earnest geologist' and an 'able philologist', an M.A. from Potomac University (U.S.A), who accepted Islam in 1882, when he was doing a series of articles on 'The Etymology of Man's Language' for the *Isle of Man Examiner*.

The American in this white Muslim line-up was Mohammed Alexander Russel Webb, 'Diplomat, Author and Journalist', editor of the *St Joseph Gazette* and *Missouri Republican*, who was born in 1846 and died at the age of 115 in 1961: a Mark Twain-like figure from 'Hudson, Columbia country' who rejected 'the drippings, or more properly perhaps the drivelling, of an orthodox Presbyterian pulpit' for Islam and spent his immensely long life in Islamic missionary work.

It was through Mr Salahuddin that I got in touch with Khalid Ishaq. Khalid Ishaq was one of the leading lawyers of Karachi. He was successful enough to give much of his time to public work. He was a member of the Islamic Ideology Council that met for ten days a month in the capital, trying to work out what should be done in the way of Islamization; he was also a member of a government commission that was looking – somewhat despairingly, I felt – into corruption.

He too was a migrant from India. He was a tall, heavily-made man in his early fifties. He had the lawyer's manner, the slow, dry humour, the eye for human quirkiness, the fondness for little anecdotes. The manner went easily with his passion for his faith. Islam, I felt, was more than a private belief for him; to him, a Muslim from the sub-continent, still insecure in Pakistan, Islam was his civilization and culture; it was fundamental to his idea of what he was; it was something, as a man and a lawyer, he had to serve and protect.

Mr Salahuddin had told me that Khalid Ishaq had a prodigious library and spent 20,000 rupees a month, 2,000 dollars, on books. This didn't prepare me for what I saw in Khalid Ishaq's house.

I said, as we drove into his yard, that he had a big house. He said in his precise lawyer's way that yes, it was a big house, but it wasn't big enough. And it wasn't. Books filled room after room; case upon case, case in front of case; yards and yards of shelves, and cupboards in front of the shelves. One big room was devoted to many-volumed commentaries on the Koran – hefty Arabic tomes. 'And,' he added, 'commentaries on the commentaries.' He bought everything.

Did his devoutness match his collector's zeal? He had a sense of humour: I thought I could put the question to him. He said, 'I wouldn't say I am very devout. I haven't missed a prayer for the last thirty-three years.' Since 1946, that was, the year before the creation of Pakistan; and he meant the five-times-a-day prayers.

We sat in his office, a clearing in the book stacks, a large room with a large desk and with seating at one end that would have done for a board meeting. We sat below fans; the whirring muffled the noise of the scooters and scooter-taxis in the street.

His explanation of his Islamic passion was simple. 'Our people emotionally reject the West. Materially, we may be dependent on the West. Our people may go abroad to better themselves. But however long they stay, they always want to come back, if only to die.' And it was out of that emotional rejection of the outside world that Khalid Ishaq conceived the need for specifically Islamic institutions – institutions not of the West, and not socialist, but institutions in keeping with the people's emotional needs.

To understand those needs, it was necessary to understand the idea of equality in Islam. 'The servant here brings us tea and sweets. That is his job. But he also knows that on another occasion we can be men together and he can sit with me.' And there was the role of the mosque: every Friday every man, whatever his condition, heard from the mullahs that the laws of men were not to be obeyed if they went against the teachings of the Koran.

So the Islamic enterprise was stupendous: it was the deliberate creation – with only the Koran as a guide – of a state mechanism that would function in the modern world and would be unlike anything else that had evolved. It was a high intellectual enterprise. Did Pakistan have the talent? Was there an intellectual life in Pakistan? Not much, Khalid Ishaq said; books were expensive, and television was putting paid to whatever intellectual life there was.

What had been achieved so far by the Ideology Council? Not much, Khalid Ishaq seemed to indicate. They were still trying to get around the problem of interest in banking. There was an idea they had put up to the government for getting everyone to wear the same clothes and drive the same make of car; but nothing had come of that.

There were difficulties, Khalid Ishaq said. First, there were the 'modernists' among the Islamizers. These were people who in old age or for some private reason had turned from secular life to religion. They read a few books about Islam, and thought they knew a lot; but they knew very little. These people were really mystics and knew nothing about institutions. (I thought I detected a criticism there of Mr Mirza.) And there were the mullahs. It was to the mullahs that the military government had turned when they had decided to Islamize.

'The mullahs really had no idea what was being asked of them. They could only think of "the good man" or "the good men" to whom everything should be entrusted. I have met these people and I really think that many of them don't even begin to have an idea of the need for institutions of any kind. They don't know what we are talking about.'

I felt, after this, that there were no Islamic experiments for me to see in Pakistan, that it was as Mr Deen had said right at the beginning: the Islamic experiments were things people were waiting for other people to start. The great Islamic enterprise of Pakistan existed, but only as an ideal, at once an expression of the highest faith and an expression of the political insecurity in which Muslims lived in the Muslim homeland.

The poet Mohammed Iqbal, when he had put forward his idea for a separate Indian Muslim state in 1930, had spoken of a Muslim polity or social order as something arising naturally out of the 'Islamic principle of solidarity'. Such a polity existed in Pakistan. But the Islamic state of which people now spoke was more abstract than Iqbal's. This Islamic state couldn't simply be decreed; it had to be invented, and in that invention faith was of little help. Faith, at the moment, could supply only the simple negatives that answered emotional needs: no alcohol, no feminine immodesty, no interest in the banks. But soon in Pakistan these negatives were to be added to: no political parties, no parliament, no dissent, no law courts. So existing institutions were deemed un-Islamic and undermined or undone; the faith was asserted because only the faith seemed to be whole; and in the vacuum only the army could rule.

Khalid Ishaq drove me back to the Intercontinental. When we were on

Club Road he turned off into the grounds of the Karachi Gymkhana, the British club of colonial days.

It was late; the lights were dim; it was quiet. There were a few elderly men in the bridge room; but the wide verandah – with an old, dark, uneven wooden floor – that ran the length of the building was empty. The British had built Karachi and the Gymkhana. The club, at this hour, still felt like theirs; but their fantasy, of empire-building, had been absorbed into another.

Ahmed was taking me to dinner at his house, and I went down to the lobby of the Intercontinental to wait for him. As soon as I sat down on the sofa a young man, whom I had barely noticed, left where he was sitting and threw himself next to me, with a movement so sudden, violent and intimate that I was startled.

He wore the long Pakistani shirt and the loose cotton trousers; he had the squat physique and the round face of the taxi-driver who had driven me round Karachi. His English was thick and hard to follow. 'Cafeteria' – was that what he was saying?

'Cafeteria,' he was whispering, 'where is cafeteria?'

I pointed to where the coffee shop was. But he wasn't interested. He said, 'Nothing else here? Upstairs?'

'Rooms.'

'Rooms. Only rooms? You live here?'

'For a few days.'

'Only rooms, eh? Pool, where is pool? You know the pool?'

'It's closed.'

'Closed. This Islamic government closed it.'

The lobby was busy. The foreign air crews – the principal users of the Intercontinental – came and went. One tall young German girl, lusciously hipped, and with her hair in a pony tail at the side, was attracting the young man's attention.

He said, 'Woman is God's gift to man. You think?'

'Yes. You come here a lot?'

'My first time.'

And it turned out that he had been in the lobby for only twenty-five minutes. He had come with a friend – that older, thinner man in a brown country outfit on the other chair.

The young man beside me said, 'We come to see the traffic.'

He said he was a student. I asked what he studied. He said he was really a shopkeeper; he had said he was a student because he wanted to be a doctor; his family wanted him to be a doctor and do well. He was twenty-four; he came from Sukkur, which he said was four hundred miles to the north-east (it was nearer). He sold cloth in Sukkur. He had come down with his brother to Karachi 'to do a little business'. He had done his business; he was a little bored; and the friend from Sukkur on the other chair, more experienced in Karachi ways, had suggested they should come to the Intercontinental to see 'the traffic'.

They hadn't yet broken their fast on this Ramadan day (there was a sign in the Intercontinental coffee shop saying that Muslims would not be served during the hours of the fast), and the friend seemed exhausted, seemed even to be falling asleep. His eyes were half-closed; he was nodding unsteadily. I said, 'Your friend is falling asleep.' I thought that the young man said in reply, 'My friend is blind, cannot see.' It looked true. But what the young man was saying in his thick accent was only, 'My friend cannot speak English.'

And the luck with the traffic came to the friend. A French group came out of the lift, a man and two women. The man was the true beauty in the group, slender, all in white, the towelling texture of his jersey contrasting with the smooth drill of his trousers. He remained standing; but one of the two women of his court sat next to the sleepy man from Sukkur.

He woke up and, sleepy-eyed as he was, wriggled until he was touching her. He knew about the traffic in the Intercontinental; he knew that foreigners and their shameless women, non-Muslims, could be treated with contempt as open as this. The woman took out some colour photographs from her bag. The man from Sukkur leaned over the woman's shoulder to look. But the pictures were not as exciting as he had perhaps expected; and sleep began again to get the better of him. He stared vacantly ahead, too exhausted to consider the traffic moving in and out of the lifts.

I introduced Ahmed when he arrived. This was a misjudgement. Ahmed was of Pakistan, not a visitor, and he wasn't amused. He said, when we were in his car, that the men from Sukkur (whom he had greeted ceremoniously, thinking they were friends of mine) were villagers, rustics. People like that came to the Intercontinental to look at unveiled women and women in bikinis. There were rich Pakistanis who came for the same thing; they rented rooms that overlooked the pool. Palestinians – Muslims – had contributed to the craze. Some of them (they sounded like guerrillas living on subsidies, but Ahmed didn't say that) had come to Karachi with European women, who had lounged around in bikinis by the Intercontinental pool; the story had spread.

For villagers like the men from Sukkur Ahmed had no regard. These were the men – villagers who had got to know about the traffic at the

Intercontinental, had the coolness to defy the doormen, and thought they had understood the world – who became communists. Politics in Pakistan could be as simple as that.

Ahmed said, 'The world is mixed up now. People are confused. There is no longer any symmetry in many people's lives.'

I put to him Khalid Ishaq's point about the emotional rejection of the West. How much of that rejection was self-deception? Could a civilization so encompassing, a civilization on which people here depended for so much, be truly rejected?

Ahmed was divided. He said he himself didn't like being abroad. He was always 'under tension'. It was because of 'the time factor'. When he was abroad, in a big city, he was ruled by the need to be on time. It weighed on him; it tormented him; he ceased to feel master of himself. Then he said, 'But when people here talk about the emotional rejection of the West, they usually mean one thing. Women.'

On the subject of women Ahmed was touchy. He saw himself as a liberal; but his liberalism was shot through, more than he might have acknowledged, with Muslim anxieties. Having grown devout in middle age, he had become oppressed by the Muslim idea of accountability. I believe he feared some retribution for his own womanizing past; and his daughters, lovely girls, liberally educated, were at the centre of his anxieties. During the Bangladesh crisis, reports that Pakistani soldiers were raping Bengali women had caused him unspeakable anguish. Rape, for a Muslim, was more than a physical assault on a woman; it destroyed her honour, and so destroyed her life; it destroyed the honour of her family. Ahmed said, 'For two months, while that was going on, I couldn't sleep.'

His house was in one of the many new housing colonies of Karachi. It was a big concrete house. But Ahmed, important as he was, lived simply. The drawing-dining room, lit by a dim ceiling light, felt bare: it had only essential furniture and two television sets, one of them broken.

Ahmed's son came in. He was in his twenties, and a doctor. He worked in a local hospital, and didn't intend to go abroad. He said he wanted to serve the people of Pakistan, and I believed him. He was smaller than his father, paler, more Aryan in features, a gentle man, as withdrawn as his father was ebullient. He was content to let his father speak for him.

Like a man still making a public statement of his faith – and his voice filled the room – Ahmed said, 'I wanted all my children to serve in hospitals. As doctors, nurses, even as sweepers. Because in hospitals you lessen the distress of others.'

Ahmed said he hadn't forced religion on his son; he had left him free to choose. And the son, with a kind of nineteenth-century earnestness, was preoccupied with the whole question of belief.

He said, 'In the beginning men worshipped stones. Then fire. Today we find those practices funny. Wouldn't men tomorrow find the practices of today funny?'

Ahmed let him say that. Then he spoke for his son again. 'When people come around to ask for money for religious causes, you know what he tells them? He tells them it is better for people to give blood for the sick.'

The son nodded, looking down, acknowledging what his father had said, but shrinking from the tribute.

The dinner was brought out by Ahmed's wife. Ahmed and I were the only persons who were going to eat. The son was only going to sit with us; and so, too, was the other man who now arrived. The talk turned, as it so often did in Pakistan, to the situation of Pakistan.

Ahmed said: 'I will tell you the story of this country in two sentences. In the first quarter of this century the Hindus of India decided that everything that was wrong had to do with foreigners and foreign influence. Then in the second quarter the Muslims of India woke up. They had a double hate. They hated the foreigners and they hated the Hindus. So the country of Pakistan was built on hate and nothing else. The people here weren't ready for Pakistan, and people who don't deserve shouldn't demand.'

It was what many conservative Muslims said: that the Muslims of India, as Muslims, hadn't been pure enough for a Muslim state.

Ahmed said: 'Then they began to distribute the property of the Hindus who had left Pakistan. So many of the people who came here from India got something for nothing. That was the attitude in the beginning. That is the attitude today. But I am too old to be unhappy now. It happens, you know. You find you are old, and you just stop worrying about certain things. It is for young people to worry. I am fifty-nine. At that age life is just death in instalments.'

There came into the house a very big man, an overgrown peasant, he seemed, and Ahmed's irritability vanished. He got up to greet his visitor, and solicitously led him in. The newcomer was immense, well over six feet, and built like a wrestler. At the top of this bulk was an incongruous babyface: a face unmarked by passion, rancour, expectation. He was in Pakistani country clothes, not especially fresh, and he wore a flat Sindhi cap. For a man so big he moved very quietly, and with small steps. He spoke no English, spoke scarcely at all; and when he sat at the table – sitting well away from it – he still seemed distant.

Ahmed said, 'You remember I told you about an old shrine in the interior of Sind that I want you to visit? I told you about the people there who have given up the world to serve the poor – you remember? He comes from that place.'

But the face was less the face of someone who had chosen to serve than the face of someone lost and patient, a man from whom some essential human quality was missing.

Ahmed said, 'I will tell you a story about this man. He developed a tumour on his leg and the doctors said he had cancer and there was nothing they could do for him. He went to the homoeopathic people. They wanted him to have an injection of snake poison: he would have to let the snake bite him.'

I made an exclamation.

Ahmed's son said, 'A snake bite is like an injection.'

(Some weeks later I read in the paper that the police were looking for a man who specialized in snake-bite injections.)

Ahmed said, 'But he couldn't face the idea of the snake bite. So he went back to his shrine and prayed. He prayed for days. And one day the courage came to him. He took a knife and cut off the tumour. And he's been all right ever since.'

Ahmed spoke in Urdu or Sindhi, and the big man pulled up his loose trousers to show the scar on the inside of his firm, elephantine thigh. The scar – irregularly shaped, the skin shiny and seamed – was six inches long and in places about an inch wide.

Ahmed's son went and looked.

He said almost at once, 'It wasn't cancerous. It was a benign tumour. See – he has another on his head, here.'

The scar was there; the act of courage remained. But the embarrassment – together with interest in the placid giant, who continued to sit at the table, but couldn't follow English – was set aside in renewed talk of Pakistan.

Ahmed said, 'Everybody fools everybody else here. Politicians, civil servants, everybody.'

And Ahmed and his other visitor (who had so far said little) agreed that people were turning to Islam because everything else had failed. Even at the universities the Islamic wave was swamping academic life.

But wasn't that, I asked, the special trap of a place like Pakistan? Couldn't people now accept that they were Muslims in a Muslim country, and that Pakistan was what the faith had made of it? Did it make sense – after the centuries of Islamic history – to say that Islam hadn't been tried?

Ahmed became grave. He said, 'No, it has never been tried.'

3

✦✦✦✦

The Little Arab

FORTY MILES EAST of Karachi was the little town of Banbhore, an ancient port-site dating back to the first century BC. Banbhore had become important because excavations there had uncovered the remains of what was thought to be the first mosque in the sub-continent, a mosque built in the first century of Islam, shortly after the conquest of Sind by the Arabs in 712 AD. Ahmed took me there on the last Friday of Ramadan, which was also the last day of Ramadan.

The Ramadan month ends, and the Id festival is proclaimed, when the new moon is sighted. Ramadan was expected to end on the Thursday; but the government moonsighting committee hadn't sighted the moon. So Ramadan in Pakistan lasted an extra day, and Mr Salahuddin, the newspaper editor, had to hold back his festival supplement and hurry through a non-festival editorial. If it had been Id on the Friday, Ahmed would have been busy receiving and paying visits and wouldn't have been able to take me to Banbhore.

We didn't go there right away. We went first to a mosque to find some people Ahmed thought I should meet. They weren't there. We drove around the sprawl of Karachi for a little. Then the time drew near for the noon prayers and Ahmed became restless and decided to drive back to his neighbourhood mosque.

I asked him whether he believed literally in the after-life.

He said, 'Oh, yes.' He widened his eyes and nodded, just as he had widened his eyes and nodded when he had said that Islam hadn't been tried. 'Oh, yes. I am curious about it. You see, I'm like a child in some ways.' Then he sought to explain his belief. 'People die. But they exist in my mind while I remember them. I cannot say they have vanished while I remember them.' It was in some such way that he expected to be remembered – but in the spirit – until the remembering agent disappeared. Simpler people had their own ideas: they believed in a paradise that duplicated this world, but with everything put right, and – with the women. But in fact, Ahmed said (or so I understood him to say),

118

the women in paradise were to be without periods: they were to be pure.

I would have liked to hear more of this idea of purity, but I felt that Ahmed, with his sensitivity about women and sex, would have thought the interest prurient. So I didn't press; I thought I would save it for later.

The mosque, in a hot, dusty street, was new, of concrete, and undistinguished, its walls ochre and chocolate. The street outside was spread with rugs for the overflow crowd. It was time for the main Friday prayers; the mullah had finished his Koran reading. Ahmed took his prayer mat from the car and knelt with the crowd in the street, in the sun. I waited in the car.

Later, as were driving through Karachi, I saw printed posters: *We Sacrificed for Pakistan Not Bangladesh.*

Ahmed didn't tell me what group was responsible. But the posters — with their hint of further divisions and animosities in his country — made him irritable. He said, 'They sacrificed nothing. If there was no Pakistan I would have been a third-class clerk. Big jobs came to people like me when we got Pakistan.' Later he said, 'In two hundred years it will be the same here.' And still later, the irritation continuing to work on him, turning to a kind of gloom, he said, 'When I was a young man I was told that my country was Hindustan and that it was the finest country in the world. The poet Mohammed Iqbal told me that. Then one day in the 1930s I was told that my country was no longer Hindustan and the people I had thought of as my brothers were my enemies. Then I was told that my country was Pakistan. Then I found that that country had shrunk. Now I can feel it shrinking again.'

For seven years, until the creation of Pakistan in 1947, Ahmed had served in the Royal Indian Navy, the navy of undivided, British-ruled India. He had taken part in the Bombay naval mutiny of 1946. But, thirty years later, his naval memories were not heroic or political; they were memories of sin. He drank. 'Whisky was three rupees a bottle. Beer was free.' And there were the women. 'My friends and I used to form co-operatives. And we would buy a woman for the evening and make love to her in turn.'

I wanted to hear more of those co-operatives — I liked the word, apart from everything else. But it was the sabbath; Ahmed was in a penitential mood, scourging himself for his past and also, it seemed, scourging himself for the state of his country.

I said, 'Age takes care of the passions.'

'You think so, you think so?'

I liked him for that.

He drove fast; he always did; there was in his driving something of the release and excitability of his speech. Karachi was enormous. The city had spread over the flat desert; there were many housing developments, and some of them looked grand; the remittance economy could suggest a rich country. At last we were out in the desert: the early afternoon heat, the openness, the flat scrub of useless trees. Without the Indus River and the lake-reservoirs there could have been no Karachi.

I said, 'What were you saying about the co-operatives?'

He said irritably, at once explaining and punishing himself, 'We did it more for the wickedness than for the pleasure.'

It was clear he was going to say no more. I couldn't ask again, and I wished I had followed my first instinct and saved the matter for another day.

Desert. But the land of Sind was old: seventeen miles from Karachi we came to a necropolis of many acres on an eminence in the wide waste land: tombs two to four centuries old, of decorated soft stone, block set on block, unmortared, to form little stepped pyramids: a dead tradition, perhaps enshrining older mysteries, but now, in modern Pakistan, just there, in the desert.

Modern Pakistan: the road led past the enormous area reserved for Pakistan Steel, the country's first major industrial project: a steel plant and a new port: a controversial project (as I discovered later), costing millions a day, and possibly in the end uneconomic, since everything would have to be imported. The Russians were building it. On the other side of the road, at some distance, were the apartment blocks for the Russians. But the port was named Bin Qasim, after the Arab commander who had conquered Sind and brought Islam to the land.

After this, still on the road to the ruins of Banbhore, a lesser oddity: a large model village, line upon line of two-roomed huts with concrete walls and red roofs, but absolutely empty, empty since it had been built six years before, and now beginning to crumble. Had the village been built too far from where people were? Hadn't people wanted to live in that bureaucratic fantasy of straight lines and red roofs? Ahmed wasn't precise, and didn't want to say too much. He only said the houses hadn't been 'allocated'.

They had been built six years before. That would have been in Mr Bhutto's time; and Ahmed was one of those who hadn't got on with Mr Bhutto. He had in fact left the government service when Mr Bhutto came to power in 1971. Mr Bhutto 'carried grudges', and Mr Bhutto felt he had a score to settle with Ahmed's family. So Ahmed resigned; he would have been sacked by Mr Bhutto anyway; his name was on the list of two thousand people Mr Bhutto wanted to sack. Ahmed said he had only a few rupees when he resigned. He was building his house, and that had taken up most of what he had. He borrowed and lived on borrowed money for a year, doing a variety of little jobs, until he got a job as adviser to an industrialist.

He advised the industrialist on the procedures of government departments. Previous advisers had claimed to be spending large sums on bribes. Ahmed bribed no one. He used his authority and knowledge of the rules to get the industrialist's work done; and the industrialist was amazed and grateful. Ahmed was soon getting a prodigious salary. He finished building his house; he paid off all his debts. And then, feeling himself near the end of his active life, he thought the time had come for him to think of others. That was why (after Mr Bhutto's fall) he had gone back to government service, where he earned a quarter of what he had been getting from the industrialist. Ahmed loved and admired the industrialist still. He was a truly religious man, Ahmed said, a devout Muslim who followed the Koranic injunction and set aside a percentage of his wealth for charity.

A sandy track off the main road led to Banbhore. It was a short run, but the track looped and forked between beach vegetation; and Ahmed had to ask the way of a barebacked peasant who was dragging freshly-cut branches. To come upon the excavated mound of a walled town with semi-circular bastions was suddenly to feel far away: a rough outpost at the eastern limit of the Arab empire, a place of exile.

The town stood on a creek, but was now some little way from the water. The creek opened out, in the distance, into the sea. In the middle of the creek were salt flats; on a whitish spit of land, which looked intolerably hot, were the contemporary houses of the salt workers; on one flat far away were little white pyramids of salt.

It could never have been a rich town. The museum displayed one gold coin; the other coins were shoddy bronze things, cast in honeycomb moulds of hard-baked ashy clay. But there was the mosque, or the floor-plan of the mosque, modelled on the mosque of Kufa in Iraq: that was the treasure of Banbhore.

Kufa was associated with the rightly guided Muslims at the very beginning of Islam; it was one of the earliest military towns the Arabs established among the conquered peoples north of Arabia; it was from Kufa that Ali, the cousin and son-in-law of the Prophet, ruled as the fourth caliph from AD 656 to 661. Conquest first, Islam later: it was the pattern of Arab expansion. So Banbhore, repeating Kufa, and in the first century of Islam, linked Sind and Pakistan to the great days. The Banbhore mosque, if it was what it was said to be, was fabulous. The remains had been made neat; the floor had been re-tiled around the few old tiles that had survived.

Fragments of decorated pottery lay all over the excavated town site. And everywhere, too, mixed with the earth, and commoner than pottery, were crushed bones, white and clean and sharp. Ahmed said they were human bones. But such a quantity! The bones weren't only on the surface; the excavation trenches showed the mixture of bones and earth all the way down, the bones like a kind of building material. Had the town been built on a cemetery? But why were the bones so crushed? If Ahmed was right, and the bones were human bones, Banbhore held another mystery.

I was keeping the Ramadan fast with Ahmed, and that disturbed him. He said again and again that he should have brought something for me to drink. He said that, but when we left Banbhore he seemed in no hurry to get back to Karachi. He, who normally drove fast, now drove slowly. I thought he might himself have been tired out by the long fasting day, and the sun and salt of Banbhore. Abruptly, after we passed the Pakistan Steel area, now called Bin Qasim after the Arab conqueror, Ahmed drove off the road and stopped the car in low bush. I thought he wished to rest. But no: he had only been looking for a place where he could get off the road and pray. He said, 'You can't stop on the road. Those fellows in the buses and cars take pleasure in bouncing you.'

I passed him his prayer mat. He walked briskly to the edge of the road, erect, military-looking in his grey-blue Pakistani costume, the long shirt and the slack trousers; and, oblivious of the passing traffic, he offered up his prayers for a long time. He said, when he came back, that if he missed a prayer during the day he grew restless in his sleep; his wife would wake him up and he would do the prayer he had missed.

We drove back fast to Karachi after that, not to his house, but to the house of the industrialist for whom he had worked. It was in one of the richer housing 'societies'. There was a wide concrete drive at one side of the big plot. Royal palms lined the front of the lawn, which went back to a terrace that ran the width of the house.

On this terrace, on an easy chair, lay an elderly man in brown; he was paralyzed. He was the grandfather, the head of the family, and once the head of the firm. Two young boys, his grandsons, were dressed like little Arabs, with the cream gown and the headgear with the black bands. They had just been to Mecca with their father, and it was clear they had done the pilgrimage in style. The father was a tall man, dressed in white, the pilgrim's colour, and with a white skull-cap. He was soft-featured, soft-voiced. He was as Ahmed had described him: in his pilgrim clothes he seemed as much a man of religion as of business.

He, Ahmed and I sat out on the lawn. For my sake Ahmed asked for some drink to be brought out. The servant brought out three tumblers of a red liquid. I was nervous of the colour, let my tongue touch without tasting, and – not wishing to appear to be spurning their hospitality – I asked whether I could have a Coca-Cola instead.

Ahmed was shocked. He said, with distinct irritation, that the red liquid was a delicacy; it was used to ease people off their fast; it was made from special herbs and was very expensive, twenty-three rupees for a small bottle. I would have liked to try it; but I felt, after Ahmed had mentioned the price, that I would have compounded my vulgarity by going back on my choice. So the astonished servant brought out a Coca-Cola. And through all this pother on the lawn about my drink – which I didn't really need – the man in the white skull-cap smiled sweetly.

I complimented him on his house. He said it looked much better after Mecca, because of the green. I asked about the hotels of Mecca. I was hoping to hear something about the effects of the new Arab and Muslim money; but he only said that the hotels nearer the Great Mosque and the Kaaba were more expensive, the ones further out less expensive.

The family had migrated from Bombay, and a branch was still in business in that city. But Muslims in India were 'not encouraged to come up'. Some had 'come up'; but generally there was no 'encouragement'. It was easier in Pakistan. Everything was new, just starting; and there were more opportunities; but there was as yet no 'infrastructure'.

I asked what difference there was for him between being in Bombay and being in Pakistan. He said that for him, as a businessman, there was no difference; business was business. But when you were in India or some other foreign country you were never sure whether the meat had been slaughtered in the correct way; you had to ask and you couldn't always get answers; you had sometimes to go without. In Pakistan there was no such problem. Sometimes when you were abroad you felt like going to a mosque. But mosques weren't always easy to find; you had to ask. Here, at prayer time, he said, gesturing to one end of the lawn and then to the other, here at prayer time a muezzin called from this side and a muezzin called from that side. There was no problem about finding a mosque in Pakistan.

I had expected someone less serene, more complicated. But Ahmed had spoken of the industrialist less as an industrialist than as a pious man, a good Muslim, someone who followed the rules in deed and heart. The rules made a man free: Mr Salahuddin, the newspaper editor, had told me that.

And Mr Salahuddin had also told me that it was possible in Islam for perfection to come to a child: as it seemed to have come to the elder and plumper of the industrialist's sons. The boy, his father said, had already been twice on the pilgrimage to Mecca; during this month of Ramadan, now about to end, he had kept the rest of them up to the mark by his extraordinary strictness. He, the dimpled boy in Arab clothes, pretended not to know that he was being talked about. Standing on the edge of the terrace, bending a length of black rubber tubing in childish sport, he went grave and withdrawn, frowning slightly, just minding his own business, being a little Arab.

It was nearly seven. Other members of the family, women, began to come out of the house on to the terrace, gathering around the paralyzed grandfather on the easy chair. It was fast-breaking time, and time for us to leave.

And yet it was strange, the Arab tilt of Pakistan: the little boy in Arab clothes, the Pakistan Steel project given the name of the Arab conqueror. The poet Iqbal, putting forward his plan for an Indian Muslim state in 1930, had said that the Islam of India was special, 'a people-building force . . . at its best'. 'I therefore demand the formation of a consolidated Muslim state in the best interests of India and Islam,' Iqbal had said. 'For India, it means security and peace . . . ; for Islam, an opportunity to rid itself of the stamp that Arabian imperialism was forced to give it.'

But the world had changed since 1930; Arabia had some say in the world again. Pakistan had changed since 1947. Seeking more than Iqbal's Muslim polity now, seeking in failure an impossibly pure faith, it called up its Arabian origins, mystical but at the same time real. At Banbhore, a remote outpost of the earliest Arab empires, you walked on human bones.

4

❖❖❖❖

Killing History

IN THE imagination the Arabs of the seventh century, inflamed by the message of the Prophet, pour out of Arabia and spread east and west, overthrowing decayed kingdoms and imposing the new faith. They move fast. In the west, they invade Visigothic Spain in 710; in the east, in the same year, they move beyond Persia to invade the great Hindu-Buddhist kingdom of Sind. The symmetry of the expansion reinforces the idea of elemental energy, a lava flow of the faith. But the Arab account of the conquest of Sind – contained in the book called the *Chachnama*, which I read in Pakistan in a paperback reprint of the English translation first published in 1900 in Karachi – tells a less apocalyptic story.

The Arabs had to fight hard. They turned their attention to Sind at some time between 634 and 644, during the reign of the second caliph or successor to the Prophet, and in the next sixty or seventy years made ten attempts at conquest. The aim of the final invasion, as the *Chachnama* makes clear, was not the propagation of the faith. The invasion was a commercial-imperial enterprise; it had to show a profit. Revenge was a subsidiary motive; but what was required from the conquered people was not conversion to Islam, but tribute and taxes, treasure, slaves, and women.

The invasion was superintended from Kufa by Hajjaj, the governor of Iraq. When, in the middle of the campaign, he received the head of the defeated king of Sind, together with 60,000 slaves and the royal one-fifth of the loot of Sind, Hajjaj 'placed his forehead on the ground and offered prayers of thanksgiving, by two genuflections to God, and praised him, saying: "Now have I got all the treasures, whether open or buried, as well as other wealth and the kingdom of the world."' He summoned the people of Kufa to the famous mosque of that town, and from the pulpit told them, 'Good news and good luck to the people of Syria and Arabia, whom I congratulate on the conquest of Hind and on the possession of immense wealth . . . which the great and omnipotent God has kindly bestowed on them.' It was open to the conquered people to accept Islam.

But the conquerors were Arabs, and the kingdom of the world was theirs.

There are resemblances with the Spanish conquest of Mexico and Peru, and they are not accidental. The Arab conquest of Spain, occurring at the same time as the conquest of Sind, marked Spain. Eight hundred years later, in the New World, the Spanish conquistadores were like Arabs in their faith, fanaticism, toughness, poverty, and greed. The *Chachnama* is in many ways like *The Conquest of New Spain* by Bernal Díaz, the Spanish soldier who in his old age wrote of his campaigns in Mexico with Cortés in 1519 and after. The theme of both works is the same: the destruction, by an imperialist power with a strong sense of mission and a wide knowledge of the world, of a remote culture that knows only itself and doesn't begin to understand what it is fighting. The world-conquerors, the establishers of long-lived systems, have a wider view; men are bound together by a larger idea. The people to be conquered see less, know less; their stratified or fragmented societies are ready to be taken over. And, interestingly, both in Mexico in 1519 and Sind in 710 people were weakened by prophecies of conquest.

There is this difference between *The Conquest of New Spain* and the *Chachnama*. Bernal Díaz, the Spaniard, was writing of events he had taken part in. The *Chachnama* is Arab or Muslim genre writing, a 'pleasant story of conquest', and it was written five hundred years after the conquest of Sind. The author was Persian; his source was an Arabic manuscript preserved by the family of the conqueror, Bin Qasim.

The intervening five centuries have added no extra moral or historical sense to the Persian narrative, no new wonder or compassion, no idea of what is cruel and what is not cruel, such as even Bernal Díaz, the Spanish soldier, possesses. To the Persian, writing in 1216, the Arab conquests – 'the conquests of Khurasan, Ajam [Persia], Iraq, Sham [Syria], Rum [Byzantium] and Hind' – are glorious; they are the story of the spread of true civilization. Conquest is pleasant to read about because conquest is 'based on spiritual rectitude and temporal excellence . . . of which learned philosophers and generous kings would be proud, because all men attain advancement to perfection by acknowledging as true the belief of the people of Arabia.' There is an irony in this praise of conquest: not many years after those words were written, the invading Mongols were to arrive in Persia and Iraq, and the Arab civilization which the *Chachnama* celebrated was to be shattered, stupefied for centuries.

The *Chachnama* begins with an account of the native dynasty of Sind that is to be overthrown by the Arabs. In this part of the narrative dates are few, and there are elements of the fairy-tale. The dynasty was founded by Chach. Chach was a brahmin ascetic who lived with his brother in a village temple. One day he went to the palace of the king and offered his services as scribe and secretary to the chamberlain. Chach was tall and handsome; he spoke well and wrote a beautiful hand. He became first a correspondence clerk; then chamberlain when the chamberlain died; then prime minister.

It happens one day that the queen, normally secluded in the private apartments of the palace, sees the handsome brahmin prime minister. She falls in love with him and makes a declaration to him. He is nervous. He tells the queen that there are four things men should never trust or take for granted – a king, fire, wind, and water. But the queen pleads; she asks only to be allowed to look at Chach once a day. And in the end she has her way. Chach, the brahmin ascetic, becomes the queen's lover, and his power in the kingdom of Sind is second only to that of the king.

Some years pass. The king falls ill and then is near to death. The queen, who has no children, fears that she will now be displaced and degraded by the king's relations. Through Chach she orders fifty sets of chains to be secretly brought to the palace. The king dies; the news is not given out; the physicians are detained. All the claimants to the throne are summoned in the king's name to the palace. As they arrive they are fettered and imprisoned. Then the king's poor relations are summoned. They have grievances; each poor relation has his particular enemy among the claimants, and now he is given the chance, as though on the king's order, to cut off the head of his enemy and take possession of his property.

When all the claimants are killed, it is announced that the king has appointed Chach as his regent; then it is announced that the king has died. Gifts are made to powerful nobles; the queen places the crown on Chach's head; and the people acclaim Chach. The dead king's brother (a ruler himself in a neighbouring state) disapproves. He marches into Sind, claims the throne for himself, and challenges Chach to single combat. Chach says, 'I am a brahmin. Brahmins do not fight on horseback.' The dead king's brother dismounts. Chach jumps on a horse and cuts off his challenger's head. And that is that.

Power is power; a king's first duty is to keep himself in power. There are no rules. A king, as Chach now is, has constantly to pacify his subjects, high and low, baron or outcaste. And in this pacification any means is permissible. 'Among the rules of conduct prescribed for kings, one is that an enemy should be reduced to submission by tricks and deceit.' A king has to be on the move; his presence must be felt in every corner of his kingdom. People must never get the 'haughty notion in their heads . . . that there is no one to exact revenue from them.' Kings need revenue, because the day may come when an enemy is too strong to be fought off and peace will have to be bargained for.

'Remember it is for a day like this that kings collect treasures and bury them underground, for by means of gold troops are collected . . . and war is carried on . . . in which they sacrifice their lives for the sake of their country and their good name. In other ways also by means of gold an enemy can easily be made to retreat. With the help of gold a man can settle all the affairs of this world satisfactorily, repulse an enemy, and satisfy his vengeance. At the same time, with its help, he can make the necessary provision for his journey to the next world.'

Chach – the queen soon disappears from the story – rules for forty years. It is Chach who repulses the first Arab attack, a sea attack on the port of Debal (which might be Banbhore). On Chach's death the kingdom passes to Chach's brother, and then to Chach's son, Dahar.

Dahar is told one day of a wonderful brahmin astrologer. And since it is good for a king to consult wise brahmins Dahar gets on his elephant and visits the astrologer. For Dahar himself the astrologer predicts nothing but good fortune; but this is clouded by what the astrologer says about Dahar's sister. The man Dahar's sister marries, the astrologer says, will rule the kingdom. Dahar is perplexed. His prime minister (who is a Buddhist) has a solution: since a king's first duty is to his throne, Dahar should go through a form of marriage with his sister. There are five things, the prime minister says, which 'have a sorry look' when they lose their proper place: a king who has lost his kingdom, a minister who has lost his post, a holy man who has lost his disciples, hair and teeth when they drop out, a woman's breasts when they droop with age.

Dahar is shocked by his prime minister's advice. The prime minister goes home, takes a sheep, scatters earth and mustard-seed in its wool, waters it. After some days the mustard-seed sprouts, the sheep turns green. The sheep is then driven about the town and people rush to see it. But after three days the wonder abates; the green sheep is taken for granted. The prime minister says, 'O king, whatever happens, whether good or evil, the people's tongues wag about it for three days. Thereafter no one remembers whether it was good or evil.' So Dahar goes through a marriage ceremony with his sister.

Much is made of this incident, though it has no important sequel. It serves only – in this Persian-Arab narrative – to stress that the kingdom of Sind is morally blighted, and the cause of the dynasty of Chach cannot prosper.

Attention shifts now to the Arabs. The narrative alters, becomes more historical, begins to depend on the narrator-chains of Arab history ('It is related by Hazli, who heard it from Tibui son of Musa, who again heard it from his father . . .'). We are at once in a more organized, more disciplined and less arbitrary world, a world of law, where men, however anxious for power, fame and wealth, also serve a cause above themselves. The soldier obeys the general, the general the governor, the governor the caliph; and all serve the Prophet, Islam and God.

After the failure of the first two expeditions against Sind, the third caliph, Osman (644–656), orders a detailed report on the affairs of 'Hind and Sind' – its rules of war, its strategy, the nature of its government, the structure of its society. The order goes to Abdullah, and Abdullah passes it on to Hakim; and Abdullah is so impressed by what Hakim has to say that he sends Hakim direct to the caliph.

'O Hakim,' the caliph says, 'have you seen Hindustan and learnt all about it?'

'Yes, O commander of the faithful.'

'Give us a description of it.'

'Its water is dark and dirty. Its fruit is bitter and poisonous. Its land is stony and its earth is salt. A small army will soon be annihilated there, and a large one will soon die of hunger.'

'How are the people? Are they faithful, or violators of their word?'

'They are treacherous and deceitful.'

The caliph takes fright at this last piece of information, and forbids the invasion of Sind.

But under the later caliphs the idea comes up again and again. The seventh expedition is led by Sinan, whose distinction now – time is passing – is that he was born in the lifetime of the Prophet and had been given his name by the Prophet. There was a tradition that the Prophet had said to Sinan's father Salmah: 'O Salmah, I congratulate you on the birth of a son.' But though the Prophet appears to him in a dream, Sinan is killed in Sind. And two expeditions after that also end badly.

Towards the end of the seventh century Hajjaj becomes governor of 'Iraq, Sind and Hind'. Hajjaj has first to deal with religious-racial disaffection in Kufa and Iraq. Then he too sends an army to Sind: King Dahar of Sind has been encouraging Muslim rebels.

Hajjaj's army is defeated by King Dahar's son. The Arab commmander is killed, and Arabs are taken prisoner. The reigning caliph wants to hear no more of Sind. The country is too far away, he writes Hajjaj; the people are too cunning, the expeditions are too expensive, and too many Muslims are being killed. But Hajjaj asks for another chance; he promises to pay back to the royal treasury double the sum spent on a new invasion. The caliph agrees; he gives a written order for the invasion of Sind. Hajjaj selects 6,000 experienced soldiers from Syria, appoints his seventeen-year-old son-in-law Mohammed Bin Qasim general, and superintends every detail of the preparations.

The army – with a full complement of pack-camels and camelmen (one camel for every four soldiers) – is to go by land. The siege supplies – including naphtha arrows, coats of mail, battering rams, and a special catapult that requires five hundred men to operate it – are to go by sea. Bin Qasim is to do nothing without the authority of Hajjaj; a system of runners ensures that letters get from Sind to Kufa in seven days. Hajjaj in his letters constantly mixes military instructions with religious exhortations. 'Dig a ditch around your camp . . . Be awake for the greater part of the night; and let those of you who can read the Koran be busy reading it . . .' The army must always camp in open ground; at times of battle the army must always be divided into five sections: centre, vanguard, rearguard, left wing, right wing, with cavalry on the wings.

Bin Qasim arrives at the port of Debal. The supplies sent by sea arrive the same day. But Hajjaj doesn't give the order to engage in battle until the eighth day. At the end of that day a brahmin comes out of the town. He tells the Arabs that the town is guarded by a talisman: the four long flags of green silk that hang down from the arms of the flagstaff on the dome of the great temple of Debal. While the flagstaff stands, the brahmin says, the people of Debal will fight.

It is the first of the betrayals that will assist the Arab conquest. But they are not betrayals, really. They are no more than the actions of people who understand only that power is power, and believe they are only changing rulers; they cannot conceive that a new way is about to come.

Bin Qasim asks his catapult engineer, Jaubat, whether he can knock down the flagstaff.

Jaubat says, 'If we remove two ramrods from the big catapult, with three stones I will blow off the flag and the pole and break the dome of the temple.'

'Ten thousand dirams for you if you do that,' Bin Qasim says. 'But if you fail? And if you spoil the caliph's catapult?'

Jaubat says, 'Let the hands of Jaubat be cut off.'

That is the compact (but it has to be ratified by Hajjaj). And on the next day, while the Arabs attack the town from four directions, the big catapult is placed where Jaubat says, the five hundred catapult men pull on the ropes and the stones are shot off and the flagstaff and the dome are shattered. And it is then as the brahmin said: the defenders of Debal open their gates and ask for mercy. But Hajjaj has issued precise instructions for this first victory: the residents of Debal are not to be spared.

The Arab army has to slaughter for three days: it is what Bin Qasim tells the people of Debal.

After the slaughter, the booty: the treasure and the slaves. One-fifth, the royal fifth, is set aside for the caliph, 'in obedience to the religious law'; Hajjaj's treasurer takes charge of that. (And it is odd to reflect that the Spanish royal fifth, set aside by Columbus and Cortés and others in the New World, should have had its origin in the religious laws of the Arabs.) The rest of the booty of Debal is distributed fairly, according to Arab practice: a cavalryman getting twice as much as a camelman or foot-soldier.

The war is far from over. Sind is big, and has many fortified towns. But Debal sets the pattern: the siege, the betrayal by nobles or brahmins or Buddhist priests who do not believe in killing; the entry by the Arabs; the killing; the checking and distribution of the booty, after the caliph's fifth has been deducted (and in one place the sharing out of the booty takes as long as the killing).

It is in the district of Siwistan that the people get to understand the nature of the invader. A spy from the Chanas tribe sees the Arabs at prayer in their camp: the whole army standing up, a picture of equality, unity and union, the general leading his men in prayer, but at one with them. The effect on the Chanas people is immediate. They go in a body to the Arabs – who are now having supper – and surrender. (Pakistanis today who have seen the Chinese soldiers building the Sinkiang–Pakistan Silk Road in the far north are similarly awed by the discipline and unity of the Chinese.)

After the massacre at Debal the killing is more selective. Traders, artisans and peasants are allowed to continue in their occupations and practise their religion; brahmins continue to be administrators. All that is required of unbelievers is the tribute and the special tax. But Hajjaj insists on the killing of the warrior class and the enslaving of their dependents. When he gets Dahar's head and Bin Qasim's report of victory he writes sternly: 'My dear cousin, I have received your life-augmenting letter. On its receipt my gladness and joy knew no bounds . . . But the way of granting pardon prescribed by the law is different from the one adopted by you . . . The Great God says in the Koran: "O true believers, when you encounter the unbelievers, strike off their heads." The above command of the Great God is a great command and must be respected and followed . . . Concluded with compliments. Written by Nafia in the year 93.' And he returns to the point even later in the campaign. 'My distinct orders are that all those who are fighting men should be assassinated, and their sons and daughters imprisoned and retained as hostages.'

So at the big town of Brahminabad, after his entry, Bin Qasim 'next came to the place of execution and in his presence ordered all the men belonging to the military classes to be beheaded with swords. It is said that about 6,000 fighting men were massacred on this occasion; some say 16,000.'

And King Dahar never understood the nature of the war, never understood that more than his throne was at stake. There was for him, in war, an element of chivalry and deadly play. He could have prevented Bin Qasim crossing the Indus River; it was what he was advised to do. But he thought that undignified. He could have retreated even then, and left the desert to deal with the invaders; it was again what he was advised to do. But again he thought that undignified. He died in battle. Naphtha arrows set the litter on his elephant alight. There were two women servants in the litter, one preparing betel leaves for the king to chew, one passing him arrows; there was also a brahmin. The elephant, frightened by the fire on its back, plunged into the shallow lake beside the Indus; and mounted Arab archers killed King Dahar while he was still in the litter. Like a warrior, Dahar had gone into battle prepared for death and the funeral pyre. His body, when it was found (betrayed by the brahmin who had been in the litter), smelled of musk and attar of roses. The women servants were captured; they later identified the king's severed head for Bin Qasim.

The sister Dahar had nominally married for the sake of his kingship burned herself to death with other women of her household. Dahar's real wife (now the property of the Arab caliph and state) was bought by Bin Qasim with part of the loot of Sind. And Dahar's two daughters were sent in the charge of Abyssinian slaves to the caliph.

They were admitted into the caliph's harem. He allowed them to rest for a few days. Then he asked for them to be brought to him at night. He wanted to know who was the elder; he wished to take her first. He found out through an interpreter. The elder was called Surijdew. When the caliph tried to embrace her she jumped up and said: 'May the king live long! I, a humble slave, am not fit for your majesty's bedroom, because the just Amir, Imaduddin Mohammed Bin Qasim, kept us both with him for three days and then sent us to the caliph. Perhaps your custom is such, or else this disgrace should not be permitted by kings.'

The caliph bit his hand. He immediately ordered a letter to be sent to Bin Qasim, ordering him to 'put himself in raw leather and come back to the chief seat of the caliph'.

Bin Qasim was on the Indian border. He obeyed. He asked his men to put him in a fresh hide, to put the hide in a box, and to send the box to the caliph. He died within two days. The body, when it came to Baghdad, was displayed by the caliph to the daughters of King Dahar. 'Look,' he said, 'how our orders are promptly obeyed by our officers.' And then Surijdew said she had lied, to be revenged on Bin Qasim. She and her sister were both virgins; they had not been touched by Bin Qasim.

'The caliph immediately ordered the two sisters to be buried alive in a wall. From that time up to our own days, the banner of Islam has been rising higher and higher and gaining greater and greater glory day by day.'

With that apparent inconsequentiality the narrative ends. The recall of Bin Qasim speaks of some political change in Iraq and Syria at the time; but the Arabian Nights fabrication, and the degeneracy it implies, is a reminder that five hundred years separate the *Chachnama* from the conquest of Sind: the Mongol storm is about to break over minaret and seraglio.

The Arab conquest of Sind is distinct from the Muslim invasions of India proper, which began about three centuries later. But the Sind conquered by Bin Qasim was a big country, roughly the area of present-day southern Pakistan and southern Afghanistan; and the *Chachnama* might be said to be an account of the Islamic beginnings of the state. But it is a bloody story, and the parts that get into the school books are the fairy-tales. An Arab ship was taking gifts to the caliph; the ship was seized by King Dahar, and Muslims were made captives. The women among them called out, 'Hajjaj, save us!' To rescue them (rather than the soldiers captured during the previous Arab expedition), Hajjaj invaded Sind.

Little things have to be changed even in the fairy-tales. The flags on the temple of Debal — the talisman knocked down by the catapult — were green (in my 1900 translation, by a Sindhi, Kalichbeg). But green is the Islamic colour; so, in at least one text book, the flags are made red, for the children. In little things, as in big, the faith has to be served.

In September 1979, on Defence of Pakistan Day, there was a long article in the *Pakistan Times* on Bin Qasim as a strategist. The assessment was military, neutral, fair to the soldiers of both sides. It drew a rebuke from the Chairman of the National Commission on Historical and Cultural Research.

'Employment of appropriate phraseology is necessary when one is projecting the image of a hero. Expressions such as "invader". and "defenders", and "the Indian army" fighting bravely but not being quick enough to "fall upon the withdrawing enemy" loom large in the article. It is further marred by some imbalanced statements such as follows: "Had Raja Dahar defended the Indus heroically and stopped Qasim from crossing it, the history of this sub-continent might have been quite different." One fails to understand whether the writer is applauding the victory of the hero or lamenting the defeat of his rival?'

The time before Islam is a time of blackness: that is part of Muslim theology. History has to serve theology. The excavated city of Mohenjodaro in the Indus Valley – overrun by the Aryans in 1500 BC – is one of the archaeological glories of Pakistan and the world. The excavations are now being damaged by waterlogging and salinity, and appeals for money have been made to world organizations. A featured letter in *Dawn* offered its own ideas for the site. Verses from the Koran, the writer said, should be engraved and set up in Mohenjodaro in 'appropriate places': 'Say (unto them, O Mohammed): Travel in the land and see the nature of the sequel for the guilty . . . Say (O Mohammed, to the disbelievers): Travel in the land and see the nature of the consequence for those who were before you. Most of them were idolaters.'

So theology complicates history for the people of Pakistan. And for people who feel that their country hasn't worked, that in the Muslim homeland they are still strangers, or dispossessed, or threatened with dispossession, for such people the wish to claim kinship with a triumphant Islam makes for further disturbance.

In orthodox theology only the first four caliphs were rightly guided. After that the caliphate becomes a dynasty; the Islamic ideals of brotherhood are betrayed. Sind, therefore, was conquered by the Arabs in the bad time; but the Arabs brought the faith, so the bad time becomes a sacred time. The Mongols destroyed the Arab empire in the east. So the Mongols were bad. But the Mongols became Muslims and established the great Mogul empire in India; so that becomes a wonderful time. The Turks displace the Mongols; but the Turks also become Muslims and powerful, and they too cease to be bad. So history – that begins as a 'pleasant story of conquest' – becomes hopelessly confusing. And out of this more-than-colonial confusion some Pakistanis fabricate personalities for themselves, in which they are Islamic and conquerors and – in Pakistan – a little like people in exile from their glory. They become Turks or Moguls. Or Arabs.

The *Chachnama* shows the Arabs of the seventh century as a people stimulated and enlightened and disciplined by Islam, developing fast, picking up learning and new ways and new weapons (catapults, Greek fire) from the people they conquer, intelligently curious about the people they intend to conquer. The current fundamentalist wish in Pakistan to go back to that pure Islamic time has nothing to do with a historical understanding of the Arab expansion. The fundamentalists feel that to be like those early Arabs they need only one tool: the Koran. Islam, that made the seventh-century Arabs world-conquerors, now clouds the minds of their successors or pretended successors.

It was the poet Iqbal's hope that an Indian Muslim state might rid Islam of 'the stamp that Arab imperialism was forced to give it'. It turns out now that the Arabs were the most successful imperialists of all time; since to be conquered by them (and then to be like them) is still, in the minds of the faithful, to be saved.

History, in the Pakistan school books I looked at, begins with Arabia and Islam. In the simpler texts, surveys of the Prophet and the first four caliphs and perhaps the Prophet's daughter are followed, with hardly a break, by lives of the poet Iqbal, Mr Jinnah, the political founder of Pakistan, and two or three 'martyrs', soldiers or airmen who died in the holy wars against India in 1965 and 1971.

History as selective as this leads quickly to unreality. Before Mohammed there is blackness: slavery, exploitation. After Mohammed there is light: slavery and exploitation vanish. But did it? How can that be said or taught? What about all those slaves sent back from Sind to the caliph? What about the descendants of the African slaves who walk about Karachi? There is no adequate answer: so the faith begins to nullify or overlay the real world.

The military rule; political parties are banned. There is fifteen percent literacy, and fundamentalism stifles the universities. There is no industry, no science. The economy is a remittance economy; the emigrants, legal and illegal, pour out. But in the Social Studies text book in the sixth class in English-language schools the child reads:

'"Uncle," said Salman, "I have read in my history book that in old times the caste system had a very firm hold in India. Everyone had to adopt the occupation of his family. He could take no other work." "Oh!" said the uncle. "Conditions in India are much the same to this day. But we are a democratic country. Here everyone is free to adopt the occupation of his choice. This is the secret of our progress."'

5

✦✦✦✦

Hyderabad Boogie-Woogie

AHMED wanted me to go to the interior of Sind, to a famous shrine near the town of Hyderabad. Sind was full of the shrines of Muslim saints. Islam had long ago taken over the old holy places of Buddhists and Hindus; but memories of old religious attitudes adhered, and Islamic purists didn't always approve of the mystical or ascetic or near-idolatrous practices of some of these places.

But Ahmed had his own reasons. The shrine or sufi centre he wanted me to see was associated with an order or brotherhood – some centuries old, he said – who had renounced the world to live in the desert and serve the poor. They ran a dispensary; every day at lunch time they fed all the poor who came. It was the idea of sacrifice and service that attracted Ahmed. And one morning he put me in a car and sent me a hundred miles north to Hyderabad.

It was desert all the way from Karachi. The 'super highway' was flat and fast. The River Indus, where it was crossed, was wide, its muddy waters choppy; little fishing boats with dingy white sails gave an abrupt antique feel to the unremarkable desert. Hyderabad – a nondescript desert town with low, ochre-distempered concrete buildings – baked. But there were pools of stagnant water here and there: the desert was waterlogged.

And when I got to the Circuit House, where I thought I was staying, there was trouble. Two civil servants, with little English, greeted me and told me that a minister had unexpectedly arrived, my booking had been cancelled, and I was to stay in a hotel. 'A class, A class,' they repeated. But the place they took me to was – in spite of the central air-conditioning – rough and dark, with a broken lavatory seat in my bathroom.

I didn't have to spend the night there, though. Razak, the young man who was to take me around, had another programme for me. Ahmed's sufi centre was to wait until the next day. Razak intended that evening to show me other shrines and religious places, hours away, and in an opposite direction. We started in the middle of the afternoon.

Razak was a Sindhi. On this religious tour with a visitor he was at once a pilgrim, who couldn't have enough of the holy places, and a bureaucrat, firm about his programme and schedule. He was intelligent and kind, but language was our mutual irritant.

I strained him right from the start. I said, seeing a man in Sindhi costume by the roadside, 'So you have Africans here too, Razak.' He said sharply, 'They are not *Africans*. They are Negroes, *local* Negroes.' Razak's English was precise, as precise as that. But several Pakistanis – a Pakistani teacher-chain – separated him from the spoken language, and what came out required a lot of attention. I said, 'Do they do anything with these reeds, Razak?' He said, 'Bar skates.' I struggled with that. After a while I said, 'What are bar skates, Razak?' And now he struggled with his irritation. He said, 'Bar skates are used for putting domestic articles in.' Baskets: a precise, but no doubt for him also a taxing, definition. And it could be like that: I being Harpo to his Chico Marx, or Chico to his Harpo.

So, though there was much that Razak could have told me, I drove ignorantly through this ancient peopled part of Sind, hardly knowing why Razak became excited at certain places: understanding only later, for instance, that the desolation of Mansura was the site of King Dahar's great city of Brahminabad.

We drew a blank at the first shrine. The holy man here, Razak told me, had a hundred thousand followers. We arrived a couple of hours after dark, and to enter the compound was like entering a medieval town. Boys opened the main gate for us, and closed it behind us. The lanes were paved, with central gutters. People were sitting on tiled platforms outside the great man's courtyard. One man took our request inside; another man came out to answer it. He was thin and oldish, in blue, with a cloth glove on his left hand. He said the great man received only in the mornings; he was now resting.

So we left and drove on to the shrine of Shah Abdul Latif. In the dark tiled courtyard of the mosque there was music: the saint's 250-year-old devotional songs. And listening to the music at the end of the long day – a small crowd, some asleep, people coming and going – I felt, as I had felt in the garden of Ayatollah Shariatmadari's house in Mashhad, that Islam had achieved community and a kind of beauty, had given people a feeling of completeness – if only the world outside could be shut out, and men could be made to forget what they knew.

In my room in the rest house the air-conditioning didn't work. If I opened the window, insects came in. And it was because of the insects that I didn't sleep outside, like Razak and the others. To sleep in the open you had to wrap yourself up like a mummy, from head to toe; that took practice. So I stayed in my hot room and rested and waited for the morning. We were to make an early start, going back to Hyderabad and then beyond, to get to Ahmed's sufi centre in time for the midday feeding of the poor: Ahmed had been particular about that.

Beyond Hyderabad there were patches of cultivation, patches of scrub, patches of sand. The brightness hurt; the heat hurt. Village dogs stood still in yellow pools. We were in one of the famous river valleys of early civilization. But there was no feeling of a valley; the land felt like an immense plain, until you noticed that the flat land was at different levels and that the upper levels were capped with rock, so that it seemed that the Indus was the merest remnant of a vaster flow of water that had flattened everything not protected by rock. For some miles we drove on the west bank of the river. In the distance were jagged hills. They were of pure rock, fractured in parts. Some great convulsion had created this mountain range, forcing up and folding over the rock strata like pastry; and then some water cataclysm had punched through the rock. The river made a bend here. And not far away was the town with the shrine.

The stalls in the main street were hung with photographs of Mr Bhutto. Mr Bhutto, during his time in office, had given or caused to be given new gilt gates for the shrine. They could be seen from the outside, beyond the outer iron gates. A plaque in the wall recorded Mr Bhutto's gift; but since his death the plaque had been covered over by a gold-fringed green cloth. Pilgrims looked both at the gates and the green cloth before they went in.

We left our shoes with the man who sat below a sheet awning. He was turbanned and dignified, brisk, a professional; he tied up each pair of shoes, gave each pair a number, and charged half a rupee a pair. The fee seemed high; there was no competition; and I asked Razak whether the pitch was hereditary or somehow protected. He said these shoe-keeping shrine pitches were auctioned by the government, and the bidding could go as high as 4,000 rupees, 400 dollars. The successful bidder was, in more than one way, in business.

It was crowded and close inside. People were sleeping on the worn marble floor. They had come from far, and for the poor there was no other place to stay: the wretched of the desert, of those scattered poor fields and villages beside the Indus, people for whom the shrine – and all the shrines that had stood here, even before Islam, between the river and the shattered hill-range of rock – had always provided shelter and comfort. The marble floor was grimy; there were babies, and many flies, seeking always to settle on the floor and the bodies.

The shrine – the tomb of the saint – was railed around in silver, beautifully worked, worn by the hands of the faithful. One corner post had been broken, perhaps by a crush of pilgrims on a particular day; there was a kind of frenzy even now. There were several canopies, one above the other, and just below the ceiling was a wire net, perhaps to catch bird droppings. A stone, clamped around with a silver band, hung by a short cord from the canopy bar. The stone was heart-shaped; it was pale-brown, and so smooth and shiny from being touched that it did seem to have a fleshy quality. I thought there was some significance in the shape. But Razak said the saint had carried this stone on his belly while he lived; the Prophet had done the same thing. (Probably, though, it was an ascetic adaptation of an old Arabian torture: Bilal, the Abyssinian slave who was one of the first to accept the Prophet's message, was exposed and tied down in the Meccan desert with a heavy stone on his chest.)

People passed their hands over the stone, caressed it, and then took their hands to their lips and eyes, or touched their heart; or they appeared to hug themselves. Outside, the Indus Valley town, blazing with heat; here, this passion. It was important to touch: not only the stone and the silver railing, but also the cloth draped over the saint's tomb, at one end of which were a mitre and cope, curiously Christian-looking, and a turban which seemed to stand for a head. It was a land of faith, but it was also a land of dust and sand and dry nostrils and nose-picking; and the peasant woman who rubbed her hand on the rail before touching her young sons' mouths with her hand, also in between scoured and scraped at her nostrils.

We went on to the *koli* or sufi centre. It lay at the end of a short bazaar lane. The dirt surface of the lane had turned to black mud, with washing-up and other water from the food stalls on either side, which were in business and active, although at the *koli* it was feeding time for the poor: brown rounds of flat bread were in many hands at the entrance.

To the right, as we entered, to noise and bustle and music, was the shrine: the tombs of the *pirs*, the holy men who had settled here to celebrate the saint, and had become rulers or governors of the brother-hood. A Mondrian of the desert had been at work with modern bathroom tiles on the shrine walls, creating a bigger and more direct version of the abstract painter's *Broadway Boogie-Woogie*: a kind of Hyderabad Boogie-Woogie, with stepped lines of yellow, white, blue, red, black and so on, delightful to come upon because it was an expression of such pure delight.

Directly in front was the feeding place, an open pillared pavilion. One man stood guard over pyramids of brown flat bread covered with a cloth, bread that by its colour suggested more than the wholesomeness of whole grain, suggested also the Indus Valley earth. One man was ladling out a thin lentil soup from a big black iron pot. In the porch of the building to the left another man was doling out water; a boy, aware of his importance, was holding the hose that led from the tap to the water barrel.

Razak had become involved with a man in a blue gown who appeared to be of authority. The man in blue was short, squarely built, and with a shaved head; there was a touch of Central Asia in his features. He said that the *pir* was out and would be back in three hours. In Pakistan the standard unit of stated delay was half an hour; three hours meant not that day. So there was no one to talk to? The man in blue said the *munshi*, the secretary, was available. He asked for our names and details. When Razak gave them the man in blue said in English, in a curiously flat way, his eyes still assessing us, that he was inviting us to stay as his guests, to spend the night, to stay as long as we liked. The *pir* would be back in three hours; in the meantime we would see the *munshi*; we would be given food; we were his guests.

He deputed someone to lead us upstairs. We picked our way past puddles (from the water hose) and were led, through a confusion of small verandahed quadrangles on the upper floor, to a clean room spread with bedding, and with two sets of bolsters and cushions. A fan was turned on; a window was opened. It was cool and inexpressibly relaxing. Two record players or amplified radios were on outside; but the fan muffled the noise; the songs – not film songs, Razak said: devotional songs – cancelled each other out; and in the coolness it made a distant, pleasing background.

The *munshi* didn't come. Not after five minutes, not after ten. But the food came, brought up by a boy or young man in a brown Pakistani costume. He was of great beauty; it was strange to think that he had chosen the life of sacrifice and service. Razak (rounding out nicely at twenty-seven) pretended to share my nervousness about the food; but then almost immediately he fell on it and ate with luxurious concentration to the end. Still the *munshi* didn't appear, and when the boy in brown came with the tea (stewed in the Indo-Pakistani bazaar way, sugar, water, tea and milk boiled together: sweet and sharp and refreshing) I made him stay and talk about himself.

It wasn't easy. Not because he was secretive, but because he seemed to carry no connected idea of his life. Experiences floated loose in his mind, and it was necessary to ask many little questions. He was oddly passive. His words (which Razak translated) were spoken softly, with downcast eyes.

He had been with the community a year. He was going to go away in a year; there was no question of a lifelong commitment. But wouldn't it have been better for him, since he wanted to get a job again, to have spent the time learning a trade or skill? He said he had been a pipe-fitter with the waterworks, earning 450 rupees a month; he could get that job again.

He came from Peshawar, in the northern Frontier Province, on the Afghanistan border. His family had a hundred acres of land, and a tractor; but there were six brothers, and he had joined the great migration south. He had gone first to Karachi (where there were said to be a million Pathan migrants from the Frontier Province); then he had come to Hyderabad. A friend had told him of the community and brought him to the house. In the house he had seen two men from his northern village. So he had come again, two or three times. But he couldn't make up his mind; he had decided to stay only after he had met the *pir*.

Experiences floated loose in his mind: he seemed to have no goal. He was a wayfarer. Through him it was possible to understand something of the wayfaring life in the European middle ages. The religious community in the desert was a staging post; it helped him through a part of his life. And no doubt in Pakistan – with its migrant movement within and outwards – there were many more like him, adrift, taking life in stages, as it came.

I asked whether foreigners came to the community and whether, when they came, they behaved strangely. He brightened at the question, looked up, became like a boy with excitement. He said there was a Bengali who came once and stayed for a month. He had no money, nothing. One day a man came in a car and took away the Bengali to Karachi. When the Bengali came back he was driving his own car.

Was it luck? Was it some deal?

There was an exciting answer, clearly. But it never came, became just then the man in blue – with the shaved head, the firm paunch, the stout shoulders, and the assessing eyes – came in. And the boy in brown grew nervous, stopped talking, looked down again, picked up the tea cups and went out.

The man in blue squatted before us, sitting on his heels, resting his knees on the floor-spread. Since (though he didn't say this) the *munshi* wasn't coming, he wished to talk to us himself.

He said in English, 'What do you want to know?'

I was surprised by the clarity of his accent: it had improved since he had spoken to us in the yard. There was aggression in this new clarity, but it was a managed aggression: it could harden or soften: he still wasn't certain about me. I said I couldn't yet say what I wanted to know; I would be happy with what he had to tell me.

He said, and the English words poured out of him, 'I will tell you.

There are different categories of believers. Some want money, some want a good after-life. I want to meet Allah. You can do that only through a medium. My *murshid* is my medium. I want to love my *murshid*. I want my *murshid* to enter my heart. Allah is with my *murshid*. And when my *murshid* enters my heart, Allah is with me. I have no doubt about that. I can meet Allah only through the medium and in the form of my *murshid*. Through the medium and in the form.'

The *murshid* wasn't the *pir* or ruler of the community, as I thought. The *murshid* was the original saint, whose tomb we had visited.

The man in blue explained with a political analogy. 'The Qaid-e-Azam [Mr Jinnah] founded Pakistan.' He was like the *murshid*. 'But today we obey the President, Zia ul-Haq.' The President was like the *pir*. The man in blue pointed at Razak. 'You obey Zia ul-Haq.' He pointed at me. 'You obey Zia ul-Haq. I obey Zia ul-Haq.' I was beginning to detect a quality of incantation in his speech.

He said, 'I haven't shown you hospitality. It is my *murshid*. I don't know you. You don't know me. But I serve you to the best of my ability because I love my *murshid*. I want my *murshid* to enter my heart.'

There were about a hundred devotees in the community. They fed from eight hundred to a thousand people every day; they also ran a dispensary (it was in a cubicle downstairs, near where the man was doling out fresh water). But where did they get the money?

The man in blue said that the previous *pir* was a saint. 'He was all the time for Allah. He fasted all day and he prayed all night. I am telling you. It isn't easy to do, to hold your hands like this.' He brought his palms together and held them open, the way Muslims do when they say their prayers, as though reading their hands like a book. And then he stood up and demonstrated the open-palmed act of prayer and repeated what he had said. 'All the time for Allah. Fasted all day, prayed all night. You try holding your hands like that for even ten minutes.' He sat down again on his heels. 'He did miracles. He took no food for fifty years. He took no water for three years. The people told him he would be useless if he took no water, and that was when he decided to take water.'

But how did they get the money to run the community?

The man in blue said, 'That's what I'm telling you. It was because of all that sacrifice that this place is now possible. Our *murshid* now has so many *murids*, followers, all over the world. They come here in lakhs. They give one rupee, five rupees, ten rupees. And we bargain for goods. I haven't shown you hospitality. It is my *murshid*. There are different categories of believers. I want to meet Allah. The important thing is that I can do this only through-the-medium-and-in-the-form of my *murshid*. Do you understand?'

I asked him to tell me exactly what he felt when he stroked the stone that hung above the *murshid*'s tomb. To my surprise he appeared not to know what I was talking about. And when I asked again he said he was too busy here, with the community.

The boy in brown stood in the doorway – eagerness on his face – but when he saw the man in blue still squatting before us he turned and walked silently away on his bare feet. I was nagged by that story about the Bengali and the car; it began to torment me while the man in blue talked on, repeating himself, mixing up the sequence of sentences he had already spoken.

He told me another miracle of the previous *pir*. A *faqir* died, one of the ascetics of the community. They told the *pir*. He went to the room where the dead man lay. As he entered the room the dead man raised his right hand in the Muslim salutation. The *pir* became very angry. He jabbed his stick at the dead man and said, 'You must learn greater control over your body. Surely you know it is incorrect for a dead man to salute me.'

I asked the man in blue whether he couldn't send up the boy with some tea for me. I asked many times. But we weren't going to have the boy in brown to ourselves again. We would have tea later, the man in blue said; but we had to visit the kitchens first, and then of course we should look at the tombs of the old *pirs*. He didn't intend to leave us now; I began to understand that it was his way of seeing us off the premises.

I tried to get him to talk about himself, and it was as hard as it had been with the boy in brown. He gave out random facts; they had formed no pattern in his mind; he knew only where he was now. He too was a wayfarer, part of the semi-medieval migrant life of Pakistan. In spite of his Central Asian features (emphasized by his shaved head) he too, like the boy in brown, came from the Frontier Province. He had studied at an agricultural college, but he didn't take a degree. He had done odd jobs for a few years. Then he came to the community. He saw the present *pir* and decided at once to stay. He didn't ask anybody's permission; he just stayed (and Razak added that he was now the *pir*'s 'right-hand man'). His father was a farmer in the Frontier Province. How many acres? Sixteen. Good land? Very good. Any brothers? No brothers. So who was going to take over when his father died? He thought I had asked whether he was needed on the farm, and he said there were contractors with machines. What was going to happen to the sixteen acres when he inherited them? He said he didn't know; he had given up that side of life.

We went down to look at the kitchens. The midday feeding was over, but cooking was going on. We had to take off our shoes to walk, in thick, tickling dust, from the main building to the kitchen shed. There they

143

were boiling tea in big copper pots; and there, among the cords of firewood, the boy in brown stood idle; he kept his distance.

In an open shed in front of the deep fire-holes a man was standing over a high marble basin, kneading brown dough, kneading up to the elbows; flies had settled on the kneaded dough in the marble stand beside him. Another man was making lentil soup; another man was in the fire-hole, attending to the oven. The heads of all were shaved; their eyes were bright; their cheeks were round. They were friendly, pleased to be observed; they were at the source of food and plenty; they knew they served the poor and God. In North Indian painting these cooking scenes recur: the very faces I felt I had seen before.

One by one, the man in blue guiding us, we touched the tombs of all the *pirs* who had been buried here in the *koli*. And then we sat in the hot tiled courtyard, in the gaiety of the stepped coloured lines of the Hyderabad Boogie-Woogie. Shyly, the boy in brown came out with the tea. He didn't go away. Our time was almost up. I asked directly about the Bengali.

The boy in brown said, 'He went to Karachi and he came back. I told you.'

'Bengali?' the man in blue said. 'We get people from all over the world here. I don't know you. You don't know me. But I serve you – ' And abruptly sitting on a white-tiled ledge, he stopped, as though enervated by the mid-afternoon heat, the dust, the desert, the life, the boredom.

When we were in the car, going down the wet, black bazaar lane with the paying food stalls, Razak said, 'You remember when he was talking about getting goods? He said he bar-gained. In the *koli* he should not be making bar-gains.' Razak was speaking as a good Muslim.

We drove back between the river and the rock mountains: neat layers of rock folded over and then breached by some water cataclysm, the rock stripped off in layers, so that in places the mountain looked like the tiers of a vast stone amphitheatre tilted sharply to one side.

We stopped at one such breach. Razak had been energized by his lunch. And a bottle of a Pakistani version of Seven-Up, Bubble-Up (it was a pleasure just to hear him speak the name), had made him frisky, indifferent to the great heat.

The mountain grew as we walked towards it. When we were in the mountain shadow it was cooler. It was a site that called up awe. But the Hindu temples, expressions of that awe, small, pyramid-roofed structures, not old, only pre-1947, had been broken, emptied, cleansed, and then defaced with Urdu inscriptions: the enemy utterly cast out. And it was a famous site: of the water turbulence that had smashed the mountain, and the lesser turbulence that had afterwards washed between the layers of rock, creating smooth holes and caverns, there remained only a salt spring, known for its healing qualities: blue-green in the mountain cleft, leaving a white slime on the rocks its little stream now slipped over and still smoothed. In this stream there were more than pebbles; there were marine fossils.

Razak had the naturalist's eye. He bent down and picked up pieces of stone on which I could see patterns of shells; he placed in my hand a mussel, fossilized whole, and a small conch-like shell. Islam, Buddhists, Hindus, Aryans, pre-Aryans; and there had been a civilization in the Indus Valley even before the builders of the ancient cities of Mohenjodaro and Harappa. But the greater wonder, that took the mind far away, was that once all this land lay at the bottom of the sea. And still this thin salt spring, rising out of hot rock, brought up evidence of the sea past in a land that was now so far from the sea, so full of light and heat, so crying out for water.

There was trouble again at the Circuit House in Hyderabad when we got back there. I had been booked in for the previous night; there was no booking for me for this night. The place was empty; no one was expected. But it took a full hour's telephoning, Razak being passed on from official to official, before permission was obtained.

We didn't have to go far in the morning. In Hyderabad itself, within one of the mud-walled forts built by the last Muslim amirs or princes of Sind, there was a shrine where the mentally disturbed went to be cured.

It was up a flight of marble steps. At the bottom were pathetic shrunken women, one with a little baby boy, waiting for alms; two or three steps up a man was beating a drum and singing. At the top were two small buildings separated by a narrow paved lane. In the building to the left the saint had meditated; in the building to the right he was buried. The tomb was barred around, and the guardian of the shrine, a fat and friendly little man, sat amid a companionable swarm of flies on the tiled floor of the pillared porch in front. To people looking for health he must have seemed like a sweet-shop owner to children, the man who had it all. He was exchanging gossip with a demented, red-eyed man, and while they talked they also appeared to be bartering or exchanging beans of some sort.

One or two people came and made the circuit of the tomb, passing slowly in the lane between the two buildings to get the emanations from both sacred places at once. They held the silver-painted iron rails of the tomb with a rubbing gesture, and then rested their heads on the metal.

At the back, two young girls with covered heads were facing the tomb. They were not ill; they were just using the shrine as a meeting place, having a little Hyderabadi chat and giggle. But a man was there with a real *djinn* or spirit on him, a young man, dark, physically wasted, his mind half gone. It was this man that the guardian of the shrine presently rose to deal with. The flies swarmed up a few inches, then settled down again.

The guardian could be heard shouting at the back. *'Come on!'* The *djinn* in the man howled, suffering from the sacred emanations. But the guardian, like a man standing no nonsense from any *djinn*, led the man on, shouting roughly all the while at the *djinn*; and the man with the *djinn* pretended to pull back. For all his distress he knew what was expected of him. And in this very ill man there was still a remnant of vanity. He knew he was a case so bad that he had to be brought to the shrine; and he looked back at Razak and me, his only audience, to make sure that we were seeing how strong the *djinn* was that possessed him, how the *djinn* howled and resisted going nearer the emanations of the saint. But there he had to go, in the lane between the two buildings; there he would stay until he was pronounced cured. *'You sit here! You hear me!'* the guardian shouted. After a little resistance the *djinn* quietened down, and the guardian, jolly once more, returned to his beans and his flies, that swarmed up six inches to greet him, and then settled down again.

An African – *sidi* was the local word that caused no offence – came. His hair was neatly dressed; he didn't look unwell. He sat beside the barred window of the meditation place, next to the man with the *djinn*, now pacific, even remote. And in a short while the African's face altered; his eyes glazed, his cheeks hollowed, his pain became apparent. A small woman came with a child on her hip. She was pregnant again. And then I saw that she was herself hardly more than a child, twelve or thirteen, but excited at the idea of already being adult enough to experience important needs. Everyone was acting (though the man with the *djinn*, after his flash of vanity, seemed a little too far away); everyone knew his role. But was it acting when the whole world, or the world you knew, was in the play?

It was the point that Razak – who was awed by the *djinn* – struggled to make with his English. He had seen two or three other people possessed by *djinns*, he said. But then he said that he was sure that in other countries, other civilizations, people would believe in other things, mental illnesses would take other forms, and there would be other cures.

To drive back through the desert to Karachi, to cross the ancient Indus again, was to drive back through ascending levels of development, to leap generations. It was easy to see how the great city – not to speak of the Intercontinental with its special traffic – drew them out of their villages, and committed so many to the wayfaring life.

For some of the way, nearing Karachi, we drove behind an open van with freshly and correctly slaughtered cattle heads, skinned, shining in the sunlight, but still with horns.

I was glad that Ahmed had sent me to the interior. I had much to talk to him about. But when I got to Karachi I found that it was Ahmed himself who had cancelled my first booking at the Circuit House – there had been no visiting minister that day. Between his sending me to Hyderabad and my arrival at Hyderabad something had happened to make Ahmed change his mind about me.

He had known nothing about me before we met. His response to me had been the pure response of man to man; and I had responded to that. But now perhaps he had been told that I was not what I said I was. He became cold on the telephone; he failed to keep two appointments. So I couldn't talk about the sufi centre with him. I couldn't discuss with him whether the mixing of the two types of religion – the religion of revelation and rules, the religion of asceticism and unconfined meditation – didn't diminish both. Nor could I find out more about the 'co-operatives' of his youth or about his idea of the period-less purity of women in paradise. As with the boy's story of the Bengali who had left penniless for Karachi and come back with a car, I had to be content with what I had.

I liked Ahmed. His withdrawal made me unhappy, and anxious to leave Karachi.

6

❖❖❖❖

The Disorder of the Law

AT THE SESSIONS COURT in Karachi – just beyond the central bazaar – the prisoners were led out into the yard, usually tied up in twos, with chains attached to their wrists, and with the free end of the chain held by a khaki-uniformed policeman. It was friendly, and in the courtyard bustle, which was like the bazaar bustle, no one stared or paid too much attention. The prisoners chatted with the policemen and sometimes they stopped at the *pan*-stalls to buy betel-nut to chew. The faces in the main were like the faces of the street; though one man had disturbed eyes, and two barefooted little fellows chained together, possibly brothers, looked mentally deficient. There weren't enough chains. Some prisoners were led along by ropes attached to their upper arms, and they looked a little like performing monkeys; but it was just as friendly.

On a platform shaded by awnings were the notaries and commissioners for oaths, waiting for custom, with their little tables and glass paper-weights and their little grubby books. One booth sold stamps and forms of all sorts. Outside, on the pavement, were the affidavit men, pecking away on old – sometimes very old and rusted – standard typewriters, filling stamped forms. And there were the letter-writers ('Respected Sir' – and I longed to stop and read more, but already I had caught the warning-off, professionally jealous eye of the writer).

Around the corner, on the pavement of the main road, were the medicine men, with their strange stock. At first I thought the heaped-up lizards were dead or stuffed, or a kind of sculpture. But then one lizard (or iguana) moved, and all moved; and there were eleven of them tied to a big stone, tied by the thick end of the tail or by the waist above the hind legs, all now striving to break free on the hot pavement. It was Nusrat who later told me what the lizards were for: virility. You bought and killed your lizard; then you ate a certain part.

I went twice to the sessions court. The first time I went alone, and saw only the tableau in the yard. The second time I went with Nusrat.

Nusrat was a journalist on the *Morning News*. He was a short, chunky man of about thirty, with big round glasses on a round face, and a thick walrus moustache. He was full of a great excited energy. He gave himself, for more than the normal working day, to his newspaper job. This absorbed some of his anxieties about his wife, who was not well, and his anxieties about what he felt to be his failings as a Muslim.

Nusrat was of mixed Punjab and Madras descent, so that in Pakistan he was half a native, half a *mohajir* or Indian Muslim stranger, half settled, half a man who felt that as a Pakistani and a Muslim he wasn't doing enough. Almost the first thing he said to me, in his brisk, throw-away manner, was that he wasn't much of a Muslim. He meant it only as an apology; he went on to say almost at once that the most important things to him were Islam and the hereafter.

And in all that bustle at the sessions court, in all the rooms Nusrat took me to, only one magistrate was sitting. In the little room, below the legal bench, there were two or three spectators, or simply people waiting. The atmosphere was casual; and the gravity of the depressed-looking man in the dock (blue shirt, loose Pakistani trousers) was slightly incongruous; he was like a man taking his role far too seriously. It was hard to know what was going on. People spoke loudly in Karachi; but in this little room they mumbled, and with the encircling hubbub it took some time to understand that they were speaking in English. It took longer to understand that it was a case of theft, that after a year the police had still not produced witnesses, and that the case had been called only to be adjourned yet again.

A federal prosecutor, who knew Nusrat, gave me a little harangue about the procedure while the case was going on. He was anxious for me to stay and see him handle his own case, which was against a teacher in government service who – anxious to emigrate – had given false information when he applied for a passport. As a government servant the teacher should have had an NOC – a no-objection certificate; but the poor wretch, no doubt despairing of getting such a certificate, had hidden the fact that he was a government servant. The prosecutor said the case was going to come up in ten minutes. But with half an hour being the standard unit of stated delay in Pakistan, ten minutes meant a long time. Nusrat and I moved on (and indeed, when we looked in a while later, there was another case going on, and our prosecutor was still waiting).

In the verandah outside we saw four chained boys waiting without anxiety on a bench, and quite ready to chat about their adventure. They worked in a hotel and had been charged with theft. They said the police had 'well' beaten them up. But they were laughing, and the policeman holding their chain also smiled, shaking his head. Next to them were two men charged with stabbing; they had unreliable eyes. At another plane of crime and vanity was the young man from the north who now came stamping by. He wore leg irons in addition to the chains on both wrists; and two policemen with rifles walked with him. His pale skin was pimply on the cheeks; his narrow almond-shaped eyes were frightening. He was aware of the stir he was creating, a man marked for the gallows, high above the world of petty crime, and he was dressed like a chieftain for this public appearance: a freshly ironed pale-blue Pakistani suit, a red turban with a tall, stiff crest. There was no question of stopping him for a chat.

Nusrat saw a man being led along by a rope, and became agitated. 'You see, there aren't enough chains. They're using ropes. I must write about this. There've been many escapes from the courts. Perhaps they've imported the chains and they haven't arrived. Perhaps they're using the chains for political prisoners.'

In a court without a magistrate, a room like a small classroom, an unveiled woman sat with her very thin young son. Her pallid face was round and small, her skin rough; neither she nor her son was getting enough to eat. She had bought a property for 4,000 rupees, 400 dollars; but there had been trouble. She had her documents in a plastic envelope, among them the precious, much-handled receipt for 4,000 rupees. For three days in succession she had come to the court, and today again there was no magistrate. She lived fifteen miles out of Karachi. She said her husband was dead, from asthma. But Nusrat didn't believe that. He thought she was divorced; but it would have been too disgraceful for her to admit that she was alone, unwanted.

And in the verandah just outside, more murder. A plump, moustached man from Swat in the far north: he had been arrested two days before. He had a good, straightforward face and seemed at ease, even with his shackled wrists. He said he was at ease because he had done nothing. The police had found a gun in his possession; but the man who had been killed was a man of bad character and there were many people in the area who would have wanted to kill him.

A *sidi* or man of African extraction, charged with murder, had a large group of *sidi* well-wishers. (So many *sidis* here, the full-blooded among them from the Karachi docks, those of more mixed race from the ancient Makran coast of Baluchistan; so many other idle people in the yard and verandahs of the courts.) A Muslim murder, this *sidi* affair, and a justified murder, according to the accused man's supporters: the murdered man had seduced an unmarried girl.

And then, led along in chains, was a Pathan boy from the Frontier Province, drawn from home by the capital and committed now to the wayfaring life of Pakistan. For him that life was turning out badly. He was barefooted and his feet were black. He had worn the same clothes for weeks; the collar of his long-tailed shirt was grimed and black, as though with engine grease. An English-speaking lawyer, a man of some style, explained the case to me. The boy was charged with trespassing on railway property. In fact, this trespassing was the boy's dangerous way of picking up a few rupees. He would board a moving train, force or bully his way into a seat, and later try to sell the seat for twenty rupees or so. It was a well-known trick. The policeman holding the boy's chain smiled; the lawyer telling the story smiled; the only one who didn't smile was the boy.

There was an office in which it was all recorded: a room that was a store-house of files, racks and racks with bundles wrapped in red and yellow and white cloth, shelves and shelves with torn and dusty ledgers. At a table in the middle of this seeming debris was an old white-bearded man with a black cap. He had a story of legal dedication and bureaucratic success to tell. He had come to Karachi at the time of the partition of the sub-continent in 1947, and he had been with the courts for thirty-two years. He had migrated from Jaipur in India, where he had had three years' experience of court work. In 1947 there were only six city courts in Karachi; now there were forty. He had worked his way up step by step; he had eventually become the chief 'reader' in the most important of the city courts. As reader, he sat beside the magistrate; he was the man who made a note of everything. Note-taking, records, had always been his vocation.

Finally he had transferred to the registry, this room of cloth bundles and ledgers and papers. It looked chaotic, but it was organized. He could find anything in fifteen minutes. All he wanted was the date of the judgement and the date of the consignment. The consignment date was the date when the records were sent down to the registry. But if the consignment date wasn't known? Then, the old man said, it would be difficult. And, I thought, impossible. He demonstrated his method, giving himself a judgement date and a consignment date, opening one tattered ledger, then consulting another even more tattered, then – black-capped, white-bearded, his index finger seeming to beat time – picking his way along a rack, until he disinterred and dusted down a bundle. I complimented him. He said he was a success by God's will; everything was due to Allah.

'Would you like Islamic laws?' Nusrat asked.

'Indeed,' the old man said, sitting again at his table. 'It would be better.' People were too wicked in Karachi; they needed swifter punishment. Many of the people hanging about in the yard were professional witnesses, appearing and reappearing in various cases; even he, taken up with his records, hidden away in the registry, had grown over the years to recognize some of those men.

How did he feel, then, living his professional life among these wicked people? He misunderstood my frivolous question; he said sternly that he had never accepted bribes. Now he was going to retire in three years. He had no plans. He left the last years, as he had left the others, to Allah.

I said, 'Your children?'

'Please don't ask, sir.'

And only now it came out that this full and successful life in the Karachi courts – the life for which God had to be thanked – was cruelly flawed. Four of his seven children suffered from calcium deficiency. He used the English words. Their bones crumbled away. Two of the children had already died. One girl was now paralyzed and helpless at home. Raising his forearms and crossing them, as though he too was shackled at the wrists, he demonstrated how her legs were. Even if a fly settled on her face she couldn't move to brush it away; someone had to do it for her.

For this girl, though, he had hopes of a medical cure in the United States. He had written letters; there had been a reply. And, sure enough, this man of files had the file to hand, on the table: handwritten letters in Urdu and a typewritten letter in English. The United States! The world of knowledge, beyond the world of faith: even here it was known.

On a bench next to the balustrade of the verandah two peasant women sat, old mother, grown-up daughter. The mother was no more than four feet high, very thin and wrinkled, and her lips were thickly coated with the purple paste of a *pan*-leaf; it stained the muslin *orhni* that covered her hair and flat chest. When she spoke she shrieked; and her daughter – her old-young face marked by sun and labour and undernourishment – shrieked as if in competition. In their patient, feminine way they were waiting for someone to show an interest. They were people with a grievance and they had grown to love the legal atmosphere; the court building was their wailing ground.

They had trouble with a tenant. He didn't want to give up the property. They had had a lot of trouble until the military had taken over and imposed martial law. So it was all right now? They had got back their property? Yes. But he hadn't paid the rent. Fifty rupees a month for five years. Five years? Had they allowed him to live rent-free for five years?

The daughter showed her documents. There was a letter in English, the work of a letter-writer. The letter – it jumped about – said that the daughter's husband wanted to divorce her, and the daughter in consequence lived in constant terror of being murdered by her husband. She had gone to the local police station and made that statement. She was now living with her mother. She had 'only three clothes'. Her husband, who wanted to murder her, had taken away all the rest, had even taken away her *burqa*, her veil.

But what did this have to do with the tenant and the unpaid rent?

Well, they shrieked at me, one after the other, it meant they had no man, no protector. It meant they had no livelihood, except the rent from the property.

And they also had trouble with the lease of that property. They had bribed someone 3,000 rupees to get the lease through. But that man had taken the money and done nothing. And they had bribed somebody else 800 rupees to get back the 3,000 rupees, and that man had also done nothing.

So they shrieked and wailed in the upper verandah of the court, the old woman spitting out the thick *pan* paste, until the *azan* sounded, the muezzin's call to the midday prayer. The government had decreed that government departments should cease work for these prayers. And in the courts, not especially active that morning, the *azan* seemed less a call to prayer than a signal to people who were not doing much to do absolutely nothing.

At lunch Nusrat said, 'Give me your advice. Should I stay here? Or should I go to the West?'

'What would you do there?'

'I could do a master's in mass communications in America.'

'And afterwards?'

'I wouldn't teach. I would travel and write. Travel and write.'

'What would you write about?'

'Various things. Afterwards I would get a job with some international body as an expert in third world media.'

'What would you do if you stay here?'

'I would go into advertising.'

'I should stay here and go into advertising.'

'But it's so dishonest.'

'Is it more dishonest than what you do now?'

'I wouldn't like it.'

'How much would you get in an advertising agency?'

'Four thousand.' Four hundred dollars. 'Now I get 2,000. But I wouldn't like it. You may not like the *Morning News*, but I am a free man on it. I couldn't do public relations. Don't you think that someone like me should go into third world media? Do you think the Americans and Canadians should be travelling around talking to us about third world media?'

'Yes. They know what newspapers should do. You wouldn't be able to tell us much.'

'Why do you say that?'

'You've told me yourself that Islam and the hereafter are the most important things to you.'

'How small you make us feel.'

I had momentarily – a number of irritations coming together: the political virulence of his paper, his wish both to remain Islamic and to exploit the tolerance and openness of the other civilization – I had momentarily allowed myself to be aggressive with him. I felt guilty.

But his rebuke was not all rebuke. He believed in the ideal of the Islamic state; he felt that Pakistan fell short of that ideal and deserved the disregard which he had read into my words. The Islamic ideal was the theme of a 1951 book, *Pakistan as an Islamic State*, which he had brought as a gift for me. It would help me to understand Pakistan, he said. And the book showed me that thirty years before, the Islamic ideal had been as vague, as much a statement of impracticable intent and muddled history (with interim wordly corruption), as it was now. The Islamic state, I read, was like a high-flying kite, invisible in the mist. 'I cannot see it, but something is tugging.'

Remember Nusrat. Six months later, when I returned to Karachi and wondered who I should look up, I thought first of Nusrat. I found him changed. That bubbling, intelligent man had gone grey. The Islam he wished to serve had pushed him deep into paranoia; and I regretted more than ever that momentary impulse of aggression towards him, who after all knew only Pakistan.

Nusrat had spoken to the black-capped man in the registry about Islamic laws. I thought they were laws that had yet to be brought in. I didn't know that seven months before, a set of ten Islamic laws had been passed by the military government: laws about Islamic courts and Koranic taxes on wealth and agricultural produce, together with laws about drinking, theft, and illicit sex. These last were hardly laws; they were more about punishments.

Drinking was to be punished by eighty stripes. The punishment for illicit sex, for an adult Muslim, was to 'be stoned to death at a public place'; for a non-Muslim, a hundred-stripe public whipping, with the possibility of death for rape. 'The punishment of stoning to death awarded under section 5 or section 6 shall be executed in the following manner namely: such of the witnesses who deposed against the convict as may be available shall start stoning him and, while stoning is being carried on, he may be shot, whereupon stoning and shooting shall be stopped.'

For theft – above a certain amount (above the value of 4.457 grams of gold), and not theft by a close relative, a servant, or a guest, and not theft of 'wild grass, fish, bird, dog, pig, intoxicant, musical instrument, or perishable foodstuffs for the preservation of which provision does not exist' – for theft outside these circumstances the punishment for a first offence was the amputation – 'carried out by an authorized medical officer' – of the right hand 'from the joint of the wrist'; for a second offence, the amputation of the left foot 'up to the ankle'; for a third offence, imprisonment for life. There was to be no amputation 'when the left hand or the left thumb or at least two fingers of the left hand or the right foot of the offender are either missing or unserviceable'.

Generally, for many offences, there was to be a lot of whipping, and 'The Execution of the Punishment of Whipping Ordinance, 1979' laid down the rules. 'The whip, excluding its handle, shall be of one piece only and preferably be made of leather, or a cane, or a branch of a tree, having no knob or joint on it, and its length and thickness shall not exceed 1.22 metres and 1.25 cm. respectively.' Whipping, if it was likely to cause death, was to be spread out or postponed. A pregnant woman was to be whipped 'two months after the birth of the child or miscarriage, as the case may be'. The weather had to be considered. 'If . . . the weather is too cold or too hot, the execution shall be postponed until the weather has become normal.' The decencies were to be observed. 'Such clothes of the convict should be left on the body of the convict as are required by the injunctions of Islam to be put on.' Men were to be whipped standing, women sitting.

From the 1951 book Nusrat gave me, it seemed that almost as soon as Pakistan had been established pious people had begun to chat about stoning to death and cutting off hands: 'classical' punishments to be worked towards as part of a far-off Islamic ideal, when men became again as pure as (in this fantasy) they had been at the beginning of Islam. It couldn't be said that that had happened in Pakistan; but from Hamid Ali, M.A., M.Ed., LL.B., the editor of Combined Set of Islamic Laws, 1979 (the book I have used here), there was a more than legal welcome for the new laws. They made the nation 'proud'. Outsiders had 'wrong notions' about Islam. 'Islam is a system aimed at bringing about a welfare, progressive and forward looking society.' It ensured 'fair play'; its principles were for all time; its penalties were meant 'to purge the society as a whole'.

But if I hadn't so far been aware of these laws, it was because in the seven months they had been in force they hadn't been applied. One case had caused a scandal. A *pir* or holy man in a provincial town had been charged with raping the thirteen-year-old daughter of one of his followers. The case against him couldn't get far in the sessions court because the new Islamic law under which he was tried required four eye-witnesses to the act.

Why four eye-witnesses? It went back to a famous incident in the Arabian desert during one of the Prophet's early military adventures in 626 or 627, when the new faith was just about establishing itself, reducing small hostile communities one by one. The Prophet's favourite wife, Aisha, then perhaps thirteen, had for some reason been left behind by the caravan one evening. She didn't join it again until the morning, and then in the company of a handsome young soldier. There was an uproar among the Prophet's companions. Ali, the Prophet's cousin, thought that the Prophet should get rid of Aisha. The Prophet – now in his mid-fifties – was distressed for days. But Allah intervened; the Prophet had a revelation that Aisha was innocent; that four witnesses were needed to prove adultery; that people spreading unfounded rumours about adultery deserved eighty lashes.

For a writer in the *Pakistan Times* – defending the government against accusations of Islamic slacking, and criticizing the mullahs who had advised the government about Islamic laws – the law about rape was faulty and absurd ('because the act is never performed in public') and was based on a misreading of the Koran. The Prophet's revelation was about 'lewdness' and feminine lewdness specifically. It couldn't be said to refer to rape. So it didn't require the four eye-witnesses. Ordinary witnesses would have sufficed; even medical evidence might have been offered.

Who, Islamically speaking, was right? The mullahs, sticking literally to the most applicable revelation in the Koran? Or the *Pakistan Times* man, bending that revelation a little to make it fit the case, and giving a modern extension to the idea of witness? It was easy to state the Koranic punishment; it was another matter to work out law. To work out law, with only the historical, geographical and cultural (and sometimes folksy) particularities of the Koran as a guide, was to become entangled in textual-religious-sectarian disputes of this kind, and very quickly to get away from the idea of equity.

The *Pakistan Times* man could not hide his rage about the mullahs. They were politically ambitious; they had 'shrewdly entrapped' the government by framing laws that couldn't work and then blaming the government for not operating these laws; they had divided Islam into conflicting sects and made Islam a mockery. The answer was to by-pass the mullahs, do away with the sects, and go back to the holy book. Do that, and 'we find the light all around. But once we wriggle out of the Koran, there is nothing but darkness and confusion in store for us.'

But was it as easy as that? To raise just one point: how old was Aisha when she married the fifty-year-old Prophet? Was she six or nine or nineteen? Did she, as in one tender story, take her dolls and toys to the Prophet's tent? The Koran doesn't help; Aisha's age has to be worked out from other sources. The question was gone into at length one Friday sabbath in the *Pakistan Times*; and the question is of more than historical interest, because Aisha's age at marriage – and there are nine different opinions – can fix the legal marriage-age for girls.

In Islam, and especially the Islam of the fundamentalists, precedent is all. The principles of the Prophet – as divined from the Koran and the approved traditions – are for all time. They can be extended to cover all disciplines. The Prophet was reported to have said that the best Muslims were going to be his contemporaries, the second best the generation after, and so on, the decline continuing till the end of time. Can that be read as a condemnation of 'Darwinism'? It is what the new, educated fundamentalists say. And it is at once sound faith, and part of their rage against the civilization that encircles them and which they as a community despair of mastering.

In the fundamentalist scheme the world constantly decays and has constantly to be re-created. The only function of intellect is to assist that re-creation. It re-interprets the texts; it re-establishes divine precedent. So history has to serve theology, law is separated from the idea of equity, and learning is separated from learning. The doctrine has its attractions. To a student from Karachi university, from perhaps a provincial or peasant background, the old faith comes more easily than any new-fangled academic discipline. So fundamentalism takes root in the universities, and to deny education can become the approved educated act. In the days of Muslim glory Islam opened itself to the learning of the world. Now fundamentalism provides an intellectual thermostat, set low. It equalizes, comforts, shelters and preserves.

In this way the faith pervades everything, and it is possible to understand what the fundamentalists mean when they say that Islam is a complete way of life. But what is said about Islam is true, and perhaps truer, of other religions – like Hinduism or Buddhism or lesser tribal faiths – that at an early stage in their history were also complete cultures, self-contained and more or less isolated, with institutions, manners and beliefs making a whole.

The Islamic fundamentalist wish is to work back to such a whole, for them a God-given whole, but with the tool of faith alone – belief, religious practices and rituals. It is like a wish – with intellect suppressed or limited, the historical sense falsified – to work back from the abstract to the concrete, and to set up the tribal walls again. It is to seek to re-create something like a tribal or a city state that – except in theological fantasy – never was. The Koran is not the statute-book of a settled golden age; it is the mystical or oracular record of an extended upheaval, widening out from the Prophet to his tribe to Arabia. Arabia was full of movement; Islam, with all its Jewish and Christian elements, was always mixed, eclectic, developing. Almost as soon as the Prophet made his community secure he sought to subdue his enemies. It was during a military march in the fifth year of the Muslim era that Aisha spent that night alone in the desert.

The West, or the universal civilization it leads, is emotionally rejected. It undermines; it threatens. But at the same time it is needed, for its machines, goods, medicines, warplanes, the remittances from the emigrants, the hospitals that might have a cure for calcium deficiency, the universities that will provide master's degrees in mass media. All the rejection of the West is contained within the assumption that there will always exist out there a living, creative civilization, oddly neutral, open to all to appeal to. Rejection, therefore, is not absolute rejection. It is also, for the community as a whole, a way of ceasing to strive intellectually. It is to be parasitic; parasitism is one of the unacknowledged fruits of fundamentalism. And the emigrants pour out from the land of the faith: 30,000 Pakistanis shipped by the manpower-export experts to West Berlin alone, to claim the political asylum meant for the people of East Germany.

The patron saint of the Islamic fundamentalists in Pakistan was Maulana Maudoodi. He opposed the idea of a separate Indian Muslim state because he felt that the Muslims were not pure enough for such a state. He felt that God should be the law-giver; and, offering ecstasy of this sort rather than a practical programme, he became the focus of millenarian passion. He campaigned for Islamic laws without stating what those laws should be.

He died while I was in Pakistan. But he didn't die in Pakistan: the news of his death came from Boston. At the end of his long and cantankerous life the Maulana had gone against all his high principles. He had gone to a Boston hospital to look for health; he had at the very end entrusted himself to the skill and science of the civilization he had tried to shield his followers from. He had sought, as someone said to me (not all Pakistanis are fundamentalists) to reap where he had not wanted his people to sow. Of the Maulana it might be said that he had gone to his

well-deserved place in heaven by way of Boston; and that he went at
least part of the way by Boeing.

'If we seek guidance from the Koran,' the writer in the *Pakistan Times*
said, 'we find the light all around.' The mullahs' laws about whipping
and stoning to death had come to nothing, but an Islamic social order was
still possible in Pakistan. A new 'methodology' was needed. By-pass the
mullahs; do away with the religious sects; give up the attempt to mix
Islam, based on the sovereignty of Allah, with western democracy, based
on the sovereignty of the people; do away with the political parties.

The political advice was followed within weeks. The elections that had
been promised were scrapped. But the state had to be governed, the
people had to be policed. Public floggings were decreed, and there was no
nonsense this time about eye-witnesses. The army sent out whipping
vans to the bazaars: instant law, Islam on wheels.

Step by step, out of its Islamic striving, Pakistan had undone the rule
of law it had inherited from the British, and replaced it with nothing.

7

❖❖❖❖❖

Basics

SIX OR SEVEN HUNDRED MILES north-east of Karachi – after Sind and the plains of the Punjab, at the end of the wide valley watered by the Indus and its tributaries – the Himalayas began. In the foothills were the small 'twin cities' of Rawalpindi and Islamabad.

Islamabad, 'the city of Islam', the capital of Pakistan, was new. It had been built twenty years before by a military government for no apparent reason except perhaps that a new, well laid-out city, separate from the messiness of Asia, appealed to the military mind, and the sudden setting down of a western-style city (like the importation of United States arms) gave the illusion that the twentieth century had been finally dealt with on its own terms, and that both Islam and Pakistan were on the march.

Rawalpindi, twenty miles away, was the older city. In one direction it sprawled towards Islamabad; but in the centre little had changed. In the bazaar there were still the high, dark-timbered, verandahed and latticed houses of the Sikhs and Hindus who had predominated in the little town before partition and had then been displaced. The old British Rawalpindi club was still in business – the ceiling lights a little dimmer, the walls a more muddy yellow, the uniforms of the waiters a little grubbier, the atmosphere at meal times more highly spiced.

The British had ruled here for under a hundred years, and more than thirty years had passed since they had left, but old Rawalpindi remained a town of British India: in the Mall, a street of hotels and gardens; in some of its old-fashioned shops on the Kashmir Road; in its military and administrative residences.

In one such residence lived the doctor. He was the chief medical officer of a small oil company that operated in the Himalayan foothills to the west. The company, once British-owned, was now Arab-controlled; but old dignity adhered to the company's senior residential 'compound'. The house of the chief medical officer had a big lawn, a semi-circular drive, a chunkily-pillared portico. The sitting room, with thick walls and a very high ceiling, was kept cool only by fans and open doors, which gave glimpses of the green just outside.

The doctor, a man of fifty, small and fine-featured, was aware of the dignity of the house. But he was not dwarfed by it: such dignity as had come to him, he said, had come to him because of his faith. The doctor was a Shia. The Shias – supporters of Ali and Ali's defeated cause (in its beginnings a political cause, an anti-Arab cause within the expanding Arab empire) – the Shias were the minority sect in Pakistan. And it was of his 'internationalist' faith, as he called it, that the gentle doctor (as though wishing to play down the excessive dignity of his residence) began to talk to me on this Friday sabbath morning.

One of the doctor's two sons was there; he was a medical student of twenty-three and, the doctor said, a 'rebel' and a rationalist. There were two journalists and their wives; they too were Shias. The sabbath gathering was more than the social occasion I had been led to expect. For the Shias it was an occasion for serious – and that meant theological – discussion.

The doctor said he had been strengthened, even in everyday matters, by his faith as a follower of Ali. There were five points in his faith: the oneness of God, justice, a belief in prophethood, a belief in imamhood (the reign on earth of an *imam* as God's regent and spiritual successor to the Prophet), *jihad* or holy war. Not the holy war the mullahs spoke about, the doctor said; the holy war he had in mind was 'the constant struggle in yourself to fight evil'.

I asked how articles of faith as abstruse as prophethood and imamhood strengthened him in day-to-day matters.

He said, 'I'll tell you. I am now chief medical officer of the company. I wasn't that always. I used for some time to be the assistant. Then the chief medical officer retired. For six months the post was vacant. But no appointment was made. The appointment should have come to me. I had done a lot of work. My work on bites was well known to my old superior, and I knew he had written a favourable report about me. Bites – it was my field. Snake bites, scorpion bites, dog bites, donkey bites, dog bites on donkeys – all these things I had done work on. Poor people suffer from these things, and I had done a lot of work among the poor. Rich people don't go about barefooted and get bitten by scorpions. They don't have to worry about dogs biting their donkeys or camels. So I had done all this work. I had treated so many people who had got bitten by snakes. They come with the blood pouring out of their nostrils and mouths. You can cure these things. That is the viper bite I'm talking about, I should say. The cobra and the *krait* are different.

'So I went to the GM, the general manager, and told him about the position, about this vacant post and my qualifications. He didn't give me any satisfaction. He suggested that what I really wanted was the salary and this big house. Well, these things are important. But not that important. And besides, a doctor can make a living anywhere. It was my faith that comforted me at that moment, in the GM's office. And when the GM said to me that if I wasn't happy I should resign – and he passed a sheet of paper across the desk to me – I wrote out my letter of resignation. He thought he was frightening me. But I had my faith. If I didn't have my faith I wouldn't have written that letter. The GM saw that. He rejected the letter I had written. That is why I am here.'

But the doctor hadn't mentioned the after-life or hereafter as one of the articles of his faith. Wasn't that essential for a Muslim?

'I don't know about the after-life. Sometimes I believe. Sometimes I lose my belief. But I feel I must believe. I'll tell you. My elder son – not the boy here: his older brother – he was studying chemical engineering. We are that kind of family, scientifically inclined. Well, this boy had done very well in the "matric", but in the "inter" he began to do badly. It worried me a lot. How could a boy who had done so well in the matriculation do so badly in the inter? That was a serious business; it was going to affect his future. I thought some minister was responsible. It's the kind of thing they do here. They want something for their own son and they get people to throw away the papers of other people. It happens.

'One night during this time I dreamt I was below a big and beautiful tree. There was a musical instrument. I remember only the black wood of the instrument – when I woke up I couldn't remember any more. Out of this came music of a sort I had never heard before. And my father appeared before me. But he appeared in the form of my uncle. Because my father died when I was two, and I had been brought up by my uncle. He said he had come to solace me. In the dream I began to cry, and when I woke up I found that my pillow was wet with tears.

'I went to my son's school that day. I met his teacher. And he told me that although my son had lost so many marks in the earlier papers he had done all right in the examination as a whole. He had made 78 percent. And just at that time out of the school building there came a man who was absolutely like my uncle in the dream. I ran to him and embraced him and said, "You don't know how happy I am to see you. I met you in my dream last night."'

That incident – and others like it – made the doctor believe in the after-life. But he was at the same time proud of the rationalism of his younger son, the medical student, who also wrote poetry in English (some of which was, at that moment, being shown to one of the journalists). In what way was the son a rationalist? The son – called over by his father to speak for himself – said that his attitude to the Prophet was historical. The great and good man existed; people added the divinity later.

The son, Syed, was taller and heavier than his father. Glasses made him look like a student; with his father's guests he had the manner of a privileged student son. He was more socially secure than his father, intellectually more adventurous, but he was conscious that he was building on the achievement of his father.

Syed said he felt isolated from his friends at the medical school. They just wanted to pass the examinations, to become doctors; they weren't interested in intellectual matters. They just wanted the skill; they weren't interested – as Syed was – in the civilization that went with the skill. (But Syed didn't put it like that.) How had he arrived at his intellectual interests? Well, he had the advantage of his father's medical background – that put him a generation or two ahead of most of his fellows. He had spent a year in England. And he had read a lot in English.

It was about his English reading that I got him to talk. And I was so taken by his account of his approach to the outer civilization – a pioneer journey in many ways, and a contrast with the blanket dismissal of 'the West' by people who often, even after travel and a picked-up profession (a single, isolated skill), had the thinnest idea of what they were dismissing – that I asked for paper and noted down Syed's words.

He was twenty-three, and he thought he had so far read about two hundred and fifty English books – apart from the Enid Blyton, which he had read until he was twelve, and the 'Biggles' books, which he had moved on to from the Blyton and had read until he was fourteen. The reading breakthrough came then, at fourteen, when his father gave him *The Good Earth*. That got him on to adult books: James Hadley Chase, Harold Robbins, Ian Fleming. Did he enjoy those books? Weren't they too strange? He said he couldn't follow the Ian Fleming; but he had read the books because they were famous, and the same was true of the Harold Robbins. He wanted to read; he was told it was good to read; the problem for him was finding things that made sense. He used to go through the best-seller list in *Time*, hoping that there might be something for him. But it wasn't always easy for him to know what the books were about.

At this period – he was fifteen or sixteen – Steinbeck was a find. *East of Eden* made a great impression. 'I loved it. This girl wanted to break away from her family, and a house burned down. That is all I remember now. It was a revolutionary book to me.' Then came his year in England.

He saw the Perry Mason series on television, and read twenty of the Perry Mason books. Wasn't the background too hard for him, too far away from what he knew? No; he understood the books completely.

It was strange, the popular English reading that had given order to Syed Hussain's expanding, shaken-up world: mechanical fantasies for the most part, making the foreign manageable, offering a mixture of the modern and the archaic, disorder and ritual: Enid Blyton, the Biggles books, Pearl Buck, James Hadley Chase, John Steinbeck, Perry Mason.

And sex. Out of the 250 books he had read, he would say that about thirty had been sex books. He read them 'to become stable'. People who didn't know sex books became over-excited when they ran across one; and they wanted to look at *Playboy*. His literary sex course cured him of that. 'I also read sex books of the academic sort. *Married Happiness*. That kind of thing.'

But nine years after he had read *The Good Earth*, Pearl Buck remained the charmer for him. He had read about six or seven of her books – and he regarded that as serious reading. 'Then I liked a lot Graham Greene's *The Wall Has Two Sides*.'

'Felix Greene, you mean?'

'Maybe. Greene something. No, Graham Greene was *The Ugly American*. I get the names mixed up. I'll tell you a story. One time I was travelling to Lahore on the train. It was at the time of the revolution in Iran. There was an American missionary on the train. He asked me to sit down, and we began to talk. He wanted to know what I thought about Iran. And I told him – I am like that – that the Americans were going to get out of Iran, that they were going to go to China instead now. He didn't like what I said. Maybe he was an agent.'

I didn't follow the story. But it was important to him, perhaps for that vision of the dangerous American: life answering literature, literature clearing up the world.

When he was done with the story of the American on the train he said: 'In between all these books I got into pop songs and western music. I really went for them. Not the rock-and-roll noisy types. But the ones which really carried a message. Not only the western ones, but the local Urdu ones. I liked very much the Carpenters, a brother and sister group. They sing about the basic innocence. That's how I get it. There are lots of songs I get which carry a message about religion, a mention of God, beliefs.'

'Beliefs?'

'Like doing something because you really believe in it. Like love. Basics.'

'But I thought you weren't a religious man.'

'In a way I'm not religious. But everything has got to have a message.'

'What was the last book you read?'

He couldn't say. It was six months ago; he couldn't remember. To keep the conversation going, he said, 'The best writer I have read is still Pearl Buck. She writes about the poor. I won't say Chinese or communists – just the poor. She writes about the poor and the basics in human relationships.'

'What are these basics?'

'Relating to people. The innocence. People are always trying to trick people. The victims and the hypocrites. Everywhere you see the big fish-small fish thing. Big countries trying to dictate to the small countries. Not Pakistan only, but small countries everywhere. They tried to do it in Iran.'

His family was Shia. Iran was the Shia heartland; there had recently been a family wedding in Iran, in the holy city of Mashhad. I said, 'Do you think it's all right now, after the revolution?'

'No. It's just a vicious circle. Something keeps going wrong all the time in Iran. So much killing can't be right even in the name of God.' He was thinking of the executions decreed by the Islamic revolutionary courts. 'A sort of eternal punishment – that is what death is – can't be right if God is so great. It can't relate to God if God is so great.'

Hypocrisy was the theme of the poem he had been showing visitors that morning – and he had spoken to me about the victims and the hypocrites.

> *The hypocrite sounds like a lark*
> *the bite is worse that the bark.*
> *A hypocrite may appear fearless and bold*
> *all that glitters is not gold.*

Cruelty, injustice, slander: these were also among his themes (and in his own language, Urdu, the play on words, the twisting of idioms would have been more unexpected and violent). Closest to him (and containing the point he had made about his isolation at the medical school) was the poem about a surgeon friend of the family who had died from a viral infection contracted during surgery:

> *His skills just anyone cannot learn*
> *if a flame of love does not burn*
> *for his was not a magic art*
> *but a beating healing heart.*

He said, talking of his poetry, 'I am empty for three–four months. I am occupied – empty from the angle of the poetry. Then it just comes. It happens. I can write two or three poems then. I don't want to do anything else. Even if I'm supposed to study I don't feel like studying after this thing happens. And then I'm empty again.'

The poem he had just written was 'The Big Black Man'. Strange theme. Who was he? Muhammad Ali, the boxer,

> *... who wouldn't break a twig*
> *but at one blow can fell a tree. Do you dig?*

At the end of the sabbath morning at the doctor's a religious discussion between the two journalists seemed to turn to an outright quarrel. The subject was Ali, the Shia hero, the cousin and son-in-law of the Prophet. The Shias think that Ali should have succeeded the Prophet as the ruler of the Muslims in 632. But Ali – stupendous though his life was: one of the earliest Muslims, one of the handful, living to see Islam become an empire – was a political failure. Three men became caliphs of the Islamic empire before him. It wasn't until 656 that Ali became caliph; even then his rule was challenged; and he was murdered in 661. And this was the sabbath debate: Ali, as caliph, had led armies, but could it be said that he had ordered men to kill? Or had he ordered his followers to kill only in self-defence?

The debate began calmly enough, in the doctor's sitting room. But soon the voices of the disputants altered: grated, quivered, became like the reciting voices of mullahs in the mosques. More than history was involved. The failure and death of Ali, the failure and death of Ali's sons, had been worked over by the Shias into an extended agony in the garden, oddly unavenged after thirteen hundred years: an agony without the resurrection. The racial dissensions of the early Arab empire (Ali the defender of the oppressed) had turned to religion; and were the source of this sabbath morning passion in the British-built residence in Rawalpindi.

The dispute went on well past lunch time. I did not stay for the end. The doctor, before I left, gave me his own copy of *The Maxims of Ali*. It was a small paperbacked booklet, locally published. It was the book that had worked wonders for him, the doctor said; it had given him the strength for that encounter with the general manager of the oil company; he thought it would do me good.

I looked at it later that afternoon when I got back to Flashman's Hotel on the Mall. Ali's sayings were famous. The first collection – a hundred sayings – had been made more than a thousand years before; thousands had been subsequently added. This was a selection, in an English translation by J. A. Chapman. At first I was puzzled.

Trust another as you would yourself. How ugly is Mr Facing-both-ways. Not every archer hits the mark. The death of one's child breaks the spine.

But there was another side to this folksy wisdom:

The greatest wealth is the wealth of wisdom and judgement; the greatest poverty is the poverty of stupidity and ignorance; the worst unsociableness is that of vanity, conceit and self-glorification.
Perfection is not of this world.
The inhabitants of the earth are only dogs barking, and annoying beasts. The one howls against the other. The strong devour the weak; the great subdue the little. They are beasts of burden; some harnessed, the others at large.
The world is a dwelling surrounded by scourges, and heaped with perfidy. Its state endures not, and all who come to it perish.
The world is like a serpent: its touch soft, but its bite mortal.

They were the sayings of a righteous man eaten up by injustice and defeat. The misanthropy, the pain! Could this give strength? But to the defeated, and the faithful, Ali would have been the good man who had suffered more; he ennobled worldly defeat and suffering. And there was no question here of forgiveness or calm: he ennobled rage. And it became clearer to me – reading in Flashman's, in my wide-eaved hotel room, screened by a free-standing wall of pierced concrete blocks from the glare of the little pool, decoratively planted at the corners with banana trees – it became clearer to me how much of this Shia and Muslim religious attitude had been bred into the doctor's son, who was a rationalist, and in whose poetry, always outward looking, I might never – without this special new knowledge – have seen anything Muslim.

No religion is more worldly than Islam. In spite of its political incapacity, no religion keeps men's eyes more fixed on the way the world is run. And in the poetry of the doctor's son, in his fumbling response to the universal civilization, his concern with 'basics', I thought I could see how Islamic fervour could become creative, revolutionary, and take men on to a humanism beyond religious doctrine: a true renaissance, open to the new and enriched by it, as the Muslims in their early days of glory had been.

The fundamentalists, insecure, with their un-historical view, feared alien contamination. But fundamentalism offered nothing. It pushed men to an unappeasable faith; it offered a political desert. It violated the 'basics'; it could never wall out the rest of the world. And I thought it was possible, looking not many steps ahead, to see how in Pakistan, by the very excesses of fundamentalism, Islam might be preparing its own transformation.

8

❖❖❖❖❖

In the Kaghan Valley

JUST TO THE NORTH the mountains began, and less than a hundred miles away were the high Himalayas. Winter came early there; snow blocked the passes for months. In September began the migration of the herdsmen and their families and their flocks from their high summer pastures to the lowlands. And to see that migration I went to the Kaghan Valley. Qazi, a professor at the university of Islamabad, arranged the trip for me. He lent me his car and his driver; they were to take me to Balakot. There I was to hire a jeep for the rough ride north, beside the Kunhar River, one of the icy, early tributaries of the great Indus.

My companion was Masood. Masood was a science student. He had been doing degrees all his adult life and now, at twenty-seven, was at a loose end. There was no post for him in Pakistan. He would have liked to continue his research work, and had been accepted for an advanced course at an English university; but the fees were beyond him.

He was a tall, thin, melancholy man with glasses and a walrus moustache. The moustache hinted at his military background: his father had served from 1941 to 1961 in the army, for the first six years in the old British Indian army, then in the army of Pakistan. Now his father was an accountant. The family had migrated from Lucknow in India; in Pakistan they were *mohajirs*, strangers.

The *mohajirs* had altered the provincial or regional cultures of Pakistan, Masood said; they had brought a new style in food, music, language. Urdu, the *mohajir* language, was now the national language of Pakistan; and Masood said – speaking to me as to a stranger who had to be put right about the country – that Urdu was a beautiful, easy language. After we passed the site of the ancient Buddhist city of Taxila and turned north, climbing, to Abbottabad, he gave me an Urdu lesson, and it was possible even for me to appreciate the clarity and elegance of his Lucknow accent. But then, as we climbed between the dry, bright hills, and as he became used to me, he became less of a spokesman for the *mohajirs*; he allowed his tone to become ironical.

Many of the *mohajirs* who had migrated to Pakistan, he said, had pretended they were nawabs and aristocrats in India. He made no such claim. His father had been in the army; but he had only been a *havildar*, a non-commissioned officer, something like a sergeant. So, in spite of his Lucknow Urdu, his military moustache, his science degrees, Masood was – in Pakistan, more feudal than India, with less of an industrial or professional middle class – of simple origins; and a man without a job.

At Balakot we parked our car. We had to bargain for a jeep at the government travel office. That was unexpected, the bargaining. And the office too was unexpected: an open room at the end of a lawn, with two upholstered chairs, two metal-framed beds with foam mattresses, two other metal beds on their sides, a couple of chairs stacked upside down at the back of the room, a little sofa at the front: an office that was at once like a waiting room and a run-down hospital ward. But it was a working place: the jeeps on the lawn were real enough.

Masood asked me to stay out of the way, and not to speak English, while he bargained. I sat in the verandah of a chalet at the side of the lawn, and after a while he came out of the office looking grim. He said they had asked for 750 rupees, 75 dollars; he thought they would settle for 700; but he had told them we would go and find another jeep in the bazaar.

A man came out of the office. He asked for 650. Masood paid no attention. He said to me grimly, in English, 'Let us go to the bazaar.' We walked through the bazaar – a blackened dirt road, blackened little shops. In a beaten-up, oil-blackened filling station a man was hosing down a beaten-up jeep; he asked for 900 rupees. So we went back to the government office and settled, not for 650, but 700.

And almost at once (the government people had never doubted that they would get us) we were off. The jeep driver was a man of extraordinary handsomeness: rich, dark-brown hair, classical Indo-Aryan features, his slender, strong physique well set off by his baggy white trousers and long-tailed tan shirt. He had a boy assistant, a grubby, square-faced little cigarette-smoker with only a thin shirt below his khaki-coloured shawl. We had started off with such dispatch that it was some time before I was aware of him holding on (for the sake of the drama) to the back of the jeep, shawl wrapped around his head and narrow shoulders; and then, for a few miles, I had taken him for a Balakot bazaar boy hitching a ride.

Soon we were beside the Kunhar River, shallow in a wide, rocky valley. And after all my weeks in sand and heat I stopped the jeep to listen to the sound of water. The road was shady with trees; they were an extra blessing. But we couldn't dally; we had far to go; and Masood said there was a lot more water on the way. We began – and, after the easy ride from Rawalpindi, it was like something theatrical, arranged – to see the shepherds driving down their flocks. They were Afghans, unexpectedly small and frail-looking, the men black-turbanned, the women in bright baggy trousers and long head-covers. Busy, the women, private, shut away in their migrant life, grimy with their bright colours (red and black), underfed, exhausted by the work and the walking, their faces tanned and lined.

The hills were irregularly marked with old, overgrown terracing. The houses, set against the hillsides, had flat, thick mud roofs, often at varying levels; these roofs rested on heavy beams, sometimes whole trunks – trees were plentiful here. Houses set against the embankment of the road often had their roofs level with the road and showed only as a kind of earthen yard: the quarters were below, hidden.

We stopped at a village to talk to some boys. They looked idle, but they wore the slate-grey uniform of schoolboys, and were not as isolated as they appeared. One boy had an uncle in Lahore; another, brothers in Karachi and a brother in Saudi Arabia. A young man who came out from a two-level, flat-roofed, stone-walled house said that he could go to Karachi any time and earn 2,400 rupees a month as a carpenter. Masood didn't think he was exaggerating: with the great migration artisan skills were rare in Pakistan. But the man's peasant arrogance added to Masood's own melancholy; he said he couldn't earn that himself.

They were not isolated. But we were, already, only a few easy hours away from Rawalpindi, in a feudal land. A very small man, less than five feet – how small these mountain people were! – walked past, leading a buffalo. He didn't own the buffalo, the boys said. The buffalo belonged to the man's master, who was walking ahead: a turbanned man we had paid no attention to, not understanding that his empty hands and casual gait were signs of his village status as an owner of a buffalo and a serf. And the house of the great landlord, the local rich man, the boys said, was there: not a flat-roofed house set against the hillside, but a house on flat land, at the end of the field: a big stone house on two floors, with a pitched roof in corrugated iron. And those stunted men now going past were Gujars: the original inhabitants of the valley, not very bright, rather backward in fact, and keeping to themselves.

The road climbed. The river dropped below us. The steep hills were welted with little strips of cultivation: maize, the late summer crop of the valley, growing wherever a little flat space could be banked up. And there were the pines. They seeded themselves on the hillsides; the seedlings, after their first horizontal thrust, straightened up and, looking for the light, grew straight and tall; they were the tallest pines I had seen. And always there were the houses, not always easy to see, camouflaged by their flat roofs and stone walls.

Sheep and goats and horses and camels came down the road constantly; the sheep's backs were dyed. The Afghans couldn't stop to talk. When they did, they didn't have much to say. They lived where it was very cold; at this time of year they moved down to avoid the winter snows; that was all. They were at one with their animals: man and beast had come to an understanding. Very small children, while still recognized as babies, were tied up with the baggage on the backs of camels or donkeys. Above that age they walked, were workers, miniature adults, with switches instead of sticks; and with their turbans and shirts and trousers looked so self-possessed and complete that it was hard, from a distance, especially if they were by themselves, to assess their age or size.

The handsome jeep driver said, with something like tribal jealousy, 'For every one of those sheep they will get a thousand rupees in Mansehra or Abbottabad.'

The busy little trotters of the sheep ground the fine dust of the road finer. And as we crawled in a cloud of dust through two or three jumbled flocks, all woolly, bobbing backs, dyed in many colours, Masood (already wounded by that man boasting about the 2,400 rupees he could earn in Karachi) said, 'Can you imagine the lakhs and lakhs of rupees on this road?' A lakh was 100,000.

I said, 'What do they do with the money?'

Masood said, 'They have their dependents. They have daughters or sons to marry off. They have wedding parties. The custom here is for the boy to make a gift of 20,000 rupees to the girl. If there is no cash then he has to build a house or make some arrangement about land. So that when he sends her away she has something. If he can't do that the girl can't marry him.'

'I thought that in Pakistan the girl had to have a dowry.'

'Dowry? I don't know that word.'

I thought Masood knew the word. I thought he also knew that the custom was not considered good. I said, 'In Karachi I was told that orthodox families give only thirty-two rupees because that was the sum given to the Prophet.'

He recognized that.

I didn't believe in that figure of a thousand rupees for a sheep. And when later we were stopped by another flock I got Masood to ask the Afghan herdsman directly. The Afghan thought we wanted to buy. He indicated one of his plumper animals and said he wouldn't take less than 300 rupees for him. And now it was the turn of the jeep driver, who had given the figure of a thousand rupees, to pretend not to understand.

The pale-green river tumbled over rocks; the water was always in movement. But at a certain height the river appeared frozen. The white eddies and swirls formed a fixed, marbled pattern – though you could still hear the noise. And it was fascinating, going down, to see the fixed pattern quicken again, to have the river noise matched by movement.

At a wide, sharply angled bend in the mountain road there was an Afghan camp. A low tent had been pitched; camels and donkeys were in a group; there was cooking. The cooking fire, the darkness of the tent, made an attractive picture, and we stopped to talk to the Afghans, after asking the jeep driver whether it was the kind of intrusion they permitted.

We spoke to a young man who was dressed in the Pakistani fashion. He was moustached, with a tanned white skin, and a jovial peasant face. But he was canny; he thought that we – in a government jeep – were government men; and the first thing he said to Masood was that the people of his camp had left Afghanistan many years before and now lived permanently on the Pakistan side of the border.

Masood, not turning away from the young man or altering his voice, said to me in English, 'He's lying. He's come from Kabul. He's just been to Kabul. But he doesn't want to get into any political trouble.'

The young man took out a brass snuff-box. It was full of a dark-green mixture of tobacco and herbs, a pinch of which was meant to be kept below the lower lip. He gave me some to try. I placed it on the tip of my tongue and as it moistened it pricked and was not unpleasant. He took in return a speck of my own brown tobacco snuff. It was too strong for him and he made no attempt to control his disgust; he sneezed and spat almost at my feet. Recovering, he first tapped the clear-lensed glasses I had in my shirt pocket, then with his own hand he took off the dark glasses I was still wearing. I had forgotten I had them on, it was so bright. I should have let him see my eyes from the start: he was right to object to my discourtesy.

He took us to the tent to let us watch. Tea had been brewed or stewed, in the manner of the sub-continent; dirty little china cups lay on the ground. A girl or young woman was making *roti*, flat unleavened bread, over a brushwood fire, flattening the dough balls between her palms, working fast, tossing and spinning the dough until it was very thin and round and then, with one gesture, draping the thin round of dough over her right forearm before throwing it on to the baking iron. The flour was of local grain, ground in village mills, worked in these parts by water, always abundant.

The hot *roti* we were offered was delicious. The tent, the cooking fire, the mountains, the river, the tea and the *roti*: I felt momentarily I could surrender to the life. But was that all they were going to have, the *roti* and the tea? Masood asked for me. 'Only *roti* and *chai*? No *tarkari*?' No savoury dish of vegetables or meat? The young man laughed. '*Tarkari*? Why do we need *tarkari*?'

The jeep driver said they sometimes ate *paneer*, cottage cheese. But there was none at that meal.

Masood said, 'That's why they are so healthy.' Masood was nervous about infected food and bad water. He travelled with pills; it was part of his general anxiety.

The women or girls in the tent were beautiful. *Roti* and tea was all they were having now; but they looked better fed and better cared-for than most of the women we had seen on the road; and the mountain sun had given a wonderful dark warmth to their white skins.

Sheep and goats were in and out of the tent. Rugs and bedding were at the back. This left-hand part of the ground at the front of the tent, the young man said, was for his father and his uncle; this middle part was for the women; and the right-hand part – but I didn't get who the right-hand part was for. There were two brothers in the caravan; they were a rich family. That plain, fierce woman sitting in her assigned place in the middle, with her heavy silver earrings and her heavy silver necklace, was the wife of the uncle. She never looked at us.

Masood, without prompting from me, asked the young man about the price of sheep. The young man pointed to the lesser encampment across the road and said that the sheep there was worth 3,000 rupees. It was big, heavy with wool, and it must have been special because it was in the living quarters of the encampment, and both its hind legs were tied to a central stake.

The camels near the main tent were hobbled in a way new to me: one of the front legs folded back and tied with rope to the upper part of the leg, so that the big animal could only hop. I noticed for the first time that there was a plug or wooden nail driven into the nose of each camel. It was to this that the lead rope was attached. The young man demonstrated. He pulled down on the lead rope. The camel neighed as if in anger, and did nothing. But then, a little while later, it squatted down on its long legs, which were bruised and calloused at the joints. Camels, like elephants, look neater from a distance; close to, their hides are broken and ragged.

The young man said that the pretty girls in the tent were his sisters. They were unmarried, and so was he. He thought he was sixteen. But this was clearly nonsense; perhaps he didn't know his age and had no means of assessing the passage of the years. The father of the family now approached. He was sour, but superb; elegantly turbanned, forbidding.

It was only when he came right up that his very small stature became noticeable: he was an inch or two below five feet. But these Afghan nomads were all small, like many of their animals – the cattle, the ponies, the donkeys; the calves were the size of dogs. Only the sheep and the goats were fine and strong. The father had pale-blue eyes, and they were freshly rimmed with kohl. His white moustache was waxed at the tips; his beard was parted and curled; below his tan his skin was white. Astonishing, the dandyism, the pride in his toilet (there was no other word), greater than that of the women in theirs, at this altitude, and among the camels and the goats!

The young man said his father was fifty. And the father – his blue eyes full of distrust, even disdain – asked his son who we were. The young man said that we spoke different languages; Masood spoke Urdu and I spoke English. It was his way of saying that Masood and I were both strangers, but of different tribes. The father – casually – offered us tea. We said no. And then there was no more to say. The father sat down in the left-hand side of the tent meant for him and his brother, reclined against some bundles, and paid us no more attention.

A donkey, followed by two or three of its tiny fellows, came into the tent to nibble at some cut grass that was possibly being saved for a more valuable animal. The father gave the donkey a loud thump on its side with his open hand. But there was no hurting intention behind the blow; the blow had been given only for the hollow, warning-off sound. One of the little boys of the family threw stones at the other donkeys, but the stones were very small, and were thrown lightly. They were all gentle with their animals. They made big and threatening gestures with their sticks, but the sticks were not used to hit; the sticks stroked, guided.

The father, reclining against the roped baggage of the caravan, began to cough. And then – with his splendid turban, his kohl-rimmed eyes, his curled beard and his waxed moustache – he spat, messily, just where he reclined. I saw that he was reclining among animal droppings; and that in the darkness at the back of the tent – more protected than the people – were the valuable sheep and goats of his flock.

Masood, looking down at the old man, said to me, 'They are like that. Have you been to Afghanistan? Kabul? The middle classes are just like that too.'

We spoke different languages. And it was as though it was understood that with our mutual interest and tolerance, stranger with stranger, there should also be disregard, and the privacy of each man within his group. Masood's contempt was not greater than the contempt for us I could read in the old man's eyes. There were so many tribes in this small area: Gujars, Afghans, Kaghanis, Pathans, Masood (from Lucknow in

India), myself. And yet the civilities would be maintained: tea would be offered, tobacco. Our jeep driver had withdrawn; the Afghans bored him already; he made no secret of that. He sat at the edge of the cliff, handsome, more evolved, his hair combed in the film-star style, dust now giving a new tone to his rich dark-brown hair.

And who was the mother of the pretty girls in the tent? The plain woman in the middle was the wife of the uncle, I knew. The young man said that the mother of the girls (not necessarily his own mother) was across the road, in the lesser encampment, where that sheep worth 3,000 rupees was carefully staked, to prevent it scrambling about and damaging itself.

We went across the road to that encampment. The uncle was there. He was simply sitting on the ground; he ignored us. Two veiled women — one of them the mother of the pretty girls — were fussing with the baggage. The veils were unusual, a sign of the status of the family. The uncle spoke to the women. Together they threw a rug on the ground. The uncle moved from where he was sitting and sat on the rug. And while he sat, the women began to set up a tent around him: canvas with ringed holes, the tent poles of bamboo, iron-shod, and linked at the top to make a tripod. The women had trouble with the poles. The uncle paid no attention. He just sat, waiting for the tent and shade, holding an old powdered-milk tin before him. The tin probably contained his money.

The women's veils fell off their faces while they tried to get the tent up. They were not like the girls in the tent across the road. Their faces were old and lined and brown. The unmarried girls were beauties. These women, wives, were workers; they were beasts of burden. Like the women of the Dakota Indians Parkman saw on the Oregon trail in 1846. But these Afghans, and all these mountain tribes, lived in terrain which only they could master. No one could say of them, as Parkman could say of the Dakota Indians, that they were going to be wiped off the face of the earth.

Masood said, while we were standing over the uncle, 'The women do all the work. The men do nothing. It isn't like that in Europe, is it?' But he was being unfair to the men. They drove themselves hard too; no one among these nomads drove anyone harder than he drove himself. Masood said, 'That attitude to women is with us too. But it is getting less in the towns.' Masood had sisters. The older ones had married and become 'housewives', as he said, had fallen into old ways. But the younger girls were students, at the university, and Masood was concerned about them.

But my attitude at that moment was not like Masood's. The Afghan encampment had taken me back to the earliest geography lessons of my childhood, to the drawings in my *Homes Far Away* text-book: men creating homes, warmth, shelter in extreme conditions: the bow-and-arrow Africans in their stockades, protected against the night-time dangers of the forest; the Kirghiz in their tents in the limitless steppes; the Eskimos in their igloos in the land of ice.

And the girls in the tent were so pretty: a peasant or nomadic longing stirred within me. In the desert of Sind, at the shrine of that saint, beside the Indus, the talk of *murshid* and *murid* had brought to mind Tolstoy's and Lermontov's tales of the Caucasus. And here, beside one of the cold rivers that fed the Indus (green water turning muddy, transported in a lined canal to Karachi on its tropical, salty swamp nearly a thousand miles away), I felt taken back to a beginning: that life of animals and tents and the daily march. But what to me was the impulse of the moment was for them a way of life. I would move on, do other things; they would continue as I saw them. And those girls, pretty as they were, with their lovely skins, were really far away, shut off in their own tribal fantasies, beauties now, well fed, conscious of their rising price, but soon to be wives and workers.

All afternoon we passed them, noted their tenderness to their animals, greater than their tenderness to themselves: those faces so lined and burnt, so old though young. Not many had the complexions and health of the girls in that encampment. Once I saw a man carrying a goat; once I saw a goat wrapped in a blanket and carried on a donkey's back. One woman walked with one shoe on, the other off, and on her head. It was a style, the shoe on the head: later we saw women with both shoes on their heads, the heels fitted one into the other to form a little arch. Shoes were worn when the ground was pebbly; when the ground was smooth or soft with dust it was better to walk barefooted. The ankles of the walkers were black with grime.

High up, at Shogran, it was overcast and cool, cold when it began to drizzle. The pines were immensely tall, and in places the land fell away so sharply from the road that it wasn't easy to look down to the roots of the pines. On the safer side of the twisting road there was peasant destruction: the barks of the great pines had been hacked away, for kindling. Kindling was scarce here, where there was so little flat land and so little vegetation, only pines growing in the thin drift of soil around rocks.

At dusk we were beside the river again. In a wide grassy clearing on the low bank many camps had been set up. Fires burned; tea was being prepared, *roti* being made; and here and there, for this evening meal, pieces of dried meat were being cut up. Camels (feeding before people) chewed their fodder. The camels of one camp were chewing holly branches. Just below the bank, on the rocks at the water's edge, in the dark all colours reduced to grey and white, were the ponies and other baggage animals, free at the end of their day.

The Afghans spread thick woollen rugs on the grass. I had noticed these rugs before. They were of undyed raw wool, dark-brown, with simple patterns in violent colours; and they smelled of sheep or goats, the Afghan smell, the smell that these nomads carried around with them. I was attracted to one rug; and at once Masood and the jeep driver – purely for pleasure, as it seemed – began to bargain for me. The old man, the head of the camp, friendlier than our earlier kohl-eyed dandy, asked for 400 rupees. The jeep driver said it was too much. But we sat down with the other men of the camp and drank cups of sweet tea.

Masood then led me away, leaving the jeep driver to complete the business. We looked at the baggage animals chewing at their leaves and branches; we walked among the tents and the cooking fires; we walked among the donkeys at the edge of the rocky river bed. When we got back, the deal had been done: 300 rupees.

Everybody was happy. Hands were shaken all round; and the jeep driver, triumphant, took up the rug as though he had really been bargaining for himself. But I must have been affected by the altitude. When I looked at the rug in Rawalpindi later I was astonished not only by its great size – at dusk, beside the river, I had thought it smallish – but also by the oddity of its pattern and colours, like the dots and wavering scrawls of an inflamed mind, work from the asylum. And perhaps to live that nomadic life is to be touched in the head in some way.

The road climbed again. Even in the darkness the river showed white, breaking over rocks. The rocks grew larger; they grew enormous; once or twice the road passed below overhangs of rock. In the flat-roofed, multi-level houses on the hillsides there were yellow lights. Lights alone marked the houses, defined interiors; and gave a feeling of bareness and solitude.

There was no solitude on the road. Sometimes people had camped just below it; in one place a man appeared to be asleep on the rock walling that shored up the road. Once we passed a whole camp spread out beside the road: twig fires, tents, sheep settled down for the night and looking in the darkness like the smooth rocks at the edge of the river bed. The camp dogs, the thick-furred dogs of the region, barked and raced after us.

Ever since the light had gone the jeep driver had been playing Indian film songs on his cassette player. Sad sweet songs of love and loss and longing accompanied us through the dark valley; and always it was a woman who lamented.

> *Tum zindagi-ko ghumka fasana bana-gé.*
> *Ankho men intizar-ki duniya jagga-gé.*
> You have made my life a tale of sorrows.
> In my eyes you have awakened a world of longing.

Untranslatable, that magical second line, with its unexpected conceit, that world (*duniya*) of longing (*intizar-ki*) awakened (*jagga-gé*) in the lover's eyes (*ankho*). It was the line that had kept the song alive for forty years; whenever the line came around again on the tape the driver's boy sang it.

> *Ik tees si dilmen ut-ti hai.*
> *Ik dard sa dilmen hota hai.*
> A sort of dirge rises in my heart.
> A kind of pain happens in my heart.

People were still on the march, though the night was now advanced; there seemed to be no set hours for marching and camping. Once we slowed down for a group chasing a bull which, all alone, had broken away from the caravan and was running back hard the way it had come.

Then we appeared to lose the road. We got out of the jeep. It was very dark. The driver sent his boy ahead to prospect, and then went to prospect himself. He came back, and drove the jeep on slowly, leaving us where we were. We lost the jeep's lights. The boy, returning, led us forward with the help of a flashlight. He offered me his little hand: his touch was unexpectedly gentle. We seemed to be walking over mud and rocks. We saw the jeep's lights again. In the blackness it was hard to assess distance. The lights of the jeep seemed far away, as though the driver had gone some way before finding the road again. But then, seconds later, the jeep was just there, a few steps ahead.

It seemed we had been walking over mud and rocks. But later, on the way back, in daylight, I saw that a glacier had come down and cut the road. The snow hung over the stone retaining wall of the road. The snow on its surface was old and dirty; but below that seemingly solid snow there was, at the end of the Himalayan summer, a great white cavern, and out of that dripping cavern there flowed a torrent.

We were now among glaciers and torrents. The chilling sound of water was everywhere.

The rest house at Naran was lit up, but no one answered. At Balakot, when we were bargaining for the jeep, the jeep driver had said there was a government hotel that charged 125 rupees for a room. Now he said the charge was over 200. Since I was calculating for four rooms – myself, Masood, the car driver who had brought us from Rawalpindi to Balakot (and had since been silent and self-effacing), the driver of the jeep with his boy – my heart sank. But Masood, who, with his anxiety about infections, also had something like a hypochondria about money, about being overcharged, Masood said that he had made it clear that the jeep driver and his boy had to make their own arrangements. But it wasn't to the government place that the jeep driver took us, but to the Park Hotel, whose bright crude boards we had seen at various places on the road.

The Park was a long low building set well back from the road; it had a dimly lighted verandah. The driver blew the horn, and a man in a blanket came out from a smaller building at the side of the plot. It was cold, had been cold for some time; but there was no warm room in the hotel to go to. The man with the blanket showed us a bedroom: two wood-framed beds, wall lights. He and Masood bargained, and Masood took me out from the cold bedroom to the freezing verandah to tell me that if an extra bed were placed in the room, I would be charged seventy-five rupees. So from being a traveller with a little caravan, faced with a bill of a hundred dollars for the night, I had become part of a dormitory and liable only to a charge of seven dollars and fifty cents. I said I would sleep alone; I said I was a bad sleeper. Masood talked with the smiling hotel man, and it was agreed that the extra room would add twenty-five rupees to the bill.

I asked for a fire in my room. The hotel man smiled and said it wasn't possible. The chimney didn't work; the room would be full of smoke if he lighted a fire. That explained the comparative cleanliness of the fireplace. I asked for hot tea. Yes, that would come, with the dinner. What about the dinner? What did I want?

Did they have eggs? No, there were no eggs. I thought of the clear river and said, 'Trout?' Masood, translating for me, repeated the English word: 'Trout?' The hotel man swung his head in affirmation and said, 'Trout.' And Masood, still translating, said there was trout.

Masood said, 'Forty rupees for the permit.'

'Permit? Do you have to have a permit for everything?' The word had made me think of the trouble I had had in Rawalpindi in posting books and changing traveller's cheques.

Masood said, huffily, 'No.'

It was too cold to talk any more about permits. I had looked forward to the cold. But now it was like pain; and the room seemed to grow icier every minute. I had no woollen shirt or pullover with me. I decided to put on a second shirt below my safari shirt. When they saw me stripping they left the room and went out to the verandah. The door remained open; it was a freezing kind of half privacy. I would have preferred the company, even a little help. My fingers were too numb to manage the buttons easily; and all around there was the very cold sound of tumbling water.

When, double-shirted, I went out to the verandah, the hotel man had four limp trout to show: he clearly hadn't had far to go. The jeep driver and his khaki-shawled boy now left us. As Masood had said, they had made their own arrangements; some warm mud-roofed peasant house no doubt awaited them.

Masood and I (and our own silent driver) went to the kitchen, for the warmth. It was in the smaller building at the side of the plot. And though we had arrived only minutes before, though the negotiations had only just been completed and the four trout had only just been bought, there was a veritable staff at work in the kitchen on our dinner, and a wood fire was burning below a baking iron, and a man in a long-tailed blue shirt was flattening balls of dough between his hands for the *roti*, the tail of his shirt jumping with every festive gesture, and the trout had been filleted and sliced and spiced and laid out on a low wooden table.

I stood before the fire, in the way of the cooks. Masood sat on a cane-bottomed chair in front of the low table. We both constantly moved to close the kitchen door; the staff as regularly, going in or coming out, left it open. Nothing was as important as the fire: not the state of the table on which the blue-shirted man was dusting the dough balls in flour, not the quality of the water, in the red plastic bucket, not the chipped low table on which the filleted trout lay.

The cook, always brisk, and satisfied now with his *roti*, used a knife to scrape off old charred fat from the round baking iron. He threw oil on the iron, withdrew the blazing wood to moderate the heat, put the fillets on the iron, put an aluminium pot-lid on the fillets, bent down to pick up an old brick from the blackened floor, and put the brick on the pot-lid.

Masood said, 'Shall we eat the dinner right here?'

He spoke my thoughts. And that was where we ate.

A big, grand-looking man came in, with a fur cap and a slate-blue shawl. He wasn't a villager or a man of the mountains. I thought he might have been a landowner or someone connected with the hotel; or a policeman, someone from an intelligence department, come to have a look at the strangers. He said he was a 'compounder', a chemist or druggist. He had a shop in Balakot, and a shop here in Naran. I said, 'So you have two shops?' He said, 'I have one shop.' The Naran shop was open in summer (officially, that was still the season); the Balakot shop was open in the winter.

There was, in addition to the trout, a dish of meat for Masood and our silent driver (self-effacing even in the matter of food: he was anxious to appear to be eating less than Masood or myself). Hunger and cold made Masood forget himself, forget his anxiety about infections. He asked for water, with his meat. The kitchen boy, who had been staring at us all the time, leaning against the fireplace platform, dipped a glass into the red plastic bucket, handed the dripping glass to Masood, and Masood drank to the end.

The compounder went away. He had had little to say, after he had told us what he did and where he lived and had found out who we were and what languages we spoke. The blue-shirted cook pulled out the wood from the fireplace. The flames were beaten out; the embers darkened fast. The kitchen was no longer open to us; we had to go out into the cold again. But the food had warmed us. It seemed less cold in the yard, less cold in the room. But Masood had been touched by the solitude and desolation of the valley. He stayed in my room to talk of himself and his anxieties.

His anxieties were about his father and his family and about money. He felt he should be supporting his family; but he was in no position to do that. At the same time he was anxious about his own scientific career, which had stalled for lack of money. He was twenty-seven; he had been a student all his life; and for some time yet, because of the field he had chosen, he had to continue being a student. It was hard on his father. His father hadn't complained; all his father's pride lay in his children and their education.

'My father can't go on working. He works so hard, from morning till night. He is a man of sixty-one.'

'But if he retires he will have nothing to do.'

'You don't understand. I have told you what my father's rank was in the army. My father was a non-commissioned officer, a very junior man. You don't know what that means here.'

At sixty-one, his father was earning 1,700 rupees a month as an accountant. And Masood was tormented by this and by his own helplessness, and also by his need to stick to his field.

'It's not an applied field. If it was an applied field, there would be money in it.'

'Do you want to leave Pakistan?'

'I don't want to leave. There are jobs here I can get. But right now the government has stopped recruiting people. It might be temporary, this stopping. But I don't know. I applied for a scholarship at an American university. They turned me down. They said that people from Indo-Pak were abusing the student's visa. They got the visa and went and worked for a month or so, and then they disappeared. I can go to England, to

Telford. They've given me a place. But where am I going to get the money? In some countries you can believe in the life of struggle. You can believe there will be results. Here there is only luck. In this country you can only believe in luck.'

He didn't know how directly he was speaking to me. The idea of struggle and dedication and fulfilment, the idea of human quality, belongs only to certain societies. It didn't belong to the colonial Trinidad I had grown up in, where there were only eighty kinds of simple job, and the quality of cocoa and sugar was more important than the quality of people. Masood's panic now, his vision of his world as a blind alley (with his knowledge that there was activity and growth elsewhere), took me back to my own panic of thirty to thirty-five years before.

Masood's parents had migrated to Pakistan from India in 1947. They had migrated, as Muslims, to a Muslim state ruled by Muslim beliefs. The state hadn't altered; but Masood, liberated by that migration, had evolved; he (and his father) needed more than a Muslim state now. The regret Masood said his father sometimes felt about leaving India was both right and wrong: Masood's father, in 1979, was not the man he had been in 1947. Masood himself, who knew only Pakistan, had no re-ligious or political heroes; his Pakistani hero was a scientist, Abdus Salam, who worked in Europe (and a few weeks later was to be awarded a Nobel prize).

Masood said, 'They can give me a job at a university. I used to have one. But I no longer have it. Everything here is politics. For people to give me a job now will be for them to get into trouble with the author-ities. I've been active in student politics.'

'How good are you?'

'I was one of the five best in my university.'

He had talked of a thesis, the work he was doing, a doctorate he might soon be getting from a local university. Now, surprisingly, he said, 'In a month I may be going away. A friend has arranged a contract for me with a West African college.'

'Which one?'

'A college.'

'What's the name?'

'It doesn't have a name. It's just a college. A secondary school. They call it a college. I've worked out how much they will pay. Thirty-six hundred rupees a month.' Three hundred and sixty dollars.

'That isn't a lot.'

'My friend says I can live on 800 rupees.'

'I don't think that will be possible.'

'So I will save 20,000 rupees.'

'What about the tax? Have you found out about that?'

'I haven't found out about that. But it will solve the money problem for me.'

'Will it damage your career?'

He said irritably, 'Of course it will damage my career.'

'Don't go.'

'It will solve the money problem. I have to look after my family. My father is a man of sixty-one.'

A year: ten months perhaps. I said, 'All right. Go. It will improve your English too.'

He didn't like that. 'In "English as a Foreign Language" I did well.' He gave the percentage. His English was variable, though. But he was a man of degrees and diplomas.

The smiling hotel man came in.

Masood said, 'He wants the forty rupees for the fishing permit now. The rest he will take tomorrow.'

He had also brought for the bed not a sheet – for which I had asked and which I thought he had promised – but a table-cloth. He took off the heavy eiderdown; spread the table-cloth evenly on the bed, as on a table; folded the eiderdown and left it at the bottom of the bed. Then he was gone.

I began to make the bed up.

Masood told me it was important to have the sheet (or table-cloth) below the eiderdown. 'You don't know who's been using it.' He demonstrated. 'Sleep in it like this. Don't let the eiderdown touch you.' This kind of bed-making was something he – like me – had had to learn. In hot countries you don't sleep below a blanket; you use a cotton sheet to cover yourself. What Masood was passing on to me was knowledge he had acquired. He had come from so far; he had had so much to learn; he had no one to follow. His simple origins showed in the way – when eating – he spat things out on the floor; his distance from those origins (mingling now with his general anxiety) was expressed in his fussiness and hypochondria.

He said, pointing to the pillow, which had a green damask-like cover, 'And cover that too.'

When he left I did that, using the safari shirt I had worn during the day, putting the outside of the shirt against the pillow. I drew the thin cotton curtains; they didn't meet. It was cold, but the eiderdown was heavy and comforting. In no time I was lulled by my own trapped warmth. I fell asleep to the roar of water. And – to my relief and pleasure – when I woke up it was morning.

I had thought it was the river roaring. I saw now that it was a waterfall, tumbling down the hill which was just at the back of the Park Hotel. At the foot of the hill, at the side of the hotel, a stone channel led the water away. In this valley of melting snow, canals were not for irrigation but to prevent flooding.

The hills at the far side of the valley – beyond the hotel yard or plot, the main road where blanketed men and boys were walking, the low houses of the little town, the hidden river – were lit up by the morning sun, and the folds in the hills were soft and hazy. The sun hadn't yet risen over the hill at the back of the hotel; the hill and the hotel were still in shadow. But a little way down, where the hill dipped, the sun shone through the branches of some pines: a narrow shaft of light, creating a transparent, ferny effect.

The smiling hotel man brought tea for three. He set the tray in my room. I went to get our driver and Masood. But Masood was locked away in the bathroom, and didn't appear for some time. When he did appear he said he hadn't slept well. His stomach was upset. What had he had that I hadn't had? The meat? The water? Yes, it was the water.

He said, 'The water here looks pure. But it has certain minerals. Have you been to Gilgit?' Gilgit was further to the north. 'The water there is *black.*'

He had his pills, though. But then, immediately afterwards, the other side of his nature coming out, he sat down and ate right through the starchy hotel breakfast of thick fried bread-slices and limp, oily potatoes, green with curry.

It was a small settlement of low stone houses, nondescript, some old, some government-built and new (the roof of the government hotel was bright red); and it ended abruptly in wilderness, after the bazaar. Some of the shops or stalls had cooking platforms. Scummy water from the shops ran out into the rocky road; there were animal droppings; the softer ground between the rocks was churned black. Sheep and cattle, even at this early hour, were being driven down.

Comfortless as the settlement was, makeshift and half ruined as the bazaar looked, the site was old, on an old mountain route. And the route was peopled: always there were the flat-roofed houses, set against the hillsides and the road embankment and half hidden, the thick roofs of insulating mud supported on heavy beams or tree-trunks, that could in addition take the winter snow. Winter kindling – drying pine branches, shrubs – lay on the roofs and was like a further camouflage.

Sometimes in pebbly, rock-buttressed terraces grew poor crops of potatoes or peppers or maize (wheat the early summer crop, maize the late summer crop, millet the winter crop). Grain and potatoes – and peppers! Pines were scattered. Grass grew in tufts on the steep mountain sides, creating a mottled effect, and suggesting, when you rose above them and looked down, hills or mountains netted with goat tracks.

Snow, melted now, had scoured and abraded the mountains. Old snow lay in clefts and the colour of this snow was indeterminate: not white, not brown, more like a water-surface catching the light. This old snow was firm on the surface; but – though winter was about to come again – the snow was melting, and each snow cleft fed a torrent. At 10,000 feet the land opened out between the mountains: blackened remnants of snow in shadowed crevices; snow thick and white on the mountain tops, softening sharp lines; moss growing on the cleansed red rock of sunlit mountain sides; and, in the middle of the openness, a green lake, with a meadow with forget-me-nots and the small yellow flowers of a summer water meadow, growing for the few weeks before the snow came again. On the far side of the lake there were a few tents, the tents of the nomads: dark triangles against white canvas. The traffic of men and animals never stopped.

On the way back, down the valley again, the jeep driver stopped near an Afghan encampment. He shouted out to the girl or woman preparing *roti* in front of her tent. When she understood what the jeep driver was saying she smiled and shook her head. Masood said he was asking for some kind of root. It was a medicinal root; it cured pain. I later thought it was probably ginseng.

The jeep driver had other concerns as well. Many times, this morning, he stopped to chat to the drivers of minibuses. He was a man of local reputation, our jeep driver; I hadn't guessed that on the way out. So he was more than a man of the mountains; his elegance – the full white trousers, the tan shirt, the beautiful hair – was studied.

The whispers now, with the other drivers! The air of conspiracy! I thought he might have been asking for another kind of root or drug, less healing. But he was talking about politics, about the local elections the military government had decreed. In spite of the goats and the sheep and the camels and the tents and the cooking fires and the Afghans with their red-and-black costumes and their silver jewellery, the valley was full of politics. The jeep driver's party was the party of Mr Bhutto. Mr Bhutto had been hanged five months before; but his party still drew the people's affections in the valley.

Mr Bhutto, the jeep driver said, was the only man in Pakistan who had ever done anything for the poor. Before Mr Bhutto, in the time of General Ayub (ruled 1958–68), poor people could get passports only for countries like Afghanistan and India, bad countries, countries with no jobs, no opportunities. In Mr Bhutto's time you could get passports for everywhere – Europe, America, Saudi Arabia, Abu Dhabi, everywhere. Now once again you couldn't get passports.

Masood (wearing a blue nylon zip-up windcheater and an embroidered white skull-cap) said to me in English, 'It's the foreign governments that stopped it. But he doesn't think so.'

The jeep driver said he was born in the valley. His father kept a shop; so he was better off than most. He became interested in politics only in the time of Mr Bhutto. 'This place,' he said (in Masood's translation), 'had big landlords in the old days. They grew their three crops a year. They sold their crops. They got local people to work for them, and the people worked for them only for food. This is what used to happen in this place.'

And that bridge there, across the Kunhar River, that bridge was built by Mr Bhutto.

The jeep driver talked on, whipping himself up. He seemed quite different from the man who had driven us into the valley, who had been playful enough to bargain for the Afghan rug for me. Masood stopped translating.

After a while Masood said, 'He's being emotional now. Very emotional. He is saying that Mr Bhutto isn't dead.'

We had travelled out with sad and sweet film songs about love: they had given a mood to the dusk and the river and the lights of the far-off houses. We were travelling back with this other passion. And I began to look at the people on the road with another eye: they were the poor, the neglected. But that wasn't quite what the driver was seeing.

'These maulanas,' the driver said, in Masood's translation, 'are using Islam as a tool. We are all Muslims. We are not Muslims in their way. They want to destroy Pakistan. Our Islam is better. We are the only people who can save Islam and Pakistan.'

We had to stop. A truck was being loaded with pine logs. The logs were being manhandled from the mountain side on to the truck. The road was narrow; we had to wait until the log-loading was completed. A red Suzuki minibus was waiting ahead of us. We got out. The road was trampled into fine dust by the flocks that had passed. The jeep driver scrambled up the road cutting to talk to the loaders, and then to sit and watch them.

Masood and I stood beside the gorge of the Kunhar.

Masood said, 'I agree with what he says about the maulanas. It is my attitude. There is fifteen percent literacy in this place.'

I said, 'But isn't it strange that the only freedom he wants is the freedom to leave the country? He doesn't have any idea that the country might be developed, that there might be jobs here.'

Masood didn't understand at first. The idea of escape was too much in his own mind. When he did understand he said, 'But the rulers of the country have never had that idea or given people that idea. Now the army is in control.'

So now, seeing them as the poor and the unrepresented, and not as people wearing a certain kind of costume or having a certain cast of features, I considered the labourers, the herdsmen, and the idle people watching the log-loading, above the green-and-white river. And something of Masood's gloom and the jeep driver's hysteria touched me.

I said, 'What will happen to these people?'

Masood said, 'God alone knows.'

Later he said, '*Nothing* will happen. *What* will happen?' And later still, after a flock of dyed sheep picked its way past us, grinding the fine dust finer, causing it to rise, colouring his white skull-cap and greying his walrus moustache, Masood said, looking down into the river, 'They have empty hands. They don't have guns. *Millions* will have to die.' And that was not rebellion speaking; that was despair. 'Do you know how many political parties there are in this country? There are ninety-four political parties in this country. *What* can happen?'

I said, 'When did you start getting worried about the future?'

'1971.' That was the year of Bangladesh. 'No, I think it was before. I think I started worrying about the future in matriculation.'

Masood had misunderstood my question. I had asked about Pakistan. But he was so choked by his own anxieties that he had taken the question to refer to himself. He had taken the question to be a continuation of our talk the previous evening.

The jeep driver was sitting on the hillside, knees up, white-trousered legs apart, watching the loaders.

Masood said, 'I used to do tuitions. I used to get 400 rupees a month for that. But I had to stop. The parents of the children treated me like a servant. They never treated me like a teacher. If I had to get to the house at four and got there at five, they made trouble. If their children failed they blamed me.'

Money, his career, his family: after the previous evening, these were the topics to which Masood returned.

He said, 'My father now asks himself why he came. "Why did I come? Where is the dignity I thought I was coming to?"' But that, as I had felt before, was only half true. Masood's father, the Muslim army sergeant, migrating to Pakistan in 1947, had found the dignity he had wanted in 1947.

The truck was loaded at last. The heavy logs were beaten into place with staves; and ropes were twisted tight around the logs. The truck moved off. The red Suzuki minibus moved off. We followed, after a tussle with the opposing traffic that had also built up.

We stopped at the town of Jared. It was famous for its woodcarving. But the examples I saw were poor – wooden daggers, trays, ashtrays: poor design, poor carving. Masood bought a walnut ashtray for fifteen rupees. Clearly there was once a tradition; now the absence of skill, eye, judgement, was like part of the human desolation.

We passed the truck with the logs again, and then again we were behind the little red Suzuki. We ate their dust.

All at once there appeared to be some kind of commotion at the back of the Suzuki. Someone was hurled out on to the road. And then someone else was thrown out.

I said, 'They are throwing people out of the bus.'

Masood said, 'A fight.'

The Suzuki was moving on. But then it stopped. We avoided the first man; he was uninjured, and on his feet again. Then we passed a young boy or man – his slack, string-tied trousers opened, his genitals exposed – lying on the road. People from the bus were already running up to him. We passed the Suzuki – there was no one in the driving seat – and stopped about a hundred yards ahead, where the road widened.

I didn't want to see blood. I was glad our driver had stopped where he had. What had happened wasn't clear. But the Suzuki's windscreen was smashed, and on the steep hillside above was the explanation: a herd of goats, part of the migration, wandering off the road. They had dislodged a stone; the stone had smashed the windscreen and wounded the driver. For some seconds the Suzuki would have been out of control on the mountain road. That was no doubt when one of the passengers at the back had thrown himself out. Then the wounded driver had fallen out; and someone, perhaps the man beside the driver, had brought the Suzuki to a halt.

The driver was now being lifted, to be brought to our jeep. And our jeep driver was climbing, surefootedly (he was a man of the region), up the rocky slope to where the goats and their herdsman were, high above the road. What was our driver doing? Why the haste? The answer was simple: it was to knock the herdsman about, to beat and drive him down to the road.

The quaint tribesman, the man driving his flocks down to their winter pasture, was now only someone very small and vulnerable. He was hit about the face and abused by our driver. His black turban – his dignity – fell loose from his bald head, became a dingy length of cotton; and he was pushed and punched all the way down, leaving his precious goats behind. There, on the road, various people from the Suzuki took runs at him and punched him and then ran back to where they had been standing. Then anger came to them again, and they ran up again to the old herdsman – crying, and without his turban looking as small as a child – and beat him about the head and chest.

I said to Masood, 'They're going to kill that man.'

Masood said, 'No. They're going to stop beating him now. You see, they've put him in the bus. Now they're going to take him to the police station.'

But it had been an accident. And what about the man's goats? But it was the custom of the place; Masood saw nothing to object to. Yet our jeep driver had spoken so feelingly about the poor. The poor were his fellows, people of the valley; outsiders were not among his poor.

They brought the Suzuki driver to our jeep. He was unconscious. One man held him in his arms in the front seat. Masood and I sat on a back seat; the jeep driver's boy held on to the back of the jeep. The wounded man wasn't bleeding.

Masood said, 'His wounds are internal. They say it was a very big stone that fell down and hit him as he was driving.'

I had thought, seeing him half-exposed on the road, that he was a boy or a very young man. I saw now that he was older; that he was very thin, with a face and body shrunken from undernourishment. He remained unconscious. The man cradling him spoke to him softly, as to a child. But the wounded man never replied, never opened his eyes.

We drove as fast as we could down the Kaghan Valley to Balakot, beside the Kunhar gorge, the lines of the hills, the tall pines, the terracings of maize, the flat-roofed houses. From time to time Masood or the jeep driver felt the unconscious man's cheek with the back of a hand. They said he was alive; but he never stirred or made a noise.

For an hour or so we drove. And when we got to Balakot, to the little grey hospital, there were only children in the yard, and no one came out to take the wounded man. The doctor had gone to Peshawar; the compounder was in Mansehra. It was to Mansehra that the wounded man had to be taken. But that was no longer our responsibility; we had to surrender our jeep.

And the responsibility of the jeep driver was also at an end. There was nothing more he could do. He had worked himself up into a political passion; he had expressed this passion in his persecution of the Afghan herdsman, his tenderness towards the wounded man. But his solicitude – and his sense of drama – could not survive the long, exacting mountain drive to Balakot. When we left him there – handsome, idle – he was like a man enervated and empty.

We drove away – in our borrowed car and with our borrowed driver –

through the late afternoon and early evening. After the mountains, the land was softer, drier, with more varied vegetation.

Neither Masood nor I spoke much. There was little to say. Masood's troubles made him heavy, made neutral conversation difficult.

The bicycles on the road carried no lights. The buses and trucks often had no lights at the back, because there was no point in lighting up where you had been. The horse-carriages had no lights at all.

I said, with sudden irritation, 'They have no lights.'

Masood said, flatly, 'They have no lights.'

I set him down on the Peshawar road – Peshawar, the military town to the west, in the flat wide valley leading to the Khyber Pass and another part of Afghanistan.

9

❖❖❖❖

Agha Babur

IN RAWALPINDI the newspapers carried news of government cuts. Six ministries were to be wound up. There were to be economies in Baluchistan: no new jobs were to be created, and there were to be no salary rises for people in jobs. Twenty-nine officials of the Weights and Measures Department were to be dismissed. The *Pakistan Times* said that the officials concerned had 'urged the government to provide them alternative jobs to save them and their families from mental agony and starvation in these days of high prices'. According to *The Muslim*, however, the officials had only asked to be relieved of 'mental agony and frustration'.

The minibuses that plied between Rawalpindi and Islamabad had gone on a one-day strike to protest against police harassment. The bus drivers told the newspapers that the police wanted higher bribes. The police said the drivers had been 'misbehaving' with passengers.

Thirty-four teachers told *The Muslim* that they hadn't been able to leave for their jobs in Oman in south-east Arabia because the emigration authorities in Pakistan had raised questions about the teachers' 'no-objection' certificates. In the same issue of *The Muslim* there was an investigative report about the high costs of an extension to a government-run tourist inn in the far north: a job that should have taken seven months had taken five years.

In the *Pakistan Times* a retired army man wrote an article about indiscipline. 'It is now openly acknowledged that ours is a corrupt society, practising every conceivable social evil imaginable. Children growing up in a domestic atmosphere where smuggling, black-marketing, hoarding, bribery and corruption . . . are indulged in quite blatantly, should not be expected to accept discipline in any form. When these children go to the educational institutions, they naturally try to project the home atmosphere there . . .' The solution was a greater firmness, 'an iron hand', in the schools (no politics to be allowed there), and in the courts. 'Imprisonment, flogging and even capital punishment will do the needful.'

On the wider subject of the Pakistan crisis there was an urgent leader-page article in *The Muslim* by A. H. Kardar, the former cricket captain of Pakistan, and an Oxford man. 'We look back in shame and anger at the utter lack of homework and preparedness of political leaders and administrators vis-à-vis economic issues . . . shame and anger at the ever-increasing shipload of imports of foodgrains . . .' What – after this passion – was his solution? Nothing concrete. Only, less politics; and a little more of what had gone before. 'Clearly, the choice is between materialism and its inseparable nationally divisive political manifestos, and the Word of God.'

With all this there was a review in the *Pakistan Times* of an Arts Council art exhibition. The artist was Hameed Sagher. It was his first show; and the reviewer was at once frank and tender.

'As one enters the aged hall of the Council's premises, and treads the wooden floor, the eye is caught by a number of bright panels and the mind is gripped by conflicting reaction to these panels. There is a bewildering variety of techniques and styles . . . To understand all that variety of styles, some of them clash with each other, one has to know a few things about the artist. Hameed Sagher was poet for some time. Then he started the vocation of art in the commercial field with a professional experience as his guide. He has no formal training as an artist . . . As a poet he is fascinated by ideas. As an artist he has to capture those ideas in colours and he feels inspired by the provocative ideas of his friends. He therefore has developed a tension with which he illustrates his ideas rather vehemently and sometimes rather obviously . . .

'His "Intellect" looks a head on fire. The panel captioned as "Struggle" in pastels is hands with fire emanating from them. "The Movement" is another rendering a political struggle in flames and smoke. Somewhere in patches the cool green tends to disturb the fiery impact of figures on fire. "The Pray" is hands in supplication, with big eyes looking in between and minaret with birds around it . . . The bright colours, the movement and the tension hold out a promise. With more experience, and less of economic pressures, Hameed Sagher is bound to emerge as a significant artist.'

The exhibition was in the Freemasons' Hall. The Freemasons had been banned a few years before as a Zionist organization (and also, I was told, because they exalted Solomon above all other prophets); and their hall had been taken over by the Arts Council.

It was in the street at the back of Flashman's Hotel, a street of shawl

sellers and carpet sellers and cloth sellers. It was a solid brick building of
the British period – Public Works Department style – with a lawn, a
semi-circular drive, arched windows and a portico. On the pediment of
the portico was still the Freemason emblem of the two dividers, like an
unfinished star. (Rawalpindi was full of these usurpations, these reminders of expulsions and the cleansed land. The president's house had
belonged to a Sikh; Poonch House, one of the palaces of the Hindu
maharaja of Kashmir, was due for demolition.)

The man responsible for the Hameed Sagher exhibition was Agha
Babur. He was a humorous middle-aged man, slender and attractive,
with a fringe of white hair, long at the back. His office was in a room off
the exhibition hall. He was busy – the vernissage was to be that
afternoon – but he gave me a little time.

A woman of some size (Agha Babur's wife: he told me later that her
health was not good) sat silent but companionable at one side of Agha
Babur's desk. A deferential man from the radio faced him across the
desk. I sat at the free side of the desk.

Agha Babur had written the short note about Hameed Sagher's work
in the catalogue card.

'I had to write it. It is important for our artists that they should have
these brochures of their exhibitions when they go abroad. They can't
just show a price list. People abroad in France and Germany and Italy
wouldn't give them exhibitions if they just show a price list. They
need these brochures.'

The Hameed Sagher prices were not high: from fifty rupees to 200,
five dollars to twenty dollars.

Agha Babur was in the army before he joined the Arts Council. 'I
came to the Arts Council because it was a sinking ship. I brought it on the
map. I was able to do so because I am a man of ideas. I will give you an
example. 1975 was the Year of Tourism. The ministry here was doing
nothing about it. Tourism in the beginning didn't do well here. I wrote
letters to all the embassies here to please get me their tourist posters. I
got posters from ten countries and we held an International Exhibition of
touristic posters. We gave prizes. We gave the first prize to Poland, the
second prize to Turkey, the third prize to Spain. We had to give it to
Spain. They had a poster of a bullfight.'

Sitting in his chair, making toreador's gestures with his hands, he did
a sudden sideways arch with the upper part of his body; and his eyes
danced with pleasure.

'Full of *movement*. So this got publicity in all those countries. I wrote
a letter to the minister here saying, "This is what I've done. Your
department is *sleepy*." And he said, "Agha Babur, you are a man of

ideas.'' I didn't leave it there. I got him to get the ministry to give me troph-ies.' He made the word rhyme with 'toffees'. 'And we gave out these troph-ies, and that was projected on the TV in Warsaw and Ankara and Spain.

'The ideas come to me just like that. In the morning, when I shave. For example. This is the fourteenth century of the Islamic *hijra*. Our President said this in Havana: "Fourteen hundred years ago a revolution took place."'' (The President had said that a few weeks before at a meeting of non-aligned countries, which Pakistan had just joined.) 'Now that gave me an idea. You're the first person I'm telling. You have that privilege. When we enter into the new *hijra* I'm going to arrange an exhibition on the calligraphy of the Holy Koran.'

In the Hameed Sagher brochure Agha Babur had written: 'Hameed Sagher utilizes a poetic atmosphere in his paintings where the retranslation of nostalgia and agony is represented in a naive style. He is searching for identity and strength . . . His work represents an individualism of the artist who is confronted with half baked, mixed feelings as if closeted and couched in the treasure cave of Ali Baba.' And it was signed, in a stylish cursive type: *Agha Babur*.

He was waiting for a response from me. I read out the last sentence to him. He seemed to enjoy it. Agha Babur, Ali Baba: perhaps the first (Agha Babur liked using his own name) had suggested the second.

We talked about English in Pakistan. I said that not many people spoke it. He disagreed, but then appeared to agree. 'The spoken language may be dying. But not the written language. Although I am proud of Urdu, I never forget I am also an Englishman.' He meant a speaker of English. 'We have this English language now. All the Arabs and Persians would like to have it. It would be bad if we lose it. Now when our Pakistani delegate gets up at the United Nations and makes a speech for two, three hours in this beautiful English, the Arabs run to him at the end and embrace him. We can't lose this English.

'My teacher was Bukhari. The great Bukhari. A terror. He would fling the paper back at you. Back in your face. "Call this writing? Call this English?" He said something that lodged in my head. He said, "Writing now is pain. All the rest is pleasure. Remember that. But the day will come when writing will be pleasure, and all the rest will be pain." Wasn't that a good thing to say? "Writing is pain; all the rest is pleasure. But the day will come – "'

He broke off and said, 'You are like my friend Caro-leen in the United States. She too used to make notes of the things I said.'

I was writing on the edges of the little catalogue card.

'She was my guide in the United States. A divorcee. I was a cultural guest of the State Department. Caro-leen said to me, "Agha Babur, most people come to the east line and feel they've seen the United States. At the most they make a trip to Los Angeles on the west line. And then they feel they've seen the United States. You are the first one I know to come to Utah. What are you interested in?" I said, "Being a Muslim, the polygamy." That was a joke. She told me about a plan for a theatre in a department store. I said, "Caro-leen, you are putting art in the window shop." The show window, the shop window. Whatever I said was correct. She was driving. She pulled out a pad with one hand and began to write. I said, *"Caro-leen!* What are you doing?" She said, "Agha Babur, I just have to make a note of the things you say."'

He took down an encyclopaedia. On the small map of the United States he had marked his cultural route in blue ink. He had also been to Florida, to Disneyworld.

The vernissage was to be at 5.30. But this was Pakistan, and the man who was to make the opening speech and cut the ribbon was the ambassador of Iraq. I thought I could get there at six. But, because the hall was so near the hotel, and because I dawdled to look at the shawls and carpets, I arrived at five past six. There was a policeman at the gate. In the lawn, for the refreshments, there was a *shamiana*, a decorated canvas enclosure. And I was hopelessly late. The speeches had already been made.

Agha Babur, with his military background, had started on time. He had asked the ambassador to arrive seven minutes after the official opening time, at 5.37; and the ambassador had done precisely that. When I went into the hall with its bare old floorboards, the official group was going round the paintings: the ambassador in a dark three-piece suit, Agha Babur in a light-grey lounge suit, the artist in a white Pakistani costume with a fawn-coloured woollen jerkin. The ambassador, thick-set, looked earnest and pained and listened with his head to one side; the artist was small, shy, overwhelmed by the occasion, and altogether winning; Agha Babur was courtly and distinguished, and artistic with his long white hair.

The hall was full. Agha Babur had done it again. In the social desert of Rawalpindi he had created another occasion. And the exhibition was a success. Twelve of the paintings had already been sold. The Iraqi ambassador had bought five (including the head on fire, 'Intellect'); the man from the Indonesian embassy had bought two; the East German ambassador or his representative had bought one, as had the Russian ambassador (who couldn't speak Urdu, but understood Persian, and had felt the long fingers of the artist and pronounced them 'artistic').

I met a friend of the artist. He was a teacher; and the small young man with him was also a teacher. The young man – black hair sprouting from his narrow chest – had been in the army, but had left to be a teacher. Now he wanted to go to England to do a thesis. Like many Pakistanis, he claimed to be more than a Pakistani. He said he was of Persian origin; his ancestor had come to India after the Indian Mutiny of 1857. (But that ancestor would only have been one out of sixteen.) He wanted to go to England to do a thesis on the political novel: E. M. Forster, Conrad, Graham Greene.

'Greene?'

'He wrote those three novels about Africa.'

'Three novels?' I tried to think.

'He wrote that novel about Africa. *Heart of* something.'

'*The Heart of the Matter*. I wouldn't call that political.'

'It is political. There is some dialogue there about natives being liars. But nobody said that it was because of colonialism that people called natives liars. People were made by colonialism. By history. But nobody says that.'

'But if you think like that, then everybody is a political writer.'

The young man – pale, thin – hadn't thought deeply about his thesis; that little idea was all that he had. Changing his tack, he said, 'What about Kipling?'

I said, 'Nobody has written as accurately about Indians. You can't fault Kipling there.'

But he didn't really know Kipling; he knew only the name. He became confidential. He said, 'I didn't want to do the English political novel. It was their idea. I really wanted to do Shakespeare's sonnets. But they said that was too much on the beaten track.'

'There's been a lot about the sonnets. What did you want to say about them?'

'I feel that Shakespeare was attracted to a young man. But people considered it unnatural.'

I thought that it might be better for him to leave the sonnets alone.

'And because they considered it unnatural – you see, I'm Persian. Do you know Hafiz, Saadi? People in Europe are very naïve about homosexuality.'

He was thirty. But he had read little; he knew little; he had few ideas. I don't think he wanted to do a thesis, really. He wanted a job; he wanted a visa and a no-objection certificate; he wanted to go away.

How could he read, how could he judge, how could he venture into the critical disciplines of another civilization, when so much of his own history had been distorted for him, and declared closed to inquiry? And how strange, in the usurped Freemasons' Hall of Rawalpindi, to talk of the English political novel and the distortions of colonialism, when in that city in a few weeks, in the name of an Islam that was not to be questioned, the whipping vans were to go out, official photographs were to be issued of public floggings, and one of the country's best journalists was to be arrested and photographs were to show him in chains.

10

❖❖❖❖

The Salt Hills of a Dream

THE EVENINGS were getting cooler in Rawalpindi; the summer was nearly over. But to take the short bus ride down from the Himalayan foothills to Lahore in the plains of the Punjab was to go down to where it was still very hot. It was also to go down from where farming depended on rainfall to where it depended on irrigation, fed by the rivers of the Punjab.

The irrigated plains of the Pakistan Punjab had been the granary of this part of the sub-continent. But the irrigation that blessed some fields cursed others. With no natural drainage in the Punjab soil, the water table had risen to within ten feet of the surface. Forty percent of the irrigated land was now waterlogged; a quarter of the land was spoilt by salt, white on the soil surface, black and more damaging below. The killer marched underground; but it was possible to see the next line of grown trees whose roots were to rot, the next area of fields where soon nothing would grow.

The village of Raiwind stood in the middle of an area of new desert. To drive out to it from Lahore was to see (because of the flatness of the land) hundreds of blighted square miles (with, here and there, rich green patches still). There was a big gathering at Raiwind. From far away it was like a fair: people going on foot along flat, straight paths to a great tent city, trucks and buses and horse-carriages, like miniatures in the distance, kicking up dust (but the ditches were full of water).

It was a religious occasion: in Pakistan the religious excitement never abated. There had been Ramadan and the festival at the end of Ramadan; there had been the excitements of the pilgrimage to Mecca; the Festival of the Sacrifice was soon to come. In the interval there was this: the assembly of a Muslim brotherhood dedicated to the idea that every Muslim was also a missionary for Islam.

They had come, at heaven knows what expense, from all parts of Pakistan and from many other countries as well. They were not among the poor, the people of this brotherhood; many of them were traders.

For three or four days they would listen to speeches and live and pray together. Raiwind, where no crops grew, provided a perfect open space. The land was so waterlogged, the water was so near the surface, that to walk in certain places was like walking on a spring mattress.

There were many refreshment tents with striped canvas walls. The main tented area was vast, with innumerable bamboo poles sticking out at varying angles from the hummocked white cover: lengths of white cotton hung on ropes tied to the bamboo poles, the cotton dipping and rising, loosely tacked together, so that in the immense covered area, where it was hard to see to the end, the white covering looked gashed and ripped, revealing bits of pale-blue sky and bits of the dazzling white of the top of the cotton where the sun struck. The gashes created irregular stripes of light that fell in broken segments on the people and the ground below. The effect below the white cotton, of filtered light rather than shade, was vaguely aqueous; and the rising and dipping of the cotton strips on their rope supports did suggest a kind of sea surface above. Here and there men were fanning turbanned holy men, sometimes with sheets; sometimes two men at a time lifted and dropped big white sheets, creating momentary canopies over the reclining holy men. There were mats and bedding rolls and water jars everywhere.

It was organized; every row had a number. I was passed from person to person, snatched at one stage from a developing conversation, and taken to the foreign enclave, where there were Arabs, Indonesians, and even Africans (clearly old hands at these international Muslim gatherings, unashamedly enjoying the ethnic sensation they and their costumes and their language were exciting). Snatched from a conversation there, I was led finally to the executive *shamiana*, where a scientist with a shaved head looked me over, before an air commodore with a wonderful white beard, sad eyes, and a tender manner came and talked to me about the after-life. That, he said, was one of the aims of the gathering, to get people to think seriously of the after-life.

They squatted before me on a cotton rug on the bare ground. The scientist said he had been to England at the end of the war; he had gone on a troopship. Even then he had seen signs of the sickness of the West, but he had held his peace; now of course the West admitted that it was sick.

The scientist said he didn't want to be 'divided', as his own father had been divided in British India: a Muslim at home, a European away from home. They -- he and everybody else at the assembly -- wanted to be Muslim in the way the earliest Muslims had been. When I asked in what detail his new behaviour differed from his old behaviour, I could get no direct answer.

THE SALT HILLS OF A DREAM

It was hot; the scientist with his shaved head was sweating. The turbanned air commodore was cooler, more impressive, too, more tormented. He wished to purge himself of thoughts of self, to do everything for the pleasure of Allah alone. But every action raised doubts; in every action he detected some debasing thought of self.

'Stay for our prayers,' he said. 'It sometimes has an effect on newcomers, seeing us all at prayer.'

But that was what I didn't want to stay for, and was anxious about: the prayers, the sight of a hundred thousand – or was it 200,000? – bowed in unison, in the avoidable desert of Raiwind.

On the way back I stopped at a village. No crops grew here now. The men were no longer peasants, but labourers who commuted to the city of Lahore, two hours away. Sub-surface water was the enemy: the simplest hole became a pool, and the village was full of stagnant pools, some quite large, rimmed with village debris. Green was missing. But somehow there were cattle; dung cakes, fuel, were drying on mud walls.

The men I talked to were sheltering from the sun in a ruined one-room building, of mud bricks, beside a pool. There was a house of some size further down the uneven dirt street. I was told it was a Muslim house. I thought it was a strange thing to say, until I understood that what was being said was that, before Pakistan, before 1947, the house had belonged to a non-Muslim. Now the village was all Muslim, pure. At prayer time – though no call came – two of the men got up to go to the mosque.

The land was salt. But the faith kept these men at peace.

And some were of such great faith that they had been taken out of the faith altogether. That had happened to the Ahmadis. It was to find out about them that I had come to Lahore.

The Ahmadis considered themselves the purest of Muslims. To their reverence for the Prophet they had grafted on a reverence for a Promised Messiah, Ahmad, who had appeared in India in the nineteenth century. Ahmad's followers, the Ahmadis, claimed that Ahmad had appeared to purify the decayed faith. To other Muslims this reverence for the Promised Messiah derogated from the Prophet's 'finality' as a prophet and was the blackest sort of blasphemy. There had been repeated campaigns against the followers of Ahmad; and in Mr Bhutto's time the hated Ahmadis had been declared non-Muslims.

My interest in the sect had begun with the Ahmadi woman civil servant I met in Karachi – the widow in the green sari. I had been struck by her education and dignity, her acceptance of persecution, her acceptance of the fact that it might be necessary for her and her children to leave Pakistan.

My hope, in coming to Lahore, was to visit the Ahmadi settlement at the little town of Rabwah, about a hundred miles away. But introductions were necessary; and it was not easy in Lahore to get introductions to Ahmadis. The Ahmadis themselves were, understandably, secretive. And Muslims not of the sect didn't want to know about them; they either pretended not to hear, or they raged.

I heard that the Ahmadis indulged in casuistry; that the man they publicly spoke about only as the Promised Messiah was accepted by them in private as a second prophet. I heard that the original Ahmad had been encouraged by the British, to divide Indian Muslims. I also heard that they were strong in the armed forces; that they were good businessmen and 'looked after their own'; that to become an Ahmadi was to be secure and looked after.

Then, through the son of a retired army officer, I met Colonel Anees, formerly of the Pakistan army. The colonel was of the sect; he had left the army because he felt that the prejudices – especially after the outlawing of the sect – were now too strong. He was forty-one, heavy but muscular, with powerful shoulders. He had a serene expression that seemed close to a smile. He had spent two years as a prisoner of war in India after the Bangladesh war in 1971. In the Indian camp he had read a lot, learned French, and done a number of fine, patient, photographic drawings in pencil. Some of his serenity would have come to him during those two years of withdrawal and mental concentration.

He was an easy man to like. It was harder to enter his prodigious faith. But he expected that: he said that to understand the Ahmadis it was necessary to know a lot about Islam, a lot. And I understood what he meant only after he had taken me to meet the Lahore leaders of the sect. He took me there late one afternoon, and left me to make out on my own.

A rich, suburban house, with three or four cars in the drive; a green, leafy garden; sliding timber-framed glass doors; a carpeted floor; reproduction furniture; low carved tables; modern Pakistani paintings; servants; tea. A strange setting – right perhaps only in its Indian-Victorian fussiness, the feeling it gave of being enclosed – for the exposition of religious mysteries that to me seemed to come from an antique world. And the men waiting for me – of varying ages: from the late thirties to the late sixties – might have been modern businessmen, from their dress, education, and manner. Some probably were businessmen. But they had an extra authority: they were men in their own estimation made tremendous by their faith.

It was not given to many to recognize a Messiah, to be among the first: to be linked in this way to the earliest believers in the Prophet's mission. The courage of those early believers was now vindicated, as theirs would be when the whole world turned to the Promised Messiah. And as a mark of their faith – in spite of persecution – some wore a very thin crescent of beard on the chin.

A hundred years before there was only Ahmad, one man. Now there were ten million Ahmadis all over the world. In a hundred years from now why not ten million times ten million? It was what the Lahore Imam or bishop (who had a crescent beard) had told a doubter in London. With that tremendous faith they could afford to laugh at scoffers, at 'vested interests'. True religion, the Imam said, was overlaid by 'culture'. Once that passing thing was seen through, religion became clear again.

There were always people who preferred to deny the signs, the Imam said. It had been prophesied, for instance, that when the Promised Messiah appeared or declared his mission there would be an eclipse both of the sun and the moon. When such eclipses had occurred in close conjunction in 1894, a doubter banged his head in frustration against a wall and said, 'Now that man' – the Promised Messiah '– is right!'But the doubter had not given up his doubt.

They laughed at the story, which they knew well. And there was a more recent story of disbelief and vested interest.

The Imam said, 'Last year there was a conference in London at the Commonwealth Centre. There were hundreds of delegates from various countries. There were scientists there. Some read papers. But the press ignored the conference. The TV people didn't send anyone.'

I said, 'What was the conference about?'

The oldest man said, 'It was about the deliverance of Christ from the cross.'

Christ hadn't died on the cross. He was only in a coma when he was taken down from the cross. The Turin shroud proved that blood had flowed from a man who was still living. Christ's broken limbs were healed and he went about preaching to the lost tribes of Israel. He made his way to Kashmir in northern India and died there at the age of 120.

I said, 'Who arranged this conference?'

The Imam was taken aback. 'We did.'

I was puzzled. But that belief about Christ was central to the Ahmadi faith.

Some Muslims believe (though there is no sanction for it in the Koran) that Christ (to Muslims, one of the prophets before Mohammed) will return to earth as the redeemer or the Mahdi. The Ahmadis say that the prophecy has been misinterpreted. For this reason: Christ is not alive in heaven somewhere, waiting to come back to earth; Christ is dead. He is dead because he was not taken up to heaven from the cross. He was taken down from the cross, healed, and went on with his preaching work until he was 120. He lived out his life as a man; it was a very long life; he cannot come back to earth for a second spell.

The true prophecy, according to the Ahmadis, was that someone *like* Christ was going to come back to earth as the Promised Messiah, to cleanse religion at a time of darkness and restore the purity of Islam. And that man was Ahmad, born in 1838 in the village of Qadian, now in India, just across the border from Pakistan. Jesus was born 1,300 years after Moses; Ahmad was born 1,300 years after the Prophet. Jesus was born in a Roman colony; Ahmad was born in a British colony. Those were just two of the numberless similarities.

Ahmad's family had been landowners. But under the British administration they had lost their eight villages, and family division of the remaining property had left little for Ahmad. Of Ahmad's childhood or early life little is said. It is known that Arabic, the holy language, came to him without instruction; and that he suffered from vertigo and diabetes and had a slight stammer. He had his first revelation when he was forty. But it wasn't until he was fifty-one or fifty-two, in 1890, that he announced his mission. It was found then that many of the things about Ahmad – including his physical disabilities and the name of his birthplace – had been prophesied.

His revelations came to him in words, and that was important. If he had claimed merely to be inspired, he would not have been able to claim much for his words. He was charged at one time with attempted murder – it was an early attempt to discredit him – but he was acquitted. He married late; had a son at the age of fifty (a year before he announced his mission); and the son became the third head of the movement (Ahmad died in 1908). All these events were prophesied.

It was a difficult story, as Colonel Anees had warned me; and I may not have got all the details right. Much of what I have written (but not all) was told me by Idrees, the Lahore Imam's brother, during a long morning drive to the Ahmadi settlement at Rabwah.

Idrees wished me to see that the faith was pure Islam, and fitted accepted traditions and prophecies. He was also, I felt, a little nervous after the outlawing of the sect, and anxious not to appear to be blaspheming. Idrees was a high-court lawyer, white-haired; his explanations could be fine and detailed.

The outlawing of the sect by Mr Bhutto had been prophesied. So had the punishment of Mr Bhutto. It had been prophesied that a ruler was going to declare them *cafars*, infidels; and that afterwards both hands of this ruler were going to be broken. 'The hand that held the declaration,' Idrees said, 'and the hand that authenticated it.'

I asked Idrees whether it wouldn't have been better for the Ahmadis to stay in India, in their original headquarters in Ahmad's birthplace.

Idrees said, 'Without Pakistan and Mr Jinnah, India would have been another Spain.'

'Spain?'

'A land where Islam has been wiped out. And now so many scholars say that the most glorious achievements of Islam were in Spain.'

Long before partition, though, the second caliph or successor (Ahmad's son) had prophesied a migration: a migration similar to Christ's, after he had been taken down from the cross. The prophecy had come to him in a dream.

The land through which we had been driving was flat. The hills, when we came to them, were abrupt. They were the salt hills of the Punjab, and Idrees said that from the air they showed as the last outcrop of the Himalayas. They were low red hills, so red that the men who quarried the salt – pure, the lumps like veined marble – were red with the dust.

Beside the hills was the Chenab River, one of the rivers of the Punjab, a river here of the Indo-Pakistan sub-continent: not a flow of water within well-defined banks, but a wide, ravaged depression, which at the town of Rabwah (below the salt hills) was two to three miles wide: most of the river bed exposed and dry, with low convex sand-banks, great grey flats of silt, blackish where soaked by water, and with water in pools, with the true river like an irregular spread of water rather than a flow, unrippled, seemingly without depth, lazily dividing around an island.

The second caliph, after he had prophesied the migration from India, had seen a landscape like this in a dream, and it did have a quality of dream, with the abruptness of the red rocky hills and the sprawling river channel after the level, irrigated Punjab plain.

'He saw that there was a huge flood,' Idrees said, 'and we were all drifting in it and ultimately we touched land at a place which was hilly, which had mounds, and some sandy area also.'

The hills were important, in this migration that had to resemble that of Christ: it was reported that Jesus and Mary, after leaving Galilee, had moved to some physically elevated place. And the river was important, because the Promised Messiah himself had prophesied that times would be hard for his people and that then, to solace them, he would appear on the banks of the Nile or a river like the Nile. In an unreal world 'simile' – to use the word Idrees constantly used – was everything. The

Nile, Idrees said, rose in the Mountains of the Moon; Chenab meant 'Moon River'.

The community had planned a housing development on the bank of this precious river. Many devotees had bought little plots. But then the Pakistan government – pursuing the community even here – had claimed the land for Bihari refugees from Bangladesh. Refugees against outcasts, the unwanted dispossessing the unwanted: the Biharis had actually built a mosque, symbol of their take-over, before the Ahmadis obtained a stay order from the courts against the appropriation of their land. In Rabwah itself the government had claimed nearly four acres of developed community land for a police station; a stay had been obtained against that as well.

Beyond the river, at the foot of one of the red hills, the light vaporous with heat, was the Ahmadi cemetery. The people buried there were people who had willed money to the community and the movement. The graves were low; the wall was low. The cemetery was like part of the strange landscape, and if Idrees hadn't pointed it out to me I wouldn't have noticed it.

Saltpetre was six inches to a foot deep on the land when the Ahmadis bought it. The land – they had bought a thousand acres – had been abandoned for centuries. Now on this land, as in places on the red salt rock, there was a lime-green growth, an extra tinge of colour. And there was a little township, with trees, though the tube-well water – which was the only water available here – was a little salt. The Ahmadi settlement and headquarters had the air of a government township: low, dusty red-brick buildings with reed curtains over the doorways; and verandahs around courtyards where, carefully watered, grew oleander, hibiscus and a kind of small palm.

Idrees settled me in the guest house – 'for dignitaries' – and went to leave his name at the office of the Imam, the current head of the sect. The Imam, the Promised Messiah's grandson, was seventy and an M.A. from Oxford, Idrees said. Pepsi-Cola was brought in for me, then tea. Soon Idrees came in to say, with some awe, that he had been 'called'. He thought that I too would soon be called.

But I wasn't. Idrees, explaining later, said the Imam was busy. He had thousands of letters and many administrative matters to deal with; and he was going to Rawalpindi the next day. Instead, I was shown a photograph – a turbanned, full-faced man – and allowed to go up to the darkened waiting room where, waiting as in a doctor's surgery, was a sombre family group with a bowed, black-veiled woman.

In the publications section – in spite of trouble with the government about a new printing press – there were booklets in stacks, and translations of the Koran. Idrees, beating away desert dust from each bulky volume, showed the Korans language by language, title page by title page. The Ahmadis were active in Africa: they had Korans in Luganda, Swahili, Yoruba. The energy, the organization in this corner of the Punjab! But the Ahmadis aimed at nothing less than the conversion of the world.

They were banned in many Muslim countries; but the work went on elsewhere. The tall man in white had come back from a missionary posting in Denmark. He made me think of a diplomat recalled home and living in reduced circumstances. He said, before getting on his old bicycle to ride away into the glare, that the Scandinavians were looking for new beliefs and he had built up a good little congregation for the Promised Messiah in Denmark.

Fatter, happier, and with a bigger story to tell, was the man who had served on and off for twenty years in London. He had a congregation of 10,000 (mostly Pakistani migrants, I would have thought); and he had not hesitated – in London – to fight for the Muslim cause. The headmistress of his daughter's school wanted his daughter to wear the skirt of the school uniform rather than the slack trousers of Islamic modesty. He had taken the matter to higher authority and won his case. His daughter wore trousers, and when word got around many Muslims sent their daughters to that school; the headmistress later thanked him. The law provided for freedom of religion, he said. He meant the law of England, the other man's law.

His big problem had been to prevent his daughter having 'a divided mind'. But she had been made restless by 'this woman's lib' and she wasn't adjusting easily to Pakistan and Rabwah. He was talking her round, showing her how much better for women the Islamic way was. He had seen the position of women go down in England during his time there; men no longer got up for them in buses, and he had read in *The Observer* that VD was now like an 'epidemic'.

But what was it about woman's lib that attracted his daughter? He didn't answer. The amplified call to the one o'clock prayer came: 'There is no God but God', melodiously and variously chanted. And the former London missionary got up. He put on his black fur cap and said – with a London-made jokeyness: he still had his London manner, his London security – that he didn't want to be late for lunch: his wife, contrary to what was said about Muslim women, was a tyrant. People in London, he said, used to ask him why he didn't take four wives; he used to tell them he couldn't cope with one.

Idrees himself believed in the strict seclusion of women; his own wife kept *purdah*. Idrees thought that my unhappiness with the London man was only an unhappiness about Pakistani migration. And, as we walked in the white light back to the guest house, he said, 'There is a tide in the affairs of men . . .' The image of the flood, the caliph's dream, the migration!

We had lunch. Idrees went off to say his prayers, adding to the three o'clock prayer the one o'clock prayer he had missed. Afterwards I went to his room in the guest house and we talked. He lay on one of the beds, now on his back, now on his side. I sat on the dressing-table stool. It was hot. The salt rock of the Rabwah hills stored and radiated heat. In summer the rocks never cooled down. But Idrees was at peace. This land of salt and rock and river was his sanctuary. He said that peace always came to him at Rabwah.

There were pinpricks; there was always persecution. He had received a little shock even that morning: a man of the town had complained to the police that he had been thrown out of a house on the orders of the head of the sect. It wasn't so; it was only a dispute between a tenant and a landlord; but people knew they could go to the police with stories about the sect. It was like the recent case he had had to deal with, of a dismissed workman who had inflicted some injuries on himself and then complained to the labour court that he had been beaten up by the sect.

He invariably came to some little piece of bad news like this. But he liked to come to Rabwah, and it was his good fortune to come about twice a month. I couldn't enter his faith. But in that room, as he lost his anxieties, I felt tenderer towards him. I liked seeing him relaxed on the bed, snatching at peace, carrying the stupendousness of his faith, his belief in the Promised Messiah who had come to cleanse and reveal anew the true religion. He became calmer; his face freshened. And I saw how I had been misled by his grey hair: he was some years younger than me. The great dry heat, the dream landscape to which men had only recently given significance, the site of deliverance and possible martyrdom: it was like being taken far back.

We talked about dreams. The second caliph's dreams had been famous even in the British time. Sir Mohammed Zafrullah Khan, one of the most distinguished Ahmadis, used to pass them on to the British viceroy, who was sceptical until he received in this way some precise information about Allied warplanes. But dreams and prophecies had to be handled with care; they couldn't be broadcast; they could be provocative. It was better for prophecies to be made public after they had come to pass — like the prophecy about Mr Bhutto and the breaking of both his hands.

But how long would the peace hold at Rabwah? Had there been any hint, any dream about a new migration?

It was like touching a nerve. That was something Idrees didn't want to think about. He said, formally, 'At the present moment this is the place which is fulfilling the purpose of God, providing guidance for the whole world and the whole human race.'

We went out into the heat. We looked at the mosque, and the big courtyard where every year there was an assembly of the faithful. We saw the school where students from different countries were being trained – training taking from six to seven years – to go back and spread the word about the Promised Messiah. We met a twenty-two-year-old Indian Muslim boy from Trinidad, an Indonesian of twenty-six. There were two Nigerians, twelve and fourteen, at the edge of the brown playing field. 'Here, here!' Idrees said to me. 'I don't want them to feel left out.' And the boys, looking orphaned, came up: nothing to say: bright eyes in sad faces, pining below the salt hills of the Punjab, in the artificial township, for the wet forests of Africa.

The sun began to go down. We left. Abruptly, as we were talking, Idrees held his open palms together in the Muslim gesture of prayer. We were passing the cemetery. It was his custom, he said afterwards, to say a prayer for them, 'that they might be elevated even higher in heaven'.

Sunset flared in the Chenab, the Moon River. And when we were past the river, sunset flared in the still pools of waterlogged fields, irrigated land dying, turning to salt and marsh, marsh clearer at dusk (water catching the last of the light) than in the even glare of day.

Idrees had talked all the way out. Now he was silent. It was as though the land called up and gave an anxious edge again to his own melancholy.

Smoke rose from cooking fires. On the road smoke was black from the exhausts of unregulated vehicles. The horse-carriages had no lights; and the trucks often had no lights at the back. They all had lights once, Idrees said. Now there was no law. 'When the law is dishonoured by the lawmakers, how can the common man obey?'

His high-court practice hadn't been growing. But his wife had some property and income. He wanted to travel; he liked travelling; he was only forty-two. He never said it; but I felt that for him, as for the Ahmadi girl in the green sari I had met in Karachi, there was now some idea of migration, of getting away from some harder persecution to come.

The lights of Lahore began to show.

He said, 'Did you make a note of that prophecy? By 1989 the world will be tired of waiting for the coming of Christ. The Iranians will get tired of waiting for the Twelfth Imam. They will then turn to us.'

III

Conversations in
MALAYSIA
The Primitive Faith

. . . A half-naked, betel-chewing pessimist stood upon the bank of the tropical river, on the edge of the still and immense forests; a man angry, powerless, empty-handed, with a cry of bitter discontent ready on his lips; a cry that, had it come out, would have rung through the virgin solitudes of the woods, as true, as great, as profound, as any philosophical shriek that ever came from the depths of an easy-chair to disturb the impure wilderness of chimneys and roofs.

Joseph Conrad: *An Outcast of the Islands* (1896)

Those communities that have as yet little history make upon a European a curious impression of thinness and isolation. They do not feel themselves the inheritors of the ages, and for that reason what they aim at transmitting to their successors seems jejune and emotionally poor to one in whom the past is vivid and the future is illuminated by knowledge of the slow and painful achievements of former times. History makes one aware that there is no finality in human affairs; there is not a static perfection and an unimprovable wisdom to be achieved.

Bertrand Russell: *Portraits from Memory*

1

◆-◆-◆-◆-◆

First Conversations with Shafi:
the Journey out of Paradise

IT WAS FROM India or the Indo-Pakistan sub-continent that religion went to south-east Asia. Hinduism and Buddhism went first. They quickened the great civilizations of Cambodia and Java, whose monuments – Angkor, Borobudur – are among the wonders of the world. These Indian religions, we are told, were not spread by armies or colonists, but by merchants and priests. And that was the kind of Indian traveller who, after Islam had come to the sub-continent, began in the fourteenth or fifteenth century to take Islam to Indonesia and Malaysia.

Islam went to south-east Asia as another religion of India. There was no Arab invasion, as in Sind; no systematic slaughter of the local warrior caste, no planting of Arab military colonies; no sharing out of loot, no sending back of treasure and slaves to a caliph in Iraq or Syria; no tribute, no taxes on unbelievers. There was no calamity, no overnight abrogation of a settled world-order. Islam spread as an idea – a Prophet, a divine revelation, heaven and hell, a divinely sanctioned code – and mingled with older ideas. To purify that mixed religion the Islamic missionaries now come; and it is still from the sub-continent – and especially from Pakistan – that the most passionate missionaries come.

They do not bring news of military rule, the remittance economy, the loss of law, the tragedy of the Bihari Muslims now wanted neither by Bangladesh nor by Pakistan. These events are separate from Islam, and these men bring news only of Islam and the enemies of Islam. They offer passion, and it is the special passion of the Muslims of the sub-continent: the passion of people who, in spite of Pakistan, feel themselves a threatened minority; the passion of people who – with their view of history as a 'pleasant tale of conquest' – feel they have ceased to be conquerors; and the passion, above all, of Muslims who feel themselves on the margin of the true Muslim world. The Persian distance from Arabia created the Shia faith, and the Persian conviction that they are

Islamically purer than the Arabs. The Indian Muslim distance from Arabia is greater than the Persian; and their passion is as fierce or fiercer.

Every Muslim is a missionary for Islam: that was the idea of the brotherhood assembled in the waterlogged desert of the Punjab. And after four days of tent life, of mass prayers, the simple men go out intoxicated by their vision of a world about to change. Some go to Malaysia; they have been going for years; and now their passion finds a response.

There are a few Hinduized architectural remains in the far north, but no great Indianized civilization grew in Malaysia, as in Java or Cambodia. The land (though touched on the coast by Europeans) was more or less bypassed and left to the Malays until the last century.

The stories of Joseph Conrad give an impression of the remoter places of the Malay archipelago a hundred years ago: European coasting vessels, occasionally in competition with Arabs, men of the pure faith; European trading or administrative settlements on the edge of the sea or the river, with the forest at their backs; Chinese peasants and labourers taking root wherever they can; Malay sultans and rajas, warriors with their courts; and, in the background, simpler Malays, people of river and forest, half Muslim, half animist.

Separate, colliding worlds: the world of Europeans, pushing on to the 'outer edge of darkness', the closed tribal world of Malays: it was one of Conrad's themes. And in Malaysia today the Islamic revolutionaries, the young men who reject, are the descendants of those people in the background, the people of river and forest. In Malaysia they have been the last to emerge; and they have emerged after the colonial cycle, after independence, after money.

There is now in Malaysia more than coconuts and rattan to be picked up at the landing stages. Malaysia produces many precious things: tin, rubber, palm oil, oil. Malaysia is rich. Money, going down, has created a whole educated generation of village people and drawn them into the civilization that once appeared to be only on the outer edge of darkness but is now universal.

These young people do not always like what they find. Some have studied abroad, done technical subjects; but not many of them really know where they have been. In Australia, England or the United States they still look for the manners and customs of home; their time abroad sours them, throws them back more deeply into themselves. They cannot go back to the village. They are young, but the life of their childhood has changed.

And they also grow to understand that in the last hundred years, while they or their parents slept, their country – a new idea: a composite of kingdoms and sultanates – was colonially remade; that the rich Malaysia of today grows on colonial foundations and is a British-Chinese creation. The British developed the mines and the plantations. They brought in Chinese (the diligent, rootless peasants of a century back), and a lesser number of Indians, to do the work the Malays couldn't do. Now the British no longer rule. But the Malays are only half the population.

The Chinese have advanced; it is their energy and talent that keep the place going. The Chinese are shut out from political power. Malays rule; the country is officially Muslim, with Muslim personal laws; sexual relations between Muslims and non-Muslims are illegal, and there is a kind of prying religious police; legal discriminations against non-Muslims are outrageous. But the Malays who rule are established, or of old or royal families who crossed over into the new world some generations ago.

The new men of the villages, who feel they have already lost so much, find their path blocked at every turn. Money, development, education have awakened them only to the knowledge that the world is not like their village, that the world is not their own. Their rage – the rage of pastoral people with limited skills, limited money, and a limited grasp of the world – is comprehensive. Now they have a weapon: Islam. It is their way of getting even with the world. It serves their grief, their feeling of inadequacy, their social rage and racial hate.

This Islam is more than the old religion of their village. The Islam the missionaries bring is a religion of impending change and triumph; it comes as part of a world movement. In *Readings in Islam*, a local missionary magazine, it can be read that the West, in the eyes even of its philosophers, is eating itself up with its materialism and greed. The true believer, with his thoughts on the after-life, lives for higher ideals. For a non-believer, with no faith in the after-life, life is a round of pleasure. 'He spends the major part of his wealth on ostentatious living and demonstrates his pomp and show by wearing of silk and brocade and using vessels of gold and silver.'

Silk, brocade, gold and silver? Can that truly be said in a city like Kuala Lumpur? But this is theology. It refers to a *hadith* or tradition about the Prophet. Hudhaifa one day asked for water and a Persian priest gave him water in a silver vessel. Hudhaifa rebuked the Persian; Hudhaifa had with his own ears heard the Prophet say that non-believers used gold and silver vessels and wore silk and brocade.

The new Islam comes like this, and to the new men of the village it comes as an alternative kind of learning and truth, full of scholarly apparatus. It is passion without a constructive programme. The materialist world is to be pulled down first; the Islamic state will come later – as in Iran, as in Pakistan.

And the message that starts in Pakistan doesn't stop in Malaysia. It travels to Indonesia – 120 million people to Malaysia's twelve, poorer, more heterogeneous, more fragile, with a recent history of pogroms and mass killings. There the new Islamic movement among the young is seen by its enemies as nihilism; they call it 'the Malaysian disease'. So the Islamic passion of Pakistan, with its own special roots, converts and converts again, feeding other distresses. And the promise of political calamity spreads as good news.

Malaysia steams. In the rainy season in the mornings the clouds build up. In the afternoon it pours, the blue-green hills vanish, and afterwards the clouds linger in the rifts in the mountains, like smoke. Creepers race up the steel guy-ropes of telegraph poles; they overwhelm dying coconut branches even before the branches fall off; they cover dying trees, or trees that cannot resist, and create odd effects of topiary. Rain and sun and steam do not speak here of decay, of tropical lassitude; they speak of vigour, of rich things growing fast, of money.

The old colonial town of Kuala Lumpur, the Malaysian capital, still survives in parts. Old tile-roofed private dwellings, originally British; the rows of narrow two-story Chinese shop-houses, the shops downstairs, the pavement pillared, the pillars supporting the projecting upper story; Malay kampongs or villages – modest but attractive houses of weathered timber and corrugated iron brown-red with rust – in areas reserved for Malays at the time of the foundation of the town; near the railway station, the official British buildings: the Victorian-Gothic-Mogul law courts, domes and arches and staircase towers.

That colonial town has been left behind by the new residential developments, the skyscrapers of the new city, the Korean-built highways that lead in from the airport, first through plantations (western Malaysia from the air is dark with forest, but it is an ordered forest, with trees in rows, and the white steam rises in pillars like smoke from chimneys), and then past the factories and the assembly plants of international companies.

In public gardens and in other places in this new town can be seen young village Malays dressed as Arabs, with turbans and gowns. The Arab dress – so far from Pakistan, so far from Arabia – is their political badge. In the university there are girls who do not only wear the veil, but in the heat also wear gloves and socks. Different groups wear different colours. The veil is more than the veil; it is a mask of aggression. Not like the matted locks of the Ras Tafarian in Jamaica, a man dulled by a marginal life that has endured for generations; not like the gear of the middle-class hippy, who wishes only to drop out; these are the clothes of uprooted village people who wish to pull down what is not theirs and then take over. Because an unacknowledged part of the fantasy is that the world goes on, runs itself, has only to be inherited.

Shafi worked for the Muslim cause. He didn't wear Arab clothes. But he understood the young men who did. Shafi had come to Kuala Lumpur from a village in the north. The disturbance of the move was still with him.

Shafi said: 'When I was in the village the atmosphere is entirely different. You come out of the village. You see all the bright lights, you begin to sense the materialistic civilization around you. And I forgot about my religion and my commitments – in the sense that you had to pray. But not to the extent of going out and doing nasty things like taking girls and drinking and gambling and drugs. I didn't lose my faith. I simply forgot to pray, forgot responsibilities. Just losing myself. I got nothing firm in my framework. I just floating around, and didn't know my direction.'

I said, 'Where did you live when you came to Kuala Lumpur?'

He didn't give a straight answer. At this early stage in our conversations concreteness didn't come easily to him. He said, 'I was living in a suburb where I am exposed to materialistic civilization to which I had never been exposed before. Boys and girls can go out together. You are free from family control. You are free from society who normally criticize you in a village when you do something bad. You take a goat, a cow, a buffalo – somewhere where the goat is being tied up all the time – and you release that goat in a bunch of other animals: the goat would just roam anywhere he wants to go without any strings.'

'Is that bad for the goat?'

'I think the goat would be very happy to roam free. But for me I don't think that would be good. If goat had brains, I would want to say, "Why do you want to roam about when you are tied and being fed by your master and looked after? Why do you want to roam about?"'

I said, 'But I want to roam about.'

'What do you mean by being free? Freedom for me is not something that you can roam anywhere you want. Freedom must be within the definition of a certain framework. Because I don't think we are able to run around and get everything. That freedom means nothing. You must really frame yourself where you want to go and what you want to do.'

'But didn't you know what you wanted to do when you came to Kuala Lumpur?'

'The primary aim was education. That was a framework. But the conflict of this freedom and the primary aim is there, and I consider this is the problem I faced and many of my friends face.'

'Other people in other countries face the same problem.'

Shafi said, 'Do they face the same restrictions of family life as I do?'

'What restrictions?'

'Religious restrictions. You have that frame with you. Religious tradition, family life, the society, the village community. Then you come into the city, where people are running, people are free. The values contradict.

'You see, in the village where I was brought up we have the bare minimum. We have rice to eat, house to live. We didn't go begging. In the city you can buy a lunch at ten dollars [Malaysian dollars, 2.20 to the American]. Or in a stall you can have a lunch for fifty cents. That excess of nine-fifty which the city dwellers spend will be spent by us on other purposes. To us, with our framework and tradition and religion, that is excessiveness.

'Sometimes my wife feels that we should go back to the village, and I also feel the same. Not running away from the modern world, but trying to live a simpler, more meaningful life than coming to the city where you have lots of waste and lots of things that is not real probably. You are not honest to yourself if you can spend fifty cents and keep yourself from hunger, but instead spend ten dollars.

'I will tell you about waste. Recently the government built a skating rink. After three months they demolished it because a highway going to be built over it. They are building big roads and highways across the villages. And whose lorries are passing by to collect the produce of the poor and to dump the products that is manufactured by the rich at an exorbitant price – colour TVs, refrigerators, air-conditioners, transistor radios?'

'Don't people want those things?'

'In the end they are going to use the colour TVs – which the people enjoy – to advertize products to draw people into wasteful living.'

'Village life – wouldn't you say it is dull for most people?'

'The village? It's simple. It's devoid of – what shall I say? – wasteful-ness. You shouldn't waste. You don't have to rush for things. My point about going back to the kampong is to stay with the community and not to run away from development. The society is well-knit. If someone passed away there is an alarm in the kampong, where most of us would know who passed away and when he is going to be buried, what is the cause of death, and what happened to the next of kin – are they around? It's not polluted in the village. Physical pollution, mental, social.'

'Social pollution?'

'Something that contradicts our customs and traditions. A man cannot walk with a woman who doesn't belong to his family in the kampong. It is forbidden.'

'Why is it wrong?'

'The very essence of human respect and dignity comes from an honourable relationship of man and woman. You must have a law to protect the unit of your society. You need your family to be protected. When the girls come from the villages to KL they don't want to be protected by the law.'

Shafi was thirty-two. He was small and slender, with glasses, a sloping forehead and a thin beard. He had at one time set up as a building contractor. But he hadn't succeeded; and he had given up that and all other business to work full time for the Muslim youth movement called ABIM. ABIM was the most important and the most organized Muslim youth group in Malaysia; and Shafi venerated the leader, Anwar Ibrahim, who was a man of his own age.

Anwar Ibrahim's story was remarkable. He came from the more developed west coast of Malaysia, and was a generation or two ahead of Shafi. His grandfather ran a little village restaurant; his father was a male nurse in a hospital; Anwar himself had gone to a British-founded college for the sons of local princes or sultans. Anwar had to pass an entrance examination; the boys of royal blood didn't have to pass that examination.

The British had pledged not to dishonour the Muslim religion of the sultans, and in the college they were scrupulous about that pledge. But Anwar thought that religion as practised in the college was only a matter of ritual, with no great meaning. So, with the help of a British teacher (who later became a Muslim convert), Anwar began to study Islam; and he grew to understand the value of discipline, unity, and submission to God's will. By the time he was sixteen he was making speeches about Islam in the villages; he was a fiery orator. Out of that schoolboy activity his movement had developed, and it was now highly organized, with a building in Kuala Lumpur, offices, staff, even a school.

He was in touch with Muslim movements abroad – in Indonesia, Bangladesh, Pakistan. He had been to Iran and met Ayatollah

Khomeini; that had added to his reputation locally. For Anwar Ibrahim Islam was the energizer and purifier that was needed in Malaysia; true Islam awakened people, especially Malays, and at the same time it saved them from the corruption of the racialist politics of Malaysia, the shabbiness of the money culture and easy Western imitation.

His office in ABIM – with staff in outer cubicles, with typewriters and filing cabinets – was like the office of a modest business executive: modern tools and modern organization to serve the Islamic puritan cause. He was small and slight, slighter than Shafi, and even more boyish in appearance. He was attractive; and it added to his attractiveness that in spite of his great local authority he gave the impression of a man still learning, still thinking things out. His grand view of Islam gave him a security that not all of his followers had; and travel had added to his vision. He disapproved of the 'faddishness' of some Malaysian Muslim groups, their religious and political simplicities. He admitted that he had not yet thought through the economic side of things; he said he was still only at 'the conscientization stage'. I got the impression that he genuinely belived that an Islamic economic system was something he might one day bring over from a place like Pakistan.

I would have liked to talk more with Anwar. It occurred to me, after our first meeting in the ABIM office, that I should travel about Malaysia with him, and see the country through his eyes. He was willing; but it didn't work out. He was busy, at the centre of all the ABIM activity; he was constantly on the move, by car and plane; he was in demand as an orator. When the second of our arrangements fell through, he sent Shafi to see me at the Holiday Inn, where I was staying.

It was only because of Anwar's recommendation that Shafi, when he came, opened himself to me. And even as it was, Shafi was diffident about putting himself forward, of appearing as a spokesman, of derogating from the dignity of the leader.

'I am not the leader,' Shafi said, with a laugh, when we sat in the Gardenia coffee shop. 'I'm only a general.'

It wasn't easy to talk with Shafi in the beginning. He spoke the abstractions of the movement, and abstractions made his language awkward. He dodged concrete detail, not because he was secretive, but because he was used only to answering questions about the faith and the movement, and not about himself.

He said he didn't like places like the Holiday Inn. I thought this was an exaggeration, until he began to talk about the wastefulness of city life. And I never became reconciled to the difference between the man who was talking to me – intelligent, self-possessed, scholarly-looking – and the slack village life he said he came out of and longed to go back to.

He wanted to go back, to have again a sense of the fitness and wholeness of things; and I could see how for him Islam was the perfect vehicle. But Shafi – a professional man, an organizer – had been made by the world he rejected; that was the world that had released his intelligence. It would not have been easy for him to separate the part of himself that was purely traditional or instinctive from the part for which he alone was responsible. And his village had changed; and Malaysia had changed; and the world had changed.

It was of that changed and urgent world that, not long after Shafi left me, I heard the Malaysian foreign minister speak, at a seminar at the university. The minister wore a flowered shirt: that was the only touch of traditional colour. He – and the Indian official from his ministry – spoke of the discussions at the recent non-aligned conference in Havana; he spoke of the disturbance on the northern borders: Thailand, Cambodia, Vietnam. Foreign ambassadors were present. The two men from the Chinese embassy, in short-sleeved grey safari suits, made notes, holding their pens straight up, in the Chinese calligrapher's way. Afterwards big cars took some of the ambassadors away. It wasn't only the rich local Chinese and the builders of highways and the manufacturers of TV colour sets that had altered the world.

It was to another kind of old life that later, at dinner at the house of a distinguished Indian lawyer, the talk turned. James Puthucheary, the lawyer, had once been active in colonial politics in Malaysia and Singapore. He said, 'I've been jailed by the British, the Singaporeans, and the Malaysians. The only people who jailed me in such a way that it was possible to be friendly with them afterwards were the British.' The British colonial secretary – in rank just below the governor – came to see him in jail one day. Before he came into the cell he said, 'Mr Puthucheary, do you mind me coming into your room?' Afterwards, Puthucheary said, they 'both went down in the world'. The colonial secretary retired and went into business; Puthucheary completed the studies he had begun in jail and became a lawyer. 'We used to meet and play bridge.'

It was an elegant and educated middle-class gathering conscious, in addition, of its racial variety: Malays, Chinese, Indians. There were many cars in the drive and on the lawn. Old battles, old rules; and it might have been said that – with the help of the money of Malaysia – these men had just arrived at dignity. The world had moved fast for them. But already what had been won was being undermined by the grief and rage of the people not represented there, the people of river and forest who had stood outside the awakening of colonial days, and whose sons now made the first generation of educated village Malays. For them the world had moved even faster.

It was possible in the morning to read the newspaper with greater understanding. *Shares worth $15m offered to bumiputras*. A *bumiputra* (the word was Sanskrit, pre-Islamic) was 'a son of the soil', a Malay; and Malays were to be given loans to buy the shares reserved for them. This was how the government discriminated in their favour, seeking to bring them up economically to the level of the Chinese. The method was ineffectual; it had only created a favoured class of Malay 'front men'. It was against this kind of racialism that Anwar Ibrahim and ABIM campaigned, setting up against it a vision of a purer Islamic way.

Mandatory Islamic studies welcome, says Abim: Islam was to be a compulsory subject for Muslims in schools. *Rahman: Don't neglect spiritual growth*: that was a government man, being as Muslim as anyone else. *Hear the call from across the desert sands*: that was a feature article, for this special day, the Festival of Sacrifice, by a well-known columnist: a good, lyrical piece about family memories of the pilgrimage to Mecca.

Only half the population was Muslim; but everyone had to make his obeisance to Islam. The pressures came from below: a movement of purification and cleansing, but also a racial movement. It made for a general nervousness. It made people hide from the visitor for fear that they might be betrayed. It led – oddly, in this land of rain and steam and forest – to the atmosphere of the ideological state.

Shafi came in the morning, dressed in formal Malay clothes for the religious holiday, the Festival of Sacrifice. He wore a pale-orange tunic and trousers (this part of the Malay costume copied from the Chinese), with gold studs in the tunic; he had a sarong around his middle like a slack cummerbund (the sarong was the original Malay dress, and Shafi's had been woven for him, in pastel stripes, by his mother); and he had a black velvet cap that folded flat (the cap was the Indian part of the Malay costume). He looked princely. With a knife at his side he might have been a raja of a hundred years before, standing on a river bank, with his own court. But he had driven up in his car; and we were in the lobby of the Holiday Inn.

He said, 'Did you read what I said last night? Did you like it?'

'I liked what you said about your family unit.'

'Do you want to ask more?' He was eager, open. The effort at autobiography, my interest in the details of his life, had excited him.

'Yes. But I know your philosophy, the ideas of your movement. I want something more personal.'

We went from the lobby to the Gardenia coffee shop, passing the bar on one side, where at night in near darkness couples sat and 'The Old Timers' – Indians and Malays or perhaps only Malays – sang amplified pop songs. In the coffee shop we sat next to the window, overlooking the small oval pool with its ancillary little oval pool for children. Everybody there was white this morning.

I said, 'What do you think about that?'

He had grown a little tense, waiting for the personal questions. He turned and looked at the people around the little pool, showing me his profile, the smooth brown Malay skin, the slope of his forehead, his glasses, the dip of his nose-bridge, the knob of his snub nose, his beard. He looked hard; his face grew serious.

He said, 'I don't know what I think. They are foreign to us, that's all. They don't belong to our culture.'

'You wouldn't like to be with them?'

'No. But the water's quite cooling. We have the same clear water in the village. More natural environment. You would see the river bed. You would see the plants, creepers by the side, on the bank.'

Across the pool was a woman in her forties in a black bathing suit. She was white, untanned, soft-bodied but still with a fair shape, and her legs were drawn up awkwardly rather than provocatively on the white plastic straps of the easy chair. Below us was a younger woman in blue, smaller, firmer, lying on her belly. Both might have aroused desire in a sexually active man.

I said, 'Do you think those white women are pretty?'

He looked at them one after the other, with the same serious expression: he was trying hard to find out what he thought.

He said, 'We don't have a sense of comparing.'

'But white men and others find Malay women pretty.'

'I have heard that. But is it true? Is that really what they feel?'

And in the coffee shop, with the Malay waitresses in long green dresses pinned with their Holiday Inn identity badges ('Beautiful and Homely'), we talked of the village. It was not easy for Shafi, though the effort of thought and memory excited him. The narrative that came out was shaped by my questions.

'I know every corner of my village. We used to go bird-hunting, catching some fish. Either in trousers or sarong. In the trousers, the pockets loaded with pebbles. We used those pebbles to catapult birds. We would go out about ten a.m. in the school holidays or much earlier in the fasting month. And returning about lunch time with the whole pocket of pebbles gone and returning without any reward. Sometimes we diverted to collecting rubber seeds. We would each put some seeds in a section of bamboo, put the bamboo on supports about four inches above the ground, and try to knock it down from a distance. The boy who knocked it down got all the stakes.

'One of the other activities in childhood was to read Koran, even without knowing the meaning of the verses. We were told by our parents to do it. We were just obeying them.'

I said, 'Don't you think that's a bad intellectual start?'

'You're right. But it's more than that when you read Koran. We were told from various sources about reading Koran. Each time you read will bring you some goodness in life. I do feel that.'

'Like magic, then?'

'It is above magic in this case. It is not written by human being. Magic is operated by human being, whereas Koran is above that. The other book we had is text written by a few well known leaders in the village. Religious texts, mainly dealing with teachings. They were printed in the town. On how to pray, on keeping yourself clean. Physically clean. If you have water you wash in water. If you don't have water you're allowed to use other things. Stones, wood, bark, leaves, paper. But not bones of animal which is not slaughtered. Basic hygiene.

'You should choose, if you don't have a proper toilet, a secluded place where nobody would see you, and not in the flowing stream where people are using the same source of water supply, and not under a house, and not any place where the faeces will give offence to the public. It is a holy teaching and it is applicable in our life. So I took it as something we've got to follow. This was when we were not more than twelve years old.'

'Was there a book like that in every house in the village?'

'Each of those who attended the course would be given the book. Part one and part two and part three. The book was written by the mullah of the mosque. My impression is that he had a big cabinet by the wall about ten feet long and ten feet high filled up with these printed books. He gave one free first. But if you lose that you got to buy. There were teaching sessions every Friday afternoon and Saturday morning at the mosque. For the children, from nine to fifteen–sixteen.'

'Did the books have anything about masturbation or sex?'

'Basically it was teaching about cleanliness. That was one part. The other part was how to pray. What sort of water is allowed for you to use for your ablutions before praying. You must use clean water. Clean water is defined mostly as running water in a stream. The volume of water will have to be a minimum of twenty or thirty gallons. Then you can say it is clean. You mustn't see any dirt, smell any dirt, or touch any dirt. Unless these conditions are met, then the water is dirty.

'If you didn't attend one teaching session without valid reasons, you would be punished. And this punishment by the mullah would be acceptable to the parents. In addition there were the Friday morning teachings by the head of the elders in the village. This was for everybody, and not only children. They taught worldly and heavenly things then. Human relations. Elders and the young, men and women. Cleanliness, prayers. During this Friday morning teaching they referred to Koran and translation and this encouraged people to read Koran and translations. Later, every day we have to go for Koran reading, morning and afternoon.

'My village is in Kota Baru. In the north-east. The people in my village I would consider quite enterprising. They do this cloth-weaving – my mother did this sarong I'm wearing. Not many of them are working in the government. Some of them own plantations, rice-fields, coconut plantations. They get the people from the village to do the work.

'There were about 2,000 people in the village at that time. Everybody had a house of their own, on their own land or the land of a relative or the land that belongs to the religious department of the government. They build their own houses. Nobody squats. And if I can remember, nobody begs. There is no beggar in our village. I would say it was quite a prosperous village. One man and his family had to leave because the land their house was on was sold. They went to another village, and when we asked them later how they were getting on they said nothing can be compared to this village. In the village they could find work easier.

'In the village there were no pollutions of yellow cultures, yellow literatures. A school where you learned to read and write, that's all. In Malay.'

I said, 'But if you have such a simple life you can't have intellectual pursuits?'

'Intellectual pursuits were nothing. I will give you an instance. There were not many young people who went out of the village for higher education. The only people who went out were the family of the mullahs. They only went for religious education, not secular education. They went to Mecca. The whole of the mullah's family went to Mecca. One of them had a relative there.

'There were no foreigners in our village. But adjacent to our village is a Chinese village. They were different, that's all. They ate pork, and we say the pig is dirty. They looked different. We didn't think they were ugly. They had small eyes and fairer skin. They're a lot dirtier than us.

Their backyards stink. Waste water from the backyard stinks. They kept pigs, and the pig-sties stinks. And whenever the pigs broke loose out of the compound into our village, then the young boys will stone them. And any stray dogs from the Chinese village will be stoned. Because it's taboo to a Muslim to have dogs and pigs. But there were no village fights.'

'Were the Chinese rich?'

'At that time they were not rich. In education they were very strict with their children. After dinner they will see that the child attend or recite their schoolbooks aloud, in the kitchen or in the front room.'

'But you were strict too? But with religious education only.'

'With us religious education is compulsory. Almost every young Muslim has to know it. It's a duty. With us the human value was being emphasized more than the religious value.'

'But you fell behind intellectually.'

'Yes, we fell behind intellectually. I would say further – in terms of pursuit for material and secular education we fell behind. But in terms of being more human, more responsible persons, being more reasonable in our conduct or way of life, I think that we are a lot better than them. Morally we are a lot better than them.'

'But you weren't technically equipped.'

'No, we weren't technically equipped. One of our mullahs in the village faced this problem. He started a coconut-oil mill-processing, as well as soap-making. And that was unsuccessful. Why? I consider he don't have the technical know-how as well as the managerial ability. I wasn't allowed to go to his factory, so I can't say more.

'But we never thought about it, technical learning. I remember one instance. When they started to build a bridge across the river in Kota Baru, the few of the mullahs and *hajis* [Muslims who had made the pilgrimage to Mecca] were shocked. And they said, "How on earth could they build such a huge structure across the river?" When they were doing the filling work – this very much shocked them.

'Basically we are good persons, but not technologically equipped, for reasons that we are self-sufficient. We don't need skyscrapers, the big lift, the road. We don't need technological.'

I said, 'Are you sure?'

'I don't think so. When we were in the village we saw a calendar with a picture of a twenty-five-story building in Singapore, and we were astonished with that. This was in 1957. In the village we feel we don't need that sort of development. The realization of the need for all these things comes from the experiences on the visits we made out of Kota Baru, to Kuala Lumpur and elsewhere.'

'How did you get that calendar?'

'A few of our relatives went for *haj* [the pilgrimage to Mecca] through Singapore, and they brought back that calendar. Singapore was a busy town – which they expressed in this way: when they sleep in a hotel they felt as if cars are passing by at the end of the bed. That bothered them in their sleep. I can remember only two or three cars in the village. The same person who described Singapore described the village now as more like Singapore – the sound of the car passing at the back of the bed.'

'You don't think the old village life is gone forever?'

'No, it should be there. We need good basic amenities. We need good bus service, good school.'

This vision of simplicity! But it required a bus – a road – road-making – machinery.

I said, 'What was your school like?'

'In the village we had an earth floor and when it rained it was always flooded. And we didn't have electricity.'

But in that simple school the new world had broken in, lifting Shafi without his knowing it out of purely village ways. There was the Scout Movement. It was part of the British system, but to Shafi it would have appeared only as part of the life of his village school. There was a scout camp-craft competition in Malaysia in 1963. It was to take part in that competition that, at the age of fifteen and as a member of his school scout troop, Shafi left Kota Baru and came to the British-Chinese city of Kuala Lumpur for the first time. After sixteen years the nervousness and upheaval of that journey were still close to him. It showed in his language.

'We came in by train. One day and one night. We expected that. We looked forward. We were adventurous. We were in a group. On the journey we were searching for similarities. For instance, good Malay restaurants – we had them in Kota Baru. We couldn't find. It was difficult for us to eat; for us we have to take Muslim food.

'When we left we could see a village scene. Towards the evening we see rubber estates and jungles and at night most of it is jungle. But in the morning, on approach to KL, we realized that we are passing by a Chinese community, Chinese neighbourhood, which is quite familiar to us, and we realized the pessimism we faced about the problems of having good Muslim food and not being able to meet more Malays. We were seeing more Chinese and Indians. Quite difficult for us to communicate. Because we don't know them. For us it's easier to talk to a Malay who knows us. It was a shock, but not an upset. Because we expected that. But we were not in the least frightened.

'We had some ideas of certain landmarks in KL, so we get around easily. But we felt we were nowhere. We were lost in the huge community. Each time we go around, out of ten people we could hardly see a Malay. We had expected that. But we were in a group and we didn't bother with them very much. We were staying right in the middle of a non-Muslim, non-Malay community, and that was the difficulty we had. We knew that there were Malay kampongs scattered about the town. But we stayed where we were because of the competition.'

Shafi was tired. The exercise of memory had exhausted him. And he was nagged by the inconsistency — as it had come out in our conversation — between his longing for the purity of village life and his recognition of the backwardness of Malays. Deep down he felt — he knew — that there was no inconsistency, no flaw; but he couldn't find the words to express that.

It was now one o'clock. Too late for Shafi to take me to his brothers, which was part of his plan for me for this festival day. Because of the festival the big Holiday Inn Friday buffet lunch had been laid out here in the coffee shop rather than in the enclosed, mirrored room on the upper floor, where on normal Fridays (for non-Muslims, or Muslims not observing the sabbath) there was a fashion show, with music. The hotel depressed Shafi because it was alien, wasteful, full of strangers without belief and indifferent to the rules: I could see it now with his eyes. We walked past the bar, dark even in daylight. On the other side of the corridor were show-cases of Selangor Pewter — locally made decorative objects on show in every hotel, every souvenir shop, advertized in every local brochure, every magazine.

It was strange to think of books being written and published in Shafi's village, books of rules like those written in Iran by ayatollahs like Khomeini and Shariatmadari, copies of which were to be found in the houses of their followers, who could consult them without shame on the most intimate matters and find out what was permitted by the Koran and approved Islamic tradition and what was not permitted. The simple life was a rigid life. It had rules for everything; and everyone had to learn the rules.

In Pakistan the fundamentalists believed that to follow the right rules was to bring about again the purity of the early Islamic way: the reorganization of the world would follow automatically on the rediscovery of the true faith. Shafi's grief and passion, in multi-racial Malaysia, were more immediate; and I felt that for him the wish to re-establish the rules was also a wish to re-create the security of his childhood, the Malay village life he had lost.

Some grief like that touches most of us. It is what, as individuals, responsible for ourselves, we constantly have to accommodate ourselves to. Shafi, in his own eyes, was the first man expelled from paradise. He blamed the world; he shifted the whole burden of that accommodation on to Islam.

That thought came later. That afternoon, after Shafi had left me, I was full of his mood. In the bar that evening I at last had the Holiday Inn's complimentary drink, 'Tropical Aura'. The Old Timers dinned away; the drink tasted of tinned pineapple juice. Later, in the coffee shop – again – I had an omelette. It wasn't good. But the young Malay waiter was punctilious and helpful. And I thought, looking at him laying the next table carefully, trying to do the right thing, 'He is like Shafi, I must remember.'

2

❖❖❖❖

Brave Girls

I AWAKENED in the morning at half past two and couldn't get back to sleep. During a previous sleepless night I had gone to the coffee shop at half past four and found it desolate, with a smell of cleaning chemical. So I stayed in my room. Just after five I ordered coffee. I had to telephone twice. The boy, when he came, was grubby, and not friendly. The milk was sour; it took away my appetite without lessening my need.

When I drew the curtain it was light, and on the racecourse across the road horses were training. It was for that racecourse view, with the Kuala Lumpur hills, that I had chosen the Holiday Inn. On Saturday and Sunday the crowd gathered in the grandstand in the afternoon, and every half hour shouted, above an amplified commentary. But there were no horses, no races. The races were being run elsewhere; the crowd was watching television, and had gathered only to gamble, because – under Malaysia's Islamic laws – gambling was permitted in Kuala Lumpur only on the racecourse. On the phantom racecourse now there were horses: first I saw two, then six, then many more. I studied the riders' stances over the horses' necks, the stirrups short, the reins horizontal.

It was overcast. The hills were smoking. Very white clouds were rising from the rifts; and above the range there was a whole level bank of grey-white raincloud, slowly lifting and fluffing out. Around the racecourse were the trees I knew from my childhood: banana trees, the frangipani, another tree with a yellow flower, the great Central American samaan or rain-tree, used in plantations as a shade tree.

I wished I was more alert, and more free in mind, to enjoy what I saw. The exhaustion of sleeplessness turned to anxieties, irritations: the bad milk that had denied me coffee, unanswered cables. When I went downstairs there was a girl at the desk. I talked to her about the cables. She directed me to the telephone operator. The door had a sign: 'For Authorized Personnel Only'. The operator, a Malay girl who couldn't speak English well, was plain, with round glasses.

While she checked her file I read the staff notices, which were in

Malay and English. There was one notice which I wished I hadn't read. 'Irresponsible staffs' had been 'urinating and purging' on the floor of the locker, and on canteen plates and in canteen glasses. Ritual cleanliness had nothing to do with cleanliness for its own sake, nothing to do with regard for the other man. There were rules for the villages; there were no rules for the town. There were hotel rules; they had to be obeyed because they were hotel rules – and the hotel maintained high standards. But below stairs, among their fellows, one or two Malays could still feel that rules had ceased to apply.

The nausea stayed with me. When I went outside I fancied there were smells; and the smells seemed to follow me everywhere, even to the Equatorial Hotel, where I went for the buffet lunch. There I met a man I knew. He told me that the town had not been built for Muslim people. Muslims had to wash ritually five times a day before they offered their prayers; they used what was available; they used sinks and wash-basins to wash their feet and genitals. So all the excitement I had felt at Shafi's story – excitement which had partly kicked me awake that morning – turned the other way.

But it was all right again when Shafi – in everyday office clothes – came to see me that afternoon. With the man before me, so frank, so attractive, my disturbance fell away. He had brought a friend, a very small and slight man of thirty-four. The friend's father had been a village mullah. The friend himself had specialized in Islamic studies and – strangely – had gone to Birmingham in England for his doctorate. Now he was a high official in ABIM. He had lost a number of teeth in an accident, and he limped. Whenever he spoke he seemed, because of those missing teeth, to smile.

I said, 'Why are you all so young in the movement?'

The friend answered, with his smile, 'Our parents were simple people. Ninety-five percent of them hadn't been to a university. And those who had, only got skills to serve their colonial masters.'

His directness was like Shafi's. All my sympathy of the previous day flowed back.

I said, 'But you are just like Shafi. You don't try to cover up anything.'

Shafi said, 'What do we have to cover up? What do we have?'

I said, 'Shafi, when I asked you yesterday morning what you thought of the white people around the pool, was it the first time you had to think of such a thing?'

'It was the first time.'

'But how, Shafi? These people are all around you. They are around us here now, in the coffee shop.'

He said, 'I never *see* those people.'

He meant it in both ways: he never had occasion to meet white people, and when he saw them he never took them in.

Neither of them had so far touched the egg sandwich I had ordered for them. They were waiting for me to eat first. I ate. But then – though Shafi's friend had had no lunch – they only nibbled. They both left most of their sandwich uneaten. It was only out of courtesy that they had allowed me to order sandwiches for them; in a place like the Holiday Inn they were both nervous of eating non-Muslim food.

To avoid the steps, when they left, Shafi guided his limping friend down the carpeted luggage ramp at the side. Beside the very small, frail man with the damaged left leg, Shafi looked tall and protective. I thought of Behzad and his limping girl friend on the platform of Tehran railway station: revolutionaries, unnoticeable now, but conscious of the truth and danger they carried with them.

Shafi had promised to take me to the ABIM school and even to find some 'brave girls' there who would talk to me. He had brought his friend to look me over. The friend apparently didn't disapprove; and early the next morning Shafi came for me in his car.

Considering the hectic, mixed, modern city, with business signs in Chinese, English and Malay; considering the traffic jams and the ex-haust fumes that quivered in the heat; considering Shafi in his car, now driving with the rest (the boy whose village school, in the far north-east, had an earthen floor that became flooded in rain); I asked whether the city still felt strange to him.

He said it didn't. But he was a stranger in his village. He meant that literally. Buildings had changed; people had gone away; he no longer knew everybody. The village had ceased to be his, in the way it had been.

At the school, which was in the three-story ABIM building away from the centre of the city, I met an Australian, a big, middle-aged man with glasses and a skull-cap, sitting by himself and apparently doing nothing. Shafi said he was trying to learn about Islam. The busy young Malay men I met were of a type I had begun to recognize: village men whose faces, at first expressionless and with a hint of suspicion, lit up with smiles when Shafi explained my purpose: old manners, old village courtesies, just below the dourness.

The secretary-general was tougher. He said, as soon as Shafi intro-duced me, that the world had gone down morally in the last two or three hundred years, with industrialization. He spoke like a man who was about to put that right. He had an executive manner and he held a number of folders in his hand.

Shafi had work to do. He left me with Nasar. And again – as with many of the others – Nasar's small physical size was noticeable, his frailty. A hundred years or more ago – when the European coastal steamers moved from landing stage to landing stage, when the British plantations were beginning and the Chinese were coming in, and administrative towns were rough settlements on the edge of the forest – Nasar's ancestor was a sheikh, a Malay who lived in Arabia and shepherded Malay pilgrims to Mecca.

That sheikh, returning to Malaysia and to his village, just six miles away from what was now the city of Kuala Lumpur, had a son. The son, Nasar's great-grandfather, married when he was twelve. In old age, in 1934, this great-grandfather founded a Malay-language paper. He tried to stir the Malays up, to tell them that they had to fight for their survival. But nobody listened to him; even his own son, Nasar's grandfather, who should have been a religious teacher, decided that the money from teaching wasn't good enough, and became instead a paddy farmer, with seven acres. The son of the paddy farmer became a government servant, an officer in the Forestry Department. He was Nasar's father. So the family, once Arabic-educated and leaders in their own way, had in modern Malaysia become 'a lower middle-class family'.

Nasar himself, after a local education, had gone to England, to Bradford, to do a diploma in International Relations. He had learnt that the big powers were not interested in peace; they cared only about their spheres of influence; they sold arms. And he hadn't liked what he had seen of English life in Bradford.

'They are too individualistic. In Bradford people would say to me, "Why don't you spend your time to go to pubs, disco?" They're trying to say to be together with others, but not with your family. They are created by their own technology. The modernization of Malaysia, if it is not checked, will follow the same pattern. We accept technology, but it must not affect the basis of the social structure. Free mixing and alcoholism are the great dangers. That goes with free mixing. Trust is the basis of family happiness. Allah created men and women so that they would get married in a proper procedure and to raise a family. That is the basis of the social structure. We must avoid having free mixing. Finally we intend here to have a separate school for the girls and the boys. We believe that unemployment today is due partly to this philosophy of female liberation.'

Women, the family: they created anxiety in these slender men who, just emerging, perhaps sensed more than their physical frailty. At the end of our first conversation Shafi had said: 'When the girls come from the villages to Kuala Lumpur, they don't want to be protected by the law.'

The men were to go to the mosque for the 12.30 Friday prayers. Just before they left, just before the offices emptied and lights were turned off, Shafi introduced the brave girls he had promised.

We sat together in the front room overlooking the highway. It was a kind of storeroom, disordered, with plastic cups of undrunk milky coffee on a table, many folders and publications, and a lopsided office chair with one castor off. Two air-conditioners muffled the traffic noise.

The girls were of different racial types. One was brown-skinned and slender; one was pale, plump, and round-faced. They both wore long dresses and had covered heads. The brown girl had a head-covering in thin black cotton that had crinkled up and looked slack; there was about her a general adolescent untidiness which was fetching. The round-faced girl was neater. A white kerchief was drawn tightly on her head and over that she had a pink head-cover that was pinned below her chin.

They were both a little nervous. They had been at the ABIM school for two years, and they had come there because they hadn't done well enough in the government school. They were both now in the highest school form.

I asked them about the head-dress, which reminded me of the women in Tehran. They gave me the Malay word for it, *tu-dong*.

The girl with the black *tu-dong* said, 'The head is to be covered.'

The girl with the tight white-and-pink *tu-dong* said, 'Not a single piece of the hair must show.'

I said to the girl in black, 'But some of your hair is showing.' And a lot of it was.

She giggled, and became girlish.

I said, 'Why must the hair be covered?'

The girl in black said, 'The hair, you know – ' And she giggled again, before composing herself and saying, 'Some girls have very nice hair and sometimes men are sexually attracted to the hair.'

She spoke in Malay to the round-faced girl in pink, and the girl in pink went out of the room.

I said 'Is that bad? Is it bad for the woman? Or for the man?'

'Bad for both. For the girl it is a sin because you make men attracted to you.'

The girl in pink came back into the room. She said, 'The hair is *aurat*.'

'*Aurat?*'

'Things that cannot be shown.'

They spoke then in duet, making appropriate gestures. The girl in pink said, 'Girls can only show the face.' The girl in black said, 'And the hands from the wrist.'

'And the feet?'

'The feet?' the girl in black said. 'I don't think so. I don't think the feet are *aurat.*' Her own feet were visible, below her long cotton dress, which was as crinkled as her head-cover; and she was wearing pretty little high-heeled shoes with a strap and a buckle.

The girl in pink said, 'The feet are *aurat.*'

Some Malay words passed between them, and the girl in pink went out again.

The girl in black said, 'Two years in this school is a short time. Because there are so many things to learn.' Then, as though making up for her uncertainty about women's feet, she said, making a gesture down her body, 'A man is *aurat* from the waist to the knee.'

The girl in pink came back and said, 'The feet are *aurat.*'

(Who was sitting outside, ready with the answers? Could it have been the Australian?)

The girl in black said, 'Some girls cover their face. There are many in this school. Though it isn't necessary.'

'Why do they do it?'

The girl in pink said, 'Maybe they know more.'

The girl in black smiled, less nervously now, as though amused by how little she knew.

Her friend, plump and tidy, seemed altogether solider. She said, 'The main aim of these philosophies is to preserve the beauty and gentleness of the women. We can preserve our beauty. It's not for showing off. It's very bad.'

'Why is it bad?'

The girl in black, the frivolous one, as I now thought, said, 'All I know it's very bad.' She laughed. 'I *know*, but I can't express it.'

'Would you like to cover your face?'

'Maybe one day. When we know more.'

'And when we find it necessary,' the girl in pink said.

'What more do you have to learn? You've been here two years.'

'There is so *much* to learn,' the girl in black said.

The girl in pink said, 'We don't know Arabic.'

'So you don't understand the prayers you say.'

'We understand those. But the Koran is in Arabic and we would like to read the Koran in Arabic.'

'Would you have liked to stay on in the government school, if you had passed the examination?'

The girl in black nodded.

The girl in pink said in her plump, stately way: 'Right now in the government schools the education system is more towards academic.'

'Science,' the girl in black said, now apparently disapproving of the government school. 'Science. Technology. You have to pass all the examinations to get a place in the varsity – if you want to have a good job or having a high standard of living, to have a good earning. This religion they are not really taught in schools. The girls don't pray. They have forgotten how to pray. And you *must* pray.'

'Do you tell the girls they are going to hell?'

'Oh *no*!' the girl in pink said. 'We never say that. We have to be gentle with them. We have to talk to them gently.'

'Do you feel sorry for them?'

'Well, yes,' the girl in black said.

'Is it bad to want a good job?'

'It isn't bad,' the girl in pink said. 'But we can't be forever chasing materialistic things in life. Because there is life after death. So in our life we must balance ourselves between life on earth and life after death.'

I said to the girl in black – with her high-heeled shoes: 'Aren't you too young to be thinking of death?'

The girl in pink answered for her. She said solemnly, 'Death can come at any time.'

'And you want to go to heaven?'

'Of course. In heaven we mix with good people. Not only with good people. We can mix with our Prophet. Have you heard of our Prophet? Everything is good and beautiful in heaven. I can't tell you how good it is. Our God promised us. You can't compare it with things on earth.'

'Do you find time to read?'

'Yes, we read,' the girl in pink said.

'We read so *much*,' the girl in black said, with a hint of complaint.

'What was the last book you read?'

The girl in pink said, '*Far from the Madding Crowd*.'

'That's a school book. I don't mean that. I mean something you read for yourself, for the interest.'

The girl in black said, 'With all the school work now, I haven't read recently. I can't think.'

The girl in pink said, 'We read Barbara Cartland, Perry Mason.'

'James Hadley Chase,' the girl in black said, suddenly remembering.

'Denise Robins,' the girl in pink said, her round face brightening as it had brightened when she described the life in heaven.

'Harold Robbins?'

The girl in black said, 'I didn't like Harold Robbins and I stopped.'
She giggled. The girl in pink smiled.

'Why did you stop?'

The girl in black said, 'I can't tell you. I can only translate what we say
in Malay. We say, "The book is dirty."'

'What about Barbara Cartland and Denise Robins?'

'Oh *no*!' the girl in pink said, melting. 'They are not dirty.' And then,
with a curious primness, 'They are for young girls.'

'But aren't the people in the books too far away from you? They are
English, European, white. They're Christian.'

The girl in pink said, and I began to detect another character below her
solidity, 'I read just to pass the time.'

'And our teacher made us read them,' the girl in black said.

'To improve our English,' the girl in pink said.

I said, 'The Mills and Boon books – do you get them here?'

These short paperback light romances, known by the name of their
English publisher rather than the names of the authors, have been
successfully promoted in many countries of the Commonwealth. They
meet the imaginative needs of people new to education and city life; they
appear to instruct in modern ways of feeling, and are read even by
university students, and even by men.

'Mills and Boon!' the girl in pink said, softly, melting again, as at the
memory of some especially sweet and rich food.

'Why are those books so nice?'

Formal once more, the girl in pink said, 'When we read, the love is nice
because it's all fantasy.'

'You mean you wouldn't like that sort of thing to happen to you?'

'No.'

'But what's the fun then?'

'We just read to imagine how nice their life is.'

'Nice?'

'They're rich,' the girl in pink said. 'They have a big house, big car.'
Her voice went soft and round: 'And they're in love.'

'Love? Wouldn't your marriage be arranged?'

'Oh *no*! Not with us.'

The big house, the big car: were these Islamic ducklings – though
learning the rules, contemplating the after-life – already secret city
swans?

I said, 'Would you like to live in a village? I have spoken to some
people here who think that village life is best.'

'No,' the girl in black said. 'I want to live here.'

The girl in pink – solid again, well-trained – said, 'The village is more peaceful. I would like living in the village.'

The girl in black seemed to change her mind. She said, 'Yes, the village is more peaceful.' Then she changed her mind again. 'But I would like to be in the town because everything happens here.'

The girl in pink said soulfully, 'It is more peaceful in the village.'

Like someone who now knew her own mind, and had found a way of saying what she felt, the girl in black said, 'I would like to be in the town because it is also the centre of the religious movement.'

I said, to provoke them, 'But there are so many strangers in the town.'

'Yes,' the girl in black said, and she was quick and firm. 'We have too many immigrants.' It was the word used by Malays to describe non-Malays – Chinese, mainly; it was the word rejected by non-Malays, who claimed a century of residence. 'The immigrants cause trouble. It's the British who brought them here. The British introduced the British system. Before that it was all Islamic system.'

I had thought of the girl in black – with her messy *tu-dong* head-covering, her high-heeled shoes, her uncertainty about the Islamic rules – as the more frivolous of the two. Now I saw that politically, racially, she was the fiercer. She took over this part of the conversation. The girl in pink merely listened, with her fixed sweet smile.

The girl in black said, 'The Chinese try to monopoly our economy. They are good businessmen. We are left behind. It isn't true what they say about Malays being lazy. We know it isn't true, but it hurts us to hear these things. If we don't have the Chinese we could be a good business people. If you look at history, in the time of the Malacca Sultanate we Malays are very well known as the best business people.'

'Why do you worry so much about the Chinese?'

'The Chinese have China, the Indians have India. We only have Malaysia.'

'Don't you have Indonesia and all the islands?'

She made a face; her young forehead creased. 'Indonesia is full of Christians – you don't know.'

'Were you born in Kuala Lumpur?' I asked the girl in black.

She was, but her family came from Indonesia, from Java. '*Long* ago,' she said.

'Before the war,' the girl in pink said.

So the girl in black, or her family, had come during the British time. She was Indonesian, but that meant she was racially akin to the Malays; and she was also Muslim. After forty years she could consider herself a Malaysian. After a hundred years and more, the Chinese – who had made her country – were still immigrants.

The inner offices were in darkness. The men were still at the mosque. The girls walked down to the road with me. The girl in pink crossed the busy road to wait with me until I got a taxi. The girl in black remained on the other side, in the doorway, the idea of feminine allure not far from her now, smiling, giving occasional little waves, friendly to me, an outsider; but full of her confused passions. Her slack, inexpertly tied *tu-dong* did not hide her hair; and below her long, drab-coloured, sack-like cotton dress – the garb of Islamic modesty, the symbol of her aggression – her pretty little high-heeled shoes showed, with their straps and buckles.

To be Malay was to be Muslim – it was written in the laws of the new state. But to be Malay was also to be denied the great rich British-Chinese city, where everything happened. Money had come to the tropical land of forest and river and villages; and money created new frenzies and frustrations.

3

❖❖❖❖❖

Between Malacca and the
Genting Highlands

THE LAND was rich: rain and heat and rivers, fertile soil bursting with
life, with bananas, rice-fields, palm trees, rubber. Grass grew below the
rubber trees; and cattle, which would have suffered in the sun, found
pasture in the shade. The heat which in the town was hard to bear was in
the countryside more pleasant. Water and sun encouraged vegetation
that sheltered and cooled; and green quickly covered the red earth where
it had been exposed by road works or building developments. The Malay
villages were never far away; the houses, with steep pitched roofs and
low timber walls, were set in little gardens. And regularly there were the
little towns of the colonial period, Chinese settlements: two-story shop-
houses, concrete and corrugated iron, the shops set back, the pavement
sheltered by the house above. The dates − painted on the shop-houses,
or in raised concrete numerals − were recent; many were from the
1930s; the colony was developed late.

I saw this on a drive one Saturday from Kuala Lumpur south to
Malacca. I went to Malacca for the sake of its historical name: the
Malacca Straits, the Malacca cane, Malacca pepper.

In the centre of the town there was a red-painted church dated 1753;
there was a museum beside the gateway of a ruined old European fort.
But elsewhere history seemed to have been burnt away in the heat. The
shore at low tide was wide and flat, of soft black mud; drains from the
town poured into it; and the black mud was dotted with the holes of
small crabs and marked with the trails of amphibious creatures, little
leaping minnows and finned black creatures that wriggled.

A ship was anchored far out. A line of barges, each with a bare-backed,
saronged Malay at the tiller, was being towed into the town canal, an
open sewer, grey rather than black or brown, that was lined with the
warehouses and houses of the recent colonial period.

The European past was older than that picture suggested. Malacca, guarding the route to the spice islands of the East Indies, was once thought valuable; and the Portuguese conquered Malacca (seven months' sailing from Lisbon) in 1511, eight years before – on the other side of the world – Cortés marched on Mexico, twenty-two years before Pizarro went to Peru. That was hard to grasp now; what was even harder was that Portugal and the West arrived here not long after Islam.

The West, after its many mutations, had remained new, prompting change, prompting disturbance, as it was doing even now. Islam had aged, had appeared to have become part of a self-contained and – to use the word Shafi was soon to give me – 'mediocre' Malay village life.

That subject of mediocrity, the contradiction between his longing for village ways and his wish to see Malays holding their own, was on Shafi's mind. He had telephoned me about it. He hadn't been happy with what he had said.

And when on Sunday I told him about my drive to Malacca and the richness of the land I had seen, he said, 'You can throw a seed and it will grow.' He made a gesture of throwing a seed into the pool of the Holiday Inn. 'You can put a bare hook in the water and catch a fish. That is why perhaps Malays have been mediocre. They live beside rivers. This will of course provide fish, fertile land for paddy cultivation, easy movement by boats. Life is too easy, compared to the Chinese, who come from a four-seasoned country.'

He had prepared some thoughts about the self-sufficiency of the village, and he wished to speak these first.

'We are a close-knit community and we know little of the outside world. You asked me why we didn't have technical men, professionals. We have on our own, to meet our requirements, builders who are themselves an architect, who can conceive plans that are required by the clients and can turn that plan into reality by his skills. We don't have doctors. But we have traditional medical practice within the community. If I can remember, there have never been chronic diseases which require immediate operation in my village.'

After he had said that, we returned to talking of his life and career. His first visit to Kuala Lumpur in 1963 with his school scout troop had been a shock. But a second visit two years afterwards was easier.

'I was getting a little more used, a little more brave. I came with an old man who was a distant relative and we stayed ten days, in various places of relatives. We stayed in Malay kampongs and also with relatives in modern situations. I can give one instance of getting more brave. I took a cab to the museum. On the way back home I couldn't figure which way to take, after walking some distance. Then only I took a cab again.'

'Why was that a brave thing to do? You were seventeen.'

'My parents did not allow me to come to KL with someone unknown to the family. And not many people like me leave the kampong to come to KL in this way. They are not frightened. They may or may not be frightened. But they have nothing to do in KL.

'So I wasn't frightened when I came to the college in KL in 1966 for pre-university education. I was nineteen. My seniors in school were all studying here in KL. I stayed in a students' house, run by the students. In 1968 I went to the Institute of Technology. There I began to be interested in student politics. That was when I came into contact with Anwar Ibrahim. I was twenty-one and he was twenty-one.'

'Did you go out with girls?'

'What do you mean by going out? You see, I admired somebody, and the person I admired was staying with a family and I could hardly take her out. So to take anybody out means being unfaithful. She was a distant relative. It was a childhood admiration. It began in my village, with family meetings.

'There were political disturbances in KL in 1969, race riots between Malays and Chinese. That was when I became a leader. A few friends invited me to go for a demonstration at a public rally, and I didn't go. I sensed that a disturbance was coming up that day. It was a demonstration of Malays against Chinese.'

'Did you have strong feelings against the Chinese?'

'Yes. I should say I grew up with a feeling against the Chinese. In terms of religious taboos. But the feelings in KL were different. They were national politics. About seven that evening, the day of that demonstration, I was in a hostel and I heard a radio announcement about a curfew being clamped on KL. This announcement justified my not going. My sense was right. I arranged group security measures around the college, got the students to have their dinner and remain calm and quiet. There were no other leaders. So I became a leader by accident. After these riots we had meetings with Anwar Ibrahim and other Muslim students' organizations. We began to talk about nationalism and Islam. And that's how it began.'

'Did you never have doubts about the faith as a student?'

'No. I questioned only the systems. Why marriage? I even proposed that there should be contract marriages. In the sense that if you long to have a descendant, you marry the person on the understanding that after you have a child the contract is over. That was wild thinking on my part. Those are the few daydreams I had.'

'You were thinking about the girl you admired? Did she respond?'

'The girl I had been admiring did not respond. After I left college I worked with a youth organization. Then after four years I went to the United States.'

This was news to me. Nothing Shafi had said had suggested that he had gone abroad.

'I approached the cultural officer of the American embassy after hearing that there was some exchange of youth workers. At first he said the places had all been taken, but after one month he came back and offered me the trip.

'The United States was a shock. Before leaving we were given literatures about what to expect. But on arrival at JFK airport the first shock was the biological shock, the time. It was one day earlier: we were still on the same day that we left. I expected JFK to be big and things to be different. I didn't marvel. From the air I saw beautiful housing estates close to the beach and I thought that was beautiful. And – arriving at the hotel – as I expected, I stayed with an African.'

'You expected that?'

'It didn't surprise me to be with an African, because I was the only Malaysian in the programme.' But from the emphasis Shafi gave to being with the African (anonymous, in his narrative), I felt that, coming directly after the long flight and the biological shock, the experience had unsettled him. 'My suspicion – for having that African to be with me – was that the organizers of the programme were trying to group the familiar people with similar backgrounds together. I expected there was going to be some segregation in the programme. It didn't make me unhappy. I thought they were putting a generalization to us, African and Malaysian, that we come from underdeveloped countries – the same state of civilization, if you want to put it that way.

'The food was all western food. Being a Muslim, it was difficult for me to enjoy the food because I had a suspicion that the food is not cooked in the Muslim way. On the second night my programme director brought me to see an X-rated film. And I felt that most of the experience I am going to face in America is not my' – he searched for the word – 'culture, is something foreign to me, that things there – whatever is yes in America is no to us in Malaysia, and whatever is no in America with us is yes. The technical developments, the material developments, is all I expected. You can get it anywhere.'

'Anywhere?' I was interested in this idea of the developed world as something just existing, just being there: part of an almost pre-ordained division of men: creative, uncreative; faithless, believing.

'When I stopped in Bangkok, Hong Kong, Tokyo, I see the same thing – tall buildings, busy people, modern technology. The thing I could not find is the person with the same religious background as I am.'

'Why were you so surprised? You had gone to a foreign country. A big country, an important country. Weren't you interested in what they had to show?'

'I am not interested in what they had to show. But I am asking why, with the sort of developments that they have, they could not even sit down for a moment to ponder the universal creation. The non-Muslims, the unbelievers in the greatness of the creator, did not even have the time to think about this creator. Later on, when I was in Chicago, I spoke to some Jews, some Negroes, and some Americans about Islam. And, compared with the TM that they practise, the Transcendental Meditation, my short explanation did really attract them.'

'What do you know about other religions?'

'I've read around at random. But how much can you think of the universe with the limited brain that we have?'

'Don't you think you may be claiming too much for yourself and running down other people too easily?'

'You can say that a man is civilized if he knows where he is from and where he is going. I could not agree that a man is educated and civilized if he spends his whole life-time studying the universe and in the end worship the stars, not knowing where he is from and where he is going. They have not found the answer.'

'Shafi, you think you have found the answer?'

'I think so.'

'Tell me more about your time in the United States.'

'Before I left KL, one reporter asked me what do I want to do there. I said to him that I wanted to study all the policies made by the civilized – by the so-called civilized – people in the modern world, so that we may not be trapped with mistakes that they have done.'

'Are you saying that you have civilization and they don't?'

'Civilization to us does not mean material development only. It means to us being able to develop the man, the person, closer to the creator.'

I said, 'So you don't think too much of me?'

'Now, please don't be emotional about this.' Shafi laughed. The sentence had come out pat; I felt he had made the joke before. 'If you stay longer perhaps I would be able to convince you. But about the US, somebody gave me a book. Basically, from the conversations and discussions with the people, they said that money is religion and sex is the prophet. Basically their life revolves around money and sex.'

'Do you think my life revolves around money and sex?'

'I would say: what is the purpose of your writing? Is it to tell people what it's all about?'

'Yes. I would say comprehension.'

'Is it not for money?'

'Yes. But the nature of the work is also important.'

I had shocked him. The idea of a vocation was new to him; and – it was part of his openness – for a little while he considered it. He relished religious debate – I could tell that now; but when he spoke again, it was not to deny or challenge what I had said about myself.

He said, with a regard that was like concern, 'I would say you are losing something. You are not doing justice to yourself. You have been searching for truth and yet you haven't got the truth.'

'Let's get back to the United States.'

'I made friends with people there. New York, Chicago, Washington, Indiana. I was working with an Outward Bound programme, a programme for the poor. But I looked forward to returning back home. I think of America now as a place to go for a short visit but not to stay. When I came back I worked for the Red Cross. Then I took up a job in a business firm, a construction firm. A Malay firm. As a general manager.'

'You were very young.'

'I was twenty-eight or twenty-nine. There the manipulations in business were without ethics. It was with corruption. Cheating in construction, not delivering work to the specification.'

'Was this because it was a Malay firm?'

'Business is such. This business is filled up with unscrupulous people. The pressures of this corruption were too great. I left the firm after about a year. I was getting quite a good salary. About a thousand dollars a month. This was in 1973–4. I tried to start up on my own in the construction business, trying to be honest. It doesn't pay to be honest. I got a contract and tried to be honest – and you are trying to be honest and you are the only honest person in that field. Say I build a house, and the specification is fixed in concrete mixture, and I try to adhere to the specification, my workers – most of them are Chinese – did not follow the instruction. And I ran into trouble. People don't believe me. The clients don't believe me and they are quite prejudiced about Malay contractors. It is true of their suspicion, because Malays are just starting in the field. Once I was six months without a job, without contracts. It was a difficult time. But it was satisfying because you are doing it for yourself and you know you are honest about it. The purpose of doing business for us as Muslims is to fulfil the requirements of the society.'

'Isn't that true of all business?'

'Some business are meant strictly for profit. At the end of my three years as a contractor I began to be associated with Islamic activities more intensely. And I feel there is a need, the need is very much to fulfil the requirements of the Islamic movement rather than that of business – which I was in.'

'What about the girl you admired?'

'On return from the US, I got married. Not the girl I admired, but a girl from a village who has probably a similar background to mine. A girl from a kampong. She comes from a poor family, from another state. Which is breaking a tradition of my family. Because none of my family, none of my close relatives, got married to somebody from outside the state. My parents did not object. But I feel I have broken a tradition. It doesn't worry me. My wife is working in a firm, a British firm. The business practices do not worry her. She is mainly doing secretarial work. We don't have a house yet. It's under construction. I bought it from a developer, for 58,000 dollars.'

'So you've given up the idea of returning to the village?'

'It doesn't matter to me whether I live in a village or in town. I love the village because it's not polluted in terms of environment, in terms of society, and in terms of resources. They are not materialist people. They are people with dignity. They are quite pious. Even in town, if I have that unpolluted community with unpolluted environment, I would like to stay. It may not be possible, but I have to be in town because of the nature of my activities with the Muslim youth movement. We have purchased eight acres of land collectively about seventeen miles from KL, and we are trying to plan for a self-contained community and for facilities run under an Islamic system. Islamic kindergarten; a co-operative; health centre, with Muslim doctors. Planning the utilization of resources to the maximum.'

'You will be trying to re-create the village life. But didn't you say that that life of your village in Kota Baru was mediocre?'

'Yes, in some ways. Because it's self-sufficient. The only difference is that we are guided by the sense of religious ways.'

'Surely all Malays are guided by that?'

'Not all Malays are guided by that. There are some communities which emphasize traditions more than religion. Some of those traditions are quite pagan.'

He meant pre-Islamic. And I began to see that, over and above his wish to preserve the Malay village community, he had a contrary missionary wish – given him by the new Islam – to purify the old ways of the village, to cleanse his Malay people of an important part of themselves. But that was another question. He knew he hadn't answered the question about mediocrity.

He said, 'This attempt to make Malays less mediocre is a difficult attempt. I have not put my thoughts.'

He had lost his village. He had married outside his state and broken a family tradition. By education, travel, profession, he had without knowing it broken other traditions. In the new world, he had failed in business. I could see how, without Islam, he would be lost. But whether he liked it or not, Shafi had entered the new world; and it was not possible in this world for him to hide. His survival depended on trying again and trying harder; it depended on vision.

As we were walking away from the coffee shop – and he was worried again about appearing to push himself forward, about giving himself an individuality above that of his fellows – I said, 'I want you to think about one thing. I don't want to argue, though I know you want me to argue with you. But I think that because you travelled to America with a fixed idea you might have missed some things. I think you are being less than fair to people outside.'

He said, 'I accept that there are dedicated people there, and good people. But I cannot compromise.'

From the *New Straits Times*, November 6, 1979:

THREE CHARGES OF DESTROYING HINDU IDOLS IN TEMERLOH
Temerloh, Mon. – An ex-religious teacher and a student pleaded not guilty in the magistrate's court here today to charges of having destroyed Hindu idols in the Temerloh district, last year . . .

This too was part of the Islamic movement among the educated young. It was a more elemental kind of Islam, and I felt that it embarrassed Shafi. He said it wasn't important. But it was important.

ABIM, Shafi's group, was not the only Muslim youth group in Malaysia; Anwar Ibrahim, with his high idea of Islam, was not the only leader. There were other leaders, with less difficult messages. Missionaries (from India or Pakistan) had brought the idol-smashing message to Malaysia. They had worked out, from various books they had consulted, how many thousands of years in paradise a Muslim earned for every idol he smashed; and they had calculated that a grand total of thirty smashed idols won a Muslim the jackpot, an eternity in paradise.

The Malay rage was really about the Chinese shrines – some no more than concrete boxes – that were everywhere in the towns (there were two just outside the Holiday Inn). But the Chinese were powerful, and had their secret societies. The Tamil Hindus were a small, pacific community. So Hindu images were smashed. On many nights – during a three-week period in 1978 – Tamil temples were desecrated.

Then, at the Kerling temple, there was a tragedy. A group of five idol-smashers (at least two university students among them) were met by eight temple guards. Four of the idol-smashers were killed. Idol-smashing stopped after that. And now – more important than the Temerloh temple case – was the trial of the eight Kerling guards on charges of 'culpable homicide not amounting to murder'.

The trial was taking place far from Kerling, at Klang, on the west coast, about twenty miles from Kuala Lumpur. It was a Tamil taxi-driver who took me there. But his thoughts were not of the trial. His thoughts were of money; they always were.

The first day I took him I said, 'You haven't put your meter on.' He said, 'My head is full of something. I am thinking about how to go to Malacca tomorrow. It will cost 140 dollars at least. I don't have the money. My sister is getting married.' I said, 'Why will it cost so much to go to Malacca?' He said, 'There are seven of us. My mother, my sister, my wife, and my three children. Seven. The fare will be twenty dollars each minimum. By line taxi.' And as we stopped and started in the fuming Kuala Lumpur traffic, he involved me in his anxiety.

I said, 'Do seven of you have to go to Malacca? Does your wife have to go?'

'She *must* go. It's her sister getting married.'

'I thought you said it was your sister.'

'Her sister is my sister.'

'All right. I can see that your wife has to go. What about your own sister? Does she have to go to Malacca?'

'She *wants* to go. She knows the girl *well*.'

'Well, let your wife and sister go. Two fares. Forty dollars.'

'What about my mother? You don't know our customs. My mother has to go.'

'All right. Why not let your mother, your wife and your sister go? You stay.'

'Three women? Going on their own to Malacca?'

'All right. You go with them.'

'But if I go, the children can't stay. They are very young and they're all girls.'

So it was seven to Malacca, or nothing. One man, with six dependent women and girls: no wonder he seemed close to gibbering.

And now, taking me to the trial at Klang, he was close to gibbering again. Money, money: he needed lots of it. If only he could get his hands on 60,000 dollars he would be all right, he said. He would give up taxi-driving and go into stationery. There was money in stationery. You deposited 10,000 with the wholesaler and he gave you 20,000 dollars' worth of goods with three months' credit.

If only, if only. And he had these seven mouths to feed; and his three children were all girls; and there was his sister to marry off. And the government gave everything to the Malays. The Chinese were much nicer. They were dangerous enemies but good friends. 'You know Malays? You like Malays? The Malays stab you in the back.' He bounced about with all his separate anguishes.

I said, 'Did you go to Malacca? Did you borrow the money?'

'From a Punjabi. A hundred. Next month I have to pay him back 125.'

'So you borrow money at 300 percent. And now you want to raise 60,000 dollars.'

He changed the subject by going back to an older one: his expenses. He said he bought ten catties of rice a week. 'How much is a catti?' – 'A kilo.' – 'So you buy *twenty-two* pounds of rice a week?' – 'Yes.' Twenty-two dollars a day for the hire of his taxi from the company, he had said; twenty-two miles to Klang, he had said; and now, twenty-two pounds of rice a week. It was his fated number.

Yet, for all his troubles, he was full of friends. He seemed to see them at every traffic jam. 'He's from my company.' Another time he said, 'You see that car. I used to drive it. Then the manager called me and gave me this one and he gave that one to that fellow. He's a very bad driver. He drinks and drives. I never do that. I just take a little toddy. Once a week. On Saturday afternoon. Two litres.'

'Two litres!'

'It's good for the body.'

I said, 'You don't have money, but you have three children. You borrow money at 300 percent to go to a wedding in Malacca. And now you tell me you get drunk every Saturday.' I saw in the mirror that one of his top front teeth was missing. 'How did you lose that tooth?'

'In a scooter accident.'

'How do all these accidents happen to you? Why don't you go back to the country and work your land?'

'Don't have land.'

And that was so. It was hard to think that – long before Islam and the coming of the West – his South Indian ancestors had spread their religion and epics and sculpture and architecture to south-east Asia. He wouldn't have known it himself. He was descended from labourers brought over in the nineteenth century and after to work on the British plantations; that was all his past. Now – in post-colonial, Muslim

Malaysia – he was squeezed out. He was as much a lost man as Shafi and the other village Malays. And perhaps he was more lost, not having a sense of community or a knowledge of a pure past, not having a faith to turn to, not being able to blame the world, not knowing who to blame. And the idol-smashing at Kerling and Temerloh, the trial at Klang – in which he pretended not to be interested: these would only have been surface anxieties to a man born with a full burden of distress.

Town followed town on this developed western coastal strip: no Malay villages here. In Klang, we had to ask where the court was. It was a calm, colonial, two-story building, some way out of the centre. There was no crowd in the yard. And upstairs, in the court-room, there was no one on the public benches. The trial made headlines; it was closely followed; people were nervous. But the event itself seemed private, as unimportant as Shafi had said it was: a Malay magistrate, two Malay policemen, a young, good-looking Indian boy in the witness-stand, an Indian woman interpreter in a yellow sari sitting beside the boy giving evidence, an Indian lawyer with sideburns asking questions.

The seven other accused men – who that night had faced the idol-smashers – were in the dock, a little timber-railed pen in the middle of the room; they seemed quite at ease. Four air-conditioners roared; it was impossible to hear anything that was said by lawyer or witness or interpreter. A private occasion; yet four lost and foolish young men, bewildered by the new world, their bewilderment simplified into a dream of thirty smashed idols and an eternity in heaven, had died.

We went back to the town centre and after a drive-around went to the jetty, which was built over a beach of black mud. Rowing boats with missing planks rotted in that mud and were the colour of the mud; on the brown water boats still in use were moored between upright poles; crows and a starved cat picked at refuse. Rain came and dimmed the view without lessening the heat, made everything grey, fleetingly pitted the almost liquid mud. It was possible to imagine this unlovely bay a hundred years before: a fishing settlement perhaps, and it would have seemed then as a place to which the world would never come.

The gap-toothed Tamil driver, lost for some time, came back, wet from the rain. He had found some crabs to buy. He said in his quick, excited way that crabs were twice the price in Kuala Lumpur.

I said, 'Are you going to sell them?'

'Going to take them home. Going to use them.'

'You will never raise 60,000 dollars.'

Far from that coast, a new-cut road led up through the forested hills to the Genting Highlands. The clouds came down over the hills; it was cool enough for pullovers. But at the end of that road, after the tall white trunks of forest trees, after the forest gloom, the creepers, the large, heart-shaped leaves, the ferns and wild palms and wild bananas; after that, there was no settlement, no town, only a vast amusement area, a concrete playground in the mist: a toy lake, toy walks, toy trains, a hotel and a casino.

The pleasures of money in Malaysia were simple. Money magnified the limitations of places like Malaysia, small, uneducated, and coming late to everything. Money – from oil, rubber, tin, palm oil – changed old ways. But money only turned people into buyers of imported goods, fixed the country in a dependent relationship with the developed world, kept all men colonials.

It was possible to understand the withdrawal of someone like Shafi; the rage of the idol-smashers; and the wish, among other Malays, to pretend that they were Arabs, living as purely as in the days of the Prophet.

4

◆◆◆◆◆

Araby

THERE WAS AN Islamic commune in Kuala Lumpur. The young Malays there were said to have rejected modern ways and modern goods; they farmed a little piece of land and lived, as they thought, like Arabs – old Arabs, not new Arabs. They did not welcome visitors. Shafi – sympathetic to the commune idea, but not wishing to interfere in the affairs of another group – passed on my name to them. For many days nothing happened.

Then Khairul telephoned me. He was of the commune. His English accent was clipped and sharp, like a Japanese in an old-fashioned American war film. And, like a character in a film, he said, 'How do I know you are not KGB or CIA?' I thought he knew. He said that some time ago they had allowed two reporters from *Time* to visit them, but they had since grown to feel that the men were CIA. (In fact, as I learned later, *Time* didn't use the story; and Khairul – like other shunners of publicity running into an unexpected silence – must have been a little peeved.)

He said he was going to bring three people to see me that evening. I asked him to bring two. I said I was too tired to face four people in my Holiday Inn room.

'What aspect are you interested in?' Khairul said, in his snapping Japanese voice. 'Spiritual, economic?'

'Spiritual.'

And then I thought I had said the wrong thing. It would have been better to talk about the economic side. From Anwar Ibrahim of ABIM I had heard a little about the economic ideas of some Islamic groups in Malaysia. They said the West was collapsing. 'And they're creating the impression that the Islamic economic system comprises mainly preparing ketchup and *halal* [ritually pure] foods. In terms of slaughtering one cow a week.'

But my worry about the choice of subject was needless, like my precaution about the number of visitors. Khairul and his men didn't come. Instead, there was a message asking me to meet a man outside the

Parliament Building at ten the next morning. I decided not to do that. I thought that if I did nothing, and kept silent afterwards, there was a chance that Khairul's interest might be piqued, and he might become the seeker. And it was like that.

One evening some days later, about half past seven, Khairul telephoned. He was downstairs, in the Holiday Inn, with his three men. They came up. Or rather, they blew in. Three of them – including Khairul himself – were quite startling with their turbans and long green gowns.

One man wore trousers and shirt. He sat in one of the armchairs. A turbanned man sat in the other armchair. Khairul, merry-eyed, sunburnt, unexpectedly jovial in his Arab costume, sat on the low table between the armchairs. A very small, bearded man, who said he was a journalist and wished to take notes, sat on the chair at the dressing table and immediately took out pen and paper.

Khairul said, 'What do you want to know?'

And the four men so filled the room, and I was still so startled by their appearance – turbans, grubby gowns – and their excited state, that I forgot again about the Islamic economic system.

I said, 'You are all different people. I would like to know how you have arrived at where you are.'

'Yes,' Khairul said, 'we're all different.'

All of them, except for Khairul, came from the state of Kedah in the north. The man in trousers and shirt – he looked more Chinese than Malay and didn't seem as excited as the others – said he was a doctor. Khairul himself was a lawyer. The white-turbanned man with a mulatto cast of face was a missionary and a *haji*, someone who had made the pilgrimage to Mecca. He was the least fine of the four, but he was the spokesman. Khairul interpreted, and soon was quite at ease, drawing up and folding his legs on the low table below the hanging light in its Holiday Inn wickerwork shade. I was on the bed, in pyjamas.

I asked the *haji* whether he had any romantic feeling for village life. He said no. Village life was not Islamic. The doctor said, 'There are many animistic and Hindu traditions.'

It was what Shafi had told me: that contradiction in Shafi's thought had come out towards the end of our last conversation. The village way was the true Malay way; but that way had to be altered. Belief had to be purified, the old pagan traditions of the village uprooted.

Khairul said, 'The wedding ceremonies in the villages are still Hindu.'

'Does it matter?'

Yes, the *haji* said. It went against the Koran.

The *haji* said his mother's family came from Yemen. They went to Kedah by way of Thailand. His father's family came from Sumatra.

They were – and the *haji* and everybody else laughed – cannibals, head-hunters. It was his grandfather who had been converted to Islam. His father had become a religious teacher. He was a farmer and poor; when he died he left exactly one dollar. He refused to send his son to the government school. He taught the boy himself.

The *haji* said, in Khairul's translation, 'He taught me everything. He taught me Koran, Arabic. He taught me about Napoleon and Hitler.'

'What did he tell you about Napoleon?'

'Napoleon evolved simple and effective laws. But he cannot be compared with Khalid, the companion and general of the Prophet. Khalid said that his moment of contentment was when the armies of the faithful and the infidels clashed and only the sound of horses could be heard and sparks flew from the clashing swords in the dark night.'

'The dark, cold night,' the doctor said.

'Compare that with Napoleon. He withdraws his forces in order to meet his love. It is in history. You can read it. So how could you compare the two personalities? Khalid sacrifices his life to uphold his religion. Napoleon thinks of his love. Women have the same physical attributes everywhere. But conviction is one.' That was Khairul's translation. 'If Napoleon was a Muslim he would have been at the back of the army and most probably would have been quarantined – '

'Court-martialled?'

'That's it,' Khairul said, accepting the suggestion. 'He would have been court-martialled for immorality.'

I wanted the *haji* to talk more of his boyhood. I would have liked to compare his memories with Shafi's. But he said he wanted to talk about bigger things. Still, I tried.

I said, 'What was it about village life you disliked as not Islamic? Apart from the wedding ceremonies.'

'Usury.'

'Who were the moneylenders?'

'Malays, Chinese.' And the *haji* stopped, to spare my feelings.

'Indians,' the journalist said, sitting at the dressing table, writing. 'Chettys. You've heard about the Chettys?'

I said I had. 'What did you dislike about the Chinese?'

'Their way of life,' the *haji* said, round-faced, smiling. 'If they became Muslims I wouldn't mind. We have no racial feeling.' (But it was said in Malaysia that if the Chinese as a community became Muslims, the Malays would become Buddhists.)

He looked after his father's cows and worked in his father's fields until he was fifteen. Then his father died. A thousand people came to his father's funeral.

'But why didn't they support your father? He was a religious teacher. Why did they let him die with only a dollar to his name?'

The *haji* didn't answer. He said he continued reading after his father's death. He read everything he could get. 'I read a book by Sukarno. *Revolution. Revolution* something.'

The doctor said, '*Under the Shade of Revolution.*' (That was a mistranslation. The title of the Sukarno book, *Dibawah Bendera Revolusi*, might better be translated as 'Under the Flag of Revolution'.)

The journalist, making notes of our conversation, had also been looking at various papers on the dressing table, and there was an anxiety in one part of my mind that he might find something he wouldn't like.

He spoke now in Malay to Khairul. Khairul asked whether I had a camera. I said no. Khairul said of the journalist, 'He has a camera, but no film. Can he buy some here?'

I said he could try; the shop in the lobby was still open. And the little gowned man left, big white tennis shoes flashing over the dark Holiday Inn carpet.

I took some snuff, explaining that it was tobacco and nothing harsher – I knew they disapproved of stimulants.

Khairul said, 'Tobacco is not encouraged by Islam.'

'Not encouraged?'

'It isn't forbidden. It's not encourageable. It's a technical word in Arabic, you understand.'

The *haji* said, smiling, 'Most of the tobacco manufacturers are Jewish and in order to destroy the Jews we must not consume their products. There is a very good book about the Jews.'

The doctor said, 'By Henry Ford.'

'The motor-car man,' Khairul said.

'Can I get this book here?'

'In the Perkim Bookstore,' Khairul said. 'You can get it there.'

The *haji* said, 'The Jews are the enemies of God. Do you know the evolution theory?'

'I know of it.'

The *haji* fixed his smiling face on me. 'Do you know why the theory was put around?'

I said, 'For a man with a farming background you know a lot.'

'I know very little. I know just a fraction of what is in the Koran.'

Khairul, cross-legged and comfortable on the low table between the doctor and the *haji*, said, 'If you know the Koran you know everything. Economics, politics, family laws – the principles are all embedded in the Koran.'

There was a knock at the door.

I said, 'That will be your friend.'

And I got up in my pyjamas to let the journalist in. With his turban, his round tinted glasses, his long, thin beard, his gown and a further sarong-like garment which I hadn't noticed before, he looked like a shrunken little sun-dried dervish, lost in the desert of the Holiday Inn corridor; and he stood with his big white shoes very close to the door as though, away from his fellows, he was really quite shy. He hadn't got any film.

I got back into bed and said to the *haji*, patient and smiling in his armchair, 'You were telling me about evolution. You were saying it was put forward for a certain reason.'

The *haji* said, 'What do you know about the history of the Jews?'

'Very little.'

'They are a genius race,' the *haji* said. 'Did you know that? This is confirmed by the books of God.'

Khairul added on his own, 'They are a genius race. Throughout history.'

The *haji* said, 'Other races are jealous of them because they are a genius race. They have contributed much in the sense of concepts. Karl Marx.'

'Engels,' Khairul said, speaking for himself.

The journalist, making his notes again at the dressing table, said, 'Tolstoy.'

'All Jews,' the doctor said.

I felt we had got far from the subject of evolution. I said, 'Would you like some tea?'

The *haji* said, 'Is it made by Muslims here? How do they make it?'

'They use tea-bags. And the boys are Malays.'

The *haji* didn't look convinced. They talked among themselves in Malay, and Khairul said, 'We'll have a bottled drink.'

I got down from the bed and went to the little Sanyo refrigerator, which stood at an angle in the corner not far from the *haji*'s chair and was labelled 'Your Private Bar'. It had a double row of miniatures on the top, and the shelves had a modest stock of drink. Beer, German wine, tonic water, Coca-Cola, Seven-Up. They chose Coca-Cola.

'One bottle would do,' Khairul said. 'It will be enough for the four of us. It is our way.'

I took the bottle to the bathroom, saying, to prevent thoughts of pollution, 'There is an opener next to the door.' I brought out one of the sanitized, cellophane-wrapped glasses and gave it to the *haji*, with the opened bottle.

The journalist was fingering two newspaper clippings on the dressing table.

I said, 'That's about the taxi-driver and the African.'

They knew the story. It had been played up in the newspapers. A taxi-driver had seen a despondent African at Kuala Lumpur airport. The African said he had lost his ticket and other papers and his money. The taxi-driver took the African home. At his own expense he advertized for the return of the papers, without result; arranged a visa extension; lent money – his own and his aunt's – for a hotel and then for an air ticket. Now, two months later, the African, a Ghanaian, had returned to Kuala Lumpur. He had given 2,000 American dollars to the taxi-driver's aunt; for the taxi-driver there was the promise of a new Datsun car.

The *haji*, passing the glass with the Coca-Cola to Khairul, said, 'Would that kind of thing happen in your country?'

'No.'

'It happens every day in Islamic countries. It is news for you. It isn't news for us.'

But the taxi-driver was Chinese and, according to one newspaper story, couldn't get a permit to own a taxi.

The *haji*, cleaning his nostrils with his index finger and then wiping the finger on the velveteen arm of the chair, said, 'We must finish the story about the Jews. Before the time of Moses there was a Jewish tribe in Arabian lands. Among this Jewish tribe there is a prophet. The prophet, through revelations from God, ordered the Jews to pray on Saturday. But the Jews ignored the commands of the prophet because on Saturday there were a lot of fishes in the sea and they preferred to go out fishing rather than make Saturday a religious day.'

I said, 'I don't know this story.'

The *haji* said, 'It is in the Koran. As a result the prophet was angry, and the wrath of God –'

Khairul had some trouble with the translation here. He broke off and talked in Malay with the *haji*. Then he carried on. 'And the wrath of God was imposed on the Jews, and God swore to convert the whole tribe to monkeys –' He broke off again, to giggle.

'Apes,' the doctor said severely. 'They were converted to apes.'

'For seven days,' the *haji* said.

The journalist said, 'And then they passed away.'

The *haji* said, 'This story is mentioned in the Torah, the Koran, the Testament – '

'The Old Testament,' Khairul said, commenting on his own translation. 'We don't recognize Luke and the others.'

'These are the three books of God,' the *haji* said. 'The people of the three books will all know this story. We Muslim people believe in the Old Testament. If you don't believe in that book you are not a Muslim.'

The doctor said, 'Because in the Old Testament there is one part that clearly mentions the coming of Mohammed.'

Khairul said, 'There is a book written on this matter by Professor Benjamin. You can get it in the Perkim Bookstore. He is a Catholic priest converted to Islam. His new name is Professor Abu Daud.'

The *haji*, who had been left out of this English by-play, said, 'The story of the Jews hasn't finished yet. As a result of being turned to apes the moral prestige of the Jews declined. To rectify this situation, because they are already degraded – '

'In the eyes of the world,' the doctor said.

' – the Jews are now pulling down the whole society with them.'

'They have that principle,' the doctor said. 'If they are dirty, let others be dirty.'

The *haji*, bright-eyed, plump-lipped, said, 'I surprised you when I said that the Jews were the enemies of God. But this is just one of the signs that show the wickedness of the Jews. You have asked me questions. Now let me ask you some. It is the way of Islam. You ask, then I ask. I tell, then you tell. Do you believe that your great-grandfathers were apes?'

'No.'

The *haji* smiled and said (Khairul, after the Coca-Cola, burping through his translation), 'That proves the wickedness of the Jews.'

I said, 'But don't men evolve? I don't mean this in a personal way' – and I appealed to all of them – 'but you told me that your grandfathers in Sumatra were head-hunters. Now you are a *haji* and an educated man.'

The *haji* said, 'That was a wrong way of life. That is why Islam came into being, to rectify the discrepancies of the way of life. For instance, before Islam, the Caliph Omar would take his daughter and bury her alive. It was a disgrace to have a daughter. It was the practice of the Arabs at that time. The Caliph Omar used to sob and weep thinking of his past, his life before Islam.'

The doctor said, 'His friends would see him in the desert crying.'

'And after he came into the fold of Islam he became the best of men.'

Khairul said, 'Have you read a book called *The Road to Mecca*? Ah, that's a book. It's by Mohammed Asad, an Austrian Jew.'

The journalist, silent for long, said, 'What was his name before? Pold something.'

'Leopold,' Khairul said. 'You can get that book too in the Perkim Bookstore.'

257

The doctor said, 'It's a biography, no?'

'Yes,' Khairul said, 'it's a biography. It's a *beautiful* book.'

The *haji*, left out again, re-entered the conversation. 'Do you believe in a creator?'

I said, 'No.'

'But that is the basis of Islam.'

'It's too difficult for me,' I said, after we had had some discussion. 'I feel lost if I think too much about the universe.'

The *haji* said, 'That feeling of loss I would describe as contentment.' And I didn't know whether he was being compassionate or critical.

'When you were in Iran, did you talk to the religious teachers there?'

'I saw some ayatollahs. Khalkhalli, Shirazi.'

'Ah, Shirazi,' the *haji* said. 'What did you talk about?'

'About religion a little bit. I believe he was worried that I might be a communist.'

They laughed.

'What's it like in Iran now?' the *haji* asked.

'A mess. No law. The factories aren't working. The mullahs don't know how to run the country. It's something you may have to face here too.'

The *haji* said, 'If Muslims live in the Islamic way, the true Islamic way – ' And again Khairul had some trouble with the translation.

'All will follow,' the doctor said.

I said, 'What's the difference between your life now as true Muslims and your life before?'

They didn't say.

The *haji* only said, 'You can see at a glance when you meet a person whether he is a Hindu or an animist or a Muslim.'

How? Did it show in the face? Was there a kind of grace or contentment in the face of the believer?

No, the *haji* meant something simple. Non-believers ate pork and weren't fussy about food.

I asked about their clothes. Was it necessary for religious people to dress as they did?

Khairul answered. 'There are five principles governing clothes. They are commandments of Allah. For men to cover from the navel to the knee. For women to cover everything except the face and hands.'

I said, 'Some women in the university are covering their hands.'

'It is better,' Khairul said.

'Why do you wear green cloaks?'

'To wear white and green is encourageable under Islam.'

'Why?'

'Because this is the way the prophets lived. Wearing a batik like yours is not encourageable under Islam.'

'Batik?' I plucked at my Marks and Spencer winceyette pyjama jacket.

Khairul said, 'A batik like that is only for ladies.'

The journalist said, 'For men it has to be plain.'

'But pyjamas are Islamic. The styles and colours are Islamic. The Europeans took the idea from places like Turkey and India.'

'They are from Islamic countries,' the *haji* said. 'But they are not from Allah's commandments.'

'You don't understand the beauty of Islam,' Khairul said. 'Once you understand the five principles, you will see the beauty of it. They apply to everything. In Islam certain things are mandatory. Certain things are encourageable. That's a technical word, a translation from the Arabic.'

'Permitted?'

'Permitted? No, encourageable is better. Then certain things are not encourageable, like your batik. Then certain things are *haram*, forbidden. Like a man exposing his knees. The fifth category is *harus*, discretionary.'

'Discretionary, discrepancy – you have quite a vocabulary, Khairul.'

He said, 'I am a lawyer.' And, boasting a little, 'I was educated in a Malay-language school. Let me give you an idea of a discretionary principle. A businessman who only really needs five shirts, but buys forty because he can afford forty. In the hereafter the extravagance will be accountable. These five principles cover all aspects of life. Everything – politics, economics, family life, even coughing. There is so *much* to learn about Islam. You can spend *years* and never come to an end.'

'Tell me about the coughing and the five principles.'

'I will give you an example. If you are in a gathering and you are ashamed to cough and three days later you wake up with a pain in your side because you didn't cough, that is wrong. It is mandatory to cough, if not coughing is going to damage your health. Coughing is encourageable if you cover your mouth and say, "Grace be upon Allah." It is not encourageable to cough without covering your mouth. But to cough in somebody's face' – he turned towards the doctor and made as if to spit in the doctor's face – 'to do that is horrible. It is *haram*. It is forbidden. It is un-Islamic and sinful.'

'What about the discretionary cough?'

'*Harus*. When you are by yourself and it doesn't offend anybody. Then you can stand up and cough or sit down and cough. It becomes entirely discretionary. All these things are regulated.'

Then it was time for them to go. The *haji* had a meeting; they said he was a great traveller and preacher. The doctor had his clinic.

'You must see his clinic,' Khairul said. 'It is so Islamic and beautiful. You are not well; I can see you are not well. He would have treated you *beautifully*. He would treat you now.'

I said, 'I am in the hands of another doctor. I can't change.'

The doctor, oddly professional now, said, 'That is so.'

The commune was on the outskirts of Kuala Lumpur, in a hilly wooded area. There was a board on the roadside some distance before. I wasn't expecting a board. But – though the commune had the reputation of being secretive – there was no point in dressing up like an Arab and hiding.

The land was perfect for a Malay settlement, for wooden houses on stilts or pillars, for green gardens and tall shade trees. But the forest had been cut down for a wide street; and the street was lined with modern Malay houses – modern because they had glass louvres instead of windows and because the downstairs, pillared part of the houses had been walled around to provide more space.

Rain had turned the dirt street to mud. Many young people were about with green cloaks or gowns and white turbans. At the far end of the street a stalled car was being pushed in the mud. Among the pushers I thought I recognized the *haji*; anything seemed possible here. I was wrong; it was only that the white turban gave a mulatto cast to some Malay faces. Other costumed figures (waiting for prayer time, like actors waiting for a stage call) were lounging about the verandah or porch of the shop at the corner, where – as part of its independent Islamic way – the commune sold little things to passing motorists.

I bought a few ounces of fried shredded sweet potato. It came in a stapled plastic packet. It tasted less of sweet potato than of the frying oil.

The taxi-driver said, 'You see the kind of bullshit we are getting these days?' He pronounced the word 'bu'shi''. I heard it as 'bushy', and thought at first it was his word for a village Malay: 'You see the kind of bushy we are getting these days?'

I offered him some sweet potato.

He said, angrily, 'No.'

5

◆◆◆◆◆

The Spoilt Playground

SHAFI came from the undeveloped north-east, from Kota Baru. I
wanted to see the village for which he grieved – unpolluted once, the
people pious, dignified and not materialist. And Kota Baru was the first
stop in a trip to the interior that he arranged for me.

It began badly. The gap-toothed Tamil driver, the man of misfortune,
was to drive me to the airport. He ran up happily to me in the Holiday
Inn lobby the evening before and told me that my airport job had fallen
to him; having involved me over many drives in all his anguishes, he
now regarded himself as my friend. And, as I half expected, something
went wrong. His car was smashed during the night (but he said he was
going to get the insurance), and in the morning I had to hunt around for
another driver.

An hour's flight took us to Kota Baru, and the monsoon. (For Shafi,
seventeen years before, it had been a journey of a day and a night from
Kota Baru, through rubber estates and then jungle, to all the shocks of
Kuala Lumpur.) The plane made two tries at the Kora Baru runway. We
landed in a downpour and the passengers went out to the little airport
shed in small groups, under gaudy umbrellas. And Rahman wasn't there
to meet me, as Shafi had arranged.

I got the name of a hotel and took a taxi there. Kota Baru was flooded:
a rickety colonial town of the 1920s and 1930s – little low shops, little
low houses, tiled roofs, corrugated iron – out of which new money was
causing a new town of concrete and glass to grow. The hotel was new,
small, with modern pretensions. And I found – it was like a little
miracle, but there was only one hotel in Kota Baru – that Rahman had
booked me in for the night.

He telephoned later. He said it was strange no one had met me. He
hadn't sent just one man to meet me; he had sent three men, three
headteachers. He had even told them that after my years in England I
would probably have a white skin. His story-telling – the opposite of
the directness of people like Shafi – was meant to be read by me as
story-telling: it was Rahman's way of letting me know that he didn't

261

want to have too much to do with me. Rahman worked for the government. He didn't want to have too much to do with Shafi and ABIM and a visitor sent out by ABIM.

The rain never stopped. Rahman came to the hotel late in the afternoon. He was a small, plump, smiling fellow in a short-sleeved blue safari suit. I was expecting to be taken to Shafi's village or a village like it. But Rahman didn't intend to do that; he didn't intend to appear in public as my guide to anything. Instead, we drove through the rain in the fast darkening afternoon – flooded fields, scattered sodden little Malay houses below dripping fruit trees – to a Muslim college where Rahman could share responsibility for me, his dangerous visitor, with two or three other people who were as nervous as himself.

They had laid out tea. The tea was sweet, milky and cold. And they, my hosts, seemed determined to say nothing. Were these Shafi's fellows, the fisher-boys and bird-stoners of his childhood? They were. Not Shafi's actual friends, perhaps; but people like them. It wasn't Shafi alone who had evolved.

There was a man who was a lecturer in philosophy. A lecturer? A man from Shafi's pastoral past? Yes; he lectured at the college about the attempts by Arab and Persian philosophers to synthesize Islamic thought with Greek thought. That seemed a difficult course, and the lecturer said that it was difficult, adding with some sadness that he still had to read a lot, especially in Greek philosophy. He had studied at the Islamic university of Al Azhar in Cairo. He hadn't liked it (but few village Malays seemed to have liked their travels). He found the Arabs undisciplined and unreliable.

I wanted to hear more about his time at Al Azhar. But he said – story-telling again – that he was busy. He had to have dinner with his wife. After dinner? After dinner he had to drive about with a message about a family death; it was a Malay custom (and that was the first reminder of the village ways Shafi had spoken about).

Prayer time came. They left me with the tea and went to say their prayers in the next room. They took their time.

When they came out again, the registrar, who wore a buttoned-up tunic and had a buttoned-up look, opened out a little. He said he had spent three days in England, in 'Queensway, WC2'. From those three days he remembered three things: people travelling underground; a speaker in Hyde Park saying that sixty percent of men in England were homosexual; and the (somewhat contradictory) sight of men and women embracing in public.

'This absence of manners,' the registrar said. 'Here when we catch a fish we clean it, we fry it, and then we eat it. There they catch a fish and eat it straight away. We are still washing the fish, while they are wiping their mouths after eating.'

Rahman, leaving out the village imagery, said, 'Here we have a room and a time for the sex act.'

'It's a private thing with us,' the philosophy lecturer said. 'Secret and sacred. We don't even tell our friends.'

'Those people are lost,' the registrar said.

We were joined by the Arabic teacher. He was taller than the others, and wore a sarong and a white skull-cap. His face was blank. He began to eat. He said that people were tired of novels and for that reason were turning to the Koran.

'It's more *natural*,' Rahman said.

But weren't there Arabic novels?

Yes, the Arabic teacher said, eating. There was an Egyptian novelist. But one book went that way and another book went another way, showing that the man himself was lost.

What were those novels?

He couldn't say. He said he was saying only what his pupils said. And he ate some more of the Malay cake, drank quantities of the cold tea, stood up, straightened his sarong and clomped away.

They were content: the word was used again and again. They wanted me to know that they were content. Rahman worked for the government and got a thousand dollars a month and had a car. He said, 'I like it here.' He didn't want to go to any other part of Malaysia. Here they didn't live competitively; here they didn't worry about the Chinese; they didn't have the problems of Malays in other areas.

It rained and rained. We went to have dinner at a Malay restaurant, run by a Malay organization. The restaurant was grander than anything Shafi would have known as a child. Its decorations were a bit neglected, but Rahman was pleased to show it off as an example of Malay enterprise. He said, 'You see, we aren't all going back to Islam.'

The philosophy teacher was still with us. He had apparently forgotten about dinner with his wife and his death duties. But that piece of story-telling had been no more than a signal to me not to press him about Al Azhar or philosophy or any other contentious matter.

And − it was part of their contentment − they all had large families. Rahman had five children; the buttoned-up registrar, who was very young, had three; the philosophy lecturer four.

'We are optimists,' the philosophy lecturer said. 'My father was a poor man. Yet I'm all right. It will be all right for our children.'

The registrar said, 'Allah has said that no living creature will be unprovided for.'

I said, 'But what about a place like Cambodia?'

'They have brought that punishment on themselves,' the registrar said. 'Allah has said that about unbelievers.'

Rahman said, 'One ant bites you on the leg. But you don't kill that particular ant. You get rid of the lot.'

I asked about an item in the morning's paper. A story had gone around that forty heads were needed for the completion of the port, and village people were keeping their children away from school.

They said it was an old story. Rahman said that when he was a child there was a similar story about forty heads being needed before the railway could be completed. Stories like that had a simple explanation. Parents wanted their children to stay at home and not wander too far, because it was dark in the village, with only a light here and there. It was also said when he was a child that if you climbed a banana tree your private parts rotted away: that was just to keep children from climbing the tree. If you sat on a pillow you got boils on your bottom: that was to keep the pillows clean.

'But now people are more educated,' Rahman said. 'They simply tell the children they will dirty the pillows if they sit on them.'

We talked; and it rained; and my chest tightened in the damp air; and I thought of my little room in the hotel where the central air-conditioning blew very chill and couldn't be regulated.

Shafi grieved for the village life he had known; he spoke about it as something in the past, something he could revive for himself only in a commune. But that life – of community, old ways, and peace – still existed for these men, in spite of the cars and the new kinds of job. It was Shafi who had changed. The Islam of these men was part of their contentment. Shafi's Islam – Islam the energizer and purifier of Malays, the destroyer of false ways and false longings – was revolutionary, serving no cause these men could understand.

It was odd for me to be regarded as an emissary of that revolution. But so I was, and after that dinner I was abandoned. Rahman telephoned the next morning to say that he had to go to the mosque at eleven and then he had a 'programme' with his wife until three. He couldn't take me out anywhere, not even to a batik factory. He couldn't even take me back to the airport.

It rained. I had to stay in the hotel. The sheet of newspaper the hotel 'maintenance man' taped over the air-conditioning vent didn't lessen the chill in my little room. To be warm I had to open the louvres in the bathroom, and that let the rain spatter in. The lobby was very small. Between lobby and dining room and bedroom I divided my time until late afternoon, when I went through the floods to the airport. The sun came out for a while; then it poured again. On the runway water fell on water, the big drops splashing high and white.

Penang was a hop away on the west coast. The west coast was the developed coast, more colonized, with the British plantations, the factories, the energetic Chinese. It was where Anwar Ibrahim of ABIM came from, and for that reason Shafi had arranged a visit there for me. But after Kota Baru I was uncertain. The plane that stopped at Penang went on to Kuala Lumpur, and it was tempting to go on. But I got off.

A short hop, but it was like being in another country. Penang had an international airport; there was no rain; and Abdullah, a man of thirty-four from the university, was waiting for me.

Factories with famous names, a busy town, elegant in parts: Abdullah, as he drove me in, spoke neutrally at first, feeling his way with me, but then his passion came out: international companies, low wages, the casualness of Malays, their inability to compete, the need for Islam. Abdullah was a pale-complexioned Malay, with Caucasian features. He was not content; he was a man saddened by his passion. Through him I met Mohammed, two years younger, more Chinese in appearance. Mohammed was a teacher; he too carried the Malay cross.

They took me to the E&O Hotel, and left me for a while. The E&O was a grand hotel of the British time, and it was still grand. To enter its great hall was to be refreshed. My sitting room opened on to a terrace with shrubs and palms; the sea was beyond, but I couldn't see it in the dark. And what a relief just then – sympathetic though I was to the unhappiness of Abdullah and Mohammed – to be away from Malay Malaysia and the contentment and unreliability of the folk at Kota Baru! The constriction in my chest slackened; and in the big dining room, where the tablecloths were crisp and the waiters were Chinese and brisk and experienced, my spirits lightened so far that I had most of a bottle of Australian Riesling.

I was still a little hazy with the wine when, punctually at ten, as they had promised, Abdullah and Mohammed came back to see me. They came to the room. I ordered tea and coffee. The Chinese room-waiter, previously friendly, even inquisitive, with me, a stranger, went blank-faced when he saw the Malays, as though he sensed what I had already gathered: that the two Malays with the handsome, melancholy faces were men with a racial and religious mission.

Momentarily I saw them – sitting in the rattan chairs – as from a distance. And, after the waiter had gone, I put to Mohammed and Abdullah the thought that had come to me in the dining room: that in an old colonial hotel like this, half desired, half rejected, a village Malay might feel that he had become a stranger in his own country.

Mohammed, the younger man, with the Chinese features, said, 'You got the term.'

'We feel strangers,' Abdullah said.

'Did you feel like this when you were children?'

'Especially when we are brought to town,' Mohammed said. 'I received my primary education in the kampong. After that I was sent to school in a little town. Butterworth.' He pronounced the English name in the local way: 'But'worth'. 'Just across the channel from here. And already for me it was a little like feeling like a stranger.' He was eleven then.

'I can still remember the first time I got to see my teachers. They were fathers and brothers, as you say. My uncle took me to the school. It was situated next to a Christian cemetery. So always next to the school is this graveyard and chapel. So there was always this atmosphere, this Christian and alien atmosphere. And of course in the morning we had to sing one of those songs.'

'Hymns. Do you remember any of them now?'

'I don't remember them.' But he remembered bits of the Christian religious knowledge he had been taught. 'Not Islam. Islam was never taught to us. This would have been about 1957. It was the time we were about to obtain our independence. This is the background that probably led to the confusion of our youth, people of our generation. You are a Muslim and you come from a Muslim and a kampong background, and you are brought – transplanted – into that environment. That's why I think until very recently my world view was very un-Islamic.'

'What do you mean by that?'

'Your idea of life in general. What do you think of man and society? What is your idea and conception of Nature? Is it part of you? Do you have to confront it, or to conquer it, or do you have to live side by side with it? And finally what is your idea of the supernatural? Is it powerful?'

'What is your own idea of Nature? As a Muslim and Malay.'

'We'll come to that later.'

'What idea of Nature would you say was being given to you at the school?'

'At that stage?' He was puzzled; yet it was he who had raised the subject. He thought for a while. 'Those ideas were not absolutely Christian. It was really a mixture of Christian and secular ideas. One idea – as it was put to us at the time – was that Nature was to be exploited and conquered. Wait – that first of all, Nature was something without soul, that only by conquering Nature you can be at peace.'

I thought about my own school-days in Trinidad, which was also a British colony, with plantations. Had those ideas been given me?

I said to Abdullah, 'Do you agree with what Mohammed is saying?'

'He got it right,' Abdullah said.

'Did you feel this at the time, while you were a child? Or do you think it now?'

Mohammed said, 'We realise it now that we are looking back to Islam.'

'But didn't they teach you at school about Wordsworth and English nature poetry?'

'That was not the focus. That was taught only when we were in literature class. And the qualification was that these people were all Romantics. It wasn't the essence of their thought. Because all the while the stress was how to develop the tin mines, how to cut down trees, how to build factories.'

And Mohammed was right. British Malaysia, on this west coast, was a plantation and a mine. Chinese and Indians and even some Javanese were brought in to work the mines and plantations, while the Malays, unsuitable for this kind of barrack labour, stayed in their green villages beside the rivers. Those Malay villages were enchanting even now, controlled woodlands with fruit trees and shade, banana plantings, pillared timber houses with breezy inner rooms for sleeping and half-walled verandahs for chatting. Not like the regimented plantations, where rubber trees were made to grow in rows and blocks and were regularly cut down and replanted, and the labourers lived in ranges; not like the mines, or the openness of the little towns with their rows of concrete shop-houses. As a kampong child Mohammed would have been aware of two worlds, two landscapes – more than I would have been in Trinidad. But how much had he really noticed? How much had his instinctive Malay village life permitted him to see?

'What was your own idea of Nature?'

He had ducked the question before. And even now he hesitated. 'At that time? I probably wouldn't have been able to say.'

'But try to do it now.'

'Formulate my ideas?' And with a frankness that was like Shafi's, he fell silent, trying to work out something he hadn't worked out before.

I said, to help him: 'Surely the Malay idea is also to cut down the bush and plant the banana trees and the mango trees around the house and to keep the bush away. Isn't that conquering Nature?'

'I would rather put it as co-existing. That is the Malay view. There was no idea of conquering Nature as such, as the westerners mean it today.'

Abdullah said, 'It is more like developing what is needed.'

Mohammed said, 'At the same time they take care of those that are not being used at the moment.'

'Those?'

'Those natural elements. Those elements of Nature.'

But now I felt that what they had begun to put forward – what they were trying to fit to a way of life without thought – were western ideas about ecology and the environment.

And when I pressed Mohammed he said, after one or two false starts, 'Currently I am still not sure what Malays have in mind with regard to man and society and supernature.'

'Supernature? Do you want to use that pop word?'

'That is a word we cannot avoid if we want to understand the world view of any particular people and in this case the Malays or the Muslims.'

So I was left with only his vague feelings.

He appeared to recognize that he had been vague. He said, 'I wish to add something to what I said about the tin mines. When our teachers taught us that Nature should be conquered, developed – these ideas are all in keeping with the industrial revolution.'

That was the schoolboy speaking, the history student. But there was something else. I felt he was using ideas twice removed from him: ideas derived from the West which the new Islamic missionaries had taken over and simplified in their many publications: ideas about the death of the West, its spiritual failure, the waste of the world's resources.

I said, 'You didn't feel any of this at school?'

He didn't answer.

Abdullah, who had been silent much of the time, answered. Abdullah said, 'At least for me, when I was in school, in form five, I begin to see all these things. I mean, we do not exist by mere accident. We have a deeper meaning than that. I was trained religiously from my youngest days, because my family had a strong religious Islamic background. By the time I was seventeen this kind of feeling began to appear more within myself.'

'There must have been something that started you off. Something that made you question what they were teaching you at school. Can you think of one particular thing?'

'I remember when I was doing this English literature we had particular book. *Man and God.* Greek mythology. About Zeus and Aphrodite and Milo and all these Greek goddesses. Apollo. These characters who, according to the Greeks, were gods who appeared in human form – and then indulging in all sorts of activities, no? Like rivalry, debauchery. Of course, besides the moral aspect, you know – so this is what I would find repugnant to me as a Muslim. For instance, I remember about Jupiter appearing in human form and seducing Princess – I can't remember her name. And then, apart from that, if we are studying about geography, and we have to study about land forms, say, how a volcano is formed – you would hear this and this and this. But in the religious class we are being taught that this is being created by someone who is administering the whole universe. So I would discuss these things with my religious teacher. I also would say that I was fortunate that we came from a big family. So at home sometimes we would talk. How could it happen suddenly, this volcano, as they said in the geography class? Surely it must be created by something.'

Mohammed said, 'My background was different from Abdullah's. I was probably more a Malay than a Muslim. My family was not that religious, I think, not that learned in the lore of Islam. And then I went to the mission school and the education I received there was a combination of Christian and secular.' Secular was the bad word with these men: it meant worldly, atheistic, western, non-Malay. 'So when I graduated from the secondary school I was secular. In that way my life was more confused. I didn't know much about Islam. So my Islamic consciousness was less. So I began to study more when I started working as a teacher.'

I said, 'In what way were you confused? My background is more complicated than yours, but I am not confused. And there are many people like me. Many people in the world today have complicated backgrounds.'

Mohammed said, 'You are not confused after second thoughts.'

I said, 'After second thoughts.'

He smiled. 'You are not confused because you accept.'

'Couldn't you accept what you were? You were a Malay who went to the mission school because it was the best school you could go to. Didn't you know who you were and what had happened to you?'

'Probably not.' And he repeated, 'Probably not.' He thought for a little and said, 'At that time I was probably not aware I was confused.' After some more thought he said, 'Although I say I come from a background that's not too religious, I knew I was praying and my family were all praying. And all of a sudden you are asked to sing this Christian song. Surely that must have made me confused. And another ideal which would have put me in confusion was this mingling of the sexes.' He had saved it for last, this big shock of the mission school. 'In the school you are always with girls. You are asked to hold hands, to dance.'

Mohammed was thirty-two. He was a teacher, with friends at the university. But after twenty years this violation of village taboo was still unsettling to him. And, as with Shafi at the Holiday Inn in Kuala Lumpur, it was hard for me to reconcile what was being said with the elegant man who was saying it: a man apparently at ease in a rattan chair, in a room that opened on to a terrace, with palms and shrubs and a pool, beside the sea.

He said, 'We've been talking for an hour and a half. And we haven't talked about the things you said you wanted me to talk about. The restructuring of the society.'

That was true. But I had preferred to stay away from that. I knew, from our short conversation earlier in the evening, that the dismantling of the society excited him more than the restructuring; that the restructuring he was interested in meant only Islam, and the abstractions of Islam. And so it turned out now. Malaysia – with its painful problems: the casualness of the Malays, the energy of the Chinese, the racial politics, the corruptions of the new money, the technological dependence of the small, uneducated country – vanished, became an abstraction itself, a land of pure belief, of total submission to Allah. In that submission everything was solved.

At midnight they had to leave. They were nervous about driving back later than that. Mohammed left two documents for me to look at. One was an essay he had written, 'Modernism Defects: The Trend of *Nahdah* (Renaissance) in the Muslim World'. It was in the style of Islamic missionary writing. One section was headed 'The Bankruptcy of the West' ('vice and lust, alcohol and women, wild parties and tempting surroundings'); another was headed 'The Perfectness of Islam'. There was a logic in this. The West, which had provided Mohammed with academic learning, was open to the criticism it had trained him in. Islam, which had not provided this learning, which provided only the restoring faith, was exempt from criticism.

The second document Mohammed left with me was a pencilled paper he had prepared for our meeting. It was an outline of what he had said about the restructuring of Malaysia; and it was just as abstract. His 'belief system' called for the worship of Allah; for the 'social system' he wanted freedom, 'no corruption or malpractices in departments', the protection of women and family life, 'no prostitution and gay quarters'; the 'economic system' insisted on 'moral earnings, no corruption, no gambling, exploitation of the poor and the low'. But there was a sting at the end of the paper. Mohammed's last paragraph, on the 'political system' of his ideal state, called for 'Imam-like leadership: Khalifah is God's representative on earth'. It called, in fact, for someone like

Ayatollah Khomeini. Khomeini ruled in Iran as God's representative. It was Mohammed's wish that someone like that should rule in Malaysia. It was his only concrete proposal.

That was where his Malay and Muslim passion, his knowledge of history, the beginning of self-awareness and intellectual life, had led him. He had no idea of reform or any ameliorative process. He didn't deal in the concrete. It was hard for him – dependent on other people's words and thoughts, fitting those thoughts to his own wordless emotions – it was hard for him to be concrete. He wished only for the world to be remade and repossessed as suddenly as (in his memory, the village boy going to the mission school beside the cemetery) it had been taken away from him. This was the promise of his Islam.

The news from the Muslim world was not encouraging. The new century of the Islamic era – from which so much was expected by the faithful – had begun with a series of calamities. A Pakistan plane carrying pilgrims who had completed the pilgrimage had crashed after leaving Mecca airport. In Mecca itself there had been a gun battle over many days in the Great Mosque, and many people had been killed. In Pakistan martial law had been strengthened. The elections had been called off; public whippings had been instituted; a well-known Pakistani journalist had been arrested and photographs had shown him in chains. In Iran the American embassy had been seized by students and more than fifty Americans taken hostage, for no reason except that of drama: the Islamic revolution had turned sour, wandering, pointless.

But Mohammed and Abdullah didn't believe in bad news from the lands of the faith. Mohammed thought that the news from Pakistan meant only that the country was at last being restructured. Abdullah didn't think that the news from Iran was being correctly reported by Reuter's or Associated Press. We had talked about it earlier in the evening, and Abdullah had said, 'We need our own news services.'

I went back to Kuala Lumpur, to the Holiday Inn.

The woman telephone operator said on the telephone, 'How are you? How's your chest? You know, you shouldn't take ice if you have asthma. And you should use bats.'

'Bats?'

'Bats. B-a-t-s. It's what the kampong folk do. You get the bats. You take out the hearts, you roast it until it is crisp, really crisp, then you

271

pound it and mix it with your coffee and drink it twice a day. It is what the kampong folk do. And it really works.'

'But a bat's heart would be very small.'

'Perhaps they use two or three, I don't know. But it really works.'

I said to Shafi, when he came to see me to find out how the trip had gone, 'But you didn't tell me about the rain at Kota Baru. It's like telling me about Greenland without mentioning the ice.'

He laughed. 'It slipped my mind. When there were floods people would go to have the feel of water in the road. It's a great thing for them. Then we go boating. There's a story – but I never experienced it – that young girls would come out of their house in festive dress, in best dress, and the boys will take the opportunity to see them. They wouldn't go any deeper than the knee. And the boating. Each house will have a boat kept under the house, will take it out and prepare for boating session. Row the boat around the village and see what it's like when there is water where water isn't normally. When the flood starts we cut banana trunks, poke a bamboo right through them, and on this raft we go paddling about.'

'That sounds like paradise to me. Your eyes light up even as you're talking about it.'

It was how he sometimes talked of his village, not like a villager, but like a romantic traveller, like a man who now looked from a distance.

'Rain was something we longed for. I always like water.'

Some days later – Anwar Ibrahim had gone to an Islamic conference in Bangladesh, and there was less to do in the ABIM office – Shafi came again. We took a taxi and made a tour. We drove about the new residential developments in the beautiful hilly land to the west of the city. I saw a well-kept city where the money seemed to be spreading down fast, but that wasn't what Shafi wanted me to see. The difference between the old and the new was the difference between Malay and Chinese. And even when the houses were new Shafi could spot the Malay house and the Chinese house.

I began to play the game with him. I was a novice; I chose easy examples. We passed a house stacked around with lumber. I said, 'Chinese house?' Shafi said, 'Chinese house.' We passed a house with rows of orchids in the front garden. I said, 'Malay house?' Shafi said, 'No. Chinese.' I gave up.

Farther out, suburbs turning to country, we passed some girls, one quite pretty, sitting in a bus stop shelter. They were Malay girls.

Shafi said, 'Timeless people.'

'How can you say a thing like that?'

But he was using the word in his own way. And he wasn't speaking as a romantic, but as a reformer. 'Timeless people. People who have no limits about time, and they are careless about time. They can afford to wait for a bus. There is no hurry for them to get things done, and in some villages you see people play dumb. Playing cards, chatting. "Where are you going?" – "I'm going to market." If you ask "For what?" they wouldn't give you specific reasons other than that of aimlessness, to see people as they go and to meet friends and say hello and after – nearing lunchtime – return home. And when they meet the friends they would say, "How are your children? How about the catch? Is there a lot of fish in the market? What is going to happen to that family? How is the flood? Fifteen feet? Nineteen feet?" Timeless people.'

We reached palm plantations. The rough-trunked trees with the dark-green fronds grew in rows. Heavy grappes of the oil-producing nuts, yellow and red, were stacked at the edge of the field, wet after rain. The sky was grey; more rain was coming. We turned back towards the city.

The driver said, 'Mushrooms!' and Shafi asked him to stop at the Malay roadside stall where the mushrooms were. They were big white mushrooms on long stalks and they were tied up in bunches.

'They are not cultivated,' Shafi said. 'They are gathered in the forest.'

I said, 'They look like flowers.'

He said, with a curious tenderness, looking at the bunches he had bought, 'They are a kind of flower.' And when we drove on again he said, 'In the village they always said, "Never use a spade to dig up a mushroom. If you do that, the mushroom will never come again." I thought that it had to do with the metal. But it wasn't that. If you dig up a mushroom with a spade you dig up the spores, the sub-soil.'

The girls were still sitting at the bus stop.

Near Kuala Lumpur, Shafi had the driver turn off the highway. We drove through a Malay squatters' settlement: people coming in from the villages. The houses were like the houses in the villages, but closer together, and without the green. The houses went up overnight, and Shafi pointed to the big sheds, with lumber and other building material, that served the squatters' needs.

'The Chinese,' Shafi said. 'Exploiting.'

'But they also provide a service.'

'Providing a service is only seventy percent with them.'

'That's enough. You want men to be perfect. That's the difference between us.'

We had lunch at the Holiday Inn. He made no trouble now about the food.

I said, 'Is it really true? You've never thought or talked about your life as you've done with me?'

'It's true. To me what is past is past. I feel I have no time to think of those things.' And he added, 'Those good old times.'

He knew nothing of history. From his parents he had heard about the Japanese occupation of Malaysia during the war; but that was all. There were old legends in other districts; but in Kora Baru there were none, or he had heard none. At school he wasn't interested in history. And now there wasn't time for learning or reading; there was his work for the movement. The rich past of his people remained closed to him: Hinduism, Buddhism, animist belief.

He existed in a limbo. He felt that as a Malay he had nothing; and in reaction he wished – as though such a thing was possible – to be nothing but his faith, a kind of abstract man. To be civilized, he had said, a man had to know where he had come from and where he was going to. That wasn't a matter of history; for Shafi that was only a question of correct religious belief. Everything flowed from the true faith. Out of love for his Malay people, his wish to put the world right for them, he wished them to be as cleansed as he thought he was. That was the great task he had set himself.

I said, 'But isn't religion diverting people from what they should be doing? Isn't it giving them an easy way out?'

He missed my point. He interpreted the question in his own way. He said, 'We are the first generation. It's only a few who can understand the complete way of life of Islam. We want to change from the normal tradition which is not the true Islamic way of life. But the process is difficult and takes time.'

I asked him about Nature. I told him what Mohammed and Abdullah had said in Penang: that Muslims sought to co-exist with Nature, and non-Muslims, especially people of the West, tried to conquer it.

He didn't take up Mohammed and Abdullah's phrases. 'I must be very frank with you. In my village there is no development. No tin mines, no rubber estates. So I have little to say about it.' His experiences were smaller and more personal. 'When I was young my impression of my surroundings was that they were clean. The streams were not polluted with any chemicals. The only polluting thing we had was the smell of the pigs and the pigs' waste in the neighbouring Chinese community. When I was fifteen people started building batik factories – three, one Malay and two Chinese – and the chemicals were being discharged into the river. And this disturbed our swimming activities in the small stream nearby. They spoilt our playground. They should have put the waste in a hole. My gang – my teenage friends – was not happy with it. That happened to be a Chinese batik factory and we despised it very much.'

'I was reading a Malay novel. The writer talks about pools of urine below the verandahs of the houses.'

'That is biological pollution and sometimes these wastes are fertilizers. Bird droppings, chicken droppings. However, the waste of pigs is not in our favour because of the religious restrictions.'

'Did you think the hills beautiful when you were a child? And the young rice plants.'

'To us it was a common sight. We never thought whether it was beautiful or not. But we read in a few novels about paddy fields and the wind blowing through the bamboos making a kind of sound, natural sound, and that made us realize the beauty around us.'

'You said this morning, showing me the houses, that the Chinese planted for commercial reasons and the Malays for aesthetic values.'

'I didn't say aesthetic.'

But he had. The word had made an impression on me. Perhaps – though the word could be justified – he hadn't used the word he intended. He meant that the Chinese house and yard was a commercial establishment; that the people in the house with the orchids in rows grew those orchids for money. The Malay yard was a garden, part of a home; it remained part of the good earth, part of Nature, even if some of the fruit and food it produced was meant for sale. There was no one word to describe that. 'Aesthetic' (though fair enough) was only Shafi's shorthand, the word he had let slip, and was not strictly defensible. Perhaps the idea hadn't been fully worked out by him. Perhaps – though the difference was real enough, could be felt and seen – there was no definition of the difference between Malay and Chinese houses that couldn't be shot to pieces.

And I wondered how far – added to the absence of the sense of history – this inability to fit words to feelings had led Shafi to where he was. Feelings, uncontrolled by words, had remained feelings, and had flowed into religion; had committed Shafi to learning the abstract articles of a missionary faith; had concealed his motives, obscured his cause, partly hidden himself from himself. Religion now buried real emotion. He loved his past, his village; now he worked to uproot it.

He said, 'Talking about banana plantings and the Malay house, I had a little disagreement with my father. I was very much attracted to beautiful flowers and wanted to plant them in front of the house. But my father made a *big* hole directly in front of the house and after a few days of burning some waste, some rubbish – banana leaves, grasses and other garden waste – he planted a banana. And I was not very happy with it.

He said, "We will have fruits from banana. We will not be able to have anything from flowers, which we cannot eat."

'I called my other sisters and brothers to be with me, defending my case, but the banana tree remain there. After a few months banana begin to bear fruit, and my father started to tease me. "Look, we have the fruit of our labour. And you don't have anything from the flower plants you have planted." Actually my father dug the hole right where I used to plant flowers. Later on, until now even, I begin to dislike planting flowers because it did not give much benefit except for beauty.'

I said, 'What do you think of the incident now?'

'My father was right. Even now, my wife wants to plant flowers in the pot, in the house here in KL, and I insist that we plant some greens, some vegetables instead.'

IV

INDONESIA
Usurpations

'The people here have lost their religion.'

Sitor Situmorang

1

Assaults

SHAFI changed his mind about me right at the end. The morning I was to leave Kuala Lumpur he telephoned to give me the names of some people in the Muslim movement in Indonesia. He said it was harder for them there. The army ruled in Indonesia and the army was hostile to the movement. Then Shafi telephoned again. He wanted me to stop at the office on my way to the airport; he wanted to say goodbye. But when, just over an hour later, I went to the ABIM building, Shafi wasn't in his office; and he didn't come down from where he was.

He sent an older man down. This man wore a black Malay cap and he had just come back from Switzerland, where he had gone on Islamic business; these new Muslims travelled a lot. (The news in some quarters in Malaysia was that Europe was converting fast to Islam. Scandinavia, always liberal and wise, had already fallen; France was half Muslim; in England hundreds were converting every day.)

The man from Switzerland talked to me about the seizing of the American embassy in Tehran. He said the western press reports were so biased he didn't know what to believe. But he had heard in Switzerland that the Americans had hired some Iranians to attack *another* Western embassy, to discredit the revolution. Revolutionary Guards had found out about the plot and had led the hired band to the American embassy instead.

And it was with a depression about Shafi – and the Islam that camouflaged his cause – that I drove through the rich, ordered plantations to the airport of Kuala Lumpur; and landed later that afternoon in Jakarta.

It had rained. The roads were edged with red mud. Long corrugated-iron fences (concealing what?); fruit vendors sitting with their baskets in the wet; buses with smoking exhausts; crowds; a feeling of a great choked city – red-tile roofs, many trees – at the foot of the scattered skyscrapers; the highways marked by rising smog. After the spaciousness of Kuala Lumpur it was like being in Asia again. Newsboys and beggar-boys with deformities worked the road intersections. Men carried loads in baskets hung on either end of a limber pole balanced on their shoulders, and moved with a quick, mincing gait. (Later, in the inland city of Yogyakarta, I tried a potter's load. The strain was less on the shoulder than on the calves, which jarred with every weighted step: it was necessary to walk lightly.)

But Jakarta was also a city of statues and revolutionary monuments: a freedom flame, a phalanx of fighting men armed only with bamboo spears, a gigantic figure breaking chains. They seemed unrelated to the life of the city, and the styles were imported, some Russian, some expressionist. But what they commemorated was real: national pride, and a freedom that had been bitterly fought for.

To be in Jakarta was to be in a country with a sense of its past. And that past went beyond the freedom struggle and colonial times. The Dutch had ruled for more than three hundred years; Jakarta was the city they had called Batavia. But the Dutch language was nowhere to be seen. The language everywhere, in Roman letters, was Indonesian, and the roots of some of the words were Sanskrit. Jakarta itself – no longer Batavia – was a Sanskrit name, 'the city of victory'. And Sanskrit, occurring so far east, caused the mind to go back centuries.

The hotel was known as the Borobudur Intercontinental, after the ninth-century Buddhist temple in central Java. The ground-plan of that great, nine-terraced temple was the basis of the hotel logo: three concentric dotted circles within five rectangles, stepped at the corners with a rippling effect. It was stamped on ashtrays; it was woven into the carpets in the elevators; it was rendered in tiles on the floor of the large pool, where the ripple of the blue water added to the ripple of the pattern.

Indonesia, like Malaysia, was a Muslim country. But the pre-Islamic past, that in Malaysia seemed to be only a matter of village customs, in Indonesia – or Java – showed as a great civilization. Islam, which had come only in the fifteenth century, was the formal faith. But the Hindu-Buddhist past, that had lasted for 1400 years before that, survived in many ways – half erased, slightly mysterious, but still awesome, like Borobudur itself. And it was this past which gave Indonesians – or Javanese – the feeling of their uniqueness.

The statues of war and revolution in Jakarta were over-emphatic; some were absurd. But they commemorated recent history; and that history was heroic and dreadful, and dizzying to read about.

It was the Japanese who, when they occupied Indonesia in 1942, abolished the Dutch language. They ordered all Dutch signs to be taken down or painted out; and overnight, after three hundred years, Dutch disappeared. The Japanese established Sukarno and other Indonesian nationalist leaders (imprisoned or exiled by the Dutch) in a kind of Indonesian government during the war. The Japanese organized the Indonesian army. This was the army that fought the Dutch for four years after the war when the Dutch tried to reassert their rule. And this was the army that afterwards, during the twenty years of Sukarno's presidency, held the scattered islands of the archipelago together, putting down Muslim and Christian separatist movements in various places.

Independence was not easy for Indonesia. It didn't come as regeneration and five-year plans. It came as a series of little wars; it came as chaos, display, a continuation of Sukarno's nationalist rhetoric. Sukarno's glamour faded. The army's power grew. It was the army that eventually, in 1965, deposed Sukarno. The army claimed that the communists were planning, with Sukarno's passive support, to take over the country. And, after the chaos and frustrations of independence, there was a terror then greater than anything the archipelago had known.

A hundred thousand people were arrested. There was a massacre of Chinese (resident in Indonesia for centuries, and traditional victims of pogroms: the Dutch themselves killed many thousands in Jakarta in 1740). And it is said that in popular uprisings all over the archipelago half a million people thought to be communist were hunted down and killed. Some people say a million. Indonesians are still stunned by the events of 1965 and later. When they talk of 1965 they are like people looking, from a distance, at a mysterious part of themselves.

Now the army rules. The khaki-coloured army buses are everywhere; and Jakarta is dotted with the barracks of 'kommando' units (strange, that this particular Dutch word should be retained) that fly the red and white Indonesian national flag. The army has made itself into a political organization, and it has decreed that it shall be powerfully represented in every government.

It is the army that holds the archipelago together. And army rule – after the Sukarno years of drift and rhetoric – has given Indonesia fifteen years of rest. In this period, with the help of Indonesian oil, Jakarta has sprouted its skyscrapers; the main roads have been paved; the beginnings of services appropriate to a big city have appeared. In this period of rest there has also grown up an educated generation, the first generation in fifty years to know stability. But the army rule chafes. And already – the trap of countries like Indonesia – with stability and growth there is restlessness.

The restlessness is expressed by the new Islam, the Islam that is more than ritual, that speaks of the injustices done to Allah's creatures and of the satanic ways of worldly governments: the Islam that makes people withdraw, the more violently to leap forward.

It is dizzying to read of recent Indonesian history. And to look at it in the life of one man is to wonder how, with so little to hold on to in the way of law or country, anyone could withstand so many assaults on his personality.

Suryadi was in his mid-fifties. He was small, dark-brown, frail-looking. He was born in east Java and he described himself as one of the 'statistical Muslims' of Indonesia. He had received no religious training; such religion as he had was what was in the air around him. He wasn't sure whether he believed in the after-life; and he didn't know that that belief was fundamental to the Muslim faith.

He belonged to the nobility, but in Java that meant only that he was not of the peasantry. The Dutch ruled Java through the old feudal courts of the country. But Java was only an agricultural colony, and the skills required of the nobility in the Dutch time were not high. Suryadi's grandfather, as a noble, had had a modest white-collar job; Suryadi's father was a book-keeper in a bank.

As a noble, it was possible for Suryadi to go to a Dutch school. The fees were low; and Suryadi, in fact, didn't have to pay. The education was good. Just how good it was was shown by the excellent English Suryadi spoke. And recently, wishing to take up German again and enrolling in the German cultural centre in Jakarta, the Goethe Institute, Suryadi found that, with his Dutch-taught German of forty years before, he was put in the middle class, and he was later able without trouble to get a certificate in an examination marked in Germany.

Early in 1942 the Japanese occupied Java. The message from Radio Tokyo was that the Japanese would give Indonesia its independence, and there were many people willing to welcome the Japanese as liberators. Suryadi was in the last class of his school. The Dutch teachers were replaced by Indonesians, and the headmaster or supervisor was Japanese. For six months classes continued as they would have done under the Dutch. Then – and it is amazing how things go on, even during an upheaval – Suryadi went to the university. The lecturers and professors there were now Japanese. But the Japanese simply couldn't manage foreign languages. They recognized this themselves, and after a time they appointed Indonesians, who worked under Japanese supervisors.

The Indonesians used the classes to preach nationalism. Already much of the goodwill towards the Japanese had gone. It was clear to

Suryadi that the whole economy was being subverted to assist the Japanese war effort. Thousands of Indonesians were sent to work on the Burma Railway (and there is still a community of Indonesians in Thailand, from the enforced migration of that time). Radios were sealed; the radios that had once brought the good news from Radio Tokyo could no longer be listened to.

Two incidents occurred at this time which made Suryadi declare his opposition to the Japanese. The university authorities decreed that all students were to shave their heads. It was the discipline of the Zen monastery. And Suryadi felt it as he was meant to feel it: an assault on his personality. And then one day on the parade ground – students were given military training – a student was slapped by a Japanese officer. All the Indonesians felt humiliated, and Suryadi and his friends held a protest demonstration in the university. Thirty of them, teachers as well as students, were arrested by the Japanese secret police and taken to jail.

In the jail they heard people being tortured for anti-Japanese offences and even for listening to the radio. But Suryadi's group were treated like political prisoners; and they continued to be disciplined in the way of the Zen monastery. They were beaten with bamboo staves, but it was only a ritual humiliation. The bamboo staves were split at the end; they didn't hurt; they only made a loud cracking noise. After a month of this Suryadi and his friends were released. But they were expelled from the university. So Suryadi never completed his education.

They had got off lightly because the Indonesian nationalist leaders were still co-operating with the Japanese. Sukarno never believed that Japan was going to lose the war, Suryadi said; Sukarno didn't even believe that the atom bomb had been dropped on Japan. It was only after the Japanese surrender that Sukarno and the nationalists proclaimed the independence of Indonesia. And four years of fighting against the Dutch followed.

What events to have lived through, in one's first twenty-six years! But Suryadi was without rancour. The events had been too big; there was no one to blame. He had no ill-feeling towards either Dutch or Japanese. He did business now with both; and he respected both as people who honoured a bargain. The Japanese had the reputation in south-east Asia of being hard bargainers (there had been anti-Japanese riots in Jakarta because of the Japanese domination of the Indonesian market); but Suryadi had found the Japanese more generous, if anything, than the Dutch.

Suryadi was without rancour, and it could be said that he had won through. But there was an Indonesian sadness in him, and it was the sadness of a man who felt he had been left alone, and was now – after the

Dutch time, the Japanese time, the four years of the war against the Dutch, the twenty years of Sukarno – without a cause. More than once the world had seemed about to open out for him as an Indonesian, but then had closed up again.

He had lain low during the later Sukarno years. Army rule after that had appeared to revive the country. But now something else was happening. A kind of Javanese culture was being asserted. Suryadi was Javanese; the Javanese dance and the Javanese epics and puppet plays were part of his being. But he felt that Javanese culture was being misused; it was encouraging a revival of feudal attitudes, with the army taking the place of the old courts. Suryadi had the Javanese eye for feudal courtesies. He saw that nowadays the soldier's salute to an officer was more than an army salute; it also contained a feudal bow. It was a twisted kind of retrogression. It wasn't what Suryadi had wanted for his country.

And he had lost his daughter. She had become a convert to the new Muslim cause – the Malaysian disease, some people called it here. At school and then at the university she had been a lively girl. She had done Javanese dancing; she was a diver; she liked to go camping. But then, at the university, she had met a new Muslim, a born-again Muslim; and she had begun to change. She went out with her hair covered; she wore drab long gowns; and her mind began correspondingly to dull.

Suryadi and his wife had done the unforgiveable one day. They had gone among the girl's papers, and they had come upon a pledge she had signed. She had pledged to be ruled in everything by a particular Muslim teacher; he was to be her guide to paradise. She, who would have been a statistical Muslim like Suryadi and his wife, was now being instructed in the pure faith.

Suryadi didn't take it well. He thought now he should have been calmer in the beginning; by making his dismay too apparent he had probably pushed the girl further away from him. He said to her one day, 'Suppose someone asks you to go out camping now, will you say, "I can't go, because I have no assurance there will be water for my ablutions before my prayers"?' He had spoken with irritation and irony. But later she came back to him and said, 'I have checked. In the Koran there is nothing that says it is obligatory if you are travelling.' And Suryadi understood then that she had become impervious to irony; that she had become removed from the allusive family way of talking. The intellectual loss was what grieved him most. He said, 'But don't you have a mind any longer? Do you have to go to that book every time? Can't you think for yourself now?' She said, 'The Koran is the source of all wisdom and virtue in the world.'

283

She had married the born-again Muslim who had led her to the faith. She had a degree; he was still only a student at the university; but, like a good Muslim wife, she subordinated herself to him. That was the new sadness that Suryadi was learning to live with: a once lively daughter who had gone strange.

Still, recently he had found a little cause for hope. He was driving her back one day to her in-laws' house, where she lived with her husband. He said, 'I have bought that little house for you. Why don't you go and live there? Why does your husband want to keep on living with his parents? It isn't right. Why doesn't he make up his mind to act on his own?' She had said then, 'He's got an inferiority complex, Father.'

And this little sign, the first for some time, that his daughter still had a mind, was still capable of judging, was a great comfort to Suryadi. She had seen what was clear to Suryadi: that the boy was a poor student, didn't have the background, couldn't cope with university life. He was still some way from taking his degree, and wasn't giving enough time to his work. During the month of Ramadan, the fasting month, he had given up his work altogether, fasting all day and going to the mosque in the evening to pray. That was easier than being with the difficult books; and his religious correctness was admired by his Islamic group at the university.

His daughter had seen this on her own. That was some weeks ago. And it was now what Suryadi was waiting for: that in time she might see a little more.

At the end, just before we separated, Suryadi said, 'But I've been lucky. I haven't been like so many others in Indonesia, switching to another wavelength under pressure.'

'Another wavelength?'

'You know how people are like here. But perhaps you don't. They turn mystical. Logical, rational people. They start burning incense or sitting up at night in graveyards, if they want to achieve something. If they feel they are frustrated, not advancing in their work or career.'

'Do you call that mystical?'

'I don't know what else you can call it.'

Islam was the formal faith of the people. But below that were the impulses of the older world, relics of the Hindu-Buddhist-animist past, but no longer part of a system. The ninth-century temples of Borobudur and Prambanam — the first Buddhist, the second Hindu — were a cause for pride. But they were no longer fully possessed by the people, because they were no longer fully understood. Their meaning, once overpowering, now had to be elucidated by scholars; and Borobudur remained a mystery, the subject of academic strife. It was the Dutch who rediscovered Borobudur and presented it to the people of Java: that was how Gunawan Mohammed, a poet and editor, put it. Gunawan – a Muslim, but in his own Indonesian way – said, speaking of the past, and making a small chopping gesture, 'Somewhere the cord was cut.'

They were a people to whom the past was at once living and dead. And – whether they were talking about the killings of 1965 or about sitting up at night in a graveyard – they talked as though they remained mysterious to themselves.

And now, with the army peace, with the growth of industry and learning, with the coming to Indonesia of the new technological civilization, the world had grown stranger. I walked one Saturday evening in the market area of central Jakarta, the Pasar Baru, the New Bazaar, with the broken pavements, the mud, the shops full of imported goods, the food-stalls, the amplified records. In this atmosphere of the fairground I came upon a bookshop. It was a well-lighted shop and it had books on two floors. There were books in English on technical subjects – medicine, psychology, engineering. There was also a large section of English books on mystical or occult subjects – Taoism, I Ching, Paul Brunton's searches in secret India and secret Egypt. This was how the new civilization appeared: technical skill and magic, a civilization without its core.

After the dizzying history of the last fifty years, the world had grown strange, and people floated. Whether they moved forward, into the new civilization, or back, like Suryadi's daughter, towards the purer Arab faith, they were now always entering somebody else's world, and getting further from themselves.

2

✦✦✦✦

Sitor: Reconstructing the Past

INDONESIA opened slowly, and when I met Sitor Situmorang I did not take in all of the man. He was a poet; he had been connected with the later days of Sukarno and, after the military take-over, had been imprisoned for ten years, from 1965 to 1975. At our first meeting – and it was hard to credit later – I missed the political side of the man, and the ten years' imprisonment, when he hadn't been allowed to write or read anything. I believe I missed that side of him because at our first meeting Sitor wished me to overlook it: perhaps at that moment that part of his past wearied him.

He came across as a writer, humane, reflective. His talk was of an autobiography he was writing and having trouble with. He was a small man of fifty-six, with a small bony face, Chinese-negrito, with bristling eyebrows; a canvas shoulder bag with books gave him an odd touch of contemporary undergraduate style.

He came from the north of the large island of Sumatra. Sumatra was physically more wild than Java. The Muslims were more Muslim; the Hindu-Buddhist influence was less; there were Christian areas; and there were still animist tribes. Sitor came from one of the tribes; he was a Batak. And his tribal origins lay at the heart of the trouble he was having with his autobiography.

I thought of the difficulties Shafi had in making a pattern of the events of his much shorter life, his progression from village to town. And that was part of the problem for Sitor. But Sitor's tribal past was further away; he had lost touch with it; and he had found that to write without an understanding of what he had come from was to do no more than record a sequence of events. That was why for some time he had put aside the actual writing and had concentrated instead on understanding his tribal background. He had gone back to his village in north Sumatra with a young Canadian woman anthropologist. She had helped to give him back some of his tribal past; and that had been an illumination.

This was what came out at our first meeting. It was a short meeting;

286

we both had other things to do. I was still at that time trying to get in touch with Muslim groups – they were being secretive.

Sitor went with me to one office; it was on his way. I thought he moved with the authority of a man who was known. But when someone waved to him from the window of an upper floor, Sitor drew my attention to it. He said, 'I don't know him, you know.' And even then I didn't fully take in how important it would have been to Sitor – after his ten years' imprisonment, his ten years' silence as a writer, from the age of forty-two to fifty-two – to have these little proofs that he was still a name.

The Muslims were elusive. Taxi-rides before and after lunch, in the humid heat, led to nothing. Travel fatigue and hotel fatigue fell over me in the afternoon. My room was on the fifteenth floor. I began to feel I had lived with the silent, air-conditioned view for a long time: red-tile roofs and trees, skyscrapers, a sign for XEROX, planes coming in to land at the domestic airport to the left, traffic on the roads on either side of the hotel garden, fumes hanging over the highways like a brown mist, rising and mingling with the clouds that held more rain. Jakarta was not a city for taking afternoon walks in.

And it was Sitor I telephoned. I didn't think of him as someone whose life had been distorted by politics and imprisonment. The impression I had had of him, after our meeting that morning, was of a man who had achieved calm, a restful, reassuring man.

A woman answered the telephone. She spoke English well. And Sitor was such a long time coming I feared I had interrupted him at his rest or at his work – his writing, his autobiography. When he did answer the phone, he was as gentle and concerned as I had expected.

He said, 'You must leave the Borobudur and stay at another hotel.'

'You mean the Borobudur puts people off?'

'No, it would be cheaper.'

But then he understood. He understood solitude.

He said, 'Come to my house. Come at seven. I am seeing a young man at six. No, come at six-thirty.'

He lived in the Jalan Maluku. Some men lounging after the heat of the day in front of a drinks-stall with a fluorescent tube directed the taxi-driver. A push-cart passed, the man knocking a piece of bamboo against his cart. These food push-carts, though part of Jakarta life, and though there was a real one for the local colour in the hotel restaurant, were absent from the area around the hotel.

It was a big new concrete house, with a gate apparently made of bamboo. Sitor came out in an Indonesian tunic. He said of the gate, 'The bamboo hides the iron.' And he said the push-cart was selling noodles;

he knew from the bamboo noise. Every street food had its own musical accompaniment.

The house was a German house, with a kind of diplomatic status. It was temporarily without an occupant. It had little furniture; but there was a piece of contemporary Indonesian sculpture and many Indonesian pictures.

We went to the back of the house. Sitor said, as if repeating and testing the English word, 'This is the terrace.' We sat there. The young man he was expecting at six hadn't come. Sitor said, 'He is a busy man. He works in human rights.'

The little house in one corner of the back garden, which was green and skilfully planted, was the 'pavilion'. That was where Sitor lived.

He said, 'Barbara will be joining us.'

Adi, the young man, came. He was in his thirties, slender, sharp-featured, his hair cut short. He said he had been working for twelve hours and couldn't stay long. If he stayed long there was going to be a little Vietnam war at home.

Sitor said, 'Adi is one of the new leaders. He is a Muslim.'

Adi said, 'I am a Muslim.'

'Why?' It was the kind of question that could be asked in Indonesia.

'My parents were Muslim. It is also more logical than Catholicism. That Trinity business is something I cannot understand. Protestantism is better. Hinduism has caste. That I reject.'

Darkness fell. A light came on in the verandah of the pavilion. And against this light, her face in shadow, there appeared a tall, slender woman in a long dress. She seemed to be attending to a hanging plant or to something in a cage.

There was a tremulousness in Sitor. Tremulous, at his age, at the appearance of a woman! He composed himself and said with some deliberation, 'Barbara is Dutch.'

Some plates with sweets were brought by a woman servant to the table where we were sitting. And Barbara came the short distance to us, losing her mystery as she moved out of the shadow of the pavilion light into the light of the main house. She was in a blue batik dress. She was young, in her late twenties, and good-looking; she had certainty and style. Sitor became calmer.

I said, asking about the sweets, 'What are those things?'

Barbara said, in barely accented English, 'They are made from beans.'

'Are they nice?'

'He likes them. They must be good.' 'He' was Sitor.

She spoke in Indonesian to Adi.

The sweets were round, with depressions, like little tennis balls that

288

had gone soft. Within the flannel-like hull was a soft filling: oily, sweet, flavourless, like the sweets I had tried in Malaysia.

Adi said in English, 'I was being interrogated about being a Muslim.'

'Oh, goodness,' Barbara said. 'Not interrogated?'

But interrogations were on Adi's mind. A cartoonist had been arrested by the authorities.

'The army has no sense of humour,' Adi said.

I said, 'Is it serious?'

'It is their way. They will arrest him for a day or two. He will be interrogated in a friendly way. Though friendly isn't quite the word.'

Afterwards, Sitor walked out with me into the street. There were more push-carts about in the evening, different kinds of noises.

Away from Barbara, in her long batik dress, there was a tremulousness about him again.

I said, 'Go back to Adi.'

'Adi is an old friend.'

'Are you married to Barbara?'

'Tribally.' He laughed in the road. 'Come on Saturday morning. I will show you the pictures. The tribe insisted. After we had been living together for two years.'

'You are fifty-five, Sitor?'

'Fifty-six.'

'And still the life of passion? So it never leaves us?'

'It was what the Canadian anthropologist asked me. "Still, at your age?" She was twenty-four.' And he laughed again, showing his teeth in his bony, Chinese-negrito face.

It was different on Saturday morning, in the daylight, in the almost empty main house. Sitor had a toothache and was taking various medicines. Barbara was in her working clothes: the paler colours of Europe. She looked slenderer. Daylight added a year or two to her face, though still showing her as a woman only in her early thirties. She was busy, businesslike, thinking of getting off to her job. She worked in a Dutch-supported centre for Indonesian handicrafts; and before she went she left instructions with Sitor about her caged birds, and especially about her red parrot.

Sitor couldn't settle down. He had his toothache; and people kept dropping in just to exchange the time of day with the famous poet. We had arranged to talk that morning about his autobiography. But he kept putting off the moment; at one stage he went to the lavatory. When we did get started, he couldn't talk. He had prepared too well, had thought too hard. He qualified every phrase almost as soon as he had spoken it, and he could scarcely finish a sentence. He began to use big words. And always there were the visitors, and the extended exchange of courtesies in Indonesian.

Through every door of the sitting-room there was green to look at: the climate wonderfully used in this small plot, creating green cool rooms, green, big-leaved shade outside every door. And all the time in the street – the morning ticking away, losing its freshness – the push-carts made their varied noises.

We decided in the end just to chat. Sitor brought out albums and showed me colour photographs of his village in north Sumatra. The photographs had been taken only a few weeks before, when he and Barbara had gone together to the village for the first time. Sitor had said he was a tribal man; he had also said that he came of a chieftain's family. The words didn't tell me much. The photographs helped me to understand one aspect of the reality: they showed that for Sitor, as a tribal man and the son of a chief, there was a part of Sumatra, a part of the earth, that was absolutely and inalienably his.

For eighteen generations Sitor's ancestors had ruled over a small area – six miles by twelve – in north Sumatra. It was a mountainous, rocky area, not worth anybody's while to conquer. The Dutch got there late, towards the end of the nineteenth century. It was Sitor's father who had fought them; he had fought them from 1884 to 1908. The dates were hard to believe, but Sitor said his father was born in 1850 and died in 1963. His father had died at 113? Yes; he was a tribal superman. Sitor had a sister of eighty; Sitor himself had been conceived when his father was seventy-three. After he had been defeated, his father was appointed administrator of the area by the Dutch. He remained a chief; things went on much as before.

The tribal area, the area ruled by Sitor's father, consisted of three valleys running down from hills 6,000 feet high to a beautiful lake. The photographs showed pale paddy fields with bunds or walls of stone down in the valleys. The paddy didn't grow thick and emerald, as it did in richer soil. The colours of this tribal landscape were oddly muted, temperate. Here Sitor had spent his earliest years, one unit in the extended family of the chief; and Sitor had no memory of any conversation with his father or mother. When he was six he was sent to a Dutch school for people like himself, the sons of chiefs and minor chiefs. But only the boys, not the girls. Which was why Sitor's sister – who was eighty – was an unlettered village woman and – to Sitor, before his anthropological illumination – part of a remote past.

They were an isolated people. But however they had arrived in their valleys, they had brought with them – or had evolved – a decorative art and extraordinary building skills. Big stone walls protected the village; the entrance gaps were very narrow and could be easily defended or sealed up. The houses were built in a square. They had horn roofs, steeply pitched, in front elevation dipping in the middle and projecting up and out at either end like the prow of a ship: a design, Sitor said, that protected the houses against the strong winds in the area.

In Sitor's village the only modern addition to this architecture was the corrugated iron for the roof. The houses stood on stout wooden pillars strengthened with mortised cross-bars or cross-beams. The walls, between pillars and steeply pitched roof, were really quite low. It was dark in the houses. There were wooden beds; they repeated, in a modified way, the horn or ship's-prow shape. And that modified shape appeared again, in the open village square, in the stone sarcophagus that contained the skulls of the chiefs. The upper half of a lizard was carved on the lid of the sarcophagus; the lizard's feet were on the section below. The lizard was the emblem of good luck.

From this life Sitor was snatched when he was sent, at the age of six, to the Dutch boarding school. It was a Christian school, but he wasn't required to be a Christian. He was, however, required to speak in Dutch, in class and out of it. The longest school holiday lasted a month. He went back then to his village. He would be greeted warmly by his father (then over eighty) and his mother, but there would be no conversation. He would simply sleep in one of the houses in the village, and eat from the common pot. There was always food, prepared by some distant relative.

He was in his last year at the secondary school in Jakarta when the Japanese came. They landed first in south Sumatra, in the middle of February 1942. Two weeks later, Sumatra overrun, they landed in western Java. The Dutch army retreated. The streets of Jakarta were empty; people stayed indoors. But one day Sitor and some of his friends went out on their bicycles. And it was near the big Dutch colonial monument, near the present site of the Borobudur Intercontinental hotel, that Sitor saw the first Japanese soldier.

The soldier was on a bicycle, one of the famous fold-up bicycles of the Japanese army. The soldier was tired and sweating; his uniform was thin and cheap, and he smelled of sweat. He stopped the boys. He made it clear – though he spoke only Japanese – that he wanted the bicycle Sitor was riding.

The Japanese fold-up bicycle was shoddily made and hard to pedal. Sitor's bicycle was British, a sturdy Humber or Raleigh or Phillips. But this bicycle, which was a little too big for Sitor, was far too big for the

Japanese. He tried to ride it but decided he couldn't. Sitor was five feet three inches; the Japanese was some inches shorter.

The Dutch monument, near where this meeting took place (replaced today by a gigantic bronze statue of an exultant man breaking chains), was of an early Dutch colonizer pointing down, as Sitor said, to the conquered land of Indonesia. And Sitor reflected even then – having kept his bicycle – on how strange it was that a man as small as that Japanese soldier should have defeated the very big Dutchman.

That was the limit of Sitor's direct contact with the Japanese. In the area of Jakarta where he was living life went on as before. So it did even in the Dutch areas; it was only later that the Dutch women and children were sent to camps. Sitor's school was closed down, though. When, after some weeks, the trains began running again, Sitor and his friend used to go to the hills outside Jakarta to get fruit and vegetables which they would then hawk about the streets. Later he got a more substantial job. The Japanese had decreed that all signs in the Dutch language were to be taken down or obliterated. So Sitor went around painting out Dutch signs.

Six months later the Japanese ordered that all non-Javanese students were to return to their own islands. The Japanese wanted to break up Indonesia into manageable occupation zones, Sitor said; they also wanted to remove unemployed students, potential trouble-makers, from Jakarta. So Sitor, taking advantage of the Japanese offer of transport home, went back to Sumatra, to the village where, since the age of six, he had never stayed longer than a month. He stayed in the village for three years. His brother had a good library; it was the library of a man who had received a sound Dutch education. So, although Sitor didn't finish school, he had read widely by the end of the war.

Afterwards there was all the turbulence of Indonesian post-war history: the proclamation by Sukarno and others of the Indonesian Republic; the fight against the Dutch; the Sukarno years; and then, in 1965, the revolt against Sukarno. The army that had been created by the Japanese now emerged as rulers. Sitor was arrested for his Sukarno connections and imprisoned for ten years, until 1975. He was not allowed to read or write. He was allowed one visitor a month, and that visit lasted fifteen minutes. What did he do? He talked to his fellow prisoners; he got to know people he hadn't known; politically and socially he learned a lot.

Whatever Sitor was or had been in Jakarta, to his village he was always a man of the tribe. And when he came out of jail he had to be re-initiated into the tribe. For this ceremony the skull of his grandfather was taken out of the stone sarcophagus with the lizard of good luck carved on the lid. Sitor held a plate with this skull and a lemon, the lemon an agent of cleansing. There was a cousin of Sitor's at the ceremony. The cousin was a medical man, and he saw that the lower jaw of the skull had slipped while it was being transferred to the plate for Sitor. He reached out and put the jaw back in place. The shaman or priest was furious. The cousin, by touching the ancestral skull, threatened to undo all the good and to bring bad luck on them all.

Sitor had a black-and-white photograph of that moment: Sitor, innocent of the drama at his back, holding the plate with the skull and the lemon at shoulder level; the shaman, fury distorting his face, moving swiftly, hair flying, to counter the effect of the cousin's irreverent gesture.

Sitor, as a politically proscribed man, couldn't get a job. But he still had a reputation as a poet. One day, about two years after he had come out of jail, he was giving a poetry reading at the house of a Dutchman in Jakarta. There were about twenty people there, mainly foreigners. Someone came late. Sitor, who had his back to the door, turned as the latecomer entered, and he saw a tall European girl whose beauty astonished him. And more than her beauty, Sitor said: her 'aura'. It transformed the room. He decided there and then that he would get to know that girl. And he had a bit of luck: the girl went and sat next to an Englishwoman who had asked Sitor to recite an English translation of one of his poems.

So Sitor, the reading over, was able to go directly to the girl. He told her he wanted to get to know her; he asked for an 'appointment'. He discovered that she hadn't come to the reading because she knew Sitor's poetry. She had come only to have a look at the man who had been connected with Sukarno and had spent ten years in jail. Sitor didn't mind that she didn't know his poetry. Barbara was Dutch. She had been sent out to Indonesia by a Dutch group to help develop Indonesian crafts; she was the equivalent of a Peace Corps worker.

They met on the twenty-fifth of May. Barbara's thoughts were of her return to Holland; she was going back on leave on the sixteenth of June. And that was extraordinary: because Sitor had been invited to Holland by a cultural organization and was going to Holland on the twenty-eighth of June. After two years he still remembered the dates. So, although Barbara could give him only two 'appointments' in Jakarta before she left, in Holland she was able to give him many more.

It wasn't easy for him to know what impression he was making on her. Barbara was Dutch and very cool. But he was overwhelmed by the new world she showed him, the new ideas she introduced him to. He had spent ten years in jail, shut away from books, living with old ideas; he had missed a whole decade of intellectual movement in the West.

Barbara was of the 1960s, the generation of 1968. She was full of Schumacher and people like that. And to Sitor, who had grown up in colonial times, Barbara and her friends appeared as a new breed of 'missionary'. The young people Barbara took him among didn't want to convert the natives, but wished in a more direct way to help them.

How had they been created? How had Europe thrown up this dazzling generation? During his time in Holland with Barbara he was in a state of high emotional and intellectual excitement: this tribal man of fifty-three, with the negrito-Chinese features (and the bristling eyebrows that at times suggested a Chinese pirate), five feet three, diabetic, politically neutered, with the bright and tall Dutch girl twenty years his junior.

They lived together when they came back to Indonesia. The tribe got to know, and the tribe insisted that they get married according to tribal rites. For this, it was necessary for Barbara to be initiated into a related but separate tribe, since Sitor's tribe was 'exogamous' – and Sitor spoke the technical anthropological word easily.

Just a few weeks before, he and Barbara had gone to the village for the ceremonies. It was wet and cool up in the rocky hills above the valleys; the photographs showed mist and cloud hanging low; the colours were soft. There was a ritual meal in one of the houses with the extravagantly shaped horn roofs. Barbara and Sitor ate with their hands; they ate pork. 'Look,' Sitor said, pointing to a photograph. 'That's *me*. In *my* village. It's real. It's not for tourists.' He was dressed like a visitor, in rubber boots, and he was looking down at an old woman working on a village loom. 'And that's my sister. She cannot read or write.' And there was a photograph of Barbara and himself standing at the door of his father's house, the house of the great chief, which now belonged to Sitor's brother: it was where Sitor had to take Barbara for the tribal marriage ceremony.

He was impressed by the journey he had made, and it was an immense journey. In one generation he had fitted in the experience that for other Indonesians had unfolded over the last four or five centuries. And yet he hadn't been able to write his autobiography. He had made two attempts in the last three years and had discarded hundreds of pages. The material was too rich, too extraordinary; the changing personality of the writer, to him the essence of the experience, was something he hadn't been able to express; he had only been able to record events.

He said, of what he had written, 'There is no synthesis in the whole. It has not become an expression of growth through the prism of me as an

individual. All that I've experienced doesn't fall into a context, artistic-
ally, personally, politically.'

He hadn't been able to define himself because he didn't know who he
was. He had been cut off from his past. He had gone to the Dutch school
when he was six; he had been cleansed of village beliefs. For a writer, his
early life had been oddly wordless: he had never had a conversation with
his parents. That was why the Canadian anthropologist had been of such
use to him.

She had spent five months in his village, and he had gone with her as a
guide and interpreter. He showed a photograph of the anthropologist: a
big and lovely young woman in a safari suit: clearly, being a Batak and
Sitor had its compensations. By her skilled questioning she had reconstructed his ancestral past for him. He couldn't have done it himself. So
now, when he tried to write the autobiography again, he would at least
be able to say, 'This was how my ancestors lived for eighteen generations.'

Sitor said, 'I am complicated. But not confused.'

Throughout the morning various people had dropped in. One man, a
German who spoke English, had come to look at the house. The other
callers were for Sitor, the poet. He cherished them all. After four years
of freedom it still pleased him to be sought out.

At midday Barbara came back. She looked after her birds, one by one.
Sitor and I went to the pavilion. The pavilion, at the end of a long garden
at the side of the main house, was decorated with the crafts Barbara had
come out to Indonesia to serve: reed mats, rattan chairs, baskets from
Timor. Barbara knew her subject; she had a good, chaste eye.

The servants (Barbara and Sitor had two) had prepared a lunch of fried
fish and rice, with pickled cucumbers afterwards. Sitor, with his diabetes, ate very little.

I asked Barbara, 'Are you going back to Europe soon?'

'I hope not.' She bit decisively on a piece of pickled cucumber.

Sitor said, 'I would like to go again. I would like to be invited for a long
time. There are too many things here that hurt me.'

Barbara's lunch hour was quickly over; she went back to her handicrafts. I had another slice of fried fish; Sitor watched me eat. On one wall
of the small room was a surrealist painting of two nudes seen from the
back, one male and brown, one female and dark-red, with birds everywhere. A painter friend had called on a day when one of Barbara's birds
had died; the picture was the gift he had been moved to make. Elsewhere
were violent pen drawings of nudes that Sitor himself had done.

The glamour of Indonesia and Sitor, the poet, for Barbara; for Sitor,
the glamour and security of Barbara and Europe. Barbara could take

Europe for granted. Sitor, at the end of his own journey, couldn't. He now possessed his ancestral village, the valleys, the lake, the stone walls, the fairy-tale houses. But he could no longer go back there; he couldn't pretend to be what he had ceased to be. Without Europe (and that meant Holland) and its cultural invitations, its interest in his 'complication', he had only Indonesia, for him a land of hurt and failure, where he could get no job now, and where he could be snuffed out, without anyone or anything to appeal to.

And it was only many hours later that I saw what had been left out of our long talk: the twenty years from 1945 to 1965. I hadn't asked Sitor about them: his beginnings and his present had interested me more. In those twenty years, the first of Indonesian independence, Sitor had written his poems and become famous. He had later become a politician and a man of power. To some people then, especially those who towards the end of the Sukarno time could be described as 'counter-revolutionaries', he had become a figure of threat. And, as I discovered later, there were people who felt that their careers had been damaged by Sitor. Some, even after all this time, had not forgiven him.

But the man who told me this said almost at once, 'I will not talk against him, though. He has suffered more than any of us.'

3

❖❖❖❖❖

Deschooling

ADI SASONO, whom I met at Sitor's the first evening, told me I would understand Indonesian Muslims better if I went out to the countryside and had a look at the traditional Islamic village schools. These schools were know as *pesantrens*. Adi had a business associate who took an especial interest in *pesantrens*; and it was this man, as devout or concerned a Muslim as Adi, who planned my journey. He thought I should see a modern *pesantren* – there was a famous one near Yogyakarta and Borobudur; and I should also have a look at a very old one – there was one near Surabaya.

These village *pesantrens* preserved the harmony between community and school, village life and education. In this they were different from western-style schools which, set down in the Asian countryside, were psychologically disruptive. Adi's friend told me that the famous educationist, Ivan Illich, had come to Indonesia to look at *pesantrens*. I hadn't read Ivan Illich's books, and of his theory of 'deschooling' I really only knew the word. But I knew that he had a high reputation, and I thought that it would be interesting to go where (to my surprise, I must confess) he had gone.

I went with Prasojo, a nineteen-year-old college student, and I could not have had a better companion. Prasojo had been to Arizona for a year on a scholarship given by the American Field Service. He spoke English well, with an American accent. He had greatly enjoyed his time in Arizona, had learned much, and remained so grateful to the American Field Service that he intended to give them part of the fee he was going to get from me.

I also felt that Prasojo wanted to give back to me, a stranger, some of the kindness he had received in the United States. For our trip he wore jeans with the AFS label stitched on the hip pocket. He was just above medium height and of Chinese appearance. That appearance was the subject of a family joke. Prasojo's father, a bulky man, undeniably Indonesian, would say, 'But eh – how did I get this Chinese son?'

We took the Garuda air shuttle to Surabaya on the northern coast of east Java. Mud tainted the coastline. The rivers were muddy wriggles in the green, over-worked, over-populated land. The land around Surabaya was a land of rice, the rice-fields in long thin strips, easier that way to irrigate, but suggesting from the air an immense petty diligence.

The houses – as we saw later, driving inland from Surabaya – matched the rice-strips. They were very narrow and went back a long way. The houses stood a little distance from the road, and the front yards were scraped clean, but shady. Banana trees grew out of the bare earth, and coconut trees, mango trees, sugar-cane, and frangipani. The rice-fields began directly at the back of the houses. During that drive we seemed to be going through one long village: Java here an unending smallness, hard to associate with famous old kingdoms and empires, a land that seemed only to be a land of people of petty diligence, the *wong chilik*, the little people, cursed by their own fertility, four million in Java at the beginning of the last century, eighty million today.

It was Prasojo who gave me that word, *wong chilik*, telling me at the same time that the word (though beautifully appropriate in sound) was both insulting and old-fashioned. It still mattered to some people, though, who were not of the peasantry, to have their distinction acknowledged. Such people called themselves 'nobles', *raden*, and used the letter *R* before their names. They also built houses with a special hat-shaped roof, a distinction I would have missed if Prasojo had not pointed it out to me, so squashed and repetitive and cozy it had all seemed: the red-tile roofs, the walls of woven bamboo for the poor, concrete for the not so poor, the yards full of shade and fruit and flowers.

Windows were an innovation, Prasojo said. In the traditional Javanese house there were none; and, with walls of woven bamboo that shut out glare and heat but permitted ventilation, windows were not necessary. In the traditional house light came through gaps in the roof. But concrete walls required windows; and I could see that glass louvres were fashionable among the not so poor.

Each little yard had its gate-posts but no gate. The posts were of a curious design, with slabbed or stepped pyramids or diamond shapes at the top, the pyramids or diamonds sometimes bisected: concrete, but concrete clearly imitating brick. These posts, which at first suggested a single ownership of land and people, perhaps by some vast plantation, were in fact the remnant of the architectural style of the last Hindu kingdom of Java, the kingdom of Majapahit, which disintegrated at the end of the fifteenth century.

This was how the pre-Islamic past survived: as tradition, as mystery. *Indrapura*, 'Indra's City', was painted on the bus in front of us; and

Indra Vijaya, 'The Victory of Indra', was on many shops. But this Indra was no longer the Aryan god of the Hindu pantheon. To Prasojo, as well as to the driver of our car, this Indra was only a figure from the Javanese puppet drama. Prasojo began telling me a local Muslim legend of five Pandava brothers, who represented the five principles of Islam. And I don't believe Prasojo had an idea of the true wonder of the legend: the story he was telling me came from the ancient Hindu epic of the *Mahabharata*, which had lived in Java for 1400 years, had taken Javanese roots, and had then been adapted to Islam. Prasojo, a Javanese and a Muslim, lived with beautiful mysteries. Scholarship, applied to his past, would have undermined what had become his faith, his staff.

And so we came in the late afternoon to the town of Jombang. It was where the famous old *pesantren* was. But Jombang, once we turned off the highway, seemed to be full of schools. There were scattered groups of chattering Muslim schoolgirls on the road at the end of the school day: little nun-like figures, with covered heads, blouses, sarongs. Where was our *pesantren*, and in what way was it different from these other academies? We raced back and forth, the driver behaving as though he was still on the highway; we penetrated murky rural alleys. And then we found out that we had passed it many times: it was so ordinary-looking, even with a board, and not at all the sylvan retreat, the mixture of village and school, that I (and Prasojo as well) had been expecting.

There was a fence. And behind the fence rough two-story concrete buildings were set about a sandy yard, which had a few trees. In the centre of the yard there was an open pillared mosque with a tiled floor just above the ground. Boys in shirts and sarongs were sitting or lounging at the edge of the floor and on the step, following an Arabic text while a sharp-voiced teacher, unseen, steadily recited.

We went past the newspaper board – in the open, with a wooden coping, and with the newspapers behind glass – to the office at the side of the mosque. There was nobody in the office. Variously coloured shirts and sarongs hung on the verandah rails of the two-story buildings. There were boys everywhere, bare-backed, in sarongs, with warm-brown skins and the lean, flat, beautiful Indonesian physique, pectoral and abdominal muscles delicately defined.

They stared back. And then, gradually, they began to gather around Prasojo and myself. When we walked, they followed. They became a crowd as we walked about the narrow dirt lanes and the muddy gutters between the houses at the back of the compound: hanging clothes or sarong-lengths everywhere, glimpses of choked little rooms (eight boys to a room, somebody told Prasojo). There was mud and rubbish outside the rough kitchen shed and the school shop; and over an open fire in the muddy yard one little saronged boy was scraping at a gluey mess of rice in a burnt saucepan. He looked up in terror, at us, at the crowd with us. Perhaps, I thought, all medieval centres of learning had been like this.

But – was it 'Illich' that one boy shouted, and then another boy?

A very small man in a black cap, a man perhaps about four feet ten, came up to us and led us back, with our following, to the front of the compound, to a building near the mosque. He opened a door, let Prasojo and me into a big room, and shut the door on the crowd. He looked quite stern below his black cap.

Prasojo said, 'He says we are creating a disturbance.'

I said, 'It isn't me that's creating the disturbance.'

Chairs were lined up in two rows on either side of low tables in this big room. We sat down.

And just as in East Africa, at certain seasons, the flying ants pile up in drifts against the windows to which they are attracted by the light, so the students of the famous *pesantren* of Jombang – attracted by what? By the visitor who proved their own fame? – piled up against the windows, mongoloid face upon mongoloid face, grin upon grin. They mimicked every word I spoke, even in the shelter of the room. And distinctly now, between the chatter and the mimicking, there were shouts of 'Illich! Illich!' Had the visit – or the reported interest – of that famous man made them so vain?

Another man came into the room.

Prasojo said, 'They say we must be registered. There is an Arabic class going on in the mosque and we are creating a disturbance. They gets lots of visitors here.'

Of course.

'We have to register in the office,' Prasojo said.

'But there is no one in the office. We went there first.'

So we sat for a while. And then it turned out that the man in the black cap had no authority at all, wasn't even a teacher, was only a student, had been one for nine years. He had brought us to this room only to have us to himself. I thought he should be made to do something useful.

I said to Prasojo, 'Give him the letter of introduction. Tell him to take it to his leader.'

A *pesantren*, being traditional and 'unstructured', as I had heard in Jakarta, didn't have a 'principal'. It had a *kiyai*, a 'leader'.

Meekly, the man in the black cap took the letter and went away.

I said to Prasojo, 'Couldn't you go and talk to the Arabic teacher?'

That class was continuing. The teacher, hidden somewhere in the shadows of the mosque, was reciting on and on.

Prasojo was horrified. He couldn't interrupt a teacher.

'What do we do?'

'We wait.'

We waited. When the Arabic class was over we went outside, risking the crowd. Bare-backed boys were lounging about the verandahs of the houses; some were smoking Indonesian clove cigarettes, sweetly scented. But the mimicking crowd, pressing all around now, made movement and speech difficult. The little man in the black cap came back, as brisk and neat and equable as ever, with the letter of introduction still in his hand. He hadn't found his leader.

Prasojo led me back to the room with the chairs. He said, and his unhappiness gave him a strange formality, 'May I leave you here for a while? I will go and find someone.'

He went out. I saw that none of the boys followed him. But they continued to gape at me. The evening was coming on, though, prayer time, food time, and interest in me began to abate. Less and less frequently, and sometimes now from far off (an idler moving away, his curiosity sated), came the shout of 'Illich!' And Indonesian courtesy wasn't dead. I was sitting alone, but someone from an inner room brought out many glasses of tea (as though a proper tea party was about to begin), set one glass in front of me without staring, and went away.

Prasojo came back with two men. One was a student, who stared and remained mute. The other was an English teacher, as small as the man in the black cap. He was all smiles, anxious to practise his English. Prasojo damped him down. They talked together in Indonesian and Prasojo said the English teacher would take us to another *pesantren*, half an hour's drive away, where we might see someone who might tell us something.

There seemed little to lose. So we drove through the dusk, past the eternal Javanese village, and the smiling English teacher, sitting next to the driver, was no trouble at all. Abruptly, after some minutes, he turned around and said, 'How many times have you visited this place?' And having framed and asked his English question, and having got a reply, he sat good and quiet for the rest of the drive.

The *pesantren* we came to looked newer and more businesslike: a well-constructed set of buildings of concrete and corrugated iron around a well-kept yard. It was the hour of the evening prayer: someone was chanting the call. The deputy leader was in the unlighted office, an old man with thick-lensed glasses and a long blue sarong. He said we were lucky: Mr Wahid was going the very next day to Jakarta. And he led us in the dark through some gardens to a private house, to meet Mr Abdur Rahman Wahid, who knew all about *pesantrens*. And it was only then that I remembered that Mr Wahid's name had been given me as a man I should try to see. There had been articles about him in the Jakarta papers. His *pesantren* work had begun to make him a figure.

Accident – Prasojo meeting the English teacher – had brought me to Mr Wahid. And what Mr Wahid – a short, chunky, middle-aged man in a sarong – said in his western-style drawing room – a dim ceiling light, a television set going in a far corner, women coming and going, family, servants, cups of tea laid out on the low table – what Mr Wahid said altered the day for me, gave order to the confused experiences of the late afternoon, and opened my mind to a historical wonder.

First, the name. In Indonesian the word for the Chinese quarter of a town was *perchinen*: *per-china-en*, 'where the Chinese were'. So, *pesantren* was *per-santri-en*, 'the place where the wise men were', *santri* being a version of *shastri*, the Sanskrit word for a man learned in the Hindu *shastras*, the scriptures.

In Java, in Hindu-Buddhist days, a *pesantren* was a monastery, supported by the community in return for the spiritual guidance and the spiritual protection it provided. It was easy for the sufi Muslims, when the philosophical systems of the old civilization cracked, to take over such places; and it was easy for such places to continue to be counselling centres for village people. It was open to a man to go at any time to the leader or *kiyai* of a *pesantren* and ask for personal advice or religious instruction. It was not necessary to be enrolled in any formal course; in this way *pesantren* instruction could be said to be 'unstructured'.

In the Dutch time, in the latter part of the nineteenth century, the villages began to change. Some people became rich, and they wanted to educate their children. It was these people, the newly well-to-do of the villages, who began to turn the *pesantren* from sufi centres into schools for children. And Islam itself was changing in Java. The sufi side, the mystical side that was closer to the older religions, was becoming less important. The opening of the Suez Canal and the coming of the steamship made Java – until then at the eastern limit of Islam – less remote. In the days of sail it took months to get to Mecca; now the journey could be done in three to four weeks. More people went to Mecca. More people became acquainted with the purer faith: the Prophet, the messenger of God, and his strict injunctions.

In the last decade of the nineteenth century the *pesantrens* began to be turned into schools. The Jombang *pesantren* school, which we had visited, had been established in 1896. But they remained religious places. They remained places which the villagers supported and to which they could go for advice. Every thirty-five days the leaders of the *pesantrens* in an area met to discuss whatever issues had arisen.

Recently, for instance, people had been agitated about long hair on men. The leaders had done the correct Islamic thing. They had gone through the Koran and other approved records of the Prophet's time and they couldn't find that the Prophet had said anything about long hair. So they had decided that long hair wasn't an issue. Why did the leaders meet every thirty-five days? That was a relic of Hindu-Buddhist times. The week then had five days, and the leaders of the monasteries met every seven weeks.

It was late. But a class was going on in Mr Wahid's own *pesantren*, in the house at the end of his garden. The *pesantren* still kept the hours of the monastery, still required a day-and-night devotion from its inmates. We went out to the garden to watch. Boys were sprawled in the front room of the teacher's little house and outside his door. The light in the room was very dim; the teacher's eyes were bad. The teacher read or chanted in Arabic, never pausing, and the boys followed in their books. It was a class in Islamic law.

Mr Wahid said the teacher was one of the most learned men in the area. He received no salary, only 500 rupiah a month, eighty cents. But the villagers gave him food; the *pesantren* provided him with transport, and had built the little house for him.

The class was over. The boys got up. Some of them hung around us. The little teacher with his thick-lensed spectacles came out of his dim little house and stood silently and meekly beside us while we talked about him. He was only thirty, Mr Wahid said, but he knew a lot of the Koran by heart.

I said, 'Only thirty, and he knows the Koran by heart!'

'Half,' Mr Wahid said. 'Half.'

I didn't think that was good enough, for a man of thirty with only one book to master. Mr Wahid and I debated the point amicably, while the teacher stood outside his house in his own dim light, silent, hunched, and modest, waiting to be dismissed: the unlikely successor of the Buddhist monks of bygone times, still living (as the Buddha had prescribed for his order) on the bounty of his fellows, but now paying them back with Arabic lessons for their children.

We drove back to Jombang with the English teacher. He got more than eighty cents a month, though he didn't say how much. But he didn't have a house and nobody gave him food. He managed, but things were tight. A bowl of rice from someone in the village cost him fifty rupiah, about eight cents; a bowl of rice with 'something' added could set him back about sixteen cents.

The Jombang *pesantren* looked different in lamplight, more sedate. The main gate was closed. That was to keep the boys in, the English teacher said. We entered by the open gate near the house of the leader; the boys were too nervous of the leader to use that gate.

The lights were dim. The compound was quieter than it had been in the afternoon. But in the house called Al Fattah they were still lounging about in their sarongs, and – as in a nature park at night, full of roosting birds – the visitor still raised a flutter. There were eight boys to a room; and the rule was that the boys – they came to the *pesantren* at thirteen, and left at twenty-five – had to be of different ages. But there wasn't always floor space for eight, and some boys slept in the mosque.

Here and there in the yard, in the very dim light, boys were pretending to study. It was pretence, because the light was so dim. The boys were looking at: a book on Islamic law, *An Arabic Grammar, The Story of Islam, How to Pray*. The last book had eight stage-by-stage drawings of the postures of Islamic prayer; and it perhaps wasn't really necessary, since the boys prayed five times a day. It was late in the evening; and the *pesantren* day began early.

The sufi centre turned school: the discipline of monks and dervishes applied to the young: it wasn't traditional, and it wasn't education. It was a breaking away from the Indonesian past; it was Islamization; it was stupefaction, greater than any that could have come with a western-style curriculum. And yet it was attractive to the people concerned, because, twisted up with it, was the old monkish celebration of the idea of poverty: an idea which, applied to a school in Java in 1979, came out as little more than the poor teaching the poor to be poor.

We spent the night in Surabaya. An imperial or world power doesn't remember all its little battles. But the local people remember. The British had fought the Indonesians in Surabaya in 1945, after the war. There were commemorative statues to see; and after we had seen them Prasojo and I started on the six-hour drive south-west to Yogyakarta. We took the Jombang road again, past the unending village, with the slabbed gate-posts that spoke of the long dead Javanese Hindu empire of Majapahit.

The Majapahit museum, where we stopped, had little. But there was a temple a short way down the village lane opposite. It was a green lane, full of shade. The woven-bamboo houses were without windows. A 'stop' sign in the lane – on a bamboo pole standing loosely in a hole – was watched by a small girl. For the 100-rupiah fee, for which she gave a receipt, she lifted up the pole: the money was for the village.

A big log hung loose from a cross-bar in a thatched shed beside the lane. This was the village observation post; the villagers took it in turn to watch through the night. The log was hollowed out, with a vertical gap cut down one side; when it was struck with a mallet it made a booming noise. It could be used to give the time, to warn of thieves or fires; fire was the main danger.

And just outside the shady village, in the open, was old grandeur: the high red-brick tower of the Majapahit temple, undecorated, geometric, strong, the ancient style that was the source of the slabbed diamonds and pyramids on the gate-posts we had been seeing all the way from Surabaya. It wasn't much, as a monument. The statues which the tower enshrined had been taken down. But after the crowding and the sameness, small houses, rice-fields in narrow strips, it gave a past to the people, and another feel to the landscape.

Prasojo didn't know the purpose or the significance of the temple. He was impressed only by the fact that it had been built without machines. Also, no mortar had been used. Lime had over the centuries bonded the bricks together: this had been the wonder of a German Prasojo had met.

We had something to eat in a Chinese café. 'Can you tell they are Chinese?' Prasojo asked, and I said I could. The village continued; people and their little houses were always with us. Then the land became broken and we began to wind through young teak forests, the teak growing straight, the leaves big and round. It was the Japanese who during the war had cut down all the teak of Java, Prasojo said. And this was interesting; because the day before, at the Jakarta domestic airport, where there were photographs of the antiquities of Indonesia, Prasojo had told me it was the Japanese who had with their swords cut off or disfigured the stone heads of the Buddhas. The subject had come up again in the Majapahit museum, and I had told him that (trophy-hunters apart) Muslims had been the great iconoclasts of history, the greatest cutters-off of the noses of ancient statues. That hadn't at first been easy for him to accept. But then, understanding, he had said simply, 'To prevent the people praying to them.'

It was noon, humid even in the teak forests. Prasojo fell asleep from time to time. He had the driver play pop music on the cassette player in the car; he slept to that. The land flattened, opened out to a wide plain with a line of blue hills on one side and high peaked mountains far on the other. It had rained; everything glittered. The green of the paddy fields was glorious. And against this green every touch of bright colour – in the dresses and sarongs of the people working in the paddy fields – was doubly glorious, reflected, with the sky, in the water. The rice grew in straight lines; different fields were in different stages of growth.

As the light changed, as the afternoon heat faded, Prasojo stirred and became alert again. Sleep had more than refreshed him: he talked poetically about the country through which we were driving. He had been educated near here. He spoke of the beauty of getting up in the morning while it was still dark and walking with palm-frond torches to the road to wait for the bus. He spoke of the 'dating' habits of the afternoon. Dating time was between four and six; there was nowhere to go after seven. The girl sat on the back of the motorbike with her legs to one side and held the boy around the waist: that was the recognized dating pleasure.

'This is the best part of the day,' Prasojo said.

The sun was red. The light was red; it came red through the trees, fell red on the road. A faint mist rose off the rice-fields; the blue hills went pale; and sun and sky were reflected in the water of the rice-fields.

'For us it isn't easy to be abroad,' Prasojo said. 'We get homesick.'

They got homesick for everything. For everything we had experienced that day, the freshness of the morning, the heat of noon, the relaxation and colours of the late afternoon. For everything we had seen on the road and in the fields: the cycle of the rice crop, the changing tasks, the men carrying loads in baskets on either end of a bamboo pole, the bicycle-rickshaws, the horse-carriages (different regions had different styles of carriage). To an Indonesian everything about his country was known; no detail of house or dress or light went unconsidered. Every season had its pattern; every day had its pattern. When Prasojo went to Arizona his first thought, waking up the first day, was, 'I am not in Indonesia.'

All this was drawn out of him by the fading light, the best time of the Javanese day. The road was full of people yielding to the pleasures of that time of day, relaxing, chatting. The horse-carriages were busy. Boys and girls rode together on bicycles – Prasojo pointed them out to me.

And he told me of some of the oddities of his time in Arizona. One morning he asked the man next door what, as a matter of courtesy and friendliness, he would have asked an Indonesian: 'What are you going to do today?' In Indonesia the man would have said, 'I will go to my rice-field. I have to do so-and-so today.' But in Arizona the reply – from a man of thirty – was, 'That's my business.' Or Prasojo would go, as he might have done in Indonesia, to the house of a friend, going for no reason, only for the reason of friendship. The boy's mother – in Arizona – would say, 'What do you want?' Which, in Indonesia, was rude. 'We are not as individualistic as that,' Prasojo said.

In Java when a man wanted his paddy cut he would send a message to his fellow villagers. They would come and help and get paddy in return. Prasojo's grandfather, a farmer, liked to have his evening meal in the front of the house, so that he could call out to his friends as they passed,

'Come and eat with us.' That, of course, wasn't possible in the town. In Jakarta you would be full up in no time. But his mother still had the sharing instinct; and that could get her into trouble with his father and sometimes lead to tears. Though, painfully, she had learned that she couldn't feed Jakarta every evening, she still, when she went on a train journey, took much more food than she needed for herself and her family, simply to have enough to give to people who might be with her in the compartment.

Yet, Indonesian as he was, Prasojo had travelled with delight. During his time with the American Field Service in Arizona he had been overwhelmed by the variety of the human race. He hadn't liked the Dutch because of the colonial past (some weeks later he told me of a disagreeable physical encounter between his farmer grandfather and a Dutchman); but in Arizona he had met a Dutch boy and had got to like him very much, and he had been glad to shake off his feelings about the Dutch. And how nice it was to be able to call a German boy 'Hitler' and for the boy to see the joke; and how nice it was, when Prasojo refused pork, for someone to say, 'Hey, when are you going to give up that religion of yours?'

He had lived first with a Lutheran family, then a Presbyterian, then an agnostic; and he had got on well with all of them. But he remained Indonesian enough to be unable to answer when someone in America asked him, 'Do you prefer the United States to Indonesia?' Prasojo didn't want to wound the American who had asked the question; at the same time he couldn't say that he liked Indonesia less than he did. Out of his Arizona experience there had come to him the wish to be a writer, and he had written a hundred-page autobiographical essay, *Merden Bukan Casa Grande*, 'Merden is not Casa Grande'. Casa Grande was where Prasojo had stayed in Arizona; Merden was the name of his village in Java.

At sunset we came to the temple of Prambanam. It was astonishing, after all the photographs, to see the mighty tower so near the main road, so much part of a village scene; it wasn't easy to believe in it.

The ninth-century Hindu temple − early photographs show only the great base, with a moraine of fallen stones − had been reconstructed by the Dutch, and not in any falsifying way: blank stones were used where the original pieces had been lost. The temple had been the centre of an enormous complex. Restoration work was still going on. The stones of smaller temples were neatly laid out and marked. Yet the village was encroaching. Outside the fenced-off monument area rubbish was burning in the remains of one of the smaller shrines which still had some carving. Prasojo said, 'That hurts me.' Yet again the wonder for him seemed to be only that men had built something so big without machines, had carved so well without machines.

A group of local girls, skittish at this time of day, ran up and down the four stone stairways, called out to Prasojo and me, and went giggling along the balustraded terrace. The sky was fading above the wet fields; the temple felt old.

The balustrade was carved with scenes from the *Ramayana*, the Hindu epic that Java and other countries in south-east Asia had made their own. A thousand years after Prambanam, the epic still lived in Java. Prasojo knew it well, from the puppet theatre. He knew the characters, the stories; he understood the moral issues they raised. Monuments like Prambanam used a difficult theology, Hindu or Buddhist, to proclaim the power and near-divinity of a king. The theology had faded; the kings and priests had gone; the softer side of the old faiths survived, as a civilization.

Prasojo was Muslim; he had friends among the new Muslims. But he was as yet far removed from the new Muslim wish to purify, to create abstract men of the faith, men who would be nothing more than the rules. Prasojo possessed his Javanese civilization too completely for that: it was his civilization that he had been talking about during the drive.

Friends and chat were important to Prasojo. He had friends in Yogyakarta. He spent the night with them, and he said later that five of them had gone to a restaurant – for an hour – and they had had a 'great' time.

He had said that he wanted us to get out early in the morning so that we could see the students of Yogyakarta cycling to school, seven abreast, ringing their bells and laughing. Why did they cycle like that in the Yogya traffic? 'Because they are so happy.' And they were happy because it was appropriate to their time of life, and that time of morning. But it was those cycling students – and the other pedal traffic – that created the jam that delayed Prasojo. So I missed the students.

Still, Prasojo had brought one of his friends: to me, from Prasojo's talk, a kind of mythical figure: the friend, part of the ritual and security of Javanese life. Prasojo could not conceal his delight in his friend. He touched him; he spoke smilingly about him to me. And the friend, while he was with us, was silent, yet never bored, content to be with Prasojo.

The Jombang *pesantren* had been a trial. But Prasojo had high hopes of the *pesantren* at Pabelan. Pabelan was the *pesantren* show-piece. It was the 'traditional' Islamic teaching institution which had been extended into a school of a sort which some thought perfect for Java: not a diploma-factory (it gave no diplomas), 'unstructured', teaching

appropriate skills, a 'co-operative', self-supporting, teachers and students working together, no one strictly only a teacher, village and school
sustaining one another, no one absolutely a villager, no one absolutely a
student. This was how I understood it to be: an educational commune, a
self-help organization, something in harmony with the village like
Prasojo had told me about.

It was an hour's drive from Yogya, on the road to the Borobudur
temple: village and rice all the way, the earth here volcanic and rich. We
turned off into a tree-hung lane, and at the end saw a number of
whitewashed Javanese houses in a large sandy compound, with coconut
trees and flamboyant trees. We found the office, in a roughish village
house, and there my difficulties began.

There were two men in the office. One of them was Taufiq. He was
thirty perhaps, small, round-faced, with a tremendous constant smile,
and an easy deep laugh. He denied that the office was an office. And that
confused me right away, because there was a glass case with many
folders.

Taufiq then said that there was no office staff. *Pesantren* people took it
in turn to be in the office, which was why – and this greatly amused
Taufiq – to some visitors the office didn't look like an office at all. Taufiq
was in the office that morning as *pesantren* spokesman only because it
was his turn.

But what about continuity? Who looked after the folders in the glass
case? Taufiq either didn't answer or I missed what he said. He introduced
the other man in the office – a well-set-up young man, speaking English
fluently – as a village leader, a village headman. This man wasn't my
idea of a village headman. And, trying to deal with all the puzzles Taufiq
had already set me, I missed some of his explanations to Prasojo about
there being no teachers in this school.

I began to listen again when Taufiq said in his equable way, 'We live at
peace with Nature.'

The ecological concern rang an alarm: it sounded modern, but it had
also been deemed Koranic, and for both those reasons it had been
incorporated into the new Islam. And I returned fully to the conversation when Taufiq said that we were strangers, but we were welcome. We
could stay for lunch, we could spend the night. It was the way of
Pabelan: to be a Muslim was to serve your fellow man.

I said, 'Is that why you serve your fellow men? Some people serve
their fellow men because they are their fellow men.'

The village headman answered. 'We are Muslims and we want to be
good.'

'What do you mean by good?'

The village headman, holding himself erect, said, 'Custom. Not causing offence.'

It was a good reply, a Muslim reply: keeping to approved Muslim
custom, not causing offence to Muslims.

I said, 'Is it good or bad to wear long hair?'

Again he didn't hesitate. 'That isn't a problem.'

He had passed his Islamic test. He relaxed. He looked at me with a new
regard. He said, 'Are you an Arab?'

'No. What makes you think that?'

'You look like our Prophet.'

Prasojo was outraged. 'You can't *say* that. Nobody knows what the
Prophet looked like.'

'Nobody knows,' the headman said, trying to steer now between
blasphemy and discourtesy. 'But he looks like what you would expect
the Prophet to look like.'

We looked at the map of the Indonesian archipelago on the wall.
Pabelan was the centre of this map. To it ran red strings from all the
districts of Indonesia – marked by drawing pins – which had sent students to the *pesantren*.

Prasojo, perhaps playful, perhaps not, pointed to a very small northern island. 'How did they get to hear about it up there?'

'Let's not talk,' Taufiq said. 'Let's go outside.'

And leaving the headman in the office, we went out into the
sandy yard. The cesspit smell, heavy in the office, lightened in the
open air. Some boys and men, among them an old man with a black
cap, were carpentering wooden bedsteads in the shade of a coconut
tree.

I said to Taufiq, 'You say there are no teachers. Who taught them to
make beds?'

'They teach one another.'

We went to the bed-makers. They, no doubt used to visitors, paid us
no attention.

Prasojo said, 'What do you want me to ask now?'

'Ask who pays for the wood.'

Taufiq said, 'People give us things. We sell things. We make furniture
and we sell it. Some people in the village don't even know I am with the
pesantren. They think I'm a trader.' And Taufiq gave his deep little
laugh; he liked the idea of the incognito, the puzzle.

'Look,' Prasojo said. 'Girls. And they're quite pretty.'

It was the nineteen-year-old eye. They were very young, the girls;
and they were squatting in the sand around a biggish hole, picking up
scraps of coconut-root and dropping them into a basket. When we went

to watch, they became languid, snapping off the limp pieces of coconut-root delicately, without haste.

Taufiq said, 'They're gathering fuel, to cook. It's a co-operative.'

Prasojo said, 'How long do they spend picking up fuel?'

'It's Friday,' Taufiq said. 'They have no classes.'

Prasojo began to worry for the pretty girls. 'You mean they spend all day?'

Taufiq didn't stop smiling. 'It's a co-operative.'

But even while we watched, the girls decided to call it a day. They stood up carefully, held their little baskets of coconut twigs against their sides, and swayed away.

The sand in places was marked with white cord: volley-ball courts. But nobody was playing. Here and there mattresses were being put out in the sun on mats, to air.

Prasojo said, 'That's the girls' dormitory. Do you want to go and have a look?'

I wasn't going to let Prasojo use me as a stalking-horse. I said, 'It might embarrass them.' And we moved on to look instead at a group cleaning a pond. A length of thick hose was attached to an inactive electric pump; and boys with nets stood in the scummy, dark-green water sieving out leaves and other muck. The work was being superintended by a middle-aged man.

Taufiq said, 'He's the man who founded the *pesantren*. In 1962.'

Prasojo said, 'You want to talk to him?'

I said no; I wouldn't have known what to say to him.

We walked around to a boys' dormitory. It was clogged with beds and suitcases. It was a dormitory for thirty-two boys, and some of them were there, lying on their beds.

Taufiq said to Prasojo, 'That boy is famous. His brother is a singer.' He mentioned a name, and Prasojo was impressed.

Outside another dormitory some small boys were standing beside suitcases and other bags and parcels. They had their little black caps on and this made them look fully dressed, as though they had just arrived and were waiting to be told where to go.

Taufiq said, 'We move the younger ones around every ten days or so. For the interaction. Here it doesn't matter whether they are Javanese or Sundanese or Sumatrans. They're Indonesians. You see that boy?' he said to Prasojo. 'He's from Timor.'

Prasojo was interested. 'Which one?'

'Timor,' Taufiq said, and laughed. 'Our newest colony. Soon we'll be colonizing Australia.'

Prasojo said, 'You mustn't *say* those things.'

I said, thinking about the boys being moved, 'But suppose they don't want to move? You say there are no teachers, that it's all co-operative.'

'That's right. It's totally unstructured.'

'But suppose they don't want to move?'

'Over there,' Taufiq said, pointing beyond the trees and a couple of volley-ball courts, 'we have a piece of land. We use it for agriculture.'

I forgot about the boys. I said, 'How much?'

'Two and a half hectares.'

A new building – which would have cost money – had musical instruments. But it was Friday and no one was playing. On a board were photocopies of articles in Indonesian and English about the *pesantren*. Three of the articles were in English. They echoed one another, especially about the 'interaction' between the school and the community, and must have been based on a handout. One of the articles mentioned Ivan Illich – it seemed hard to avoid his name in a *pesantren* – and suggested that the Pabelan *pesantren* was a perfect example of 'deschooling'.

Taufiq and Prasojo waited while I read.

I said, 'You say it's unstructured and there are no teachers. How long do students stay here?'

Taufiq said, 'Six years.'

'I don't think I am understanding what I am seeing.'

'Look,' Prasojo said. 'A wall newspaper.'

In a rough village shed with a dirt floor, the dust thick and hummocked with footprints, three boys were putting together the wall newspaper. The items were typewritten, the margins justified right and left: which meant that somewhere in this settlement of Javanese huts and houses there was an electric typewriter and someone who could use it.

We passed an old hut with coconut-matting walls. An old man was sitting just outside.

'Who is he?'

'A villager,' Taufiq said, pleased I had asked. 'And that's a villager too. Village, school, no difference.'

I said, 'Prasojo, I believe I'm getting a cold. I think we should be going back to Yogya.'

Taufiq didn't try to keep me. We walked back in the direction of the office. We stopped in front of some wooden crates on battens.

Taufiq said, 'This is where we keep our rice. The villagers give us. And when they want, we give them.'

This was Taufiq, setting me puzzles even at the end.

When we were in the car I said to Prasojo, 'I think it's a bad school. Why go to all that trouble just to do that? Why don't they simply build a proper school? Is anybody there getting an education? Or are they just playing at being villagers?'

'You can't say that. You can't spend fifteen minutes in a place and make up your mind about it.'

'We didn't spend fifteen minutes.'

'I don't think you understood what you saw.'

'That's what I feel too.'

'People didn't make beds at my school,' Prasojo said. 'They didn't make them and sell them. That's a new idea.'

I said, 'I did woodwork in my school.'

'You did?' He went silent.

We crossed the dug-up river bed with its litter of black lava rocks: one of the lava channels of the Mount Merapi volcano.

I said, 'Have you heard of an English writer called Charles Dickens?' I felt it as absurd, asking this as the Javanese rice-fields rolled by. 'Well, in 1837 or 1838 Charles Dickens wrote a novel called *Nicholas Nickleby*, and he described a school like that. It was run by a man called Mr Squeers. He believed in learning by doing. Botany – go out and garden. Biology – go out and brush down the horses.'

'I have heard of Charles Dickens, but I haven't read *Michael Nickleby*.'

'*Nicholas Nickleby*. I would hate to be forced to stay in a place like that.'

'It would be *criminal* if you went away and wrote that. Nobody's being forced to stay there.'

'I didn't mean it like that, Prasojo. I meant if I was a boy, and my parents sent me to a place like that, I would hate it.'

I had offended him; I had strained his Javanese courtesy. He believed in the *pesantren* system, as a Javanese system and a Muslim system. He hadn't been to Pabelan before, and perhaps he was as puzzled as I was by what we had seen and what Taufiq had told us. But he respected the reputation of the place.

A little later – Yogya getting near, billboards appearing – he returned to the subject, but obliquely. He said, 'What would you say is the difference between education and knowledge?'

And for the first time, thinking around that sentence of Prasojo's, I thought I could see what Taufiq might have been trying to tell me.

But it wasn't the kind of discussion I liked. I said, 'I don't know if I can answer that. It is a false question. Education and knowledge aren't always different things.'

He pretended to understand. As we entered Yogya in the midday heat – the scooters and the smoking buses, the Dutch-style bakeries, the advertisements for Indonesian clove cigarettes, the cycle-rickshaws with their high saddles at the back (the strain of these rickshaws less on the calves than on the arms, from the pressure the rickshaw-men constantly exerted to hold down the front part of their rickshaws) – as we entered Yogya, Prasojo pretended to play with what I had said.

But when the car stopped at the hotel he couldn't restrain himself. He said, 'I didn't want to be a guide, you know. I *ditched* school for a week to be with you. My teacher thought it would be a good idea, for me to be with you. And it was because of that the headmaster gave his three stamps.' And unexpectedly then, with this attack, he threw in an apology. 'I am sorry I took you to that batik place this morning. You didn't ask to see batiks. It was a waste of your time.'

I held his arm, offering in this way my own apology. And he let me hold his arm for a while, before he opened the car door.

But wasn't the idea of the village educational commune – if what I had heard was correct – no more than the idea of the community of low skills, an abuse of the poor?

A little of the mystery was cleared up in the evening when we went to a gathering at the house of Umar Kayam. Umar had been named by his parents after the Persian poet, but in Indonesia he was a name in his own right. He was a big, attractive man in his late forties, a teacher at the university in Yogyakarta and also a writer; Prasojo held him in awe. And Umar and his friends – one of whom had studied at Pabelan – took Prasojo's side.

They said I had misunderstood Pabelan. I had gone on the sabbath, when there were no classes; and I had been misled by language. There were teachers at Pabelan. When Taufiq had said there were no teachers he had probably only meant that there were no religious teachers, nothing like an *ustad*, whose word in the old days was law. Pabelan was mainly religious and Islamic, but it taught other subjects as well; it had a library and a laboratory. The attempt to establish a school like that in a village, using village resources, was new.

I said, 'But, Prasojo, didn't Taufiq tell us there were no teachers and that the place was unstructured?'

'Perhaps Taufiq didn't know too much. I told you you were being too quick to make up your mind. You are free to do that of course. But you were too quick.'

But wasn't it also that at Pabelan they had told me things they thought I wanted to hear? When Taufiq and the village headman had thought I was a Muslim, possibly even an Arab, they had pushed the Muslim side.

Later, assessing me differently, Taufiq had used, perhaps too loosely, modern-sounding words: 'co-operatives', 'no élites', 'unstructured'. Perhaps it was only Javanese courtesy – there were Indonesians in Jakarta who cursed it – that had confounded me.

Much of the talk at Umar Kayam's was about the Javanese village. There was a new strain of rice. It grew twice as fast as the old and gave two crops a year. The food was necessary, but the two crops were breaking up the rhythm of the old life, interfering with the festivals and the puppet dramas that were so important to the Javanese. There were too many people, and the extended family was going: relatives were no longer called in to cut rice and get part of the crop in return. The ritualized community life Prasojo had spoken about with such feeling was breaking down. And the Islam of places like Pabelan was part of the response to this breakdown.

Prasojo was nervous about it, but we went back the next morning to Pabelan, to see what I had missed.

I had missed the high gateway at the entrance to the village lane, the welcome sign. The coconut trees and the red-flowered flamboyant trees and the tiled roofs of the school compound made a more picturesque impression. There were fewer students about. The porch of the mosque building was empty. Through an open door at the back of the office I saw some girls sewing. They said they were making a welcome banner for the minister for religious affairs, who was due that day. Then they giggled and ran.

The man in the office that morning, as secretary and spokesman, was smaller than Taufiq and wore a black cap. I felt that he was going to confuse me too. We could hear an Arabic class going on, young girls chanting responses to a teacher, but the man in the office said that classes hadn't started. I asked whether the students were in the fields. It was a provocative question, but he gave a serious reply. He said the students went to the fields in the afternoon. I asked where Taufiq was.

'He is washing.'

'Bathing?'

'He is washing clothes.'

'Does he wash a lot of clothes?'

'He washes a lot.'

It seemed the kind of thing Taufiq would like to do in the *pesantren*. I said, 'I want to go and see Taufiq doing his washing.'

We walked around to a lane at the back. A concrete gutter discharged dirty water from a house into a sodden black ditch.

'What is that?'

The office secretary said, as though it was an English-vocabulary test, 'A water-channel, a canal.'

'Is it a school building?'

'It belongs to a villager.'

Next to that was a row of concrete bathrooms, and in front of the bathrooms was a series of open, half-walled washing places. In the lane between bathrooms and washing places I saw Taufiq with a red plastic bucket: Taufiq plump-cheeked and as merry as ever.

He said, 'Good morning. How nice to see you again. I knew you would come back. But you must excuse me now. I have to do some washing.'

Just beyond the bathrooms some boys were cutting the hair of other boys. One boy of eighteen, with a towel over his shoulders, was waiting to get his hair cut. He came from Sumatra and was going back to his village soon. He said he intended to do good for the village. This was correct and polite; but I wanted something more specific. He thought and said he was going to be a teacher. He couldn't say more.

Prasojo and I and the secretary turned back. We saw Taufiq again, just his head and shoulders above the concrete wall of a washing place. He was in a red tee-shirt. He gave us his smile and said, 'I am doing my washing.'

I asked the secretary, 'Does he do a lot of washing?'

The secretary understood the drift of my question. He said, 'It's his own clothes he is washing.'

We came to the new building where the girls were chanting Arabic. Their tight head-covers, denying them hair, gave them all blank mongoloid faces. The class was almost over; the teacher was stacking up copybooks. It sounded as though every line of this last part of the girls' chant began with *Allah*, but Prasojo said this was wrong.

I said to the secretary, 'Taufiq told me yesterday there were no teachers here.'

The secretary talked in Indonesian to Prasojo as we walked. Prasojo translated. 'What Taufiq meant was that he was a teacher, but at the same time he learned from others, people like the leader. So he was also a student.'

We passed the Javanese-style house which had been shown me the previous day as the very first building of the *pesantren*. On the door someone had painted, in English, *Ancient House*. The walls were of woven-bamboo panels. In the middle of the undivided space were four wooden pillars with cross-bars at the top to support the tiled roof. On three sides was a continuous bamboo platform, elegantly made: thick bamboo supports, thinner lengths of split bamboo for the platform, polished by use. Twenty-two boys slept on this platform. Against the woven-bamboo walls were many little cupboards painted in different colours. This was the original *pesantren* school idea: the village building where village boys came to learn Arabic and to chant the Koran after a village teacher.

There was a lot of bedding on the bamboo platform. But what looked like a bundle of bedding in one place turned out to be a boy, and he had a white cloth wrapped around his head as a sign that he was ill. He had fallen ill the day before; the doctor was going to come that afternoon. It was unimportant.

We stepped out again into the newer world of 'interaction'. In the shade of the coconut trees they were still making beds: seven or eight men, of varying ages, sawing and planing.

'Are you going to sell those beds? That was the impression I got yesterday.'

'No, the beds are for us. We need a lot of beds in this place.'

'Where did you get the money to buy the wood?'

'That I don't know.'

'So these men are workmen? You pay them?'

'They are from the village. And they are being paid.'

'We were told yesterday that it was a co-operative venture. Taufiq said they were students and villagers and they were learning from one another.'

The secretary was silent. We looked at the men sawing and planing. They, like busy workmen, didn't pay us too much attention.

Prasojo tried to save the situation. He picked up a mattock and said, 'But this belongs to the *pesantren*, doesn't it?'

The secretary said absently, still thinking, 'Yes.'

I said, 'What nice planes they have.'

Prasojo said, 'You would like to buy one?'

But now the secretary was speaking. 'What Taufiq meant was that some of these men had never made beds before. Perhaps they made chairs. Perhaps they built houses. They learned about making beds only when they came here. In that way they are students. I think that was what Taufiq meant.'

Prasojo said abruptly, as though he had just worked it out, 'The place is like a campus. But a campus where the students also work.'

It was a campus, though, with a feel of the farmyard. Outside the girls' dormitory (which Prasojo had wanted to visit the previous day) there were puddles, and in these puddles there were ducks and many ducklings. We picked our way through the mud, past the heaps of refuse, past the lines of washing. The fish pond was as green and dark as it had been before the cleaning. The Honda pump was still there, with the attached hose in the pond.

We jumped down the wall at the back of the girls' dormitory, and now, at this lower, dirtier level, in a farmyard smell, were village houses with village women who smiled and called out to us from the garbage that was spread about their yards and out of which their houses seemed to grow.

'Do they work for the *pesantren*?'

'They are villagers. If they have free time they work for the canteen.'

The canteen was not far from the cow-pens. The place here was full of villagers digging, cleaning, toting; and in the background was the chant of another Arabic class. The campus turned farmyard was now like a medieval manor farm, humming with peasant activity. And, as if called up by the thought, a line of medieval-looking villagers came in toting awkward lengths of wood.

Prasojo, acting on his own, stopped one man. The man was broad and muscular and not young. Burdened as he was, he still had the Javanese politeness; and he told Prasojo yes, he would like to be a student. But he didn't have the qualifications and couldn't raise the ten-dollars-a-month fee. He earned 500 rupiah a day, eighty cents; but he also got food.

The Arabic chanting came from a new school building. In the verandah a group of happy, inquisitive women were stuffing mattresses with kapok, fluff from which flew dustily about.

Prasojo talked with the secretary, and afterwards Prasojo said, 'They have seventy teachers here. And they keep attendance registers, and every student has a record. The place is not unstructured at all.' Prasojo giggled. 'It's *very* structured.' The teachers were volunteers. At the end of their time in the *pesantren* they stayed for a year or two to teach; they got from eight to forty dollars a month.

Such effort, such organization, to duplicate the village atmosphere, to teach villagers to be villagers!

When we were going back to the office we saw Taufiq, his washing done, his plastic bucket and basins left behind. He had shed his red tee-shirt and was in a fresh flowered shirt and pale-lilac trousers that were tight over his thick little thighs. His round face was closely shaved. He looked ready for the day ahead – perhaps even for meeting the minister for religious affairs. He gave us a big smile.

He said, 'The leader was expecting you to spend the night here. He personally prepared a place for you to sleep. But you went away. He was expecting you to stay for lunch. He had the boys catch the fish and everything.'

Fish! I had thought those boys in the pond were cleaning the pond. It was what Taufiq himself had said.

I asked whether I could get copies of the articles that had been published about the *pesantren*. I especially wanted the article in which Taufiq had spoken about the *pesantren* as 'a learning community'. Taufiq said he would get me the articles, and went away.

We waited.

I asked the secretary, 'You think he's getting me the copies?'

'Yes. He's gone to the copying room.'

The copying room! A modern copying machine here, where they were learning about Islam and working hard at being villagers!

Taufiq came back with the copies, not only of the articles, but also of a letter he had just got from Australia.

We went out into the yard again, to the car. A ragged little village boy went by, carrying an enormous green fruit on his back.

I asked Taufiq, teasingly, 'Is he a student?'

Prasojo giggled.

Taufiq said, 'He is a villager and student.'

Taufiq smiled. But the smile didn't mislead me: Taufiq was speaking seriously. I was glad we were leaving, because in another five minutes Taufiq, with his high philosophical way with language, would have confused us again.

In the car, going through the village, I looked at the letter from Australia. It was three weeks old and was from someone at a university. Had Taufiq really read the letter?

'Dear Taufiq, Once again I must thank you for the time we spent together. It was all too short but I hope we can continue our dialogue in letters As I reflect on my visit to you all at Pabelan I am still confused . . . What is it that you would like the students to do when they leave Pabelan? . . . He has the skills to develop the village but what can he do for those with little or no land? What kind of Islamic principles has he learned at Pabelan to help him in this situation? . . . What does Islam tell you about Indonesia and what to do about poverty?'

319

4

The Rice Goddess

AND THAT was the problem. What message did Islam have for the villages?

A week later I went back to Yogyakarta to go with Umar Kayam to one of the villages below the volcano of Mount Merapi. Merapi had a long, easy slope; a wisp of vapour always hung about its cone, and sometimes the cone was lost in cloud. Lava made the earth rich. The wet soil that the men in the paddy fields ploughed deep with bullocks or lifted with mattocks was black and volcanic. The mud-walled rice-fields came right up to the villages, so that from the air the villages – red-tile roofs among green trees, shade in the tropical openness – had sharp, angular boundaries.

To enter one of those villages was to find more than shade. It was to enter an enchanted, complete world where everything – food, houses, tools, rituals, reverences – had evolved over the centuries and had reached a kind of perfection. Everything locked together, as the rice-fields just outside, some no more than half an acre, fitted together.

Every house, with concrete walls or walls of woven bamboo strips, stood in shade; and every tree had a use, including the kapok, new to me. There were many kinds of bamboo, some thick and dark, almost black, some slender and yellow with streaks of green that might have been dripped by an overcharged brush. These bamboos made beds, furniture, walls, ceilings, mats. But rice ruled. It was the food and the cause of labour; it marked the seasons. In the traditional house there was a small room at the back of the pillared main room; this small room, in the old days, was the shrine-room of the goddess Sri, Devi Sri, the rice goddess.

Umar took me to Linus's village, and Linus went with us. Linus was a young Yogya poet whose only income so far was from his poetry readings. Linus was a Catholic; his full name (he had an Indonesian name as well, but he didn't use it) was Linus Agustinus. Linus's mother was a Catholic; it was to marry her that Linus's father had converted. They were a farming family. Linus's father was the village headman.

Since the military take-over this had become an elected post, and the headman had to see that the government's projects were carried out – getting the farmers to plant the new rice, for instance. The headman, while he held his post, had the use of twelve acres of land; in central Java that was a lot.

The village was off the road to Pabelan, and Umar knew the area well. During the revolution – the war against the Dutch – the Dutch had invaded Yogyakarta, and the revolutionary army had moved out into these villages. Umar was in the students' army at the time; they were billeted on the villagers.

I asked, 'Were you well organized?' Umar laughed at my question. 'What do you think?' It had been a time of chaos; and it was hard, as it is in most places in a time of peace, to think of war in such a soft setting: such small and fragile villages, such vulnerable fields, requiring such care.

Linus's family house was of concrete, on low pillars, with a concrete floor. But it was of the Javanese pattern. There was a Catholic icon above the inner door. And on a wall was a leather figure from the Javanese puppet theatre: the figure of the black Krishna, not the playful god of Hindu legend, but the Krishna of Java, the wise, far-seeing man, and therefore a suitable figure for a poet's house. In the bookcase were Linus's books from school and the university, and also *The Collected Poems of T. S. Eliot*, a gift from the BBC: Linus had won second prize in a poetry competition sponsored by the BBC Indonesian Service.

Glasses of tea with tin lids on the top were brought, and a plate piled high with steaming corn on the cob, and then a plate equally laden with a kind of roll. It was the Indonesian ritual of welcome, the display of abundance. It called for a matching courtesy in the guests. No one wished to be the first to eat or drink; and it often happened that the tea, say, was drunk right at the end, when it was cold.

One dish was brought out by one of Linus's younger sisters, a pretty girl of ten or twelve in a frock. Then another girl, much older, came out to look at the visitors. Her face was twisted, her teeth jutted; her dress hung oddly on her. Her movements were uncoordinated, and her slippered feet dragged heavily on the smooth concrete floor. She sat on a chair in the other corner and looked at us, not saying anything; and then, after a while, she lifted herself up and went out with her dragging step.

Some minutes later Umar said, delicately, 'You may have seen that sister of Linus's. She is not well.' She had fallen ill when she was young. They had taken her to a doctor, and the doctor's assistant had given a wrong injection, which had damaged her nervous system. So the house of the poet, the house of the village headman, was also a house of tragedy.

Linus's mother arrived: the woman for whom the father had converted, and because of whom the family was Catholic. Umar got up, with a definite stoop, and did a shuffle sideways, a big man trying to make himself smaller than the small woman. And a stream of musical speech poured out of both of them before we all sat down.

She was small and slight in the Indonesian way, and she might have passed unnoticed in the street. But now, detached from the Indonesian crowd, in her own house, and our hostess, her beauty shone; and it was possible to see the care with which she had dressed – blouse, sash, sarong (her daughters wore frocks). It was possible to see beyond the ready Indonesian smile (disquieting after a time) to her exquisite manners, and to see in this farmer's wife the representative of a high civilization. Her face was serene and open; she held her head up, with a slight backward tilt; her bones were fine, her eyes bright, though depressed in their sockets, and her lips were perfectly shaped over her perfect teeth. Her speech – without constraint or embarrassment – always appeared to be about to turn to laughter.

She and Umar talked for some time in this way, and it seemed they had much to say. But it was all part of the ritual of welcome, Umar told me later. They had used the polite Javanese language, which was different from the everyday language; and they had said little. Linus's mother had said that she had had to go to the school of one of her children to get the child's report; that was why she hadn't been able to welcome us when we arrived. She was ashamed to welcome people as distinguished as ourselves in a place that was hardly a house, was a mere hut. And Umar had been equally apologetic about our intrusion, which was perhaps upsetting the harmony of her household. That was how it had gone on, apology answered by apology.

One concrete thing had come out, though. Umar mentioned it afterwards, when we had left the house and were walking through the village. Linus's mother was worried about Linus. He didn't come to the village often; he stayed in his little house in Yogya; he wasn't married; and he didn't have a job. And she had a point, Umar said: Linus was twenty-eight.

I said to Linus, 'But isn't she secretly proud that you are a poet?'

Linus said in English, 'She wouldn't have even a sense of what being a poet is.'

Umar said, 'There is only one way Linus has of making her understand. And that is to say or suggest that he is being a poet in the classical tradition. But that would be nonsense. She would reject it as an impossibility.'

For someone like Linus's mother, living within an achieved civilization, poetry was something that had already been written, provided, a kind of scripture; it couldn't be added to.

But something was about to come up for Linus. A Yogya paper had asked him to do a cultural page, for twenty-five dollars a month. It was a short bus ride to Yogya, but the life that Linus was trying to make for himself there – poetry readings, newspapers – seemed a world away from the tight, rice-created village.

The shady village lane twisted. The earth was lava-black, and swept. The gutters were full of racing water – without water there can be no rice. The mosque was a plain shed on low pillars: no dome, no special roof. Islam didn't come to Java as a civilization; it came only as a faith, or a complement to the old faiths; it used what was already there. The mosque was open; inside there were a few bamboo mats, nothing else. A few steps away, at a bend in the black-earth lane, was the Catholic church, a plain shed like the mosque, but with a corrugated-iron portico over the concrete steps and with a cross at the top.

The mosque was open, as mosques should be. The church was locked. It wasn't much of a lock, though. Linus broke a twig off a hibiscus bush, pushed the twig into the keyhole and turned. The church was almost as bare as the mosque. It had a crucifix. High up on the walls were three small framed pictures of the stations of the cross. The glass was flyblown and cobwebby; the pictures had lost their colour and two had slipped in their mounts. The wire-netting at the top of the wall, just below the eaves, was torn in many places.

Christianity had come to Indonesia not long after Islam. It was the religion of the colonizing power; but, like Islam, it had also come to the villagers as a complement to the old faiths. And it was Islam, as the formal faith of the people, that had served Indonesian pride during the Dutch time. Not far away – the village was small and the walk was short, but it was like a walk through Javanese history – was a house with a board that said it was the office of the *Muhammadiyah*. This was a reforming, nationalist Indonesian Muslim movement that had started in the Dutch time; it was now said to be 'conservative'.

A small village, a short walk; and now – in this village of perishable buildings – centuries were added to history. We walked through the village to the house of the Muslim *koum*. Umar Kayam translated this as 'elder', and he gave me some idea of the *koum*'s duties. He was called in by Muslim families on important occasions – a birth, a funeral, an anniversary, or simply when a family wished to have a religious ceremony; and he performed then the *salamatan* ritual. This ritual had to do with the consecration of food and the distribution of the consecrated food. From my Hindu childhood I recognized the ceremony as a Hindu survival, and I thought of the Muslim *koum* as a kind of successor to the Hindu priest.

It was a surprise to find him living in a hovel at the end of the village, just next to the rice-fields, his house decayed, the inner room dark, junk in the verandah, the bamboo walls sagging, the whitewash turning to black some way above the black earth.

He didn't invite us in. He came out and stood in the front yard, on the damp black earth, in the shade of trees. He was in shorts and a white tee-shirt. His wife, not introduced to us, stood in the verandah and watched. He looked more a farmer and a peasant than a priest. And it was a further surprise to learn of his other duties: as *koum* he washed the bodies of the Muslim dead and shrouded them for burial. In himself then, the Muslim *koum* combined the ritual duties of priest and untouchable. He embodied, and in an extraordinary way, this man of ritual, what had been preserved of the Hindu system of caste.

He was sixty-four, small, muscular and still sturdy, his brown skin shining with sun, with only a looseness of skin around the knees to hint at his age, which showed more in his face. His cheekbones jutted like shelves; that, and a paleness of forehead, and his flat hair suggested that he wore a heavy hat while at work in the sun.

It was of his corpse duties that he was now speaking to Umar, and his speech was jovial, as though he was about to break into laughter. His duties did not abash him. He had inherited his position as *koum* from his father, and he had also inherited an acre of land. That explained his physique, that labour in the rice-field. He had done well. He saw himself as a successful man who had lived a good and useful life.

So he had no regrets? Things had gone well for the country?

He seemed to explode into laughter. Gone well? Things had got better and better. Life had never been better; he lived in the good time. What was there in the past for him to regret? There had been the Dutch; and when he was twenty-six the Japanese had occupied Java.

What was that time like? How had he got on with the Japanese?

Again his speech was like an explosion of laughter. It was a *dreadful* time, he said. Everything was short. They had no cloth. They had had to wear pants of sacking. And after that there was the revolution, the war against the Dutch. The village was one of those the Dutch regularly searched after they had invaded Yogyakarta; he had often had to run away and hide. No, this was the good time.

What of Sukarno, the leader against the Dutch?

And the reply of the old man, the peasant standing beside his hovel, was astonishing. His face softened; his voice softened. He said, 'Ah. He was a handsome man. He spoke well.'

Umar said after he translated, 'Beauty is important here. A leader has to be good-looking. But I suppose that is true in most countries.'

Yet it was strange, even in Java, with its ritual and courtesies: beauty and a gift for oratory leading a colonized people through cruel wars. Wouldn't there have been more to Sukarno in the early days, in the 1930s?

'Ask him when he first heard of Sukarno.'

The reply came, and Umar laughed. 'He says 1945. I must say that's news to me.'

I said, 'I was expecting to hear about the young Sukarno in the 1930s.'

'I wasn't expecting that. Sukarno was exiled for much of that time. There wasn't that amount of media coverage in those days. And what there was the Dutch controlled. I was expecting him to say that he first heard of Sukarno during the Japanese occupation, when the Japanese brought him back from exile.'

So the old man had heard of Sukarno only after independence had been proclaimed in August 1945. Sukarno had appeared suddenly, the leader, not only a man with an army, but also a man to follow because of his looks and because he spoke well.

Two white cows at the other end of the yard were eating cut grass. The tinkling of the bells around their necks accompanied the old man's bubbling talk. Life had turned out well for him, after all, better than he might have expected during the Japanese occupation, when times were hard and he had no knowledge of the existence of a leader.

But why, though being so well-to-do, with his acre of land, which was a lot, and his duties as *koum*, why did he live in such a poor hut?

Umar and Linus talked, and Umar said afterwards, 'It's a matter of a particular life-style.' Then Umar put the question to the old man, and the old man said, 'It's the way of Islam.'

It was a way that was no longer being followed, he said. Only a third of the Muslims lived as Muslims; only a third went to the mosque. There was a change among the young, though. Why? Perhaps, he said, it was because in the government school religion was being taught as a subject, and the young people had to study it if they wanted to get good grades.

He and Umar talked some more. The slender, long-legged cocks of Java walked about the damp yard; the cows' bells tinkled; the old man's wife watched us from the dark, junk-filled verandah and smiled.

Umar said, 'I've been asking him about the *wayang*.' The puppet theatre. 'Whether as a Muslim he objected to the Hindu stories. He said no; they were just stories.'

We made our way back to Linus's house – more tea, more steaming corn, a plate of hot chips made from some kind of dried fruit. Linus's mother walked out with us when we left. Shelled corn-cobs were drying on a mat in the front yard. The cobs were to be sold, to be crushed for oil; everything had a use here. And this time I took in the little roadside shack which was the family shop: Linus's family were also traders.

Umar wanted to show me the traditional Javanese house. Linus knew where one was. The house was not prepared for a visit, was cluttered; but the woman of the house smiled while we looked around, and showed us where the shrine to the rice goddess would have been. And it seemed to me that after this intrusion, Umar, as we left, made an especially low bow and did an especially long sideways shuffle. Such archaic elegance; and the ordinary main road, with its scooters, was only a few minutes away.

Here we had created a disturbance, though. The children had come out to watch. Every little girl had a doll, but it was a living doll: a little brother or sister held on the hip.

It was only half an hour to Yogya. But not all could make the journey from village to town as Linus had done. Linus was privileged. He was a poet; he had a sense of who he was; he could be a man apart. Not many villagers were like that. They had been made by the villages. They needed the security of the extended family, the security of the village commune, however feudally run, however heavy the obligations of the night watch or the communal labour in the rice-fields. For such men the villages were indeed enchanted places, hard to break out of. And if a man was forced to leave – because there simply wasn't the land now to support him – it was for the extended family – and something like the village again – that he looked, in the factory or the office, even in Jakarta.

Islam, like Christianity, complemented the older religions. The religion of the village was a composite religion; the idea of the good life was a composite idea. People lived with everything at once: the mosque, the church, Krishna, the rice goddess, a remnant of Hindu caste, the Buddhist idea of nirvana, the Muslim idea of paradise. No one, Umar Kayam said, could say precisely what he was. People said, 'I am a Muslim, but – ' Or, 'I am a Christian, but – '

And Umar told this story about the Prambanam villagers. In 1965, after the military take-over, the government, nervous of the communism of the late Sukarno period, required everyone formally to declare his religion. The people of Prambanam were in a quandary. In one way they were Muslims, believing in the Prophet and his paradise. But they didn't feel they could say they were Muslims: they broke too many of the rules. They knew that their ancestors had built the great ninth-century temples of Prambanam – which people from all over the world now came to visit; and though they no longer fully understood the significance of the temples, they knew they were Hindu temples. They liked watching the puppet plays based on the *Ramayana* and the *Mahabharata*, and they knew that these were Hindu epics. So the Prambanam people felt they should declare themselves Hindus.

The trouble then was that they didn't know what they should do as Hindus. They had no priests and no idea of the rituals they should perform. They sent for Balinese Hindu priests, and the Balinese came over with a Balinese gamelan orchestra to instruct them. But it didn't work. The past couldn't be reconstructed; the old rituals and theology couldn't take again. And so the people of Prambanam had returned to being what they had been, people of a composite religion.

On Thursday, at that time of late afternoon which Prasojo had said was the most beautiful time of the Javanese day, a woman sat outside her little shop in one of the main streets of Yogya, making up little banana-leaf sachets of rose petals, jasmine and the sweet-smelling lime-green flowers of the ylang-ylang. She was pregnant and she sat with her legs apart. The banana-leaf pieces were in a basket; the petals and blossoms and other things were in separate dishes. She worked fast, taking two strips of banana leaf, pinning them together at the bottom in a pocket with a piece of coconut-leaf rib, throwing red and white petals into this pocket, adding jasmine, sometimes perfume from a bottle, and then pinning the pocket at the top. Sometimes she added a yellow paste or a piece of a brown stick – it depended on what the customer wanted. The waiting customers were girls and women. The sachets cost fifteen rupiah, under three cents. They were flower-offerings to be made to the spirits of the dead; they were to be used in houses or placed in graveyards; and Thursday evening was the time to buy because Friday, the Muslim sabbath, had become the holy day.

Umar Kayam lived opposite a Chinese cemetery. It made for openness and quiet, but some of his relations didn't want to visit him. He told them that the Chinese were industrious and successful and Chinese graveyard spirits were likely to be good spirits. But some people didn't want to hear.

The religion which at one end was the religion of unfettered awe was at the other end a religion of extraordinary refinement. The people who lived close to the spirits of the dead also possessed living epics that had become moral texts. The rituals and difficult theology of Hinduism couldn't be re-established. But Hinduism had left Java its most human and literary side, its epics, the *Ramayana* and the *Mahabharata*; and the epics lived in the puppet plays, the *wayang*.

The *Mahabharata* was longer. It took nine hours, and was 'heavy' for a puppet-master, who had to do all the characters, all the different voices. The *Ramayana* was done more often; and everywhere in central Java the word *Ramayana* appeared – on the backs of buses, on shop-boards. The stories, re-worked and added to over the centuries, had become part of the common imagination. The characters were at once divine and human. Even in the programme notes for the abbreviated tourist *wayang* across the road from the Sheraton hotel, the characters were referred to as R. Rama, R. Lesmana, R. Hanoman – R. for *raden*, a noble, as some people still liked to label themselves – so that the archaic, stylized puppet shadows on the white screen, while connecting people to a heroic past, remained related to the present.

The stories were more than stories. They were not flat. They offered ambiguities. Here, from *Human Character in the Wayang*, a book of reprinted newspaper articles by Sri Mulyono, a puppet-master, is one little part of the *Ramayana* story. King Rahwana of Alengka has abducted Sinta, the beautiful wife of King Rama of Mangliawan. King Rama invades Alengka to rescue his wife. Wibisana, the younger brother of King Rahwana, rebukes Rahwana for abducting the beautiful Sinta and pleads with him to return Sinta to her husband. Rahwana pays no attention, and Wibisana joins the invading army. Was Wibisana right to serve what he saw as the good cause? Or was Wibisana's act an act of betrayal? Need he have acted at all?

The invading army begins to win. King Rahwana in despair turns to his other brother, Kumbakarna. He tells Kumbakarna, 'You are my last resource. My generals are dead. Our country is being destroyed. Help me.' Kumbakarna says, 'Return Sinta to her husband. You still have time.' Rahwana refuses. He tells Kumbakarna, 'Your sons have been killed by the invaders.' Kumbakarna, in a frenzy then, goes out to fight the invaders, and dies horribly. What cause has he served?

The good puppet-master, whatever his interpretation of the story, political, mystical, leaves the issues open. Everyone watching responds according to his character and circumstances. And the story is denser than appears in this account. Because every character trails his own ancestry and dilemmas, even the wicked Rahwana, even the beautiful Sinta. Everyone is engaged in his own search, and at his appearance in the story is in a crisis; so that, as in the profoundest drama or fiction, every encounter is charged with meaning. The epics are endless. The puppet plays bear any number of repetitions; because the more the audience knows the more it understands; and interpretations of motive, of what is right and wrong or expedient, will constantly change.

Salvation is the ultimate good, nirvana; it is to be achieved by the conquest of the senses – a way that is full of self-deceptions. And the Islamic idea of paradise fits easily into the Buddhist-Hindu dream of the life without worldly entanglement and stress. The Islamic idea of the omnipotent God merges into the more mystical Hindu concept of Wisnu, Vishnu, who, as Sri Mulyono says, is 'Truth . . . Reality, the source of all things and all life'.

The open-and-shut morality of Islam, always with its answers in the book or in the doings of the Prophet, gives way in the puppet theatre to something else. Hinduism and Buddhism shed their complexity. It is as if, at this far end of the world, the people of Java had taken what was most human and liberating from the religions that had come their way, to make their own. Umar Kayam saw the *wayang* and the epics as the core of Javanese religion and civilization. They explained the ritual, the courtesies, the constant preoccupation with human behaviour.

There was another side to this concern with beauty and correct behaviour. In 1965, when Sukarno and his communistic government had been deposed, between half a million to a million people were slaughtered in Indonesia. All the frustrations of over-refinement came out then; every kind of private feud was settled. In Hindu Bali, which the tourists now visit, the killing was as fierce as anywhere else. But there, to give a touch of ritual to the butchery, the village gangs took out the gamelan orchestras when they went killing.

Islam was part of the composite religion. And the questions raised by the Australian academic in his letter to Taufiq remained. What did the new missionary Islam, the Islam of the *pesantren*, have to offer these villages? What new ideas of land tenure, what kind of debate did it offer to these villages which were not as enchanted as they looked, where the balance was broken?

There were too many people. But the government family planning programme was threatening the extended-family system, the protection that system gave. More food was needed. But the new rice that gave two crops a year destroyed the old rhythm of village life, interfered with the festivals, didn't give people the time for the puppet plays, and in this way was undermining the old civilization, breaking up the bonds between men. The farmers were in debt. The two crops a year made them borrow from the bank for fertilizer and seed. The extension of rural banking was meant to help, but to borrow from the bank was not like borrowing from the village moneylender, whom everyone in the village knew. To borrow from the bank was to become the puppet or victim of an impersonal institution.

The *koum* of Linus's village said that young people were learning more about Islam at school and for that reason were becoming more interested in the faith. But the *koum*'s Islam was the old Islam of the village; and the *koum*, with his fees for his religious services, his acre of land, and with his knowledge of the past, saw himself living in the good time. There were many people now who knew nothing of the Japanese or the Dutch, many people for whom there was no longer room in the village, people who were being ejected or banished from the only way of life they knew. They lived in a bad time; and the Islam that spoke to them was not the *koum*'s Islam, but an Islam that sanctified their sense of wrongness.

At Pabelan I had been given a copy of an article from an unnamed magazine. It was an interview, by 'a Christian lay person', with a Muslim *kiyai* or *pesantren* leader. 'You ask me the situation of the farmers today and how the *kiyai* can change this unjust society? The farmers today do not receive justice. Most of them are poor because they have no land. There are more farmers now who have no job. The landlords use machines, instead of the farmers, in their farms. The farmers receive very low prices for their products. Meanwhile, the rich in our society are so rich. They get their wealth from the money that is given or lent to our country by very rich nations. Now, how can a *kiyai* help in the changing of this kind of society? How can he make the landlords and the rich give up their properties which, according to Islam, belong to Allah and must be given back to the people who are creatures of Allah?'

But who were the creatures of Allah and who were not? What land was there to give back in over-peopled Java? Java was not Malaysia. Most of the people in Linus's village farmed half an acre. Were these people rich? The *koum*, with his acre, considered himself well-off. What land did he have to give back?

The Islam that was coming to the villages – brushed with new and borrowed ideas about the wickedness of the machine, the misuse of foreign aid – was the Islam that in the late twentieth century had rediscovered its political roots. The Prophet had founded a state. He had given men the idea of equality and union. The dynastic quarrels that had come early to this state had entered the theology of the religion; so that this religion, which filled men's days with rituals and ceremonies of worship, which preached the after-life, at the same time gave men the sharpest sense of worldly injustice and made that part of religion.

This late twentieth-century Islam appeared to raise political issues. But it had the flaw of its origins – the flaw that ran right through Islamic history: to the political issues it raised it offered no political or practical solution. It offered only the faith. It offered only the Prophet, who would settle everything – but who had ceased to exist. This political Islam was rage, anarchy.

Suddenly in Yogyakarta there were tourists, tours from Japan, Germany, Taiwan and Australia; and the Sheraton began to fill up. What was there for them in Yogya? What did the Australians do? Where did they go? The visitors I saw at the temples of Borobudur and Prambanam were Indonesians, with a few Germans. The gamelan orchestra played in the Sheraton lobby for an hour and a half in the morning and an hour and a half in the afternoon; but no one seemed to listen. In the restaurant on the seventh floor there was classical Javanese dancing of a high order for an hour in the evening; but there were always empty tables there. Yogya, in fact, was only a halt for the tours, something thrown in. The true goal was Bali, of the enchanted name: Bali for Christmas.

I wondered about the Australians. But I knew what one of them was doing. He was preparing a scholarly paper on the charcoal-burners of Java. It had been discovered that they were a disappearing species, with the cutting down of the forests of Java; and apparently there were people in Jakarta who, though selling tomatoes or repairing shoes or pushing food-carts, insisted that they were charcoal-burners. I had heard about this sad idiosyncrasy from a pretty woman sociologist who had contracted typhoid from being in the field, padding about a Javanese village. And I had thought that that was all that could be said.

But the Australian I had then met had already spent two months researching into that very matter. Two months! He laughed at my exclamation. Two months were nothing. A scholarly paper required interviews, questionnaires, tables. The academic life might appear leisurely, but it had its severities!

He telephoned the evening before I left Yogya. He had actually seen a man in the street that afternoon carrying a load of wood on his back. He had felt like running after the wood-carrier, clearly a charcoal-burner, someone with charcoal to burn, and interviewing him. But he hadn't. He was with Javanese friends – at that pleasant time of day; he had let the moment slip. He had watched his rare quarry – who knows, perhaps the last charcoal-burner in central Java – walk away below his load in the dusk, disappearing in the black exhaust of the Yogya buses and scooters.

But the Australian had made his arrangements. In Yogya he had a kind of tenure. I hadn't. On Christmas eve the Sheraton threw me out and I had to go back to Jakarta, to the Borobudur Intercontinental. So the royal palace of Yogyakarta remained unknown to me; its Buddhist mandala unexplored; the nine gateways that matched the nine orifices of the human body, the rooms that symbolized so many things, the trees that held such varied meanings; all the mingled Hindu-Buddhist-Muslim mysteries of kingship in Java, matching the wonder of the unique civilization.

5

◆◆◆◆

The Loss of Personality

THE Borobudur Intercontinental in Jakarta changed its character at Christmas. The men from the multinational companies, and the foreign economists and advisers, left. Many of them were solitary, middle-aged men. Some went home; some went to the cooler hills or to the islands. The Borobudur offered cut-price holiday deals for local people; and the local people came, with their families; it was a recognized way, among the well-to-do, of spending the holidays.

Children ran up and down the carpeted corridors and played with the elevators. Nannies or ayahs, some of them barefooted, dandled babies. One Chinese family, doing the right thing for the holidays but not enjoying it, spent a whole morning sitting silently on the upholstered benches outside the elevators on the fifteenth floor. The head of the family, an old man with a ravaged face, wore a singlet without a shirt. From the fifteenth floor the black-haired heads in the pool with the rippling Borobudur design seemed unnaturally large, and (also because of their number) suggested tadpoles. One morning I counted sixty-three heads in the pool.

Simple pleasures; but they were feeding resentment. Resentment of Chinese; of foreigners; of people with skills Indonesians didn't have. Resentment, perhaps, of the skills themselves, and the new order they were bringing in, which no one yet fully accepted: new men, new status, new power, new money. Wrong men had money. Wrong men gave themselves feudal airs. Wrong people romped about the Borobudur and showed the other side of the new society.

'Cheap for you,' the girl said at the hotel shop, when I bought a bottle of port for the holiday. 'But not for us.' And her big smile – yet not her old smile, not the smile I knew – was chilling.

The feeling of wrongness was there. All that had been done during the fifteen years of peace could be ignored. The richer the country became, the better it was made to run, the easier it was for its creative side to be taken for granted, the easier it was for the new inequalities to show. And

333

people could long for 1945, when everybody was equally poor and everybody had the same idea of what was right and wrong. In the town, as in the villages, every improvement made matters worse, made men more uncertain.

'The loss of personality', the loss of the shared feeling for good and bad: this was Darma-sastro's theme.

Darma-sastro was a high civil servant in one of the new departments concerned with technology. He had been described to me as one of the gifted new men of Indonesia; and he saw me in his office one evening after hours. He was in his late thirties or early forties. He smoked aromatic Dutch tobacco in American corn-cob pipes; this, in Indonesia, gave him a distinct air. He was not a handsome man, but he had authority and a presence. He was connected with the upper nobility. He mentioned this only to play it down; but it was this connection that no doubt gave him his detachment from the new élite – 'ten thousand, no more', as he said – to which he also belonged.

Darma-sastro said: 'Among us there are now people who have lost their personalities or their identity. They don't belong to the village any more. They have become too rich or too important. To them going back to the village would be a degeneration. They have lost the sense of security provided by the mutual-help society of the village. At the same time they are not individuals in the western sense. They cannot stand on their own and as individuals interact on an equal basis with others.

'Some of them have been abroad, but there are many people whose bodies have been abroad but whose minds have stayed in the country. How do you tell these people?' It was the way Darma-sastro talked, asking questions and answering them. 'They continue to congregate among themselves. They continue to eat the same food. They will not mix with westerners. They will not subscribe to the newspapers. I have known Indonesians who have spent three years in the United States without looking at an American newspaper. What do they look at? They look at television. The contact with the West is minimal, and that's the way they want it to be. They can't function outside Indonesia. They remain villagers. They are there in the West only to get that diploma and to return to Indonesia with that ascriptive dignity.

'But here they are not members of the nobility. They don't have the feudal values of *noblesse oblige*. So, with their new dignity, they seek power and wealth, mainly. This is the cancer. In the old days important people had a responsibility to the society. If you were nobility you were supposed to give an example. The people I'm talking about cannot function now as arbiters of right and wrong because they themselves cannot distinguish between right and wrong any more. Why? In their loss of identity they have lost all values except those associated with power. They are people continuing to look for their own security.

'It's not yet become a jungle, but we could get there. There are millions of people who are morally good, but they are powerless to enforce the good. There are thousands – and this is important – who are powerful but are not willing to enforce the good. So you feel adrift. Feeling adrift is like this. You know you should do good and avoid the bad. But now you have to think. And when you find yourself thinking about it, that is when you start feeling adrift. That is when you start feeling that the whole society is adrift. I am telling you: it takes a conscious mental and moral effort for someone like me to do the good. Which is wrong.

'Where does the money come from, that's encouraging all of this? It comes from oil.' He walked about the panelled office, pointing to the steel cabinets, the modern equipment. He began to act out his words. 'I live from oil mostly – the government revenue from oil and the tax on other exports. That's when I'm here, in a town. When I'm outside the big cities I live off the land. We live off the people. I tax them, you see. I impose taxes on them. These people have to understand that I have my needs – they cannot come empty-handed to me.

'I am surprising you? In Europe in the old days the importance of a noble was measured by the extent of his land. In Java the importance of a noble was measured by the number of people on his land. Because people meant wealth: unpaid labour, part of the produce, army. We are not nobles now, but we haven't forgotten that people mean wealth.'

From high up Jakarta was a spread of trees and red-tile roofs. But the Jakarta map showed only a few main roads. These were the roads along which the traffic flowed, past the new skyscrapers and the parks and the monuments. The city was contained within these roads. Jakarta was a city without a focus, a cluster of urban kampongs or villages, and these villages preserved the haphazard structure of country villages. No street map could record the twists and turns of lanes and alleys.

In the centre the villages were of concrete. But further out they could still be areas of green: houses in unfenced gardens, in the shade of fruit trees, with yards swept twice a day. These villages were still communities, still with their appointed 'leaders'. Such areas needed little to put them right. But many of these urban village communities were unstable. Land near the centre was valuable; villages could be bought up for development; and the community then had to move further out. And families multiplied; land was divided and divided again; houses shrank, and the lanes between houses became narrower and narrower.

No question then of garbage collection: that was left to the rag-pickers, the men with the finely made bamboo baskets on their backs, who would sift through the garbage for everything that could be sold, every tin, every bottle, every scrap of paper that could be flattened out and sold to somebody as wrapping paper. The precious fruit trees were fenced around, the bounty of a little piece of Java behind barbed wire, surrounded by little houses. And always children, in every open space, in little broods, as numerous as chickens.

One little brood was at the foot of a rambutan tree, on the morning Prasojo and I walked through. An old man was up in the tree, using a bamboo rod to pick clusters of the spiky red fruit. Prasojo and I stopped to watch. The man's son saw us. He saw we were strangers; he took a bunch of the fruit his father had picked and offered it to us with the Javanese-Hindu gesture of courtesy: the fruit in his extended right hand, the fingers of his left hand touching his right elbow.

The fruit was money to the family; it was being picked to be sold. Just a few hundred yards away, beyond the maze of the village, was the main road, black with diesel exhaust and lined with little stalls. Jakarta was a city of five million. Here, among people close to the abyss, were still, miraculously, the manners of the country village, the graces of an old civilization.

Prasojo was less moved than I was by the offer of the rambutan. He saw it only as correct behaviour. He said, 'It is how I behave myself. It is the behaviour of a man still in a community. In "society" that same boy would probably steal your fruit.'

The man in a community still lived in the old co-operative Javanese village way. The man in 'society' was a man on his own, a man who had left his village and his fellows and cast himself into the town. Prasojo thought such people were 'gambling' with their lives; he called them gamblers. They were the men who became rag-pickers. They were the men who could be seen picking up cigarette butts (but using two long bamboo sticks like long chopsticks) to sell the tobacco for a kind of cigarette for the poor. They were the lost people of Java, and some of them were even without 'papers'. They were the people squeezed out by the fertility of Java from the civilization of Java, people at the very bottom who had lost their personalities as much as Darma-sastro's people at the top. With their baskets on their backs, their long sticks, their minute diligence, their eyes forever on the ground, like people withdrawn from the bustle and the crowds, they were a warning to everybody else: things could easily go wrong.

Jakarta boomed. The city and the country needed wealth and skills. But these things created wounding divisions, and there was rage about the loss of the old order, the loss of the old knowledge of good and bad.

The holidays ended. The new rich and their children and their ayahs left the Borobudur Intercontinental. The pool was drained for its annual overhaul; where water had rippled blue, white tiles glared, and workmen chipped and hammered. The men from the multinationals and the advisers and the economists returned. There was peace in the corridors. It was back to business.

6

❖❖❖❖❖

Mental Training in Bandung

IT WAS the rainy season. Even on bright days south Jakarta was hidden by cloud, skyscrapers and greenery and red roofs fading away. The land seemed flat, but there were hills to the south, and they showed when the cloud lifted. Up in those hills were the holiday bungalows of people who wanted to get away from the heat and humidity of Jakarta.

A freeway, cutting through agricultural land – the cause of student protest at one time, but now the freeway took much traffic – led part of the way to the hills. When the freeway ended it was crowded Java again, with a narrow road winding up through an unending village (occasion-ally densing up to little towns), past vegetable and fruit stalls, to tea plantations, over which rain-cloud and mist drifted, mixed with the black exhaust of buses and trucks and scooters. Here and there the sodden earth at one side of the mountain road had slipped, and the roots of a tea bush, surprisingly thick and long, hung loose above the road.

From tea and mist the road dipped to a flat clear valley of rice, and then it climbed again, through sharp cone-shaped hills, to the plateau with the town of Bandung: Bandung of the famous post-colonial conference of 1955, with President Sukarno and Mr Nehru; Bandung of the cool climate, one of the many Parises of Asia that people spoke about in colonial times; Bandung also of the famous Institute of Technology, founded by the Dutch, and inevitably the forcing ground of revolution. Sukarno went to Bandung; his title of 'Doctor Engineer' came from this Institute.

And Bandung still had a radical reputation. It was one of the centres of the Islamic revival in Indonesia. Many of Prasojo's Jakarta friends had gone there for the holiday weekend. to attend a three-day Islamic 'mental training' course at the mosque of the Institute of Technology.

The course was being given by a man famous among Indonesian Muslims, Mr Imaduddin, an electrical engineer and an instructor at the Institute. Some people in Jakarta thought Imaduddin brave; others thought him dangerous. He had been released from jail five months before, after a year inside. His name, Imaduddin, Arabic rather than Indonesian, hinted at the kind of Muslim he was.

The outskirts of Bandung were more Javanese than Parisian in the dusk, with the dirt sidewalks and the makeshift roadside stalls. But it was the charmed hour, the 'dating' hour Prasojo had spoken about, and for some time we trailed a dating couple on a scooter, the girl carefully made up to ride (arms on her escort's waist) through the smog and the traffic din, sitting with her legs to one side, her slippers dangerously dangling.

Prasojo said to me, 'You were asking about the *langsat* complexion. She is *langsat*.'

The colour of the langsat fruit was considered the perfect colour for an Indonesian woman. The fruit was pale ochre, a pale adobe colour; and the girl on the scooter had a clear, southern-Chinese complexion.

The girl was embarrassed by the scrutiny. When our driver played his headlights on her, her escort, already preoccupied by the traffic, became agitated; more than once he turned around to scowl. When at last they swerved away the *langsat* girl, slippers dangling, wickedly smiled, and Prasojo said, 'Did you *see*? Did you *see*?'

We had to ask our way, street by street almost, to the Institute and the mosque. It was in the older, colonial part of the town: impressions, in the darkness and lamplight, of wide, silent streets, houses set back, and of a big administrative building in whose carved roof Java had become only an architectural motif, a piece of Dutch colonial exoticism.

The cylindrical tower of the mosque was 'modern'. It was past seven, and in the open paved spaces between the mosque and its ancillary buildings groups of the mental training class, boys and girls, were waiting for the evening session to begin. Soft girls' voices called from the shadows, 'Prasojo! Prasojo!' The success of that boy! Girls liked Prasojo as much as he liked them; and now they thronged about him as though he had been away from them for weeks. The gaiety of the group was like the gaiety of campers. They were Jakarta young people, children of the middle class. They were not like people of the *pesantren*, or like the more austere, closed Muslim groups.

Imaduddin was telephoned, and someone led us to his house. Before we could get out of the car Imaduddin himself came out of his house to greet us, a man of medium height, broad-shouldered, wide-faced, smiling, open; and he swept us inside.

It was the house of a university lecturer, with plain chairs, shelves, but also with an Indonesian feature: two girls, relatives or servants, sitting on the floor at the far end of the room. They rose, just after we came in, and went away, no doubt to prepare the tea of welcome.

Imaduddin read the letter of introduction Prasojo had brought. His face lit up as he read; he said he was honoured. He looked less than his forty-eight years. His skin was smooth, his dark eyes bright, and he had a wide, humorous mouth. He was attractive, full of welcome. But how, he asked, had I got to hear of him? I mentioned the name of a Jakarta journalist, and Imaduddin said, with a laugh, 'But tell him I am still fighting for my freedom! After five months. The Institute hasn't given me any duties this year.'

'Why do you think they are afraid of you?'

'I don't know. I suppose they're afraid of my popularity with the students.'

I asked about his name.

He said, 'It's Ima-dud-din. It means the pillar of the faith.'

'Did you take it yourself?' Some Indonesians did that. Prasojo had given himself a name, and told his parents about it afterwards.

'No, my father gave it to me. He was a student at Al Azhar in Cairo. I have been Ima-dud-din all my life.'

The tea of welcome came, in china cups, not glasses. The food of welcome was biscuits, of two kinds, in jars. This was not the hospitality of the village.

The interrogations had been tough in jail. The first had lasted twenty hours, but Imaduddin had no stories of maltreatment. Among his fellow prisoners there were some famous men. Imaduddin had met and talked with Dr Subandrio, who had been foreign minister at the time of the army take-over in 1965. Dr Subandrio had been accused by the army of plotting a communist coup with others and he had been sentenced to death. Three days before the execution Queen Elizabeth of England had made an appeal for his life, and he had been reprieved. And for all this time – virtually forgotten by the world – this former colleague of Sukarno's had been in jail: it was not an easy thing to contemplate, sipping tea in Imaduddin's university house.

And it was strange, too, to think of Imaduddin, the new Muslim, and Subandrio, the old man of the old left – their causes opposed, and both causes deemed harmful to the Indonesian state – coming together amicably in the army-run jail.

How had Imaduddin been allowed to talk to Dr Subandrio? The warders had become friendly after a time, Imaduddin said; and he had been given certain privileges. The time in jail didn't sound so bad. And, in fact, for Imaduddin it hadn't been all that unwelcome. Just before he had been picked up, Imaduddin had visited certain Arab countries. The Arabs had fed him and fed him. Nobody had told Imaduddin that when you ate with Arabs you had to eat very slowly, that you watched your host, because while your host ate you had to eat. So, seventy kilos, 154 pounds, when he had gone among the Arabs on his Islamic business, Imaduddin had risen to 172 pounds, seventy-eight kilos, when he left them. That was his size when the police had come for him; that was the weight he was still trying to lose. He had lost some in jail; the army doctor who had examined him had been pleased with his progress.

But he hadn't been given any duties at the Institute of Technology after his release. All he was doing now was his Islamic missionary work among the young. His mental training courses were well known. He had started them seven years before and had even done a few for Muslim student groups in England. The demand in Jakarta was high. Sixty-seven people had applied for this particular course; he had been able to take only forty-seven.

A further sip of tea, a bite on a biscuit, and then it was time momentarily to split up – I to look for a hotel, in this difficult holiday season, Imaduddin to go to his mental training course.

Prasojo said, 'You can see why he is so popular. Did you notice the way he shook your hand? He shook my hand as though he had known me a long time, as though he was really pleased to see me. I suppose that is how I should behave, if I want to get on with people.' Prasojo's American experience was strong on him. He had brought albums of photographs of his time with the American Field Service in the United States: international student parties, the Grand Canyon, snow.

The mental training had been going for an hour when I got back. The class was in the shed-like clinic building attached to the mosque. The floor was tiled; the green blackboard was written on already; the lights were fluorescent. The trainees sat on folding metal chairs with broad shiny backs. There were more girls than boys, and the girls sat on the right, the boys on the left. The girls wore head-scarves or head-covers in pretty colours – yellow and green and lilac and pink and purple and white. Every trainee carried his name on a green card. The instructor was a small moustached young man in a flowered shirt.

Imaduddin was sitting at the back of the room. He told me when I went and sat beside him that we were witnessing an exercise in 'communication'.

Four or five trainees were sent outside, and the instructor, a tape-recorder in his hand, read out a story – an account of a motor accident – to a young man. One of the students outside, a girl, was then called in. The young man began to tell her the story. She asked questions; he became confused; the class laughed. The trainees were used to the puppet shows; they had the instincts of actors. The mental training class became more and more like a puppet show; and the hilarity increased as the story was passed on, more and more distorted, from one trainee to the next.

Imaduddin said, 'All this is being recorded. At the end it will be played back, so that they can see how much the original story has changed. It is to help them when they go out into the world to start preaching Islam.'

But the exercise never got to the play-back stage. It wasn't necessary. The puppet-show instincts of the trainees took over; and the point – the distortion of a tale twice and thrice told – became the subject of much comedy.

Then it was time for the serious part. And like good trainees, who had had their fun and were now willing to find virtue in that fun, the trainees settled down and told the instructor what they had learned from the exercise. They had learned important things: the value of inquiry, rational analysis.

It seemed to me that the deductions might work against them, because the message they were going to take to the world was extraordinary: a divinely inspired Prophet, arbitrary rules, a pilgrimage to a certain stone, a month of fasting. But we were well within Islam now, and its articles were beyond question. Inquiry and analysis were for internal matters: the *hadiths*, the traditions and reports about the Prophet. Some *hadiths* were more reliable than others; people who went by unreliable *hadiths* could easily find themselves committed to un-Islamic ways. And the trainees had gone straight to the point: the game they had played had led their thoughts directly to the *hadiths* and even to certain passages in the Koran. These passages were read out. And the *langsat* girl on the back of the scooter seemed far away, part of another, frivolous world.

The moustached young instructor with the Japanese tape-recorder was pleased. Imaduddin was also pleased. He hadn't made the game up himself; he said he had got the idea from various sources. But the Islamic adaptation was his own idea.

The instructor spoke again. The trainees stood up and the metal chairs were noisily rearranged by them in roughly circular groups of five – five was the Islamic number. I had so far seen the backs and coloured scarves of most of the girls; now I saw their faces. There was nothing like a *langsat* complexion among them. Most of them seemed to come from Sumatra, more Muslim than Java.

I said to Imaduddin, 'I believe I have identified six stages in the game. The instructor tells the story; the story gets distorted; the class comments; the inference is drawn about the *hadiths* of the Prophet; the relevant verses are read from the Koran; and now the trainees sit in groups of five.'

'That's right. But this sitting in groups of five is a new game.'

They were given envelopes. Each envelope contained variously shaped pieces of paper, and the point of the game was to make squares with those pieces of paper. No single envelope contained a complete square, but the pieces had been distributed in such a way that a group of five, using all the pieces it had received, could make five squares.

Imaduddin said, 'They have to co-operate without talking. No one is allowed to take a piece of paper from anyone in his group. But he may accept what is given.'

We walked among the groups of five, their heads bent close together, with here and there a clown, a boy, exaggerating his puzzlement, deliberately making absurd patterns. One boy, I was happy to see, did a swift cheat, taking a piece from a neighbour and adding it to another's pattern. There was a shout and clapping from a group of girls: they had completed. It was like bingo. More shouts, friendly squabbles between boys and girls: the air was charged with adolescent sexuality. And then, once more, the serious side: the chairs rearranged, the instructor calling for comments. One by one the comments came. And it was amazing what they had got out of the little game, how far it had taken them along the way of Islam.

The instructor wrote the comments on the green blackboard. Imaduddin translated for me. They had learned five things – five was a sound Islamic number, there being five Islamic principles. 'Co-operation indispensable for the common goal. Those who give up easily cannot achieve. You have to give others without asking. Knowing each other is also indispensable. Perseverance.'

I said, 'But they have already said that about perseverance. "Those who give up easily cannot achieve."'

Imaduddin agreed.

But the trainees had only momentarily lost their way. A girl with a saffron head-cover raised her hand and spoke; the instructor wrote at the bottom of the board; and Imaduddin said, 'This is important. The sense of belonging.'

All that had come to them from the game. Even with the little cheating that had taken place they had gone straight to the Islamic idea of unity or union: men abased together before the creator, and bound by rigid rules. There was an unspoken corollary: everything outside that community was shut out, everything outside was impious, impure, infidel. They were the righteous and the secure; they were happy in their reinforced faith. And again pertinent verses from the Koran occurred to some trainees. Again there was that display of scholarship and

343

inquiry as the pages of the book were turned, and trainees and instructor read various verses.

Some duplicated foolscap sheets were passed around by the chattering instructor, and Imaduddin said, 'The instructor is calling upon me to read a poem. It is by Iqbal. This is the last session of the mental training course, and I always end it by reading that poem by Iqbal. I chose it because it is very emotional. It was written in Urdu, as you would know. Translated into Arabic by Effendi, and translated from the Arabic into Indonesian by Mohammed Natsir.' Iqbal, the ideologue of Pakistan; Natsir, once the leader of the banned Muslim party of Indonesia.

Imaduddin — Indonesian courtesy making him delay while he explained the poem to me — then went to the desk. He put on his glasses and began to read, and he was transformed. All his social graces, all his apparent humour, were submerged in this new personality, not of the actor or the puppet-master, but the mullah, the man in a mosque, reciting the Koran on some day of Muslim passion. He had said the poem was emotional; and as he read his voice broke. At times he seemed about to sob: Islam as anguish, hell, heaven, redemption. And that, as I understood, was the theme of the Iqbal poem: how, without the Prophet or knowledge of his mission, could the world be endured?

He had said the poem would take six minutes. It took more than ten. It was now past ten-thirty. The mental training class had been going on for more than three hours. The course was at an end. But the trainees had to be up again at three in the morning. Not, as I thought, for the discipline and self-denial that encouraged union; but because, as Imaduddin told me, it was laid down in the Koran that special prayers should be uttered in the middle of the night, and the middle of the night meant between midnight and six.

The trainees didn't seem to mind. They were like happy campers, thrilled by the drama of the final early rising. They got up from their metal chairs and went away hesitatingly, the girls to one part of the mosque area, the boys to another. They were children of the Jakarta middle class, people faced with the special Indonesian threat of the loss of personality. In Islam, the life of the mosque, with its rules and rituals, they found again, or reconstructed, something like the old feudal or rural community that for them no longer existed.

Imaduddin said he wasn't going to get up for the three o'clock prayers with his trainees. But he was up at three-thirty. On Mondays and Thursdays he did that, because he fasted on those days. The custom was peculiar to the Muslims of Indonesia, and I had been told that it might have had its origin in animist practice. The fast was not strictly a fast; as in the fasting month of Ramadan, it was possible to eat before sunrise and after sunset. A refinement for some on these fast days was to eat only white foods, white being the colour of purity, and also convenient, since it enabled an Indonesian to eat as much as he liked of his favourite food, rice. But I heard about the white foods afterwards, and couldn't ask Imaduddin about them.

He said, when I saw him the next morning in his office, which was adjacent to the classroom of the previous night, that he fasted on Mondays and Thursdays because the Prophet fasted on those days. It wasn't in the Koran, but there was a reliable *hadith* about it. And Imaduddin was also concerned about his weight. In addition to his Islamic fasts, he jogged. He said he had to look after himself; he was nearly fifty. He didn't think he had fully recovered from his Arab over-feeding. But that had occurred nearly eighteen months before. His paunchiness made me feel, rather, that twice a week, during his fasting days, he built up an overwhelming appetite.

He was so varied. He used tape-recorders and western psychological games for his Islamic mental training. He had a mullah's passion; but he also jogged. He had lived through a tremendous period of Indonesian history; he had been acquainted with great Indonesians. He had bene-fited from the independence of his country, from its stop-and-start development, from the opening up of the world for people of his genera-tion. He had become an electrical engineer; he had travelled; he had studied for a higher degree in the United States.

He had lived in many eras; he had been part of a great flowing together of the world. But Imaduddin was indifferent to the wonder of his life; he took his new world for granted. There was no development to explore. Imaduddin was born a Muslim in Sumatra. Everything was contained in that beginning: to that beginning there had only been added events, tools, and age.

Imaduddin's father, as he had told me the previous evening, was a graduate of the Islamic university of Al Azhar in Cairo. He was import-ant in the Muslim *Masjumi* party.

'My father was a religious teacher, attached to a religious school run by the sultanate in the Dutch time. It was a famous school, and my father was the principal. During the revolution, the war against the Dutch, I was involved in the Muslim army, *Hizbullah*. I was trained for two weeks in 1946 as a guerrilla fighter, and they gave me a star and a stripe as a first sergeant. At the age of fifteen! *Hizbullah* actually means the soldiers of God.'

'Why do you say Muslim army? Weren't you Indonesians, fighting for Indonesian independence?'

'There were so many groups in the revolutionary army at that time. The communists, the PKI, had their own army; they called it the Red Army. The socialists had their own groups. The nationalists and Sukarno owned their own. We fought each other sometimes – when the Dutch were away.

'After we gained our independence I went back to high school. In 1947 the revolutionary government had opened the first secondary school in our area. So I went to this school and I stayed there until 1953.'

'What made you decide to be an electrical engineer?'

'In 1952 Dr Hatta, the vice-president, visited Sumatra and he talked about developing the country. He visited the largest waterfall close to Medan in Sumatra, and he gave a talk about the importance of electricity. I was spellbound by this speech. In the following year, 1953, I finished high school. I got the highest mark. When I asked my father to send me to Bandung he said, "I don't have the money. But if you want to go by yourself I give you my permission – and my prayer."

'My mother sold one of her rings, and I went to Jakarta with just enough money to buy the ticket for the ship and to buy food for one or two months here. The ship started from Sumatra in the evening about six. We sailed for three nights and we reached Jakarta in the evening. I was amazed by the crowds.

'We reached Jakarta at night, but the port was closed, and we were allowed to land only in the morning. Actually there were four of us on the ship who had graduated. So early in the morning we went to the Ministry of Education, and I went straight to the scholarship department. I showed them my marks and my letter of recommendation from my high school. One of my friends had a friend in Jakarta, but he wasn't sure whether the friend would be able to accommodate all four of us in his house. But fortunately the friend accommodated us. We slept on the floor of the sitting room. The house was actually the private house of Mr Sutan Sjahrir, the secretary-general of the Indonesian Socialist Party.'

I said, 'But that's a famous Indonesian name. You can't drop it so casually.'

And it was astonishing that he should speak it like that: Sutan Sjahrir, one of the early nationalist figures of Indonesia, exiled by the Dutch from 1934 to 1942, and prime minister of Indonesia in the first year of independence.

Imaduddin said, 'Actually, Sutan Sjahrir had visited us in Sumatra. I was one of the leaders of the students in Medan in my high school and I met him there. He was on the look-out for promising young men – the socialists were like that. And you can imagine what it was for a young-ster talking to that great man.

'We left Jakarta that same day and went to Bandung with an introduc-tion to the secretary-general of the Socialist Party in west Java. And we were accommodated by him also for a few nights. And we came to ITB, the Bandung Institute of Technology, and registered ourselves.'

'But this is a wonderful story about Sutan Sjahrir.'

'The socialists were like that. Always looking for supporters. Actually I couldn't be a socialist because I am already Muslim. The good ideas of socialism I can find in the Koran.'

'But the Koran doesn't give you the institutions. That's what social-ists try to do. You want more than the ideas.'

'For the institutions, it's up to us. *Hizbullah*, the Muslim army, was created by the *Masjumi* party. My father was one of the leaders of that party, representing his region, north Sumatra. And he sat in the highest council of the Muslim clergy. So, although I was attracted by Sutan Sjahrir and his manner and his intellectual capacity, I couldn't be a socialist because I was already a Muslim. I admired him as one of our national leaders, but nothing more than that.'

'Did you in *Masjumi* actually have a programme?'

'They did. Decentralized government. Two chambers. Co-operative economy. The natives of a region participating in the economy.'

'Is that Islam? Or regionalism?'

'They stressed rural development. Most of the Muslims are in the rural areas.'

Muslims, Muslims: he used the word where other people might have said Indonesians.

And on his first Friday at the Institute of Technology in Bandung Imaduddin had a shock.

'It was very secular here in 1953. You couldn't find any mosque round here. You would have to walk three kilometres down to the village to find a mosque. Most of the professors at the Institute were Dutch – and they were here until 1957, when Sukarno kicked them out. Most of the lectures were in English. That was the rule, for people who couldn't talk the Indonesian language. I found on the first Friday that some of the professors were giving lectures during the prayer time. I was from Sumatra, and I was brought up in a strict Muslim family. So to me not going to the mosque for Friday prayers was quite a mental shock.

'I stood up and asked permission of the Dutch lecturer to go to the mosque. He seemed very friendly and allowed me to go. Two or three students followed me out. I went to the mosque, but I lost the lecture. So I always had the choice on Fridays – mosque or lecture. That was why it started the idea in my mind of having a mosque close to the campus. That first time only three or four of the students followed me out. Now – I believe the *New York Times* did a survey and they said that two thousand students go to the mosque.'

'You applied for a scholarship. Did you get it?'

'After two months. My mother's money, the money from the ring, lasted two months. It was five hundred rupiah.' Eighty cents now, after all the devaluations. 'The scholarship was three hundred rupiah a month, which was enough. The boarding house cost about one hundred.'

Some people came into the office. Among them was a middle-aged man, small, carefully dressed, perhaps of simple origins, perhaps the father of a student. He was respectful towards Imaduddin; and Imaduddin, with the prompt courtesy that had made such an impression on Prasojo (and me) the previous evening, excused himself and got up to greet his visitors.

I gave up my armchair and sat at the desk while Imaduddin and his visitors talked. There was a duplicated, letter-headed sheet at the top of some letters. It wasn't quite the public circular I thought it was. It was personal, from the United States, from a university professor sending season's greetings with an end-of-the-year round-up of family news. American coziness, goodwill to all men of all cultures: here, on Imaduddin's desk. American teacher and Asian learner, infidel and missionary: in what degree of misunderstanding had they come together!

In 1947 the revolutionary government, in the midst of all its troubles, had established a secondary school in Sumatra. Ever since then Imaduddin had been academically on the rise; and in 1963, ten years after he had come to Bandung with 500 rupiah, the Bandung Institute had sent him to the United States to get a higher degree. He had spent three years there, at first in Iowa, and then in Chicago. In the summer of 1966, at the end of his course, he got a holiday job at Cornell as a consultant in the Indonesian language. He got 100 dollars a week for nine weeks, and with the 900 dollars he went to Europe and then to Mecca.

'I cried in Mecca. The first time I entered the mosque there, the place with the black stone, I cried. And I also cried when I was about to leave.'

That was the way, after his visitors had gone, he told about his first three years abroad. That was the emphasis he gave: the three years of higher study, the luck with the Cornell holiday job, the climax in the Great Mosque of Mecca.

'Actually, that letter you looked at' – so he had noticed – 'was from my professor. He's a Christian. He wrote a letter of protest to the government when I was arrested.'

348

After that time abroad his Muslim interests became more inter-national. At Cornell he had met a man from Malaysia. In 1971, through this man, he went to Malaysia to help with the conversion of a polytechnic into a university. Imaduddin stayed for two years in Malaysia, until 1973; he became involved with the Muslim youth movement there and still looked upon the people of that movement as his 'brothers'. He felt that it was from that time that he had become suspect to the Indonesian authorities – they, and others in Indonesia, were nervous of 'the Malaysian disease', and they were especially ner-vous of radical developments in the Bandung Institute.

1973 was the year of the oil-price rise, the year when money for Arab oil seemed to come like a reward for the Arab faith. Muslim missionary activity picked up; in a dozen foreign countries half-evolved Muslim students, until then shy in the new world, hardly able to relate their technical studies to the countries where they were, felt the time had come to proclaim the true faith. Imaduddin travelled, to Libya, to England, rising higher in international Muslim students' organizations, more and more in demand for his mental training courses, that gave a now necessary modernity to old-fashioned mullah's teachings.

His imprisonment had not arrested his rise. His card, white, black and green (the Islamic colour), said: *Muhammad Imaduddin Abdul Rahim – Secretary General – International Islamic Federation of Student Orga-nizations*. He had no Indonesian name.

I said, 'But all your names are Arab.'

'They are not Arab names. They are Muslim names.'

The midday call to prayer came from the mosque tower – the mosque that hadn't been there when Imaduddin first came to the Bandung Institute to study electrical engineering. He said he would be back in fifteen minutes, and he left me to the books in the bookcase.

Some, in English, were the bread-and-butter books of Islamic missionary work: *The Myth of the Cross, Jesus Prophet of Islam*. Others were Indonesian translations published by the movement, paper-backs. One book was by Qutub, an Egyptian. I didn't know about Qutub; Imaduddin said he had been killed by Nasser. Another book was by Maulana Maudoodi. He was the Indo-Pakistani fundamentalist, so extreme that he had opposed the idea of Pakistan, because Indian Muslims weren't pure enough for a Muslim state. For thirty years, after Pakistan had been created, he had agitated (though never offering concrete sug-gestions) for Islamic laws and an Islamic state. Entirely destructive to Pakistan, he had at the end flown to a Boston hospital, surrendered to western science, and died.

Imaduddin came back. We were now well into the lunch hour of this fasting day of Imaduddin's; and I felt that now, especially after his prayers, he was aware of doing without.

I said, 'Is it only Islam that moves you?'

'I like some western music. *Messiah* by Handel. I like Bach. The religious music.'

But he was not happy about the attention paid in Indonesia to the monuments of the old faiths.

'You've been to Canberra?' he said. 'You've seen the Indonesian embassy there? It's a Hindu building. This isn't a Hindu or Buddhist country. This country is ninety percent Muslim.'

'Borobudur and Prambanam are great Indonesian monuments.'

'Borobudur is something for the international community to look after.'

The international community, the universal civilization: providers of tape-recorders and psychological games and higher degrees in electrical engineering; and now, also, guardians of Indonesian art and civilization.

For Imaduddin, as a Muslim and a Sumatran, Indonesia was a place to be cleansed. His faith was so great that he could separate his country from its history, traditions, art: its particularity. His faith was too simple for Indonesia, certainly for Java, too simple even for the *koum* of Linus's village. And Indonesia – overpopulated, with so many people squeezed out, with only the army to hold the country together – was too fragile for his kind of protest.

'You go around Jakarta. For fifteen or twenty kilometres around Jakarta you could find the real story of what is happening here. The land is not owned by the people who work on it. According to my understanding of Islam, I cannot own a stretch of land if I cannot cultivate it. Only Allah has that right. So if this is run as an Islamic state, the state should arrange the land so that landlordism cannot exist.'

'Is there an Islamic state where that has happened?'

'Yes. In the time of Abu-bakr and Omar and all the first four caliphs.'

Right at the beginning of Islam, then, in the thirty-year period that ended with the death of Ali, the Prophet's son-in-law, in 661 AD. It was the reply I would have got from a village mullah in Pakistan. It wasn't the reply I was expecting from Imaduddin in Bandung.

'I will tell you this story,' Imaduddin said. 'One of the closest friends of the Prophet was a man by the name of Bilal. He was a Negro slave and he was freed by Abu-bakr and he had the job of calling the people to prayer. When the Prophet and his companions migrated to Medina, the Prophet gave Bilal a stretch of land for him to cultivate. During the time of Omar, the second caliph, Bilal was old and weak and couldn't cultivate all the lands. And Omar took part of the land and gave it to another.'

'Do you think a country can be run like that now? By one man?'

'That fitted the need of the time. And we were talking about land reform, not leadership. And even Omar had a kind of advisory council.'

'Why did that system of rule break down?'

'It was broken down by the fifth caliph. He was interested in having a dynasty. The first feudalism in Islamic history.'

'And Islamic rule has been like that ever since?'

'Yes, I think so. So if you want to practise Islam right now you have to build a state on the basis of a republic.'

'Aren't you saying that Islam has failed?'

'No, not Islam. The people. The Muslims.'

'You think you can get them to do it now?'

'I think so. Especially Indonesia. Because the political structure quite resembles the Islamic teaching. The president, the council or parliament, the army. What we need now is the men behind the structure. They must be true Muslims.'

'Is this why the government is nervous of you? Is this why some people say you are brave?'

He seemed surprised. 'I am not brave.' And he meant that: he was only doing what he had to do.

Some of the trainees came in to say goodbye. Their faces were bright, awed. The course had been a success. All the *Revival of Islam* tee-shirts (the words in English) had been sold. Imaduddin was as moved as the trainees. He walked with them to the doorway and stood in the sunlight, chatting: white shirt, grey belted trousers, strong, attractive, reassuring.

'I am preparing the next generation of leaders of Indonesia,' Imaduddin said, when he came back. 'I believe that the constitution has some Islamic value in it. I am preparing the new generation to replace all this.'

To replace all this. But for what, and by what? Not by new institutions, but only by men as pure and cleansed as himself. 'I am just a teacher, an ordinary teacher, at least to my feeling,' Imaduddin had said. 'I am interested in educating the youngsters. Because I believe that what we need right now is a true Muslim leader.'

Out of this, as in the days of Omar and the other rightly-guided caliphs, all good would flow. It was where his fundamentalism led: the need for the pious leader, not a man of individual conscience, compassion or wisdom, but a man who lived according to the book, the man who could stand in for the Prophet, the man who knew the Prophet's deeds and revelations so well that he would order affairs as the Prophet himself might have ordered them. It was the idea of piety and goodness that separated Islam from other ethical systems.

The logic of Imaduddin's faith, and his own integrity, was simple: injustice was un-Islamic, and Indonesia was full of injustice. And the Imaduddin who grieved about injustice at home could travel without pain to Muslim despotisms abroad. To these countries he travelled as to lands of the achieved faith. In such lands you did not look for injustice; you considered only the leader, and felt cleansed by the purity of his faith.

He told me he had spent a couple of days in Pakistan. Of Pakistan's founding and history he appeared to know little. To him it was only a Muslim state, made special by the poetry of Iqbal. Of the institutions of Pakistan, of its phantom Islamic laws, its martial law and constitutional breakdown, its political abjectness, the public whippings, the censorship, the humiliation of its intellectuals – of this he knew almost nothing.

Why did he know so little? He said; 'Perhaps it's because of the western press.' And it was because of his suspicion of that press that he remained uncertain about events in Iran. He received only a little information 'from inside'.

A Muslim editor of Jakarta, to whom I reported this, said, 'Nothing's keeping them out. They can send people to find out. If they don't know it's because they don't want to know. It doesn't serve their cause.'

And indeed that cause was well served by the western press. *The Revival of Islam*: the English words on the tee-shirts sold at the end of the mental training course had been made familiar by the cover-stories of many international English-language magazines. Imaduddin himself, speaking of the attendance at his own mosque, had referred to the *New York Times*.

In Jakarta the president of an important youth organization attached to a mosque in a middle-class area, one of Imaduddin's former trainees, said that Islam was the great new movement in the world, winning converts everywhere. Both *Time* and *Newsweek* had said so. And *Newsweek*, in a feature, had included the Prophet and one other Muslim in a list of fifty people who had most influenced the history of the world. 'It's in history now,' the young man said, meaning only that it was in *Newsweek*. (History like a divine ledger, guarded, like so many things, by the other civilization.) He was middle-class, the young man, tall, of *langsat* complexion. Since his mental training course with Imaduddin he had become obsessed with death and the after-life. But there was still a corner of his mind open to worldly pride.

Newsweek and *Time* were helping to make the history they recorded. Islam was pure and perfect; the secular, dying West was to be rejected:

that was the message. But the West was taking a long time to die. And more and more people were being drawn into the new world. In this new world, whose centre seemed so far away, so beyond control, newly evolved men like the president of the Jakarta youth organization felt only their inadequacies. These men were not peasants or *pesantren* boys. They aspired to high western skills; they took encouragement from, they needed, western witness. It was part of their great dependence. This dependence provoked the anguish which (like adolescents) they sought to assuage in the daily severities of their new religious practice: the five-times-a-day prayers, the unnecessary fasts. The religion which was theirs but which they had disregarded had now become an area of particular privacy. It gave an illusion of wholeness; it held a promise of imminent triumph. It was also where they became interesting to themselves – and, as the newspapers made them understand, to others – again.

Rejection and dependence: it was hard for the half-evolved to break out of that circle. One of the girls at Imaduddin's mental training course – she had sat separate from the boys and had covered her head and had drawn Koranic lessons from the western psychological games – one of the girls was going on to London. She said it was to model. But it was only to do a modelling course. The Indonesian-European modelling business was becoming organized. I saw a brochure. Its appeal was to the middle class, the half-evolved. Attractive now, this modelling business, to girls and their parents, an easy step forward into the new world. But it needed little imagination to see that a girl or two might become lost, and that one day that step forward might be another source of communal pain.

7

◆◆◆◆

The Interchangeable Revolutions

To replace all this. Islam sanctified rage – rage about the faith, political rage: one could be like the other. And more than once on this journey I had met sensitive men who were ready to contemplate great convulsions.

In Iran there had been Behzad, who had shown me Tehran and the holy cities of Qom and Mashhad. He was the communist son of a communist father, and not a Muslim. But his communism was like a version of the Shia faith of Iran, a version of the Shia rage about injustice: a rage rooted in the overthrow by the Arabs of the old Persian empire in the seventh century. Good Muslims believed that the best time in the world was the time of the Prophet and the first four good caliphs; Behzad believed that the best time was in Russia between 1917 and 1953. Darkness had been dispelled; an unjust society had been overthrown; and the jails and camps of Russia were full of the wicked. For Behzad the idea of justice was inseparable from the idea of punishment. Ayatollah Khomeini spoke in the name of God the avenger; Behzad, the communist, spoke like Khomeini.

In Pakistan, in the Kaghan Valley in the far north, I had talked to the gentle Masood. He was only sentimentally a Muslim. But, standing beside me above the gorge of the cold, green Kunhar River, he had allowed anxieties about his family and his own future to flow into a wider political despair about his country, and he had said: 'Millions will have to die.'

And something like this was said to me in Jakarta by a businessman. We met late one afternoon in the restaurant of the hotel. He had been described to me as an economist, someone in touch with government departments, a man planning for the future. He was all that, but he also had the Indonesian feeling of things going wrong. And he was full of rage: against the Chinese (too gifted for Indonesia, 'like Rolls-Royce spare parts in a Japanese car'), the multinationals, the successful, the ignorant men who were now running his country.

He said, 'The leaders of the developing countries – most of them – are prosperous outside, but very poor inside.' And he touched his heart. 'They can buy the Mercedes, but they don't have the true feeling for it – they cannot appreciate the ingenuity and the work that has been put into that appliance. There is no point in buying an IBM typewriter if your speed is forty words per minute.' He was not a humorous man, but his anger (and his fondness for scientific metaphor) appeared to give him a kind of wit.

He was a Muslim from Sulawesi, formerly the Celebes, where – as in Sumatra and west Java – in the 1950s there had been a strong Muslim separatist movement. And there was more than a remnant of that rage in him, though he had benefited from the holding-together of the Indonesian state. Starting from nothing, he had become educated; he had studied abroad, in the United States; he had prospered in the business he had established; he had shared in the development of the country after the waste of the later Sukarno years. But it was not enough. His success had been dislocating. It made him see more clearly the kind of people who had got ahead, and of all these people he wished to be rid. He wished now to pull down the state that had enabled him to rise.

He said, 'We have to kill a lot of people. We have to kill one or two million of these Javanese.' Everybody who had risen, like himself, had to be killed: everyone in the government, the good jobs, the universities, the nice houses. 'I feel in Jakarta I have lost my sensitivity. I have an office on the ninth floor of one of these big new buildings. It is centrally air-conditioned. I go to the office in an air-conditioned car. Going back to my place, I stay at home reading. I look at television. Where am I living? I cannot grasp poverty. How can I grasp the complaint from the society?'

There was too much injustice. Too many people were unemployed, and their number grew year by year. Not enough jobs were being created by the government, the multinationals, the Chinese entrepreneurs from Singapore and Hong Kong. Rage was the response of this man: rage, seemingly political, that was really Islamic, an end in itself; and racial rage.

'Most of the Ph.D.s are Chinese. They are like a cancer cell, ever growing and powerful, and they will destroy their surroundings, and we cannot stop it. If these people enter *any* system they always outdo and outsmart.'

'But you need gifted people.'

'These people' – and he was talking now not only about the local Chinese, but also about people from the multinationals and all foreigners – 'are actually like electric current with 220 volts. However, the existing wiring of the society is capable only of 110, so any direct contact with the 220 will spoil the 110. You need a transformer. The transformer is supposed to be the government sector and the young intellectuals. However, due to impatience to attain material goods, this sector most of the time affiliates with the 220 volts instead of with the 110. Because these young technocrats, if they're starting to drive, they want Rolls-Royce or, if not that, Volvo.'

So it all had to go. 'The fight that's coming will be between the people in the universities and the people in the *pesantren*. One day the students from the *pesantren* will come to Jakarta and burn down this nice hotel. Islam can become a cocaine. It makes you high. You go to that mosque and you get high. And when you get high, everything that happens becomes Allah's will.'

It had happened before in Indonesia, this mass slaughter. In 1965 the communists had been wiped out. A million people had been killed, he said, not half a million, as was now given out. And more should have been killed: there were two and a half million communists at the time. So a million and a half had escaped killing, and many of them were still around.

I said, 'If the killing starts, you may go yourself.'

'I might. I hope not. But I might.'

'I was told that in 1965 some people took out the gamelan when they went killing.'

'Of course. To add to the beauty.'

It was after tea, and the Brasserie of the Borobudur Intercontinental – gardens behind the glass – was full of the people he was talking against: local Chinese, well-to-do Indonesian businessmen, the middle-aged men from the multinationals. He was speaking loudly, and in English.

I said, 'Do you talk like this when you talk to the government people?'

'No. I talk to them of facts and figures, plans and studies.'

'Why do you talk to me like this, then?'

'You are not a scientist. You want to find out about me. You are playing a game of chess with me. So I talk to you of the other side.'

I was playing no game of chess with him. He had been told before he came what my purpose was. Perhaps he didn't believe. He was unusually small, with a slight but noticeable facial disfigurement. It would have worried him; in Indonesia they loved beauty. He wished in the Brasserie to draw attention to himself. He had the Indonesian feeling for drama. But his rage was real enough; and his fantasy of violence could become reality. 1965 had occurred.

I talked one day with Gunawan Mohammed, editor of *Tempo*, the leading weekly magazine of Indonesia, about the 1965 killings. Gunawan was twenty-five at the time. (Indonesians have lived through so much: it was only later that I remembered that on another occasion Gunawan had told me that in 1946, during the revolution, when Gunawan was six, his father had been executed by the Dutch. But Gunawan had no ill-feeling towards the Dutch. He said, 'It was a war.')

Gunawan's explanation of the killings of 1965 was simple. 'Fear. I cannot tell you how frightened people were of the communists. They were so strong, and nobody knew what they were going to do.' The communist youth building was not far from Gunawan's house, and during those days of fear Gunawan sat with a gun in his house. 'I believe *I* would have killed, if I had to.'

An Indonesian book preceding those days of fear came my way. It was *Contemporary Progressive Indonesian Poetry*, an anthology of Indonesian communist poetry in English translation, and it was published in 1962 by the League of People's Culture. Old history, it might have seemed; but everything issued by the League was still banned. And it was only in December 1979, while I was in Indonesia, that the most famous writer connected with the League, Pramoedra Ananta Toer, was released from confinement, together with the last of the 20,000 (the official figure given) who had been detained since 1965 as communists – the Indonesian government, it was said, yielding to pressure from President Carter.

Pramoedra's later life scarcely bears contemplating: imprisoned at forty-one, returned to the world at fifty-four, his early books banned, the years of his maturity wasted. He was like Sitor Situmorang, whom I had met only a few days after I had arrived in Indonesia, whose history I hadn't fully appreciated at the time, and whose intellectual and social graces I had taken too much for granted.

In 1962 Sitor was a man of power in Indonesia. He had made his name with his early lyrical poems. He was now more political, general secretary of the League for National Culture; and he was represented in the anthology by three poems he wrote after a visit to China.

> Zoila is a maiden from Cuba
> in Peking. With pride
> she hands me the banner
> of her country, celebrating
> the victory of her land
> over American aggression.

It was sad, and scarcely believable, that simplicity like that could have led to such pain for Sitor and his country. But Sitor was not to be reproached now: as someone had said, he had suffered too much. And I was willing to look for other things in these political poems of his.

He had said to me one day, 'The people here have lost their religion.' He was speaking as a man who had been cut off from his tribal past, snatched from his village at the age of six and sent to a Dutch boarding school. He had felt the need to reconstruct or understand this past only when he had come out of jail, and was trying to write his autobiography; without knowing what he had come from he hadn't been able to make sense of his life. And it seemed to me that in 1962 socialism or communism had given him – a man without a past or a community – a substitute wholeness. In China he had visited a commune.

> *Social life, solidarity and hope*
> *I encountered and felt*
> *in this commune. Hence:*
> *I want to drink from the warmth*
> *of your hopes*
> *I want to press your hands*
> *so busily at work.*
> *I want to eat this bread*
> *the bread of the commune, as a token*
> *of social life, solidarity and*
> *human hopes regained.*
> *Freedom together in love, in*
> *ideals and the reality of the socialist world.*

The bread of the commune; social life, solidarity and hope: the theme wasn't Sitor's alone. It was the Indonesian theme, now more than ever. It was the theme of the Muslim *pesantren*. And that was the surprise of this communist anthology of 1962: many of its themes and moods were Muslim and Indonesian, still.

Injustice (all the translations are by Bintang Suradi, and are given with his punctuation and use of capitals):

> *In bali too the rice ripens for miles around*
> *but in bali too thousands of peasants die of hunger.*
> *We come to bali and there are dancers*
> *we come to bali and there are temples by the score*
> *both are typical of bali*
> *we come to bali and the peasant dies*

not because the crop failed to ripen
This too is typical of bali
this too has meaning
(Putu Oka: 'Bali')

The Indonesian and Muslim lament about the loss of simplicity and brotherhood:

Life should not be measured by luxury
though luxury is the aim pursued
but by whether poverty repeats its cycle
and spreads conspicuously across the earth.
in the restaurant a gentleman dines lavishly
on the ground a beggar with a tin
is there a deal of life?
(Putu Oka: 'Life')

Rage and revenge:

Lovely Periangan, burning, reddened by fire
the peasants trapped, scorched on their native earth
comrades, brothers, against this challenge the will is
                                                   supreme
resistance, revenge in every heart
(Sobron Aidit: 'Sad Memories of a Tijandur Peasant')

Political pain turning to a religious wound:

Mother!
year after year you have waited
an endless longing in your heart
but your suffering has only augmented.
Sweat and toil, blood and tears
terrorists, usurers and landlords
join one another to suck out your blood.
Is it true Mother
that all creatures on earth have your love?
(Rukiah Kertapati: 'Indictment')

The saviour:

And then, when the names of paltry judges have
                                          all disappeared
forgotten, burnt or eaten by the rats
your name will still live on, – Son of the Masses
born of a powerful womb

your name will live forever, death it shall not know
for you are life itself
(M. S. Ashar: 'Freedom and Prison')

Revenge, with the promise of restored 'union':

We possess nothing
but burning hearts roughened by suffering
that may turn into lava, fire and thunder
destroying foes, grinding them to dust.
We the downtrodden shoulder freedom
without rank, nameless
we've kept our country from becoming a prison
(Sabarsantoso Anantaguna: 'The Downtrodden
Shoulder Freedom')

And, finally, the complete faith:

The society of my class, long have I dreamed of
the sunrays
of a future for Udin and for the others
who yearn for friendly love binding equals to
each other
ah, how black and soiled it is today
but wait, for the boil will burst, molten fire
will burst forth
the time will come when the enemy meets death at
the point of the dagger
the battles for the people were not in vain
they have fertilized the sturdy seedling planted
by Lenin

In the *pesantren* at Pabelan I had been given a copy of an interview, perhaps from a Christian magazine in the Philippines, with an Indonesian *kiyai*, a *pesantren* leader. 'Now how can a *kiyai* help in the changing of this kind of society? How can he make the landlords and the rich give up their properties which, according to Islam, belong to Allah and must be given back to the people who are creatures of Allah? How can the *kiyai* make the farmers see their importance as human beings who must be given justice?'

The creatures of Allah in 1979, the creatures of the earth in one of the poems of 1962. And point by point the similarities could be seen: the true faith, injustice at home, the uncritical journeys to the lands of the achieved faith.

Imaduddin had said he couldn't be a socialist because he could find the good ideas of socialism in the Koran. He said more than he knew. The Islam of protest was a religion that had been brushed by the ideas of the late twentieth century. Men no longer simply found union in a common submission to Allah. Men were the creatures of Allah; and the late twentieth century extended the meaning of the words: these creatures of Allah had 'their importance as human beings who must be given justice'. The land and its wealth belonged to Allah and not to men: the late twentieth century made that a political rather than a religious idea.

After a generation of peace, the revolutionary current of 1965 flowed again. It was Islamic now, but it was like what had gone before: as though rage and the wish for revenge were always to be tapped in this overcrowded, once-feudal land, where many men were squeezed out, the old balance was broken, where every step forward took men further away from safety, where the new world brought new gifts but made difficult demands, and all men, whether at the top or at the bottom, lived in fear of personality loss.

REPRISE
The Society of Believers

1

Submission

KARACHI, PAKISTAN, six months later. Many things had happened in those six months; the Muslim world had been on the boil. The American embassy in Tehran had been seized by Iranian students and more than fifty embassy staff held as hostages. There had been a siege and gun battle in the mosque at Mecca, hinting at underground movements in the kingdom of Saudi Arabia. The Russians had invaded Afghanistan.

In Pakistan itself there had been changes. In August and September there had been talk of elections. Those elections had been cancelled; martial law had been tightened; the newspapers were censored; there were public whippings. A well-known journalist had been arrested, had appeared in court in chains, and had been sent to jail for a year. Crowds – seeing an American hand in events in Mecca – had attacked American embassy buildings in the northern cities of Islamabad and Rawalpindi. A Pakistani scientist based in Europe had won a Nobel prize; but he belonged to the proscribed Ahmadi sect, who venerated their own Promised Messiah; and his visit to Pakistan had led to a student riot.

It looked like terror and despotism. But the state still proclaimed its goal to be the true Islamic way. And that had to be taken seriously. In Indonesia, Malaysia, Iran, Islam served or contained other causes. In Pakistan – though there were politicians and ambitious people among the fundamentalists – the faith served itself.

In the Muslim world Pakistan was special, the creation of the Muslims of India, a minority, who had never ceased to feel themselves under threat. And there were people in Pakistan who had taken the faith to its limit. To them Islam was more than personal salvation, more than a body of belief; it had become country, culture, identity; it had to be served, at whatever cost to the individual or the state itself. The poet Iqbal, outlining his plan for a separate Indian Muslim state, had said in 1930: 'It is no exaggeration to say that India is perhaps the only country in the world where Islam, as a people-building force, has worked at its best.' And, near the end now of my own Islamic journey, I felt that to be so.

Karachi had been green in August, after the monsoon. No rain had fallen since then, and now, in February, the gardens were brown, the trees dusty, some of them leafless; and no rain was going to fall until June.

I thought I would go and see Nusrat. He was the journalist from the *Morning News* who had taken me to the Karachi courts. I remembered his abrupt way of speaking, his round cheeks, his walrus moustache. In the courts he had exclaimed about the shortage of chains for the prisoners, some of whom were being led about by ropes tied to their upper arms. He had said he was going to write about that – the shortage of chains, the slackness of the prison authorities. Nusrat was always on the look-out for newspaper stories. He worked hard; he liked his job; he was driven by some kind of anxiety. He was a man of the faith. Almost his first words to me were that he was a bad Muslim – meaning that he wasn't good enough: because to him, as he then said, Islam and the afterlife were the most important things in the world.

I had been aggressive with Nusrat. He had said that he wanted to go to the United States to get a degree in mass media or mass communications and then perhaps to get a job with some international body. The assumption that – while Pakistan and the faith remained what they were, special and apart – the outside world was there to be exploited, had irritated me. I had said that he wasn't qualified to do what he said he wanted to do. And that impulse of aggression towards him – so friendly, open, anxious – had worried me.

I took a taxi to the *Morning News*. A long board on the upper floor spread out the name of the paper; there were a number of small shops at street level. Steep concrete steps led up from the pavement. It wasn't like the entrance to the office of a daily paper. It was more like the steps to an unimportant government office. And that was how it felt upstairs: an old tiled floor, the colours of the tiles faded, as though ground away by dust; beaten-up office furniture; old distemper on the walls; a few men sitting without urgency at tables.

It wasn't the building I wanted, as it turned out: it was only the advertising department. The editorial department was in a building at the back. I went down by an iron spiral staircase. The iron of the steps had been worn into holes here and there. A sweeper was sweeping the concrete steps at the side of the editorial building, sloshing down one step with blackened water from a pail, working that into the concrete, sloshing down a lower step: it explained the faded tiles in the advertising department. He paused; I picked my way up.

It was a new building, but the atmosphere in editorial, at this early hour of the morning, was like the atmosphere in advertising. In a room full of files – dusty, as though what had been filed had been put away forever – a girl was sitting at a desk. She worked for the children's page of the *Morning News*. She was answering children's letters and – as though fitting the tool to the job – she was using a typewriter that was very small. She wasn't veiled: it seemed strange. On other tables were typewriters in varying stages of decrepitude – like the machines I had seen in the typewriting stalls of the Karachi bazaar (a businessman in one stall one evening, grandly dictating to a male secretary) near the law-courts. Karachi, where iron steps wore out and tiles faded, gave its own atmosphere to offices: the editorial room of the *Morning News* had the feel of the court registry I had visited with Nusrat.

The girl telephoned Nusrat's house for me. Nusrate was not at home. He had already gone out, chasing some story. That was like Nusrat. I left a message for him with the girl from the children's page. He was keen on his job, always on the go; it was strange to think that this was the room to which he brought back his hot copy.

Later he telephoned.

'I've just come in. I didn't expect you back. I thought we had put you off for good. And now you've altered my life.'

I recognized his fruity voice, his brisk delivery. The hyperbole – which was the hyperbole of Urdu poetry – was especially touching. Because I had already had some idea of his misadventure.

The office looked run-down. But just a few months before there had been a drama. The *Morning News* had made a slip on the woman's page. They had reprinted an article from *Arab News* about a great Arab woman. The woman was the great-granddaughter of the Prophet. And the article for various reasons had outraged the Shia community. There had been demonstrations and threats, and the government had had to act. They had closed the paper down for three days; they had ordered an inquiry.

It was a time of danger. If the authorities hadn't acted as they had done, and if the *Morning News* had had a weaker editor, there might have been a calamity. Ghauri, the editor, had taken full responsibility for what had appeared in his paper; he had acted throughout as a man of courage and honour. He was a very sick man. He was only in his late forties, but he looked much older. He had been in the hands of doctors for months; his illness did not allow him to sleep regularly. When I saw him he seemed to be in some physical pain, and was hardly able to sit upright. But he had found the strength to guide his paper through its many bad weeks until the affair had been cleared up by the inquiry.

The matter was now closed. But for Nusrat the matter was not closed. It was Nusrat who looked after the woman's page. It was he who had made the slip, had passed the article from *Arab News*. For weeks and months Nusrat had lived with danger and guilt; the editor had seen him shrink into himself.

What was the offending matter that the *Morning News* had published? To understand, it was necessary to go over a little of Islamic history. For the Shia Muslims, Ali, the Prophet's son-in-law, should have been the first temporal successor (or caliph) to the Prophet. He was passed over three times; he was only the fourth caliph, and then (after a reign of only five years) he was murdered. Ali had two sons. Neither was granted the caliphate. The first was poisoned. The second died in battle when he tried to claim the caliphate. This second son, Husain, had a daughter – Ali's granddaughter, the Prophet's great-granddaughter. The offending article was about her.

There is some controversy between the two main Muslim sects about this woman. The Arabians (or orthodox) try to suggest that she was not interested in the cause of her father Husain, or her grandfather Ali. They say that, after her father's death, she settled down happily in the Arabian city of Medina; that Medina, bursting with the wealth of the Arab conquests, became in the eighth century a city of luxury and culture: musicians, singers, courtesans, slaves, exquisite brothels; and that Husain's daughter, many times married, queened over the city.

To the Shias, grieving for Ali and his sons, this story about Ali's granddaughter adds insult to injury. They reject it. They say that the girl never grew up, died as a child. But the article on the woman's page of the *Morning News* – reprinted from *Arab News* – gave the Arab or orthodox version of this woman's history, made her a beguiling, luxury-loving patroness of the arts in eighth-century Arabia.

The article could not have appeared at a worse time. It was the month of Mohurram, when the Shias mourn the deaths of Ali and his sons for ten days. Under the martial law regulations of Pakistan, crowds were not allowed to assemble; but the Shias were free to meet during this month of mourning in mosques or parks or playgrounds, and there they became worked up against the *Morning News*. Forty or fifty students marched to the paper one day; there were threatening telephone calls; there was talk of leading a procession of 40,000 to the *Morning News* and burning it down. At another level, there began to be talk of an international conspiracy against the Muslim world. The siege of the Mecca mosque had just taken place; the American embassy had been seized in

Tehran; a Pakistan plane with pilgrims had crashed after leaving Mecca airport.

It was a bad time for the paper. It might have been closed down for good, and many people would have lost their jobs. And there was the physical danger from the enraged Shias of Karachi. And not only Shias: in the month of Mohurram feelings about Ali and his sons run high among the orthodox as well. Nusrat must have lived a nightmare. He wished to serve the faith above everything else; and in the land of the faith he must have felt quite alone. The world would have changed for him: the appearance of the streets, the crowds. At any moment he might have been set on.

Ghauri said – was it with despair or fatigue? – 'There are four versions of this lady's story. One version is as was printed. The second version is that the lady died at nine and a half. The third version is that she died at eleven and a half. The fourth, and most likely, is that she didn't exist.'

'You've altered my life,' Nusrat said on the telephone. But he meant something else.

And when we did meet he was immediately recognizable. He was in a bright plaid tweed jacket, his tribute to the Karachi winter or, as the British called it, 'cold weather'. I hadn't seen the jacket before, but it was in character, bold, like Nusrat's round tinted glasses and walrus moustache.

He said, 'I am dead on time.'

'You are five minutes late.'

'Yes. I'm five minutes late.'

We took the elevator up to the Chandni restaurant, on the roof of the Intercontinental.

'How is the paper?'

'Not so good. I closed it down for three days. But you must have heard.'

He spoke jauntily. He might have been speaking of some trade union activity, some victory over the management. And I was prepared to leave it at that.

And it was only in the bright rooftop restaurant, when we were going around the Intercontinental buffet, a little more meagre than I had remembered it in August, it was only then – Karachi browning all around us, the cold weather burning away fast, the February sky already very bright, the restaurant door open, the air already warm – that I saw that Nusrat had gone grey. In five months he had changed.

'You've gone grey.'

'You've noticed? It happened,' he said. 'There is no reason. Don't think there is any special reason. I like grey hair. I like to look grey.'

'It looks nice on you. How old are you?'

'Thirty-three. I was grey before, when you saw me. You mightn't have noticed, but I was grey then.'

When we were at the table he said, 'I didn't intend to go to the office until four that day. The day I got your message. So it's a bit of luck that I am here. I could have been out of Karachi. I could have missed you. Doesn't that make you believe in a chain of events?'

'You are working too hard.'

'I work very hard. There is pressure on me. The other day, on the entertainments page, do you know what I did? I put in a picture of an Indonesian actress in her national dress. It would have gone to the printers if someone hadn't pointed it out to me. It showed up the outlines of her body. I didn't see that. I just saw the national dress. What am I to do? I don't know how far I can go on the entertainments page. I don't even know whether an entertainments page is desirable in an Islamic society.'

He broke off, waiting for me to give an opinion. I didn't say anything.

He said, 'This is serious. This is something that has to be discussed in our society. And what about the position of women? Should they do jobs? Or should they stay home? Should men teach women? Should women teach men? These are important questions.'

'Why are they so important?'

'Because we have to create an Islamic society. We cannot develop in the western way. Development will come to us only with an Islamic society. It is what they tell us.'

We had talked of this in August. He knew where I stood. For a second or two I wondered whether he was speaking ironically. But he was in earnest. The jauntiness suggested by his round cheeks, his moustache, his man-about-town jacket was false. He was grey and tormented. In five months he had changed as much as the Karachi landscape.

In August, in the gardens at the back of the Intercontinental, I had seen men using a bullock-drawn grass-cutter to cut the grass. Now there was no grass to cut; but the men were still at work, pulling a heavy roller over the heath-like ground.

I said, 'When will it rain?'

'In June. Or July. Next month it will start getting hot. Then there will be a water shortage. Everybody talks about Afghanistan now. But when it gets hot and there is a water shortage, people will talk of that first.'

This was more like the journalist, the columnist. But then he said,

'There's the question of banks and interest. That's what the economists should be thinking about. That's what we have to work out, how to create a banking system without interest. Right now, when I get my 248 rupees from the bank I get so happy, getting this money for nothing. And my wife says, "I don't know why you should be so happy." And she is right. It is wrong. My wife is a good Muslim. And, as you know, I am a bad Muslim.'

'You can't say that. When we met you said that Islam and the hereafter were the most important things to you. Do you remember?'

'But I was educated in a secular school. I don't always say the prayers.'

Later he said, 'I feel they must feel I am all right.'

'Who are "they"?'

'Civil servants, bureaucrats. They change, I know. But the file remains. So I meant the file – my file – must be a good file. God has his own ways of being kind. When certain things happen you have to believe. Think of my luck, meeting you the last time, getting your message this time – I didn't intend to go to the office until late that afternoon. And now having lunch with you and talking with you. Think of all the links in that chain.'

I looked at his distressed face. I said, 'I think you should go away for a little. Go to another country for a little. You are beginning to fight phantoms.'

'No, no. If I go, I should go for good.'

'You should take a rest.'

'You are right. I am doing too much. Only this morning I thought, "If you go on like this, you'll fall ill." What's worrying me now is that I don't like people. I don't see anyone, you know. I came here only because it's you. I can hate people. Get irritated by them. Like the other morning. I went to a slum colony in Clifton, not far from the Bhutto house. For a long time I've wanted to write about them. I should have been sympathetic to those people. I wanted to be sympathetic to them, and I am sympathetic to them. But I found myself getting irritated with them. How could they live in those conditions for thirty-two years? Just two minutes from Mr Bhutto. Why didn't they march to his house? So I got irritated and I didn't like myself for getting irritated. That was the mood I was in when I went to the office and got your message. That was why getting your message just then was to me a piece of luck.'

He had brought a file of the columns he had written over the last few months. He did a kind of gossip and comment column once a week for the *Morning News*. He wanted to make a book of the pieces and wanted me to look them over. He thought they were a record of an important period.

SUBMISSION

They were not that. But they were the work of a professional. There was nothing in the columns that referred to his own troubles during this time. He wrote of social events; he wrote of his pleasure in the Karachi cold weather, getting out his tweed jacket; he wrote of the sugar shortage. There was something about 'girlie' magazines – unsuitable in 'these changing times': that was the closest he came to his own troubles.

A column that began with a paragraph about a public flogging turned out to be a piece about the inadequacies of public transport. People couldn't go to the flogging because there weren't the buses. There was no irony. In Nusrat's writing, as in Nusrat himself, in spite of the apparent jauntiness, there was a certain humourlessness. It was part of his candour, his attractiveness. There was no question, with Nusrat, of self-censorship. Nusrat was an accepter: he lived with his country and the faith of his country. Pakistan, committed now to the way of Islam, was an ideological state. Nusrat accepted the ideology. He was a citizen of an ideological state, a believer, just the kind of man who would have been tormented by being cast out. The distrust of his fellows would have been punishment enough for him.

I told him when I saw him again that I didn't think his newspaper pieces would make a book. He didn't like that.

I said, 'It leaves everything out.'

'But people like Art Buchwald bring out their articles in books.'

I asked about his wife. I remembered that she hadn't been well in August.

He said, 'She had an operation for an ulcer. I try to avoid discussing the negative side of human existence with her. For instance, I wouldn't tell her what you think of the columns.'

'They are good newspaper columns.'

'If someone were to beat me up today, I wouldn't go home and tell her. Of course, if I went home battered and bleeding I wouldn't just sit in a chair and say nothing. I would have to say something. But normally I wouldn't. She really gets a little more worried than I do.'

So during all his crisis he had had no one at home to turn to. And yet, as his editor noted, he hadn't broken down. He hadn't tried to influence any of the important people he knew; he had kept on doing his work. It was only at the end that he had broken down. After the government inquiry was over, and the matter had been laid aside, Ghauri, the editor, asked him home to dinner.

Ghauri said, 'It's all over now. The paper will continue. But tell me, did you do it deliberately? I give you my word that whatever answer you give, I will take no action against you. I just want to know.'

Nusrat didn't understand that the question was being seriously asked.

371

When he did he burst into tears. The idea that the editor, who had risked so much to defend him, might have had some doubt about him was too much to bear. Ghauri didn't press; his question had been answered. Mrs Ghauri had to comfort Nusrat.

I saw the offending article. It was illustrated with a nineteenth-century European painting, by an unnamed painter, of an Arab woman, unveiled but fully clothed, reclining on a settee. The illustration had been taken, with the article, from *Arab News*. But what could pass in Arabia now was still provocative in Pakistan. There was little in the article itself that couldn't be found in Philip K. Hitti's *History of the Arabs*, a standard text-book. But the woman in question had been the Prophet's great-granddaughter; and there were people in Pakistan – of both sects – who felt that even to say that she was beautiful was to show disrespect.

The faith was pushing men to extremes. With only the Koran and the traditions as a guide no one could ever be sure that he was good enough as a Muslim; no one could ever be sure that he had completely submitted to Allah and that he was entirely selfless. Men like Nusrat made greater and greater demands on themselves. To a man anxious to submit, to be pure in heart and mind, the world was full of traps: like Nusrat's joy in his 248 rupees interest from the bank, his irritation with his fellow Muslims in the slum colony.

I said, 'You are accident-prone, aren't you, Nusrat?'

I had touched something. He said, 'I went to a mosque to attend a wedding last week. A friend's sister. The bridegroom was late. It was prayer time. So my friend said, "Let's go and pray." So I did the ablutions. It was a cold evening and the water was cold. I picked up a straw cap or hat – a topee – from the mosque and put it on my head and began praying. When I bowed down the straw hat came off and I thought: "God knows I hadn't come prepared to pray." I saw a hand move and I thought someone was about to interrupt me. But it was only a hand putting the cap on my head. When I bowed down again it fell off again, and I saw it roll towards the corner. I said to myself: "The prayer can be accepted even without the cap, if one's intention is to pray." The incident went unnoticed. But why do these things happen to me? It is amazing I haven't had a road accident. And I think this is God's mercy or blessing or whatever.'

I asked him about the journalist in Rawalpindi who had been sent to jail for a year.

He was cool; I was surprised.

He said, 'Perhaps he said it too often. Perhaps he shouldn't have written it for a foreign paper. Some things can be all right in a local paper but bad in a foreign paper. And *vice versa.'*

He still had plans to go abroad and study mass media. But he spoke about it differently now. He was a penitent, and he wished now to serve his country and its ideology.

'We are building our societies anew and we have to shape the media accordingly. We have to see how far, if at all, the western liberated concept of the mass media integrates with the developing countries in general and Muslim countries in particular. Maybe it does. Maybe it doesn't.'

But buried in that new personality was still the man who read Art Buchwald and wished to bring out books like Buchwald's.

The last time we met he said, 'No one has noticed that I have gone grey, or mentioned it to me.' And before we separated he said, 'Can you arrange for me to go to a place where I can read, write and study for five years? Because, in five years, if you see me again, I may have become a cement dealer or an exporter of ready-made garments. Where I wouldn't be able to have time like this, to sit and talk and share with you.'

2

❖❖❖❖❖

Islamic Winter

IN AUGUST, at London airport, the Iranian passengers for Tehran had been loaded with the goods of Europe. Later that month, at Tehran airport, the Pakistani migrants going home had been loaded with the goods of Europe and Japan. Goods: they made the world go round. And now, in February, at Karachi airport, was the complementary sight: Pakistani migrants and their families leaving the land of the faith for the lands of money.

They had their no-objection certificates and their certificates from the Protector of Emigrants. But still they were not certain. They knew only that in a crowd they had to push forward or be lost; so they pushed, and held out their precious papers; and the officials checked. One woman was taking five of her children. Many of the women were in veils, some dingy white (with a kind of cotton grille-work over the eyes), some black.

Women and children filled the no-smoking area of the Boeing 707 and gave it the atmosphere of the zenana, the women's quarters. The smoking area was virtually empty. I changed seats.

From the air, in August, the wastes of Baluchistan and Iran had been brown and black, but pale in the heat. Now, travelling in the other direction, I woke to snow. Snow covered the mountains. The plains were bare, but every little eminence was dusted with snow. Flying over snow-covered mountains, we came to Tehran, still, in winter, the colour of sand. And the girl said it was zero outside.

Brothers, guests, welcome to the Hijra [the new century of the Islamic era] *and the revolution*, said a handwritten sign in the arrivals hall. There were still the big photographs – from the Shah's time, and the colours had faded – of Persian antiquities. A coloured photograph of Ayatollah Khomeini was taped over one of those photographs at the entrance to the immigration booth.

We were a small queue. Not many of us had come all the way to Tehran. The Japanese ahead of me had given his profession as 'correspondent'. This was causing some trouble. He was beckoned out of the booth by another official. And then I was in trouble. I was a 'writer'. I needed a visa; without a visa I couldn't stay.

My passport was taken from me and I was sent to a little room at the side of the hall. It was full of officials, some with jackets and stars on their shoulders, some in shirtsleeves. They were all friendly. My passport lay with three or four others on a table, and no one seemed to be doing anything about them. Officials with jackets and without jackets were milling around; there was a lot of talk.

The Japanese correspondent was saying to someone, 'But you're a revolutionary people. In Japan we are interested in revolutionary people.'

A big, moustached man in a yellow pullover was saying to two or three Iranian officials, 'But you can't send me to Syria. They won't let me land in Syria.'

'First plane out,' one of the Iranians said. 'The whole world wants to come to Iran.'

'But they won't let me land in Syria. They'll send me back here.'

A woman of about thirty, in tight jeans and with a coppery skin and reddish hair (hair and skin suggesting a henna staining), said, 'I'm Turkish. I'm Turkish.' As though appealing to Muslim solidarity.

I was in danger of being forgotten. I spoke to the man who had taken away my passport. He was standing behind the table and apparently doing nothing. He asked me – with a smile – to take my Lark bag out of the office, which was indeed a little crowded. I took the bag outside and put it down on the wet floor: a man was cleaning, and after all that I had read about Iran this seemed surprising: that people were still doing jobs, maintaining things.

I was stunned, passive. The six-month journey I had done had been a series of gambles; what had come my way had come my way. And I had hardly slept. It had been an early morning flight, and I had had a late night in Karachi. I was content for the journey to end in the way it seemed about to end.

The man who had taken my passport followed me out. He said, 'What airline did you come by?'

'PIA.'

The Iranian girl who was the PIA representative was at the other end of the hall with her clipboard: the flight had brought a few problems. The man hailed her; she came over; they talked.

She said to me, 'You have to go back.'

'I'll leave.'

'You are a writer and you don't have a visa.'

'I know. Can you put me on a flight to London?'

'That's not possible today. You can go back to Karachi.'

'I don't want to go back to Karachi. There is no room. A pediatric conference is starting today at the Intercontinental and all the rooms are booked.'

Where else could I go that day? What were the visa-less airline cities?

'Can I go to Athens?'

I didn't particularly want to go to Athens. The name had come to me only because, from my compulsive reading of airline advertisements during the last six and a half months, Athens seemed a city to which many airlines went.

The girl seemed to like the idea of Athens. She held her clipboard against her chest and said, 'There is a Japan Airlines flight on Thursdays.'

'Book me on that.'

'That's tomorrow, though.'

'But today is Thursday.'

She said, sharply, 'Today is Wednesday the thirteenth.'

'Where can I go today?'

'There are no flights today. There's only the Karachi flight now. Are you sure you don't want to go to Karachi?'

I said, undoing fate, 'You know, I came in in August without a visa.'

She behaved as though I had solved her problem. 'You came in in August without a visa? Did you tell them?'

'It shows in my passport.'

She went to the crowded room and came out soon afterwards and said, 'They've made a mistake. They'll let you in.'

And when I was called into the little room everybody seemed genuinely pleased that they had found a way around the recent directive from the ministry about journalists and visas.

'But *you*,' an official said to the Japanese correspondent, who was still in the room, still arguing, '*you* will have to go back.'

The red-haired Turkish woman had also been let in. Why had they thought she was a journalist? She was at the customs counter with an enormous amount of stuff, goods from Taiwan and Japan, much of it brand-new, still in cardboard boxes and polystyrene moulds.

I entered the other lane, and studied the back of the customs officer, a young woman in a heavy woollen skirt and pullover, her own clothes, not a uniform. She sat casually on the counter, her legs crossed, while she examined. Her pullover was tight; her skirt was tight over her thighs; she was stylish.

I had only my Lark carry-on bag. A man spoke to the customs girl and

seemed to suggest that I should be allowed through. The girl swivelled –
not a beauty, alas – and glanced at the passport I carried, and then
showed me her back again.

When at last my turn came the customs girl said, 'You English?'

'No.'

'But you have this passport.'

'That's my citizenship.'

'Open.'

The sight of my Marks and Spencer winceyette pyjamas – the un-
Islamic 'batik' of which Khairul and his Arabist group had disapproved in
Kuala Lumpur, when they had surprised me in my room at the Holiday
Inn – the sight of those pyjamas softened the daughter of the Iranian
revolution, possibly made her think of father or brothers.

'This all you have?'

'Yes.'

'No wine?'

'No wine.'

'You're okay.'

Outside, in the cold air, were the well-fed bandits of the Airport Taxi
Service, more flourishing now than in August, with Iran big in the news
again and journalists flying in and out by the score. They wanted 800
rials for the 500-rial run to the town. I bargained, but feebly; they
knocked off a hundred.

One man said, 'That hotel you're going to. It's closed.'

'Closed!' It was in pretty poor shape in August, I remembered. 'All
right, I'll go to the Intercontinental.'

'You have a reservation?'

'No.'

'Then it's closed for you. There are only five hotels in Tehran open for
you.' He reeled off some names.

I understood that he was using 'closed' and 'open' in a special way,
that he was diverting traffic to certain hotels. I stuck to my hotel. He
didn't seem to mind. He had done his duty by his hotels; it was cold; he
went back to his shed.

The same traffic jams, the same exhaust haze; the same crazy driving,
cars handled like push-carts; the city of concrete and brick, in winter as
in summer the colour of sand, the bare trees as dusty as the cars, winter
mud drying out, the fruit displays of stalls and shops – oranges and
pale-yellow apples – catching the eye, the multi-coloured slogans and
the stencillings and posters on walls like mixed colours on a palette, part
of the general impression of muddiness. In a traffic jam I studied a
winter-clad, fresh-complexioned man using a twig broom to sweep the

dust off the streets into the concrete gutter at the side: again surprising, this evidence of municipal life going on, apparently separate from the events that made the news.

I had arrived in August on an election day, a Friday, the sabbath. The streets were without their workaday traffic; the shops were shuttered. Tehran had looked like a place that had closed down for good; but in the evening I had seen ballot boxes being taken into cars, watched over by men with guns. The election that day – after an earlier referendum about an Islamic republic – was for an Assembly of Experts, people who would work out an Islamic constitution. Khomeini had asked people to vote for the clergy. And the clergy had won.

The Assembly of Experts had deliberated on a constitution, and they had given Khomeini a place above everyone else, even above the President. Khomeini had become the regent of God, the representative on earth (or in Iran) of the Twelfth Imam (in hiding or 'in occultation' for a thousand years). Then there had been a referendum on this constitution; municipal elections; a presidential election. The clergy had lost the presidential election. In August the stencilled portraits on walls had been mainly of Khomeini; now there had been added the portrait of the man who, a few weeks before, had been elected President. And in a few weeks there was going to be another election, for the national assembly.

In between all this voting, the American embassy had been seized, and the first anniversary of the revolution had been celebrated: in the crush on that day some people had been killed by a tank. The people of Tehran lived with excitements. After three months the American hostages story was like a popular but very slow serial, to which the man in the street could turn when there was no bigger drama.

The hotel wasn't closed. There were people at the entrance lodge; there were cars within. The front garden had browned down with the winter. The oval-shaped lawns were brown, with green patches, oddly like shadows, below shrubs and trees. Rain and snow and soot had muddied the laurel and other evergreens and the fir trees; and the winter sun and the dry air of the Tehran plateau had turned that city mud to fine dust. But hands were still at work. The drive was swept; the rose bushes had been pruned.

The lobby was reassuringly warm, and the elevator that took me up to the eighth floor worked better than in August. There was a metal bed on its side in the corridor. But no chambermaid had been doing private washing for a hotel guest, as my chambermaid had done for me, once, in August: there were no clothes hanging out to dry on the door-knobs of unoccupied rooms.

My room hadn't been properly cleaned. A curtain had lost some hooks

and drooped at one end. There were no ash-trays now; no hotel literature, no directory of services, no stationery; no card on the television
set, as in August, giving programme details of the already suspended
'international' service of Iranian television. But the furniture was good,
the fittings sturdy. In six months there had been little deterioration.

The middle-aged hotel man, though, tall and thin and bald and with
glasses, was absolutely wretched. It was as if the empty hotel, and his life
in it, had been too much for him; as if he had deteriorated more than the
hotel or his bell-boy costume. I gave him 100 rials. Too much; but it
made no impression on him. He said, 'Give me something. My head not
good. You give me something.' I gave him some headache tablets. It was
that, the medication and the attention, rather than the rials, that he
wanted.

Later I went down to the tea lounge on the mezzanine floor. In August
this had been a place of especial desolation, staffed by men who had
grown weary with idleness and seemed to have lost faith in themselves.
It was empty now. A few of its many tables were laid with tea cups and
tea plates and paper napkins; but no one was having tea or coffee.

At an unlaid table a man in black trousers and a grey jacket was
apparently asleep, drooping over his arms. A figure of extravagant
despair, he seemed, someone enervated by the drama of Tehran. Was he
a waiter? Or a customer? Either was possible. The centre of his collapsed
head was bald, his sideburns very bushy. The mixture of pathos and
flash was affecting.

He wasn't asleep. He lifted his head; his surprised, bleary, reddened
eyes, set deep below a jutting forehead, took time to focus on me. The
top button of his white shirt was undone, his black tie was slackened.
Still propped on his arms, he said at last, 'You good? You all right? You
come from?'

I told him.

'You want something?'

It seemed an imposition. But he was anxious to serve. And the coffee,
when it came, wasn't bad.

'Coffee good? Service good?'

'Yes, yes. But how are you?'

'Not good. Cold. I have cold.'

He had more than a cold. He was desperate for a second job, and he
thought I could help. In the end I had to hide from him.

In August there had been twenty-seven guests, in a hotel that could
take four hundred. Now – as I saw when I went down to the telephone
room, where the girls were eating watermelon seeds from a pink plastic
bag and trying to cope with the ITT equipment – there were forty-two.

Not enough to make a difference. But the hotel people were trying. In the lobby there was a table with a free telephone below a sign that said *Reporters Welcome!* and then, in English, French and Italian, *Direct Line for journalists.* At the back of the reception desk, around a bar with an espresso coffee machine (the area had been closed off in August), there was an attempt at gaiety, with little handwritten mobiles dancing away and offering *Persian Tea.*

Like the immigration people and the customs girl at the airport, the hotel people gave the impression now of being a little bit at play. Everybody was less scratchy, friendlier, jauntier. In August the hotel had had no management, had been watched over by a revolutionary *komiteh.* On Fridays the radio in the dining room had boomed out with the speeches being made at the mass prayer rallies in Tehran University. But with freedom and religious exaltation there had been practical anxieties. One of the men at the reception desk – traditional Persian skills reviving in him – had taken to dealing in old coins. Another man at the desk, always rude, had spoken frantically one day (when he was doubling as a hotel taxi-driver) about his children's future. He had asked for my advice and we had talked about universities in India. When I raised the subject now he fended me off. The education of his children was a private matter again.

In the hotel – no longer ruled by a *komiteh* – they were like people who had got used not only to crisis but also to freedom, freedom inside the hotel and freedom outside it. They were like people returned to themselves. A waiter, to whom I had given fifty rials for bringing a pot of tea to my room, came up again almost immediately with two cup cakes on a plate, saying in English, 'You are my guest.'

In August there had been a revolutionary poster on the glass front door of the hotel: Yasser Arafat of the Palestine Liberation Organization on one side, Khomeini the avenger on the other side. There was no poster on the door now. Instead, inside, there were large framed portraits of Khomeini, official portraits of the man who was more than head of state. His eyes were no longer unreliable with anger; his old man's eyes held victory. No frown, no gesture of defiance, no clenched fist: the hands were the hands of the man of peace, the man at peace. They lay on his knees, and the fingers were long and delicate.

There was snow on the mountains to the north of Tehran. Morning light, falling on the snow, revealed the direction and line of every ridge. Then the smog of the city of motor-cars banked up and screened the mountains. In the summer the smog had been like the colour of the mountains; and it had seemed then that it was only the summer haze of the dusty plateau that hid the mountains. Now the smog could be seen rising against the snow like a dark cloud. By the middle of the day mountains and snow could no longer be seen, until, for a few minutes at the end of the day, the setting sun fell red on the snow of the highest ridges, and they were like a red cliff suspended over the clouded city, darkening fast, pricked here and there with electric lights, and soon jumping with neon lights: the old glitter, remarkably surviving.

The city was free, but it remained the Shah's creation. A year after the revolution it was still awaiting purpose. To many – like the hotel people gathering to chat in unoccupied, half-serviced rooms, like the man in the ITT-built telephone room sleeping on the floor, as on the desert sand, covered from head to toe by a blanket – to many people the city was still like a camping site.

Here and there were small-scale building works. But the cranes on tall unfinished buildings didn't move. With the rain and snow metal girders had rusted; and unplastered, roughly-mortared brick walls looked weathered. The shops were full of imported goods: it was there the money was going, the oil money that gushed up every day like magic. Sudden great wealth had created – had imported – the modern city, and bred the inequalities and alarms that had led to the revolution. That same wealth had bought time for the revolution.

On Revolution Avenue (formerly Shah Reza) south of Tehran University the picture-sellers still offered views of Swiss lakes, of forests; pictures of animals; a little boy zipping up his trousers, a little girl trying on her mother's shoe; pictures of children and beautiful women with tears running down their cheeks. Side by side with this was still the theme of revolution. The cassette-sellers played Khomeini's old speeches. Some people still offered old picture albums of the revolution: executions, bodies in morgues, blood. There were pictures now, too, of Che Guevara, and coloured posters illustrating various kinds of machine-gun. And still, every few yards, solid piles of Russian communist literature in English and Persian – in spite of the cartoon that showed Iran, a sturdy peasant figure, fending off two snakes, one marked Russia, one marked America; in spite of the helmeted skull that in another cartoon stood for the composite enemy: Russia in one eye-socket, America in the other, a scarf below the helmet flying the Union Jack at one end and the flag of Israel at the other.

It would have seemed like play – if there hadn't been a revolution and real blood. Blood seemed far away from this atmosphere of the campus and the winter street fair. At street corners and on the pavement there were candied-beetroot stalls, smelling of hot caramel: spiked rounds of beetroot set about a bubbling cauldron of syrup, the beetroot constantly basted and candied over and kept hot with the syrup: a winter food, better to see and smell than to taste, almost flavourless below the caramel.

At the Friday prayer meeting at Tehran University there was still a crowd, but nothing like the million or so I had seen on the second Friday in August, when I had gone with Behzad, my interpreter and guide, and for two hours we had watched the men and black-covered women stream up in separate columns until they had filled the university grounds and choked the streets, when the sound of walking feet had made a noise like a river, and dust had risen and hung above the crowd in the university. That kind of enthusiasm – the perfection of Islamic union, as some had seen it – couldn't last. And the much-loved ayatollah, Taleqani, who had started these meetings, had died; and it was winter, and not easy to sit and listen to revolutionary speeches by lesser ayatollahs who used guns like pastoral staffs.

The revolutionary activity this winter Friday was at the front gates of the university, where supplies were being collected for the flood victims of Khuzistan, the oil province in the south-west. Volunteers were waving down traffic; others were tossing up or manhandling bundles into vans and trucks, where other volunteers, far too many, were waiting to stack them. There were too many volunteers altogether, too much shouting, too many people trying to control traffic, too many people being busy and doing nothing.

What was going to happen to that carload of flat Persian bread? It had cost money; it had been brought hot; it steamed as it was shouldered out in the cold air; and then it was frenziedly stuffed – as though it was a matter of life or death – into plastic sacks and dumped into a truck with blankets and clothes. Wouldn't that bread have turned to brick by the time it got to Khuzistan?

But the bread didn't matter. The gesture and the excitement mattered. These volunteers in quilted khaki jackets and pullovers were revolutionaries who, one year on, were still trying to live out the revolution, still anxious to direct traffic (to show their solidarity with the police, now of the people, not of the Shah), still anxious to demonstrate the Islamic 'union' that had brought them victory. They were revolutionaries – like those who had stormed the United States embassy and taken the hostages – whose cause was dwindling.

Behzad had said in August, of that great prayer meeting, 'This is not a religious occasion. It is a political occasion.'

The communist son of a persecuted communist father, Behzad had read Islamic union in his own way, had interpreted Shia triumph and misanthropy in his own way, had seen a revolution that could be pushed further to another revolution. And these Islamic revolutionaries, in their Che Guevara costume, did see themselves as late-twentieth-century revolutionaries.

The Shia faith of Iran, committed after 1300 years to the lost cause of Ali (denied his worldly due, murdered, his sons also killed), was the religion of the insulted and the injured. 'The inhabitants of the earth are only dogs barking, and annoying beasts. The one howls against the other. The strong devour the weak; the great subdue the little. They are beasts of burden, some harnessed, the others at large.' This was from *Maxims of Ali*, which had been given me by the gentle Shia doctor in Rawalpindi in Pakistan. It was his book of comfort; he thought it could also be mine.

Injustice, the wickedness of men, the worthlessness of the world as it is, the revenge to come, the joy of 'union': Behzad was a communist, but the Shia passion was like his. And in August Behzad, like a Shia, was collecting his own injustices: Khomeini's revolution had begun to turn against the men of the left.

We had gone together to the holy city of Qom, a hundred miles south of Tehran. We had met theological students; we had been to see the Islamic judge of the revolution, Ayatollah Khalkhalli. On the way back through the desert to Tehran we heard on the car radio that the left-wing paper Behzad read, *Ayandegan*, had been closed down, its offices occupied by Revolutionary Guards.

Later we had gone to the holy city of Mashhad, far away in the north-east, near the Afghanistan border. We had travelled back by train with Behzad's girl friend. She too was a communist, the daughter of a family who had once been big landowners. During the journey she had ostentatiously read some local communist pamphlet. And she and Behzad had played cards until a Revolutionary Guard had come into the compartment and told Behzad that card-playing was banned during the month of Ramadan, and especially on that day of mourning for Ali. Behzad had raged afterwards. He hadn't seen the Guard as a man of the people; he had seen him as a servant of the oppressor class.

And he was to return to further trouble in Tehran. Revolutionary Guards had seized the headquarters of Behzad's communist group. Later I was to see the scene: sand-bags, machine-guns, young men, Islamic revolutionaries, in guerrilla clothes on one side of the busy road; the ejected, unarmed men of the left on the other side of the road, dressed like students or city workers, just waiting. And Behzad himself was to join the waiting men that afternoon.

The picture I had carried away was of Behzad and his girl friend on the platform of Tehran railway station, after the overnight journey from Mashhad. Friends of the girl were waiting for her; and she and Behzad walked ahead of me. He was tall, slender, athletic from his skiing and mountain-climbing. She was small, with one bad foot, and her hip on that side was shrunken. She was the daring one – without a veil, leaving the communist pamphlet face down on the seat in the train so that anyone in the corridor could see the red hammer and sickle on the yellow cover. He was the protector, slightly bending towards her as they walked, happier in her company than she appeared to be in his.

Behzad had moved, and he was busy with an examination. When at last I got him on the telephone, and asked how he was, he said, understanding my concern, 'Don't worry. Nothing has happened to me.'

The next day, two days before a six-hour examination, he came in the early evening to the hotel, to take me to the apartment he was sharing with a friend. I had remembered someone boyish, someone giggling in a railway compartment and playing a simple card game with a girl. The Behzad who met me in the lobby was a man, and grave. He was wearing a jacket; in August he had told me he didn't have a jacket. He also seemed to have more hair.

'Have you curled your hair, Behzad?'

'It was always like that.'

'You look older.'

'I'm twenty-five. That's not young.'

We went out and walked towards the Avenue of the Islamic Republic, formerly Shah.

I said, 'The hotel people seem a lot happier.'

'Everybody has begun to understand that life is going to go on.'

'I feel they've got used to their freedom.'

'Freedom for them, maybe. But not for people like us. There will have to be another revolution.'

We crossed the avenue, Behzad leading me through the traffic, as he had done in August, and we waited for a line taxi. The ones that weren't full moved on and left us when Behzad told them where we wanted to go. It was cold; I had no pullover or topcoat. We were standing on the road itself, two or three feet away from the traffic, and just behind us was one of the deep gutters of Tehran, now running with muddy water.

I said, 'Let's go back and take a hotel car.'

He said, 'This is how the people of Tehran travel. We will get a taxi.'

Eventually one of the orange taxis stopped. A fat woman in black, who had been waiting a few feet ahead of us, moved to get in.

I said, 'How will we sit?'

'I will sit next to her.'

When the taxi moved off I said, 'How is your girl friend?'

'I don't see her any more. It happened not long after you left. I've seen her only once.'

'Since Mashhad?'

'Since I stopped seeing her. I hear she has a new boy friend now.'

'But why? What happened?'

'It was my decision. It was a matter of the personalities. They didn't fit.'

We were in the early evening traffic of Tehran. The shops were bright: a metropolitan glitter. Eight years before, in Buenos Aires, a city which Tehran in some ways resembled, an Argentine had said to me with some acidity during the rush-hour, 'You might think we are in a developed country.' I thought of those words now, sitting beside Behzad, feeling his new gravity, trying to look at his city with his eyes.

He said after a while, 'But I love her still. I still think of her.'

'How often do you think of her? Every day? Once a week?'

'I think of her when my mind is clear. There are many things now. But I think of her.'

We got out at the street called Felestin, Palestine, so named because the office of the Palestine Liberation Organization was now there. It was darker, quieter, and lined on both sides with plane trees.

I said, 'Was it political, this incompatibility of the personalities?'

'There was that too. I wanted to start some organized political activity. She didn't want that. She wanted us to continue as we were, fighting the régime wherever we could.'

'Guerrilla activity? Drama?'

'Something like that.'

It fitted: the revolutionary who was also the landowner's daughter, the educated woman in a Muslim country, the woman driven for many reasons to exaggerate her position. She would want to look for the fire.

Behzad said, 'But it wasn't that that came between us. Politically there's no difference between us. It was the personality thing – you should understand.'

We turned off into a side street and then into a lane. It was an area of apartments in low buildings. Cars were parked right against the buildings. It was quiet and dark, with few street lights, and little light coming from the curtained apartments.

In the darkness Behzad said, reflectively, 'I feel I may not be able to finish my course. If I could have got a job I would have given up already. But there are no jobs.'

'How long have you been doing your course?'

'Five years.'

'How much longer do you have to go before you finish?'

'A year.'

'Then why give up now? A year is nothing.'

'Even if I finish there will be no job.'

'But it wouldn't always be like that. Whatever happens, whatever political activity you take up, it will always be better for you to have a definite skill.'

'Yes, it would be a waste of the five years.'

It was like something he had reasoned out many times before.

We came to Behzad's building. An apartment on an upper floor was lit up, the curtains open, and there was the sound of pop music.

'What sort of area is this, Behzad? Middle-class?'

'No, no. We're right in the centre of Tehran. This is an upper-class area. Isn't it strange that I should be living in an upper-class area?'

(But was it strange? The revolutionary son of a provincial teacher; the university in the capital; the girl friend or former girl friend from a landowning family, the expanding circle of acquaintances, the foreign contacts: wasn't Behzad moving in the only direction he could move, if he wanted to be with people like himself?)

An upper-class area, but the rented apartment was sparsely furnished; and it looked like the apartment of two bachelors sharing. A central living area suggesting – in spite of the furniture – space waiting to be filled; a glimpse of a bedroom – or a room with a bed – on one side; the kitchen on another side. A desk, spread with Behzad's books and papers, was in the far corner, next to a small bookcase with many big text-books and dictionaries. It wasn't warm.

From the kitchen, where he went to make tea, Behzad said, 'There was a strike and we had no heating oil. No oil in Iran. Yesterday there was no heating for twenty-four hours. It's on now.'

But the radiators were cold. The music we had heard in the lane was directly above, and loud.

Behzad said, 'They're a divorced couple, and they have parties every night.'

'A divorced couple?'

'They were married. Then they got divorced. Then they began living together again, and now they have parties every night. It is very distracting.' He came out from the kitchen and said, 'I've been so busy in the last few months. There are so many things. But I just think and do nothing. I don't know what to do.'

'You mean political activity?'

'It's such a mess. I spend so much time thinking of what to do. You wouldn't call this a political activity, but it is. You have to know where you are going. Nothing has changed here since the Shah, you know. The workers and the lower classes are living under the same conditions. Nothing has changed for them. So for the third time in this century the people of Iran have been broken. This is what I think about every day. It prevents me studying sometimes. Seventy years ago we wanted to get rid of the Qajar kings. We got a constitution then. But it was never carried out. That was the first time we were broken. The second time was in 1953, when we wanted to get rid of the Pahlavis who had replaced the Qajars. The American coup d'état broke everything. And now for the third time you see what's happening. A revolution, and then nothing. Khomeini is a petty bourgeois. They are going to start the whole system up again and they're going to call it Islamic. That's all.'

They were thoughts, I felt, that had been gone over many times.

I said, 'It's a strange way of describing Khomeini.'

'He's lived two lives. He was the revolutionary leader against the Shah. We must never take that away from him. None of the American journalists who have come here have really understood about Khomeini, his greatness as a revolutionary. But he's lived two lives, before and after the revolution.'

'The kettle is boiling.' It was roaring away in the kitchen.

'It isn't boiling. I know that kettle. It makes another noise when it is boiling. In Iran and countries like Iran there are three classes, mainly. The bourgeoisie, the petty bourgeoisie, and the proletariat. In a bourgeois democratic revolution the petty bourgeoisie can be revolutionary. But when it seems that the system of the country is really going to be changed, this class, the petty bourgeoisie, resists the revolution. Khomeini belongs to this class. He is a petty bourgeois and he cannot accept socialism.'

'But didn't you always see it like that, Behzad? When Khomeini talked about tyranny and brotherhood and equality, didn't you know he was talking about Islam? Islam can sound like a political ideology. Didn't you know that?'

'People find different ways to say what they want. And so the petty bourgeoisie say, "We are Muslims. Islam is not for socialism."'

'Wasn't the mistake yours? When we went to Taleqani's prayer meeting in August you said it was a political occasion. I didn't see it like that.'

'Perhaps I don't see it like that now. But I said that, because religion all over the world is dying. There are a lot of people trying to keep it alive, but they cannot. Even the Americans now are trying to keep it alive, coming and talking to us about Allah. But they cannot.'

He decided that the kettle was boiling, and I went with him to the disordered little bachelors' kitchen. After he brewed the tea he used the aluminium kettle like a samovar, inverting the lid and resting the teapot on it – so often, in Iran, were these reminders of the nearness of Russia.

We drank the tea from glasses.

Behzad said, 'There is no freedom for us now.' He meant his group. 'They closed down our paper. That was in August. You remember we heard the news when we were driving back from Qom. Then they took over our headquarters. You remember the morning we came back from Mashhad? Some friends of my girl friend – my old girl friend – came to the station to meet her. They told her the news and took her away with them. I joined the demonstration against the seizure in the afternoon.'

'That was when I got worried about you.'

'That demonstration lasted for three days. On the third day they called for a public demonstration against us. It was a very big demonstration, very powerful. We couldn't resist. They broke us. And now we can do nothing.'

'But the booksellers outside the university are full of communist literature. Nobody seems to be stopping that. And there are all those cinemas showing Russian films.'

'Selling the communist literature is nothing. You can read and write as much as you want. But they won't let you do anything. Two months after they threw us out of our headquarters in Tehran, there was that trouble in Kurdistan. Did you read about that? Khomeini appeared on television and said the army was to crush the movement with all the power it had. They sent in tanks, helicopters, 106 mm cannon. They killed at least five hundred. Then Khomeini said he had made a mistake; he had been misinformed of events there. Do you know about the executions there? Shall I show you the pictures?'

'Don't show me. I've seen too many of those pictures in Iran.'

He didn't listen. He went to the bedroom – the pop music above us dinning away – and came back with two photographs and a photocopied pamphlet in Persian. The photographs were not as gruesome as I had feared. In fact, I had seen them before. They were official photographs: ten blindfolded men awaiting execution by Revolutionary Guards standing a few feet away. The scene had been photographed twice, once from the right, facing the men to be executed, once from the left. In the second photograph a man had been killed and was on the ground; a few feet away was the crouched Revolutionary Guard with the levelled gun: an intimate act, nothing neutral about that killing. As affecting as that was the figure of one of the blindfolded men on the right: he was holding his head high. It was a good way to die. But to what purpose? Had he even served his cause?

Behzad said, 'The people you see in these photographs are all left-wing people. Some were executed four hours after they had been arrested. Khomeini sent in Khalkhalli and he arrested everybody.'

Khalkhalli, the judge, the hatchet man of the revolution: the fat, jolly peasant from Azerbaijan who had never had any doubts about himself, who, from being a shepherd boy (yet never thinking of himself as poor), had risen to power, and killed Hoveyda, the Shah's prime minister.

I said, 'In August you told me Khalkhalli was a clown, that he had no power.' But that was in August, when Behzad had his own idea of where the revolution might still go.

'I was wrong. You remember he told you he had the gun with which Hoveyda was killed. You know who actually killed Hoveyda? It was a mullah, one of these men with beards and turbans. A young man, in his thirties. He is known.'

The photographs of the execution were official photographs, but Behzad's copies were holy documents, perhaps at some future date to be put into another Iranian album of revolution and martyrs. In the official photographs the blindfolded men were anonymous, just rebels. In Behzad's copies there was an Arabic numeral above each blindfolded man: they were all known. They were middle-class, city people. And though Behzad didn't tell me, they were (as I learned from another source) that section of his group that had opted for guerrilla activity, attaching themselves to various ethnic minority movements. The leaders had gone underground; one of them was a woman.

Friends had died, and – having broken with his girl friend – he had remained in Tehran doing his studies and earning what money he could. Since October Behzad had fretted over his own inactivity.

He pointed to the Persian pamphlet. 'There are fifteen hundred political prisoners in Iran right now. I tell you, printing and selling the communist literature is nothing.'

The hot tea had been welcome in the cold apartment. He went to the kitchen and filled the glasses again. He dropped the sugar cubes in his tea and stirred.

I said, 'Don't you hold the sugar in your mouth and drink the tea through it?'

He smiled. 'Sometimes.'

'What was your girl like intellectually?'

He paused. It seemed he hadn't understood. But then he said, 'She was all right. We were all right, in every way. It was just what I told you. The personalities.'

'You told me her family was very Muslim.'

'Only her brother. He didn't get on with me. He's a businessman. But he had nothing against me. He just thought I was a boring man, always interested in politics.' His face brightened; he smiled. 'Her father liked me, though. I think he liked me a lot.' He pointed to the booklet on the low table between us. 'You remember we talked about that man?'

The booklet was in Persian. It had a photograph of Stalin on the front cover, and another picture of Stalin, a Russian-realist pencil portrait, on the frontispiece. I had seen the booklet without taking it in: it looked so much like the books and booklets on Revolution Avenue, opposite the university.

I said, 'Where was this one printed?'

'Tabriz.' In Azerbaijan, in the far north-west.

'What do you think of him now?'

'I *love* him!' Behzad said. 'The more I read about him, the more I love him. He was one of the greatest revolutionaries. Do you know his speech at the beginning of the war?'

'1939 or 1941?'

'When the Germans invaded Russia.'

'1941.'

'"The Motherland calls . . ." Don't you know that speech?'

'Why do you say he was one of the greatest revolutionaries?'

'Because he constructed socialism in Russia. That was the first socialist revolution in the world, and it was the greatest turn in human history. Maybe he made some mistakes. But I can say he was the most suitable man to do what he did. What he did in Russia we have to do in Iran. We too have to do a lot of killing. A lot.' He began to smile, as though he was worried that I might think him ridiculous, dreaming in his present helplessness of such a big task. 'We have to kill *all* the bourgeoisie. All the bourgeoisie of the oppressor class.' And he smiled as he had smiled when he said that his former girl's father had liked him.

He couldn't walk back with me to the Avenue of the Islamic Republic, to put me in a line taxi. He had to stay with his books. He called a hire car for me.

He said, 'Someone's giving a party tomorrow. I know my old girl friend is going to be there. And the person giving the party telephoned me to ask me to come. I said, "But you know I don't see her any more." She said, "That's why I'm asking you." What do you think of that?'

I left him to his books and papers. His mathematical work was in his fine Persian script, with western (or Arabic or Indian) numerals. Many of his text-books were American. He had been fed by so many civilizations; so much had gone into making him what he was. But now, at what should have been the beginning of his intellectual life, he – like the Muslims to whom he was opposed – had cut himself off.

Behzad and the other students of Iran, and the estimated 300,000 Iranian students abroad – were all really the Shah's children, the first intellectual fruits of the state he had tried to build. But they were too new, too raw, unsupported by an intellectual tradition; they were too many; and neither they nor the state had been able to cope.

The Royal Tehran Hilton, high up in the north of the city, and with snow on the ground, was now the Tehran Hilton International. In August it had only ceased to be Royal. The word – in oriental-style lettering – had been taken down from the sign over the drive and from the marble wall at the entrance; but in both places the raised letters had left a ghostly impression. That was no longer so. The marble wall at the entrance had been polished up and fitted out with the new name; and winter rains had washed away the dusty shadow of the old word from the white sign over the drive.

The hotel had a new monogram. But THI had been made to look so like the old RTH that it took some time to see that the paper napkins in the coffee shop were still Royal. They must have been part of some vast stock – like the currency notes, most denominations of which still carried the Shah's picture.

In August the Hilton had appeared a place of gloom. Now it had revived. It advertized a one-hour laundry service. The shirt I gave in was returned to me in the coffee shop (where the china was Rosenthal) half an hour later, laundered and ironed and packed.

Behzad had told me that the hoteliers of Tehran had grown anxious since some students had occupied a well-known hotel. People who had been complaining about empty rooms had begun to jump about a bit, switched on lights at night in empty rooms, and generally tried to suggest – like the people in my own hotel – that things were all right with them.

But real life had come to hotels like the Hilton, and it had been given by the journalists and television teams who had flown in for the American embassy story – the American television networks had been especially extravagant. It was strange: Americans held hostage in one part of the city, Americans made more than welcome in other parts. And not only Americans: there were Japanese and French and British and

Spanish correspondents. Some of them, the newspapermen, had been ground down by the story, which now hardly seemed to move. The television people, with all their attendants and all their equipment, could appear to be more exciting than the events they reported on. Like the French correspondent I saw one day speaking his piece to his camera right in front of the Intercontinental: the scene oddly inconsequential to me, coming out of the hotel only after the buffet lunch.

The drama of the seized embassy and the hostages behind the walls was always available. It was a short drive away; the hire cars were always ready to take you there. And – as with some too-famous tourist spot – it seemed a little shaming to go for the first time. The old hands no longer went; after three months there was nothing for them to see.

A long red-brick wall; the low embassy buildings behind the wall; a background of snow-covered mountains – and here, in the north of the city, the mountains were quite close, with no smog or tall buildings to block the view. The long embassy wall was daubed with slogans in Persian and English; and there were more slogans on cotton banners, grey and dingy after more than three months. The pavement was roped off, the rope running from tree-trunk to tree-trunk, and armed young men in khaki trousers, black boots, and quilted khaki jackets stood at every gate. Outside the main gate the pavement ropes gave way to tubular steel scaffolding, erected less for security, it seemed, than as a form of crowd control.

The first day I went, at sunset, prayer time, there was a little demonstrating group, chanting responses to a leader as they might have responded to a mullah in a mosque; and the responses were mixed with the sounds, on many radios, of a broadcast call to real prayers. The guards remained unsmiling in the face of the indirect tribute of the little crowd. Evening clouds built up in the cold sky; evening light fell on the snow-covered mountains. The demonstration, like the radio prayers, ended. The crowd chatted and drank tea.

Except for the government crafts shop, which was, curiously, having a one-week bargain sale, the shops on the other side of the road seemed to have closed down, and some windows were blanked out on the inside with paste or paint. On the pavement on that side of the road, and on part of the road itself, there was a fairground atmosphere: book-stalls, food-stalls (mainly buns), tea-stalls (tea-bags dipped in glasses of hot water).

Beyond the scaffolding at the main gate, the embassy wall was hung with a polythene-covered display of photographs of revolutions and atrocities: Vietnam, Africa, Nicaragua: the late-twentieth-century causes to which these Muslim students wished to attach their own cause.

There were sand-bags at the angle of the embassy wall, and the lane that ran down that side of the embassy compound was barred off and guarded.

Across that lane, there was another book-stall, then a picture-stall: the beauty of tears again, inexplicable tears running down the cheeks of beautiful women and innocent children. But that Persian sentimentality, the other side of Shia misanthropy, here served the revolution: one picture, all in brown, was of a crying, ragged child, eyes blurred with tears, shirt cuffs frayed, jacket worn out at the elbow, resting a small hand on Khomeini's shoulder. He, Khomeini, frowned, and seemed to look beyond the child; he was like a man meditating revenge. It was a powerful picture. A middle-aged woman in a black *chador*, catching sight of it in the near-darkness, gave a start, and put her hand on her left breast.

The television service ended that evening with a five-minute camera study, without comment, of Khomeini resting in his Tehran hospital room after his heart attack. He was sitting in an easy-chair; his legs and feet were covered with a yellow blanket. The camera moved slowly from the man to his bed and the simple furnishings of the room and back to the man. Once the camera rested on his left hand: long fingers, the skin extraordinarily smooth for a man of eighty. Once or twice the little finger lifted, as if involuntarily, and then fell back. There was no other movement from him during the five minutes of this camera study, no sign of any emotion. He was not a man meditating revenge; he was a man whose work had been done. And all the time, in the background, a male choir sang a three-word song: 'Khomeini e Imam! Khomeini e Imam!' 'Khomeini is the Imam.' The ruler above everyone else, the deputy of the hidden Twelfth Imam, the regent of God.

The second time I walked past the American embassy there was a smaller crowd, and no demonstration. In a green tent not far from the main gate a young man and a young woman in quilted military clothes were selling big, four-colour posters: the hands of the Iranian people around President Carter's throat, the president's mouth opening wide to half disgorge a small Shah, leaning out of the president's mouth with a money-bag in each dangling hand.

A tall foreign photographer in a brown leather jacket, with his equipment slung from his shoulder, was talking to a guard at the main gate, apparently pleading to be let in. The gate opened, but it was only to let another guard in. No drama, nothing more to see.

That came later, on my way back to the hotel. On Revolution Avenue, one cross-street down, in an area of once-elegant shops, part of the great middle-class city the Shah had created in North Tehran, a small boy sat on the pavement not far from plastic sacks of store rubbish. He had lit a fire in the middle of the pavement, using rubbish from the sacks.

The fire was new. Sparks and burning paper blew on to passers-by. The boy, who was about ten, sat right up against his fire. But he wasn't warming himself. With a face of rage, he was tearing at his shirt; and he was already half naked from the waist up. It was very cold; there was a wind. The boy, sitting almost in his fire, with two boxes of matches beside him, tore and tore at his shirt. His bare feet were grimy; his face was grimy. People stopped to talk to him; he looked up – staring eyes in a soft, well-made face – and continued to tear at his shirt; and the people who had stopped walked on. A hunchback, mentally defective, appearing out of the pavement crowd, walked around the boy and the fire, hands dangling, mouth agape; and walked uncoordinatedly on.

A fire in the middle of the rush-hour crowd: a signal of distress, but there was no one who could respond. It was only in pictures that the tears of children were beautiful. The hysteria of this child, stretched to breaking point, would have matched the mood of many of the passers-by; and was too frightening.

It was frightening to me, too. And without the language I could do even less than the people who had, at the beginning, stopped to talk to the boy. I walked on along Revolution, turned down Hafiz, dodging the traffic in the cross-streets (one, formerly France, now re-labelled Neauphle-le-Château, after the French town from which Khomeini, in exile, directed the revolution); walked past the long brick wall of the Russian embassy (something like a water-tower being installed on the top of a modern apartment block: the embassy compounds of the nineteenth-century powers, Britain, Russia, France, Turkey, occupy great chunks of central Tehran); and at length, after the boutiques and the shops and typewriter shop and the French bookshop and the shop with a big stock of electrical goods (a little girl, wrapped in a flowered cotton *chador*, sitting in the doorway and selling chewing gum from one little box), came – in the shadow now of the very big traffic flyover whose pillars marched down the middle of a much dug-up Hafiz Avenue – to my hotel, behinds its own high wall.

If I had followed my original plan, if I hadn't been put out by the boy with the fire, I would have walked down Revolution Avenue to Tehran University. And there I would have come upon the big event of the day. Sixty thousand *Mujahidin* students had gathered in the university grounds. The *Mujahidin*, 'soldiers of the faith', were Muslims, but they were also of the left, and for that reason not acceptable to everybody. Elements of the Tehran street crowd, 'the people', had set upon the

Mujahidin, and there had been fighting with sticks and knives and stones. Thirty-nine people had been injured.

Of that great disturbance just a short walk away not a ripple reached the hotel. And if I hadn't heard about it later that evening from a foreign correspondent I might never have known. The next day was Friday, the sabbath, and the English-language *Tehran Times* didn't publish on that day.

One year after the revolution Tehran was still drifting. Everybody was free; everybody was waiting; everybody was nervous. The city could appear to be without event. But it was a battlefield, full of private wars.

The drama – of the American embassy – that had brought hundreds of journalists to Tehran had, ironically, shattered the local English-language press. Where was *The Message of Peace*, so combative in August, so full of the rightness of the faith and the wrongness of everything else? And *Iran Week* (cover lettering like *Newsweek*) – such new offices, and the people inside a little vain of their revolution – why was *Iran Week* so hard to find? *The Iranian* (*New Statesman*-like) was considered the better weekly, but the issue I bought turned out to be the last. The decision to close must have been taken in a hurry: the back cover invited subscriptions, the half-filled editorial column said goodbye.

The daily *Tehran Times* had shrunk. It was now four pages, a single folded sheet. In August it had been a paper of eight pages, bright with advertisements and writers and religious features. It had been a paper of the revolution and the faith. The office had been busy; there were even some Europeans or Americans giving a hand (one American, reportedly a Shia convert, out-Shiiteing them all). Mr Parvez, the editor, busy with his proofs, had thought, when I went to see him, that I wanted a job. And, kindly man that he was, he seemed ready to give me one.

No such mistake could be made now. There was no such busyness. Mr Parvez wasn't sitting at a proof-strewn desk. He was walking listlessly about the empty room. He didn't remember me, but he seemed glad to see someone, glad to talk. He sat down at his bare desk, and invited me to sit on the desk.

Things were bad, Mr Parvez said, very bad. Since the students had seized the embassy many foreign firms had closed. He had lost advertisements and readers. The circulation of the paper was now only 13,000, and he wasn't even recovering his printing costs. He lost 300 dollars with every issue. So that for him, and his business associates, Friday, the sabbath, when the paper wasn't published, was truly a day of rest.

I said, 'Why don't you suspend publication until times are normal?'
'No, no. I say that if we miss *one* issue – '
He didn't finish the sentence. To speak of disaster was to bring disaster closer.

He was forty-nine. In August I had understood him to say that he was an Iranian from India. Now, less professionally pressed, more nostalgic, he said he was from Bhopal in central India. He had begun his literary career in that country as a poet, in Urdu, the half-Persian, half-Indian language that is especially dear to Indian Muslims. Parvez was his pen-name from that Indian time. In Iran, where he had become naturalized, he had turned to English-language journalism. All the money he had made from earlier ventures he had put, after the revolution, into the *Tehran Times*. He hadn't got any of that money back so far. 'I haven't touched a rial.' To fail now would be to lose everything.

'We will borrow some money, find money somewhere, and continue until the New Year.'

The Iranian New Year, in the third week of March, five weeks away: it was the magic date of which many people in Tehran spoke. On that good day, it was felt, things might change. Something might be worked out and the American hostages might be released, and the country might get started up again. The revolution within the revolution had laid the country low. The students who were holding the hostages had become a law unto themselves. They called themselves 'Muslim students following the line of Imam Khomeini', but there was no telling who controlled them and what they might do. They were critical of everybody; they were using embassy documents to make 'revelations' about everybody; they had even made 'revelations' about the *Tehran Times*.

Mr Parvez said, 'They might hold the hostages for a year.' His voice went very thin. 'The hostages might even be killed.'

He sat quite still in his chair. But his face, not always turned to me, quivered with nervous little movements: the grey eyebrows, the eyes, the corners of the mouth. He spoke softly, surprise always in his voice, as though from minute to minute he awakened afresh to his calamity.

He said, 'We were thinking of expanding to twelve pages. We had a meeting in October. From the first of January we were going to have twelve pages. Then this happened.'

Posters were still on the windows facing the street. *Everybody is reading the Tehran Times. Ask for it everywhere every day. We've got news for you.*

Uncovered typewriters were still on the empty desks. Across the room was the standard typewriter at which Mr Jaffrey worked in August. It was to Mr Jaffrey that Mr Parvez had passed me when he understood that I only wanted to talk to someone. And Mr Jaffrey, though with a half-finished column in his machine, had given me a little time.

'How is Mr Jaffrey?'

'I've had to let him go. I've had to let them all go. There used to be twenty of us.'

Like Mr Parvez, Mr Jaffrey was a Shia from India. He had migrated to Pakistan before coming to Iran, the Shia heartland. It was Mr Jaffrey who had introduced me to the queer logic – as queer to me at the end of my journey as it had been at the beginning – of the Islamic revival. Speaking of the injustices of Iran, Mr Jaffrey had said he had begun to feel, even in the Shah's time, that 'Islam was the answer'. This had puzzled me. Religious assertion as an answer to political problems? Why not work for fair wages and the rule of law? Why work for Islam and the completeness of belief?

But then Mr Jaffrey had revealed his deeper longings, the longings that had lain below his original, political complaint. As a Muslim and a Shia, he said, he had always longed for the *jamé towhidi*; and he had translated that as 'the society of believers'.

That society had come to Iran: ecstasy in the possession of a true Imam, mass prayer rallies, the perfection of Islamic union. But out of that society had not come law and institutions; these things were as far away as ever. That society had brought anarchy, hysteria, and this empty office. And now Mr Jaffrey's typewriter, out of which Islamic copy had rolled, was still: uncovered, askew on the empty desk. (No office boy now, bringing a plate of fried eggs to the desk of the harassed journalist.) That typewriter, the modern office, the printing equipment, advertisers, distributors, readers: that required the complex, 'materialist' society – of which, unwittingly, Mr Jaffrey was part. This complex society had its own hard rules. It required more than faith; it required something in addition to faith.

I said to Mr Parvez, 'Is it hard now for Mr Jaffrey?'

'It is hard for him. It is hard for everybody.'

'His typewriter is still there.'

Mr Parvez considered the office. His eyelids trembled. He said, and his voice broke, 'That – that was a special area.' With a slow, Indian swing of the head, he said, speaking as of a very old and very sweet memory, something that might have been the subject of his Urdu verses, 'It used to be our city room. And that' – the room at his back – 'was our reporters' room. Now there are only two of us.'

'Who writes the editorials?'

'I write them.'

'They're good.' And, in the Iranian minefield, they were.

397

'I can't concentrate. The financial problems are too great, too complicated.'

'This is where you need your faith.'

But after three months he had been worn down. Every day, since the embassy had been seized, there was some statement or incident that encouraged him to think that the crisis was about to end; every day that hope was frustrated. And there were family problems as well. He had a son who was studying in the United States; fortunately, the boy had written that he didn't need money from home just yet. Another son had been about to get a student's visa for the United States when the embassy was seized.

I said, 'Mr Parvez, you are a good Muslim and a good Shia. Your paper used to be full of criticism of materialist civilizations. Why are your sons studying in the United States?'

It wasn't the time to push the question. He was too weary. He said, speaking of the second son, the one who hadn't been able to get the visa, 'It's his future. He's studying computer engineering. And Britain – it's expensive.'

So, deep down, he was divided. With one part of his mind he was for the faith, and opposed to all that stood outside it; in a world grown strange, he wished to continue to belong to himself for as long as possible. With another part of his mind he recognized the world outside as paramount, part of the future of his sons. It was in that division of the mind – as much as in the excesses of the Shah – that the Islamic revolution had begun in Iran. And it was there that it was ending.

In the *Tehran Times* the next day there was an interview with a visiting Indian Muslim. Non-Muslims, the visitor said, were always impressed by 'the comprehensive system of Islam' when it was outlined to them; but then they always asked in what Muslim country the system was practised. 'The answer to that important question could best be given by Iran,' the *Tehran Times* said, reporting the visitor's words, 'because the Iranian nation launched the unique and most courageous revolutionary movement in the history of mankind to establish the rule of Islam.'

High words still; but in Iran and elsewhere men would have to make their peace with the world which they knew existed beyond the faith.

The life that had come to Islam had not come from within. It had come from outside events and circumstances, the spread of the universal civilization. It was the late twentieth century that had made Islam revolutionary, given new meaning to old Islamic ideas of equality and union, shaken up static or retarded societies. It was the late twentieth century – and not the faith – that could supply the answers – in institutions, legislation, economic systems. And, paradoxically, out of the Islamic revival, Islamic fundamentalism, that appeared to look backwards, there would remain in many Muslim countries, with all the emotional charge derived from the Prophet's faith, the idea of modern revolution. Behzad, the communist (to whom the Russian rather than the Iranian revolution was 'the greatest turn in history'), was made by Islam more than he knew. And increasingly now in Islamic countries there would be the Behzads who, in an inversion of Islamic passion, would have a vision of a society cleansed and purified, a society of believers.

August 1979–February 1981